RAF BOMBER COMMAND
Reflections of War

RAF BOMBER COMMAND
Reflections of War

Volume 1
Cover of Darkness 1939–May 1942

Martin W Bowman

Pen & Sword
AVIATION

First Published in Great Britain in 2011 by
Pen & Sword Aviation
an imprint of
Pen & Sword Books Ltd
47 Church Street, Barnsley, South Yorkshire S70 2AS

Copyright © Martin W Bowman, 2011

ISBN 978-1-84884-492-6

Typeset in 10/12pt Palatino by
Concept, Huddersfield

Printed and bound in England by
CPI UK

Pen & Sword Books Ltd incorporates the Imprints of Pen & Sword
Aviation, Pen & Sword Family History, Pen & Sword Maritime, Pen & Sword
Military, Pen & Sword Discovery, Wharncliffe Local History, Wharncliffe
True Crime, Wharncliffe Transport, Pen & Sword Select, Pen & Sword
Military Classics, Leo Cooper, The Praetorian Press, Remember When,
Seaforth Publishing and Frontline Publishing.

For a complete list of Pen & Sword titles please contact
PEN & SWORD BOOKS LIMITED
47 Church Street, Barnsley, South Yorkshire, S70 2AS, England
E-mail: enquiries@pen-and-sword.co.uk
Website: www.pen-and-sword.co.uk

Contents

We were men before a firing squad of erratic marksmen.
Kill us tonight or tomorrow night they might;
kill us by next month they could scarcely fail to do.

No Moon Tonight by Don Charlwood

Acknowledgements

Gebhard Aders; Harry Andrews DFC; Frau Anneliese Autenrieth; Mrs Dorothy Bain; Günther Bahr; Charlie 'Jock' Baird; Harry Barker; Irene Barrett-Locke; Raymond V Base; Don Bateman; Steve Beale; A D 'Don' Beatty; Jack Bennett; Andrew Bird; Peter Bone; Alfons Borgmeier; Jack Bosomworth; Len Browning; Don Bruce; George Burton; Jim Burtt-Smith; Maurice Butt; Philip J Camp DFM; City of Norwich Aviation Museum (CONAM); Bob Collis; Jim Coman; B G Cook; John Cook DFM; Rupert 'Tiny' Cooling; Dennis Cooper; Ray Corbett; Coen Cornelissen; Leslie Cromarty DFM; Tom Cushing; Hans-Peter Dabrowski; Rob de Visser; Dr. Karl Dörscheln; J Alan Edwards; Wolfgang Falck; David G Fellowes; Elwyn D Fieldson DFC; Karl Fischer; Søren C Flensted; Vitek Formanek; Stanley Freestone; Ian Frimston; Prof. Dr Ing. Otto H Fries; Air Vice Marshal D J Furner CBE DFC AFC; Ken Gaulton; Jim George; Margery Griffiths, Chairman, 218 Gold Coast Squadron Association; Group Captain J R 'Benny' Goodman DFC* AFC AE; Alex H Gould DFC; Hans Grohmann; Charles Hall; Steve Hall; Jack F Hamilton; Eric Hammel; Erich Handke; James Harding; Frank Harper; Leslie Hay; Gerhard Heilig; Bob Hilliard; Peter C Hinchliffe; Neville Hockaday RNZAF; Werner 'Red' Hoffmann; Ted Howes DFC; Air Commodore Peter Hughes DFC; John Anderson Hurst; Zdenek Hurt; Ab A Jansen; Karl-Ludwig Johanssen; Wilhelm 'Wim' Johnen; Arthur 'Johnnie' Johnson; John B Johnson; Graham B Jones; Hans-Jürgen Jürgens; Erich Kayser; George Kelsey DFC; Les King; Christian Kirsch; Hans Krause; Reg Lawton; J R Lisgo; Chas Lockyer; Günther Lomberg; Peter Loncke; George Luke; Ian McLachlan; Nigel McTeer; B L Eric Mallett RCAF; Len Manning; The Honourable Terence Mansfield; Eric Masters; Bernard 'Max' Meyer DFC; Cyril Miles; Colin Moir; Frank Mouritz; Friedrich Ostheimer; Maurice S Paff; Simon Parry; Path Finder Association; Wing Commander David Penman DSO OBE DFC; Richard Perkins; Peter Petrick; Karl-Georg Pfeiffer; Eric Phillips; Vic Poppa; John Price; Stan Reed; Ernie Reynolds; Peter Richard; Albert E Robinson; Heinz Rökker; Squadron Leader Geoff Rothwell DFC;

vii

Fritz Rumpelhardt; David M Russell; Kees Rijken; Eric Sanderson; Klaus J Scheer; Dr. Dieter Schmidt-Barbo; Karl-Heinz Schoenemann; Jerry Scutts; Johan Schuurman; Group Captain Jack Short; Leslie R Sidwell; Don L Simpkin; SAAF Assn; Albert Spelthahn; Dr Ing. Klaus Th. Spies; Dick Starkey; Squadron Leader Hughie Stiles; Mike 'Taff' Stimson; Ted Strange DFC; Maurice Stoneman; Ken Sweatman; Paul Todd; Fred Tunstall DFC; Hille van Dieren; George Vantilt; Bob Van Wick; Andreas Wachtel; Georg Walser; David Waters; H Wilde; John Williams; H J Wilson; Henk Wilson; Geoffrey and Nick Willatt; Dennis Wiltshire; Louis Patrick Wooldridge DFC; Fred Young DFM; Cal Younger.

I am particularly grateful to my friend and colleague Theo Boiten, with whom I have collaborated on several books, for all of the information on the *Nachtjagd* or German night fighter forces contained herein. And, aviation historians everywhere owe a deep sense of gratitude to his and all the other valuable sources of reference listed in the end notes; in particular, those by the incomparable W R 'Bill' Chorley, Martin Middlebrook and Chris Everitt and Oliver Clutton-Brock. Finally, all of the late authors' books, as listed, who are beyond compare. This book is dedicated to their memory and all of the casualties in the Appendices.

Almost an Epitaph
by Irene Barrett-Locke

My two sons and grandchildren seem to have what I can only describe as a sort of 'second hand nostalgia' for the Second World War. I have sometimes wondered why and the only conclusion I can come to is that it is similar to my own questions to my father and his friends about life in the trenches in the First World War (perhaps a yearning for a time when issues in life were simpler). Their recollections always seemed rather disjointed and I was invariably disappointed. One of my grandsons at West Point military academy in the States asked me about this and I pointed out that a RAF officer's wife was hardly the person to consult on strategic matters. My own memories are equally disjointed. It would be nice to think that fifty years later my thoughts have become crystallized: that I have gained some perception or insight from living on the fringe of Bomber Command. But even today I have not reached any special conclusions and cannot provide them with a coherent version of it all. The simple fact is, it was a vivid but disjointed series of events and remains so in my mind.

I was watching one of those old black and white wartime romance films on television one night. There was a whole spate of them produced in the late forties–early fifties. You know the sort of thing – the chance meeting on a darkened wartime railway station, the dim lights, the elegant young woman in her pill box hat and veil pretending she is older and more sophisticated than her years. Through the steam drifting across the platform from the waiting railway engine emerges the dashing young airman. All very romantic and about the only part of the whole film I could relate to because you see that is how I met him, Daniel Angus Barrett, born 11 February 1919. He was a WOp/AG.

The next six years of my life bore very little resemblance to the rest of the film and if there were people like Jack Hawkins or Trevor Howard on aircrew then, I must have missed them, because for the most part they were quite ordinary men caught up in extraordinary circumstances.

I left my home in the Forest of Dean at seventeen in 1937 for London. The general feeling seemed to be that I was about to embark on a life of sin, but nothing could have been further from the truth. I had very little idea of what 'Sin' entailed. Sometimes innocence is its own protection and if 'Sin' was lurking around the corner it must have missed me altogether. London was certainly a very civilized place to be in the late thirties. Looking back on it today I find it amusing that my mother's letters to me often recounted some thoroughly lurid goings on amongst the news from Gloucestershire but would end up with severe and dire warnings about the perils of life in London. I had virtually no qualifications and the idea of learning to type or work on a switchboard did not appeal to me. One thing, which was not lost on me as a little girl from the country, was that I possessed a very pretty face and quite nice legs. It took me sometime to realize this. I traded on these assets quite ruthlessly and I'm sure it is the same today, women's lib notwithstanding. (Say one thing about being over seventy, one can afford to be objective.) The net result was that I became the first dining car stewardess on the Great Western Railway. It was quite an interesting job working between Paddington and Worcester – a breakthrough at the time and my picture appeared in the London papers in my smart uniform. Rather the equivalent today of becoming an air hostess.

1938 passed happily exploring the world as an adult, earning my own money and devoting my free time to clothes, parties and dates and examining the infinite variety of men. If the proverbial 'storm clouds' were gathering over Europe, they had little bearing on my own life. It was not until early 1939 that I began to get an inkling of what was coming and it happened in the strangest way.

I had a brief love affair with a naval officer named Ivor. I enjoyed being taken out to small restaurants with him and remember Maxims in Wardour Street, also the Cafe de Paris, which was bombed one night soon after we had dined there. Ivor had studied archaeology at Cambridge and as we walked around London, diving into air raid shelters when the sirens went, he explained the different styles of buildings. I think he must have thought me very ignorant on the subject. This happiness could not last. One day he told me he had to go to a place called Sarisbury Green in Hampshire to report to his MTB unit. I went with him from Worcester to say goodbye. We hitch-hiked most of the way, easier then, especially for a man in naval uniform. It was very late when we arrived in Fareham. He booked me into a hotel and we watched the bombs raining down on Portsmouth. I remember he left saying he would return in the morning, after breakfast. I was surprised to find a letter at the reception desk for me the contents of which I can even now, fifty years later, remember word for word. I returned to Worcester in tears. How painful is young love and I never saw him again. Over a year later while visiting my mother with my new husband she quietly told me that a letter written by me to him had been returned stamped on the envelope 'missing while on active services'. In her wisdom she had burned it.

Anyway, to return to the railway station. I was in the buffet on Paddington station one day when a crowd of boisterous young airmen came in having a quick beer between trains. They sat at my table and amidst all the commotion there were the usual veiled and not so veiled propositions which young men *en masse* tend to make. Receiving little encouragement they lost interest. All but one.

I gathered that they were on their way back from a gunnery course somewhere in Wales. He spoke with a pronounced American accent and I was curious as to why he would be in the RAF. It turned out he was a Canadian. He agreed that a lot of people made the same mistake about his accent. In that direct North American way they have he said he would like to see me again. Without much conviction I said 'Yes, that would be nice' knowing that their train would be leaving in a short while. Suddenly there was a mass exit as the train was about to leave. The whistle blowing, doors slamming. I could hear shouts. Something about 'Come on Dan, you'll miss him'. I looked through the window and as the smoke and steam cleared the Canadian sergeant was walking back alone into the buffet. He had missed his train for me. So that was really how it all started. I don't remember what we talked about for the twenty minutes or so until my train came in and I suppose he got a later train. But I had given him my address in London.

So you see, the first five minutes of the wartime romance film were reasonably accurate. It was from that point on that the script and my own life began to diverge.

From time to time, when he could afford the money and the time, the young RAF sergeant would come down to visit me in London. I behaved abominably. There is no other way of putting it. I was vain, selfish and totally self absorbed and he was a RAF sergeant with little money and none of the social graces of the young men I graced with my company. An orphan from Montreal from the depression did not count then in my general scheme of things. He was not even an officer. (I found it interesting that one of my granddaughters who is a 22-year-old actress, making her way in films and the theatre in the West End of London said something similar to me: 'He's not even a producer!' I understood her well.)

With the callousness and abandon which only comes with, I was told, a perfect Welsh nose and the eyelashes, I cheerfully stood him up after his long journeys to London. At this time I shared a flat in Sussex Gardens with a friend I called 'Chick', a young woman of my own age and similar outlook; a most attractive brunette. One Sunday night after I had stood him up again and been away for the weekend, I returned to find 'Chick' curled up in our corner seat eating what the sergeant called candies. There was also a bunch of flowers in a vase. The thought struck me that 'Chick' never bought flowers. Although Chick and I shared clothes and make up I took exception to sharing my young men! From what I could gather an RAF sergeant had arrived asking for me: and as I was absent had, on his limited budget, taken her out to dinner. She rhapsodized about the young sergeant and his aspirations. I sat in my little bedroom and fumed: how could they have done this to me? I felt a sense of betrayal. To cut a long story short we met again and I married him and became what I sometimes referred to myself as a camp follower.

In the little church where we were married my family sat on one side of the aisle and his aircrew sat on the opposite side. It was the only family he had. They were partly drunk and cheering him on. Fortunately he did not insist on taking his crew on our honeymoon which I heard happened sometimes. (My father found his rear gunner still asleep a day later in a chicken coop at the far end of our garden and put him on a train.) I have been a very lucky woman. I'm not particularly religious but I cannot help feeling that if there is a God, he had some plan for this vain little creature in 1939. I remember going through the litany about 'love, honour and obey' without much conviction on the altar because we had already made a commitment which I had taken more seriously one Sunday afternoon on a bench in St. James Park. It was quite simply that we would try never to be parted. And that's really what my little story is all about. To do all we could to stay together.

Aircrew on active duty were 'discouraged' from living with their wives. As usual with the RAF I never got to the bottom of what 'discouraged' really meant. I suppose it meant whatever the CO decided it to mean depending on interpretation. Whatever, the edict was indeed a discouraging experience.

Anyway, I took that private little vow very literally with very little understanding of what the consequences would be. The result was that I joined a very small group indeed of air force wives who followed their husbands illicitly from the vicinity of one RAF Station to another throughout the war. I only ever met one other wife who admitted to doing the same thing. It meant trekking around from one Station to another with a baby searching hopelessly sometimes for accommodation. I got to know many of these Stations: Scampton, Waddington, Bardney, Dunholme Lodge and so many others. I became quite expert on the flora and fauna of the north-east English countryside while pushing a pram and I developed a hatred for trains which is with me to this day. It was bad enough that the trains never ran on time during the war (not that they do these days but at least then they had a reason). What made it worse was sitting in some siding, cold, sometimes without much light, wondering if he would be there to meet me and where the hell would I live.

It is here again that the romantic war films and I again part company. You know how for dramatic effect or contrast the 'hero' is shown returning to a peaceful country cottage in his sports car and is greeted by an adoring little wife. It is either that or a luxurious flat in London. The general impression being that he has returned from an extended business trip. Well for me in my furnished room or run down room in a farm cottage it wasn't like that at all.

One of the most vivid memories I have of a journey while following my husband was when he went to Brighton on a conversion course to Lancasters.

It was November, the baby was seven months old, I left Middlewich in Cheshire one morning in freezing fog, placing carry-cot in the pram, and carrying a suitcase I reached the station.

The journey was cold, there were no refreshments and in any case I had little money.

Then I eventually arrived. Brighton looked very depressing with barbed wire protecting the coastline. I found the hotel that my husband had reserved a room in. The owner 'alas' was not very welcoming, denying all knowledge of the reservation and saying, they didn't take children. Eventually I was given a room at the very top of the hotel and I staggered up the stairs with the carry-cot and then went down and asked for some warm milk for the baby, only to be told they were too busy. This hotel was typical of so many small hotels which sheltered residents who had fled from the bombing of London. They all looked very prosperous to me; the small dogs they carried were accepted but not a harassed mother with a small baby. However when I heard his footsteps outside the door, it all seemed worthwhile. I spent the next few days in Lyons teashops, waiting for the evening. We left together for Lincolnshire where, as I have already explained, I illicitly attached myself to Bomber Command.

We couldn't afford the luxury of sitting back on overstuffed rose covered settees with slip covers asking sensitive, introspective questions about 'how it was all going' or 'when do you think it will all end?' The fact was that I was living it every day and although my concerns usually centred on such things as my triumph at finding a place which had at least a toilet roll, in 1942 my assessment of the war was probably as good as the cabinet's. In 1941 I had seriously thought about my role in the war effort. The idea of working in a munitions factory did not appeal to me and I was unqualified to become a nurse. I seriously considered trading on some naval officers I had known to become a WREN, or at least using their recommendations. Above all, I liked their uniforms. So you see by 1941 I had not changed that much.

Biology solved the problem for me. I became pregnant, which the government was good enough to consider my war work. When you are five foot two and give birth to a ten and a half pound baby boy, I think that is definitely work. It is fashionable today to be explicit about one's sex life. All I can say is that even today the workings of the hormone system in human beings is one of the least understood fields in medicine. I think it manifested itself in an urgent need to procreate at that time and when my first son was born in the maternity ward it seemed as if everyone was having boys. A girl baby was an exception. Perhaps in a mysterious way nature was replenishing itself. There is one other aspect to this in that in the same way that the men in their uniforms became intensely masculine; we reciprocated by becoming intensely feminine. At times there were massive conflicts of will between the sexes but certainly never any question of identity.

Late in 1941 he was still flying on Wellingtons. He watched one day from 28,000 feet Manchester being bombed. There was nothing he could do but sit and watch. I asked what he thought about it all. He said he thought they were doing a very good job, which only goes to show how distorted our values had become.

In 1942 my husband converted to Lancasters and I was relieved because I thought he would be safer every few days when I kissed him goodbye. I needed to believe that. He was commissioned and later got a DFC, neither of which seemed to impress him, although it did me. By that time whole squadrons of men were gradually dwindling down and being replaced. It is hard for me today to realize I am the same woman who would kiss him goodbye in the front garden as he rode off on his RAF bicycle and shout 'see you in the morning, honey'. Someone stole his bicycle and he would hitch-hike to work. Fortunately his Wing Commander who had a car would pick him up on the country road at the same time and place each morning and studiously avoided any questions as to where he had been. I found out later that the Wing Commander was also flouting RAF regulations and trying to live a domestic life at the same time, so a conspiracy of silence existed between them.

A few times I found a place close enough that I could see the aircraft returning in the distance. I would stand in my dressing gown at dawn watching them gradually straggle in. Sometimes one would be trailing smoke. Sometimes they seemed to be coming in without undercarriages. But my husband would laugh and say that the good landing was the one you walked away from. I should explain that my husband was very superstitious. By this time I no longer believed he would be safer in these big black Lancasters.

We both believed that as long as he had his lighter with him he would be all right and return to us. One morning after I had kissed him goodbye, imagine my horror when I saw the lighter lying on the table. I jumped on my bicycle and peddled furiously to the base praying that I would get there before they took off. I could see him and I stood there at the fence screaming his name. Somehow he heard me and I was able to pass the lighter to him through the mesh. He returned from that trip. On another occasion at another base he told me to find someone to look after the baby and to come out to the base that afternoon. I found a chambermaid in the hotel to look after the baby and took the bus out to the airfield. When he saw me he came over to the fence and handed me the little tins of Sunkist orange juice they were given for the flight. He said this is for Peter and we kissed through the mesh.

And while I think of it, there was a funny sequel to the DFC involving warts of all things. They were great big ones, which suddenly erupted on his left hand. The MO attempted to remove them and bandaged his hand but it was that afternoon he was meeting me at another railway station. I don't remember where. With his usual gallantry he picked up the baby in his right arm and my case in his left. A man stopped him on the street and said 'Excuse me sir but do you realize you are bleeding?' We looked back and there was a trail of blood all the way along the pavement. The medical officer was furious and to prove his point put my husband's arm in a sling. With the little purple and white ribbon with its diagonal stripes he looked good. In pubs it was amazing how everyone seemed to know what the little ribbon represented. He also had a broken nose, which was strangely attractive, from when an ice hockey puck was driven into it as a boy. And a few scars on his cheek from a time in Quebec in the thirties.

In pubs we made an ideal couple; me with the glamorous young flying officer with arm in a sling. We had enough money for our half pints of mild and bitter and really just wanted to be alone. As honest as he was, he protested that the sling on his arm was due to his warts. But the habitués of the pub knew modesty when they saw it and the table was usually filled with drinks. So much so that petrol rationing apart, they drove us home. To some awful place where the driver of the car would say, 'Why don't you stay with us?' We never accepted their offers or any of the black market goods to which I was offered. I tried to match his integrity with my own. I was beginning to realize what total war was all about. I mashed carrots and coddled eggs and poured them over mashed potatoes. Sometimes it would be stewed apples or dried fruit from an American sergeant, a six foot one.

I have another criticism of the black and white film I watched. They are all sitting around the breakfast table. It was Sylvia Sims or somebody like her. He is home on leave and there was some dreary, introspective, philosophical debate about 'when will it all be over and life can return to normal?' Well first of all, we couldn't afford the luxury of philosophical debate about when it would be over because it had become the only life we knew. One night he brought his bomb-aimer back and they were drunk and depressed. From what I could gather there had been a heavy German cruiser called *Prinz Eugen* and I think it was in Gdynia in the Baltic. They had looked at the photographs and in his bomb aimer's words: 'it should have been a direct hit.' I went upstairs to bed and could still hear the two young men discussing it. In the morning I made them omelettes with a pack of dried eggs. I don't think they sell them anymore but someone should because they make a perfect omelette.

I should point out that I was not a security risk. Although he would tell me where he had gone the previous night you could read about it in the papers the next day anyway.

And so I continued to follow my husband around all the little airfields, which have long since gone. By '43 I had watched the appalling losses of Bomber Command. I think he knew his days were numbered and so did I. Sometimes they would ask me to comfort some bereaved woman. I did not offer any trite words of sympathy. It was mainly because I didn't want to hear anyone telling me the same thing. I do wish I could put all these things into chronological order. The simple reason was that by 1944 there seemed to be no kind of order to anything. Suddenly the people one had met and liked were just not there anymore.

I remember once in the 'Saracen's Head' in Lincoln when a sergeant came up to my husband and said 'Did you see Dave go down?' I knew David well but thought it best to stay silent.

At a celebration party before, Dave had gone out and cut out a large paper 'Gong' which he had pinned on causing howls of laughter. There was a callousness coming over him and probably me too.

He became morose and distant. And for me, well the baby kept screaming. Sometimes I would say, 'Where was it last night?' The answers were monosyllabic: 'Wuppertal, Bochum, Düsseldorf, Essen, Cologne, Dortmund, Hamburg, Mannheim, ploughing up and down 'Happy Valley'. I began to feel that I knew all those cities well. We knew the odds were against him. I was no longer surprised by anyone's absence. As I said, the flighty little girl who lived for dancing had changed. The constant anxiety was showing.

I began to wish I had become a WREN, a nurse trained in clinical detachment. And then there was the famous pilot with whom my husband sometimes flew. Only on one trip did I have a dreadful presentiment. It coincided with my husband having a really dreadful attack of sinusitis. The MO grounded him and that night the pilot came down and was given the VC. We didn't regard any of this as heroic particularly. By this time I was becoming tired of the stress and counting every trip on a calendar. Even when on leave I worried about our return. Vera Lynn used to sing 'I won't complain; I'll see it through.' It was all very well for her to sing those lyrics on a long distance radio I thought.

He bombed Danzig one night. I heard on the radio that sixty bombers had failed to return. I committed the cardinal sin of calling the Station. A WAAF answered the phone and said she would find out if he was there and severely reprimanded me for ringing. She put the phone down and standing in the booth I could hear her heels tapping down the corridor. I felt strangely calm and thought it had only been a matter of time. I was outraged when she came back and told me he was asleep in his bed! Without realizing it had been a fifteen-hour flight, I became infuriated when he finally returned. I did the same thing when he drank his tin of orange juice over Berlin, which was always saved for our baby Peter.

Usually he would return in the early hours trying hard to be cheerful. To this day I will never know how he managed to have a few hours' sleep and then at 11 o'clock after he had washed off that terrible smell, sit with me and the baby in a cafe pretending we were just another normal couple having our morning coffee. By late 1944 not much touched me anymore. I was no longer the little girl who had sat in St. James Park. Unlike Vera Lynn I complained frequently and was not so sure I would see it through. Apparently in the 15-hour flight to Danzig they had crossed Sweden to get there. He muttered something to me about the way the Swedes knew which way the wind was blowing and the search-lights and flak went deliberately off in another direction.

I didn't cry anymore, except one morning when he returned very late and looked sick and old beyond his years. Apparently they had been coned and badly shot up. They had barely made it home. He tried to explain that the searchlights had locked on them over Duisburg. This was the night he earned his DFC. I think what had most upset him was seeing other aircraft going down in flames. Well, we still went to our cafe and tried to pretend. I was twenty-two years old at this time and he was twenty-three.

How I wish there had been another wife to talk to but I didn't know any. I had the baby and apart from that I waited. In 1944 he was becoming paranoid about the German night fighters and envied the Americans with their long-range fighter escorts. I don't think flak bothered him much anymore or if it did he never talked about it. So you can see how divorced we were becoming from reality.

One night I watched some programme on the BBC debating some sort of moral issue about the bombing of Dresden. Their little academic pronouncements made about as much sense as asking whether Rome should have destroyed Carthage. I also have not noticed Rome having problems with Carthage today.

After his first tour on ops my husband had a wonderful posting to a small village in Oxfordshire, Chipping Warden, not far from Banbury. Six months' rest from flying for him but heaven for me. We lived in a very old cottage with roses around the door, yellow jasmine around the 'privy' at the bottom of the garden and hollyhocks as well. The RAF sanitary squad dealt with the 'privy'. The cooking facilities were primitive: a small fire and a straight chimney going up to the open sky. Soot fell regularly. We were at the bottom of a hill and in the autumn when the drains were blocked with leaves, the rain water rushed straight into our cottage through the ill-fitting door. It took weeks to dry out. I didn't care, for I was happy. On summer evenings we cycled along the lanes and walked in the fields full of poppies with sandwiches and flask.

I tried to ignore the war news but began counting the days when I knew this peace must end. It did: one night we heard heavy tanks and lorries rumbling through the country lanes. This went on and on, night and day. The preparations for D-Day had begun. Sure enough he was recalled to start his next tour of ops.

It was Berlin, Berlin: the great thousand bomber raids had begun. Sometimes now I didn't see him for days, but still living in dread of inevitable news as the huge Lancasters lumbered with their heavy loads, an impressive sight. He survived all this physically.

I had severe anxiety neuroses later on but as I have said before, that is another story.

One night I was awoken at two in the morning by a strange flickering, which even seemed to be coming through the blackout curtains. I peered between the curtains and the entire opposite side of the street, similar three story buildings, were in rubble and flames. I ran down to the shelter and slept there. They told me in the morning that some rockets or bombs or whatever had gone over my flat and straight into the opposite side.

After the first exultation that the war was over, it would be nice to think that there were 'Bluebirds over the White Cliffs of Dover'. That life could return to normal. But by that time none of us knew what normal was anymore and we regarded peace with the same apprehension. It was anti-climactic and all I saw among the men was an aimlessness and lack of purpose. I hated how cynical I had become and tried to tell myself thus if we bought furniture we could start a 'normal life', whatever that was. I wasn't that far wrong, because right afterwards the Berlin Airlift started, followed by Korea. We would talk late into the night about what to do. The American Air Force was willing to take him, and as a Canadian, the Canadians would take their son back into the RCAF. We needed the money. We certainly needed the money. Then in their wisdom the RAF offered him a permanent commission and he took it.

The RAF were a strange assortment of men. Fighter Command may have been accurately portrayed in films but the men who relentlessly went up and down the Ruhr did not indulge in glamour. I knew so many of them a bit too well. To this day I know about growing oranges in Rhodesia, sheep farming in New Zealand and the lumber business in Canada and mining in South Africa. I should explain here that he was based on a Rhodesian Squadron, 44, (5 Group) and we were living in Lincoln on Nettleton Road, in rooms of course.

I have left a great deal unsaid, I had three of his logbooks, two of which have been lost with so much else. I do remember one entry however describing seeing Düsseldorf burning two hundred miles away from the Dutch coast. How ironic that after the war we should know Düsseldorf so well when he was posted to Mönchengladbach in the intelligence section.

I could not help wondering what his feelings would be regarding the country he had so ruthlessly bombed in the line of duty, I must say he never expressed any personal hatred of the people.

We had taken our caravan and our two sons Peter and Jeremy for a holiday before he reported to Rhiendahlen HQ. His Quebec French was fluent but his German poor. It rained heavily so we found a small *Gasthaus* frequented by *Wehrmacht* men in the bar.

We lived there as our house was not ready. Our sons returned to Boarding School and as he was still on leave we explored Holland in the beautiful autumn sunshine. I have had a love affair with Holland ever since. Once we had settled in our quarter we sometimes had a German officer to dinner. He wore spectacles and smoked through a holder. The two men talked into the night and laughed; they certainly bore no malice. Another friend from Venlo – a Dutchman, Peter – would visit us, bearing bunches of tulips. He also wore thick spectacles and had been in the Dutch Resistance. His poor sight we were told (not by him) was the result of interrogation under 'The Lights'.

Forty years later Jeremy and I scattered his ashes in the Forest of Dean. A beautiful place and only one mile from the little church we had married in that perfect June day in 1941. Incidentally the day Germany attacked Russia. 'The best wedding present you could have had', said my farseeing Father as we held our reception in the Speech House.

Later I was to realize why he liked the Forest of Dean so much. It reminded him of the Laurentian Mountains in Canada, where he had been taken for six weeks of summer while he had been living in Weredale House, a 'Boys Home' in Montreal after becoming an orphan at the tender age of nine years: I always felt God surely owed him something.

The time spent alone after his death forced me at last to the grim reality that here was a posting I could not follow and the only thing which could have parted us. I like to think of him reunited with all those gallant men gone before. *Per Ardua Ad Astra.*

I later met a very kind and understanding man while having lunch in a Gloucester Hotel. Harold had been born not far from me and we seemed to have so much in common that our meeting might have been arranged. How strange fate is. He also had been in the RAF in North Africa, though was very reticent about what he actually did and so I married for the second time in a small eleventh century church.

This marriage has brought me peace and security in my late age. I have always thought that one of the most beautiful words of Christ was: 'Blessed are they that mourn for they shall be comforted.'

I feel I have found exactly what was meant by those words.

CHAPTER 1

'I'll Gladly Pay You Tuesday'

It is as well for the man in the street to realise that there is no power on earth that can protect him from being bombed. Whatever people may tell him, the bomber will always get through. The only defence is in offence, which means that you have to kill more women and children more quickly than the enemy if you want to save yourselves.

Stanley Baldwin, during a House of Commons debate
in November 1932

Perhaps it was because he had grown from childhood to teenager in the air age that Peter Bone wanted to join the Royal Air Force. The aeroplane had, in the interwar years, captured mankind's imagination as it swiftly replaced the ocean liner as the link between the continents. The 16-year-old had never been mechanically minded and had never handled any kind of firearm when he left school in 1938 to begin a four year apprenticeship as a junior reporter on a local weekly newspaper near his hometown 10 miles south of London. That was what he felt he was good at – writing about other people and their activities. In 1939 the prime minister, Neville Chamberlain, had finished his radio address on that quiet, sunny Sunday morning of 3 September in which he had declared war on Nazi Germany, when the air raid sirens sounded. This was it! Everyone expected a devastating attack on London, just as Warsaw had suffered just two days earlier. But it was a false alarm and for the next nine months, the so-called 'phoney war' period, enemy air activity over Britain was negligible. Both sides adhered to international prohibitions on bombing civilians and their property but Hitler and his fellow dictator, Mussolini, had contravened that prohibition in recent years. Mussolini, in 1935, by using his military aircraft to subdue spear-carrying natives in his campaign in Abyssinia, and Germany when it had tried out its new dive-bombers on the defenceless citizens of Guernica in 1937 in support

12

of the Fascist overthrow of the democratic government of Spain. On 1 September 1939 Germany had used them again on the defenceless citizens of Warsaw, Poland. In May 1940 the Dutch city of Rotterdam was dealt with in a similar fashion.

Hitler had, by June 1940, overrun Norway, Denmark, Belgium, Holland and France, but he still had some admiration for the British and their far-flung Empire and hoped up to the fall of France, that Britain would come to terms with him. In return for a free hand in Europe and Russia, he said he wouldn't interfere with Britain and its possessions. This might have worked with Chamberlain's government but when Chamberlain was ousted and Churchill became prime minister, Hitler realized there would be no deal. The gloves came off and the Battle of Britain began in mid-July. Although the *Luftwaffe*'s objective was to make RAF fighter airfields and radar installations unusable in order to attain air superiority as a necessary prelude to invasion and occupation, the action most visible to people on the ground took place thousands of feet above them. Occasionally they heard the faint rattle of machine gun fire or the zoom of an aircraft engine, but when a plane came spiralling down trailing white smoke, it was just as likely to be a Spitfire as a Messerschmitt. Few realized that the outcome of the battle would dictate the future course of the war and how it would end.

By then, Peter Bone was nearly eighteen. He told his friend, who wanted the same, that yes, he would be a fighter pilot, but he was not one of those steely-eyed, firm-chinned heroes portrayed in Hollywood films. He had never gone out of his way to look for trouble; live and let live was his motto. But, he did not like being pushed around. It did not cross his mind that within a year he would be called upon to lend a hand and when he was called upon to don uniform and take up arms, he saw himself as something like a gladiator of old, not on horseback but in the cockpit of a fighter plane. Not for him the horrors of hand-to-hand combat with a rifle and bayonet – that was too personal a way to be killed or to kill. He wanted to fight his war without seeing his opponent's face, his hatred, or perhaps his fear. He would be firing at another fighter plane, not at another young man of about his own age.

Often outnumbered and nearing exhaustion, RAF fighter pilots did not win the Battle of Britain but they prevented the *Luftwaffe* from winning it.

Without air superiority, Hitler tried a different tack. At the end of August 1940 a small *Luftwaffe* force bombed London throughout the night. Although little damage was done, Bomber Command, which up to now had confined its bombing to enemy naval targets on the Baltic coast, retaliated on the next night by sending about 100 aircraft to bomb Bremen, Cologne, Hamm and Berlin. Again little damage was done but Pandora's Box had been opened. Hitler, incensed by the bombing of his capital, ordered the *Luftwaffe* to switch from day bombings of British fighter airfields in southern England to night bombing of industrial cities, beginning with London. What came to be known as the *Blitz* began. The Battle of Britain and now the *Blitz* seemed to crystallize Peter Bone's thinking and that of his friend. They would both be fighter pilots. Cycling in the country lanes of north Kent that sunny Saturday afternoon of 7 September, Peter Bone and his friend Geoff Willis noticed numerous black dots in the sky, in perfect formation, heading towards London. It was the vanguard of about 600 fighters and 300 bombers on their way to attack the capital's dockland area. As the boys raced home, the air raid sirens wailed all the way to London. And, that night the sky over the capital was a smoky red. The fires that had been started in the late afternoon guided the night bombers to the target.

Because their house was 10 miles south of London, Peter Bone's family were spared the full force of the *Blitz*, but being on the flight path of the bombers, it received its full share of broken roof tiles, smashed windows and downed ceilings caused by bombs jettisoned by *Luftwaffe* pilots who turned for home over the suburbs rather than face the anti-aircraft fire and night fighters over the city. Several members of his family sustained minor injuries. Peter was now working as a junior reporter on a weekly paper serving a rather down-at-heel working class district of south London popularly known as 'Crystal Palace' after the exhibition complex that had burned down in 1936. He wrote many stories of tragedy and heroism played out in those dingy back streets. Some were written sitting at the living room table before the sirens bade them to take shelter under it, in the steel cage that offered protection only from falling debris. They knew there was scant protection from a direct hit.

The *Blitz* took the lives of about 43,000 citizens throughout Britain before it petered out in May 1941 when Hitler turned his attention to Russia. He moved the bulk of his military forces east but left enough aircraft on the French coast to mount sporadic sharp attacks on Britain, to remind the British that the *Luftwaffe* was only 20 minutes' flying time from London.

At the outbreak of war the overall strength of Bomber Command stood at 55 squadrons. On paper this sounds a respectable figure, but by the end of September it was down to 23 home-based first-line squadrons. These consisted of six squadrons of Wellington Is and Ias of 3 Group (with two in reserve) stationed in East Anglia; five squadrons of Whitleys in 4 Group in Yorkshire and six squadrons of Handley Page Hampdens of 5 Group in Lincolnshire.[1] Under the RAF Bomber Command 'Scatter' plan, the majority of bomber squadrons were immediately dispersed to satellite bases. Like Germany, Britain's first bombing operations of the Second World War were made in daylight, and just like the *Luftwaffe*, the RAF was soon forced to switch to bombing by night.

Who were the pilots and crews who flew these operations? In the 1930s for anyone who wanted to fly, the RAF was considered to be the best

'Flying Club' in which to do just that. Born in Simla in India on 12 August 1918, Guy Gibson had joined the RAF in 1936, being commissioned in 1937. He had one aim: to fly. His father, Alexander, was an official in the Imperial Indian Forest Service who moved his young family to Porthleven in Cornwall in 1921. Guy was sent to Folkestone in Kent at the age of eight to attend St George's Prep School and he went on to St Edward's in Oxford. Gibson had average grades in education but was good at sports.

On 31 August 1939 he was sailing off Monkstone Beach near Saunders-foot in South Wales where his father had once owned a bungalow. Ann ('blonde and pretty') was asleep at the back of the boat. Suddenly, a young boy swam out to them with a telegram in his mouth. The telegram told the bomber pilot to return to 83 Squadron at Scampton immediately. Freddy Bilby, just down from Oxford, arrived in his 1928 Alvis and the two pilots set off at speed for a pub near St Edwards for a rendezvous with friends, some in the Oxford University Air Squadron. After they had downed a few beers and a 1928 Burgundy, Gibson caught the train to Lincoln and he reported to 83 Squadron at Scampton.

The Handley Page Hampdens were standing by on 3 September, the first day of the war, but were not sent until the next day when with Blenheims and Wellingtons they were ordered to attack German war-ships in the Schillig Roads at the entrance to the Kiel Canal. At Scampton the Station intelligence officer read a pamphlet, which said it was best to attack from 3,000 feet, above the height of machine gun fire and below the heavy flak. On no account were they to bomb civilian targets. Gibson and the other Hampden crews had their take-offs delayed and they never reached the target as the weather was bad. Willie Snaith, the 83 Squadron CO, aborted the operation. Other aircraft did attack and two bombs were dropped in the Danish town of Esbjerg, 110 miles away, killing two people.

Young RAF bomber pilots like Gibson were enthusiastic and confident in their aircraft and equipment. The strategy was that bomber aircraft did not need fighter escort to reach and destroy targets, but as the *Luftwaffe* discovered in the Battle of Britain, this was all wishful thinking. The Hampden and the Vickers Armstrong Wellington, Armstrong Whitworth Whitley and Bristol Blenheim, all twin engined bombers, were the main-stay of Bomber Command early in the war.

'Stately' was the only word to describe the elderly Whitley's progress through the air, its basic shape giving it that extraordinary 'nose-down' flight attitude. Crews were surprised to find that it felt just like that inside too! In a Whitley one attained the rear turret down a long, low tunnel on a small trolley running on rails and this too was a source of some amusement.[2]

The Wellington was affectionately known as the 'Wimpy' after the American cartoon character J Wellington Wimpy in *'Popeye'*, who was always eating hamburgers and saying, 'I'll gladly pay you Tuesday'. The

Wellington had been conceived by R K Pierson and his design team, who had used the ingenious geodetic framework devised and developed by brilliant British scientist, Dr Barnes Wallis, in the design of their high wing monoplane bomber.

The Wellington and the Hampden and the Whitley were weakly armed but it was these bombers' exploits which featured in the headlines in the British press and sometimes in German papers as well. Wellington and Blenheim operations against elements of the German fleet at Brünsbuttel and Wilhelmshaven on 4 September 1939 met with stiff opposition from fighters and flak and two Wellingtons and five Blenheims were lost. Worse was to come. The 3 Group Wellingtons in Suffolk, Cambridgeshire and Bedfordshire and 5 Group Hampdens in central Lincolnshire kept searching for the German navy in daylight during the remainder of September 1939 but serious losses inflicted on the 29th, when a complete formation of five 144 Squadron Hampdens was destroyed over the German Bight between Heligoland and Wangerooge Island by Bf 109s of I./ZG26, soon convinced the Air Staff that a profound change of its daylight policy was necessary. After the Wellington and Blenheim losses in daylight the ancient Whitley squadrons in 4 Group in north and east Yorkshire were immediately employed in night leaflet dropping or *Nickeling* operations over the Ruhr and north-western Germany and made no appearance in daylight at all.

The first leaflet raid took place on the night of 3/4 September when the war was not yet 12 hours old. The route ran from Leconfield to Borkum, an island off the estuary of the Ems, south along the frontier of Holland to Essen and then along the Ruhr Valley. Release height was set at 16,000 feet. *G-George*, piloted by Flying Officer J A 'Tony' O'Neill, was one of three Whitley IIIs on 58 Squadron that took off from Leconfield in the late afternoon. Four hours out and the Whitley was over the Ruhr. There was no oxygen in the long fuselage and no portable oxygen bottles. Two crew members began posting bundles of leaflets out and in less than 10 minutes they were exhausted. Two others took their place while those relieved went forward to plug into the main oxygen supply. It was then that the port engine showed the first signs of failure. O'Neill decided to head for Rheims and he crossed the Belgian border, past Liège and into France. Then the port engine failed completely, the propeller began windmilling violently in the slipstream and the starboard began to show signs of strain. O'Neill made a wheels-up landing in a cabbage field at Dormans near Epernay in the heart of the Champagne country. There was a loud thump and the tearing of metal as *George* skated across the field with cabbages bouncing about the cockpit like 'short-pitched cricket balls' as the broken bomb aiming window sheared them off like 'a harvester's knife'. The crew escaped injury. They had been airborne for seven and three quarter hours. On 5 September a DH Rapide flew O'Neill's crew to Harwell and they were soon back at Leconfield.

Seven such raids took place on the first seven nights of the war. In the Whitley, leaflets were discharged from the gun-turret under the fuselage known as the 'dustbin'. The Whitleys operated in the leaflet dropping role on 22 nights between 4/5 September and 23/24 December and a total of 113 sorties were flown. From all these all operations, 11 Whitleys failed to return, the first on 8/9 September when the Whitley piloted by Squadron Leader S S Murray was shot down near Kassel and all the crew were taken into captivity. On the same night Flying Officer W C G Cogman on 102 Squadron force-landed at Nivelles aerodrome in Belgium. Flying Officer G L Raphael, returning from Essen, landed at Buc aerodrome in France and taxiing in poor visibility he collided with a parked Dewoitine aircraft. The Whitley was later written off. Cogman's crew meanwhile, were interned for a time and when they were eventually released the Whitley was left behind in Belgium.[3] Two nights later Sergeant A G E Dixon's crew were injured when their Whitley crashed on take-off from Rheims-Champagne and burst into flames. On 15/16 September Flying Officer Roland Williams on 77 Squadron was shot down near Frankfurt on the sortie to Munich. Williams was killed and his crew were taken into captivity.

It was said that while Poland bled and burned we were bombarding the Germans with nothing more lethal than copies of Mr Chamberlain's broadcast, and the War Cabinet suspended *Nickeling* operations. With the resumption of operations on the night of 24/25 September the Whitleys carried their bundles further afield and on 1/2 October three Whitleys from 10 Squadron at Dishforth were the first British aircraft of the war to fly over Berlin. Australian Flight Lieutenant John William Allsop and crew were lost without trace. Weather conditions that night were particularly severe. One aircraft arrived over the German capital at 22,500 feet. The oxygen supply momentarily failed; two of the crew collapsed and part of the mechanism of the rear turret froze such that the air gunner could not open his door. The pilot carried on and the navigator went back to assist the two unconscious members of the crew. He dragged one 12 feet along the fuselage into the cabin and connected him with the oxygen supply. He then threw overboard two-thirds of the leaflets before collapsing in his turn. The pilot brought the aircraft down to 9,000 feet and at this height it became possible to open the door to the rear turret. The air gunner climbed through to the assistance of the navigator, who, however, had already recovered and returned to duty.

Besides this raid on Berlin, leaflets were dropped on eight more occasions in the month of October by aircraft operating mostly from an advanced refuelling base at Villeneuve-les-Vertus near Paris. On the night of 24/25 October, when Whitley Vs of 77 Squadron took off from Driffield in Yorkshire on *Nickel* sorties, Pilot Officer Philip Edwin William Walker and crew were lost without trace. At 17.00 hours on the evening of 27 October, five Whitley IIIs from 51 Squadron, which had been standing by for the past three days at Villeneuve awaiting suitable weather, were ordered to take off before dark to reconnoitre southern Germany and to drop leaflets over the Düsseldorf–Frankfurt area. This despite the afternoon weather forecast, which included the promise of: 'rain, hail and sleet showers, risk of thunder; cloud 7 to 9/10ths, low base 1,000 feet but 500 feet in showers; freezing level 1,500 feet; heavy icing anticipated in shower clouds up to 12,000 feet'. Better conditions, however, were expected over base for the return; and with this consolation the crews took off as dusk fell. They had eaten nothing since midday and had had no time to pick up the usual sandwiches and hot drinks before departure. The weather was soon too much for one crew who turned back. The remaining four carried on. The ceiling of the Whitleys was only 17,000 feet in the best conditions and over much of the route the snow clouds rose a thousand feet higher. Trouble began for the first aircraft near its objective, Stuttgart, for it was impossible to use oxygen during the unloading of the leaflets and the two unloaders – the navigator and wireless operator – became very sick. Owing to the intense cold, it was almost impossible to lower the turret from which the pamphlets were discharged. The temperature varied between minus 22 and minus 32° centigrade.

One of the Whitleys engaged on the Munich operation experienced icing in cloud at 1,000 feet. It climbed to 20,000 feet, where it was still in cloud with severe icing conditions. Crystalline ice formed on the leading edges of the wings, over the gun turrets and on the cabin windows. The front gun was frozen up and rendered useless. The aircraft's trimming tabs were jammed by ice and the 'dustbin' turret stuck about a third of the way down its travel. The ceiling of the bomber was reduced to 16,500 feet and it was forced to remain in cloud. After two and a quarter hours in the air the oxygen supply in the cabin was exhausted. Such was the condition of the navigator and wireless operator at this stage, that every few minutes they were compelled to lie down and rest on the floor of the fuselage. The cockpit heating system was useless. Everyone was frozen and had no means of alleviating their distress. On the way home the Whitley descended to 8,000 feet, but icing conditions grew worse and the rear guns now also froze. The windows became completely covered and lumps of ice could be heard coming off the blades of the airscrews and striking the sides of the nose. Continuous movement of the controls was necessary to prevent them from freezing up. Nevertheless, the Whitley successfully homed on to a French base.

The Whitley flown by Sergeant J H P Wynton had a relatively uneventful outward journey to Frankfurt, where the crew successfully released leaflets over the city. After that the trouble began. First the 'dustbin' turret, lowered for the dropping of the leaflets, stuck fast in the down position. Eventually the combined strength of the crew got it up again, but the navigator fainted from the effort. Then, after five and a half hours' flying, the exhausted captain handed over the controls to Sergeant D C Hide the second pilot and collapsed. When Wynton recovered, flames were pouring from the starboard engine. At that time the Whitley was in thick cloud and ice about six inches thick formed on its wings. The starboard engine was at once switched off but the second vacuum pump had now gone, the blind-flying panel was no longer functioning and with ice on the wings the aircraft soon went into a steep dive. The full strength of both pilots was required to pull the aircraft out of the dive and recovery was made at 7,000 feet. It was then found that the rudder and elevators were immovable. The wireless operator sent a signal to say one engine was on fire and tried to get an immediate 'fix' but had no means of knowing if he was transmitting as the instrument glasses were thick with ice. The aircraft at this stage was on an even keel but losing height at 2,000 feet per minute. The port engine had stopped and four inches of ice was observed protruding from the inside of the engine cowling. The airscrew, leading edges and windscreens were covered thickly with ice. Wynton gave the order to jump, only to cancel it when he got no response from Aircraftman First Class Albert James Heller and Corporal Ernest Short, the front and rear gunners. The front gunner was unconscious due to a blow on the head from an ammunition magazine and the rear gunner was unconscious from a blow on the head from the turret due to the dive and subsequent recovery.

The Whitley then assumed a shallow high-speed dive towards a forest. The top hatch was opened to see where they were going and Hide opened the side window. The aircraft emerged from the clouds in heavy rain at about 200 feet above the ground. All they could see was a black forest with a grey patch in the middle, for which they were heading; the second pilot pulled the aircraft over the trees brushing through their tops and the aircraft dropped flat into a field, travelled through a wire fence, skidded broadside on and came to rest with the port wing against the trees on the further side of the clearing. It was then found that the starboard engine fire was increasing in severity. The half-stunned crew crawled out as quickly as they could and attempted to put out the flames, but were unsuccessful. The captain returned to the fuselage to get the extinguisher but found it had already discharged in the crash. On seeing the fire the wireless operator obtained the extinguisher from his cabin, climbed on to the engine cowling and extinguished the flames. It was then ascertained that all members of the crew were safe and unhurt. The crew spent the night in their half-wrecked aircraft and the next morning a Frenchman solicitously asked them what time they would be taking off![4]

Another of the Munich-bound crews was even less fortunate. On the way out ice blanketed the windows of Sergeant Thomas William Bowles' Whitley and there was snow on the floor of the front turret. He and Sergeant Alan Arnold Emery, the second pilot, and the rest of the crew kept up their spirits with songs like *Roll out the Barrel, Hang out the Washing on the Siegfried Line* and *East of the Border* – a slight geographical adaptation for operations over the Franco–German frontier. But when the *Nickel* dropping was done the 'dustbin' remained frozen in the down position and the effort to move it manually soon reduced the crew to complete exhaustion. Then the starboard engine gave trouble and near the frontier a cylinder head blew off. As the Whitley lost height, it descended into thicker and thicker snow clouds and the port engine began to fail. Finally, at 2,000 feet and with hills ahead, Bowles ordered the crew to abandon aircraft. One by one, with varying alarms, they did so, Bowles trimming the aircraft to a slight descending angle before he bailed out. When all this was done the Whitley glided down, bumped heavily and burst into flames, and from the rear turret stepped Sergeant A Griffin the tail-gunner. Blissfully ignorant of the parachute descents – his intercom point had failed at the last moment – he dashed to the front of the burning aircraft to save his comrades. The cockpit was empty. Dazed, cut, burned and more than a trifle puzzled, the sergeant limped his way to the nearest village: here he found the rest of the crew safe in a café, where they exchanged experiences. The front gunner had been knocked unconscious by his parachute which, when opening, hit him on the head. He regained consciousness lying on his back in a field among a herd of curious but friendly cows. The wireless operator was not so lucky. Landing in a field full of curious but hostile bulls, he took successful avoiding action by sprinting for the hedge in full flying kit and cleared a four-foot hurdle. Bowles landed softly and was unhurt and the navigator sprained an ankle. The whole crew after their reunion in the café, were taken, 'complete with bouquets,' to a French hospital, whence, after treatment, they returned the same day to their Squadron.[5]

The only flowers for Squadron Leader James Aldo Bartlett Begg's crew on 77 Squadron following the *Nickeling* sortie from Villeneuve on 10/11 November were at their funeral at Charmes Military Cemetery after their Whitley crashed at Bouxurulles, killing everyone on board the aircraft.

On the evening of Sunday 17 December, 34-year-old Wing Commander Richard Kellett AFC, a distinguished pre-war aviator, now commanding 149 Squadron at Mildenhall, was summoned to 3 Group Headquarters at Beck Row, along with Squadron Leader Paul Harris and the Squadron commanders and section leaders of 9 and 37 Squadrons for a briefing on another raid on Wilhelmshaven the following morning. Unfortunately, there would be little cloud cover, for the weather forecast for 18 December predicted clear conditions. At Honington 9 Squadron was to supply nine Wellingtons for a force of 24, with nine from 149 Squadron and six from 37 Squadron at Feltwell.

Returning to Honington aerodrome after time off on the night of 17 December, 19-year-old Aircraftman First Class Charles Ronald Driver learned that the Wimpy crews on 9 Squadron had to report to the crew room, which he did without delay. For a time, after leaving school, Driver helped in the office of his father, a Yorkshireman who was a wool buyer, but in November 1938 he joined the RAF and before a year had passed he could write the words '1st Class' after his title of Aircraftman. Tall, of fine physique, with black, wavy hair, dark eyes and an open countenance, Driver was delighted and excited, as were all the other members of the crews present, to hear there was a chance of finding the German Fleet in Heligoland Bight and that they would all be on operations next morning.[6] There were the usual preparations and quests for information arising from such an order and then they were all dismissed to bed.

At 04.30 on the morning of 18 December they were roused, and after breakfast, went to the crew room where they stood by until 08.27 when the order came through to take off. They crowded out to find their nine Wellingtons (for a force of 24) all bombed up and ready to depart. Driver clambered aboard 35-year-old Sergeant Jack Ramshaw's Wimpy to make his way to the twin guns in the front cockpit which, with doors closed and the canvas door drawn at the back was entirely separated from the rest of the aircraft by an inch or two of space. The second pilot and navigator was 24-year-old Sergeant Bob Hewitt, whose wife Helen Annie in Glasgow was expecting a baby. Driver's great friend, 21-year-old Leading Aircraftman Walter Lilley from Kippax, was the rear-gunner, Leading Aircraftman J Conolly being the wireless operator. By 08.35 they got away. They were all in the best of spirits, laughing and joking and no doubt wondering what they would do on their leave, which was due next day. Their aircraft was one of a formation of bombers detailed for the raid. It was a fine day, with a good deal of cloud when they started, and these conditions persisted as they climbed steadily while crossing the North Sea. About 10 miles from the German coast, however, the cloud cleared and the sun shone in a clear sky which gave them no cover whatsoever. It was unfortunate for them that just where clouds would have been welcome they vanished from the heavens and left them very vulnerable to attack.

As they flew over the centre of Heligoland Bight they saw below them about eight German destroyers, which quickly put about and made for port. The Wellingtons carried on over Wilhelmshaven where the first Bf 109 which came up to intercept them was met with a burst from one of the aircraft which sent him down. For about fifteen minutes the Wellingtons went inland, flying in close formation at 18,000 feet. Then they ran into a terrific barrage. Without a wisp of cloud to veil them, they made a perfect target for the German gunners. Just as they were wheeling on the instructions of their 28-year-old Canadian Squadron Commander, Squadron Leader Archibald John Guthrie (who was killed moments later), a piece of shell hit Ramshaw's Wellington and put the wireless out of action. As they were completing the turn they saw the enemy fighters coming up at them. There were droves of them taking off in the distance and climbing to intercept. Most of them were Messerschmitt 110s.

This was the beginning of a terrific air battle. The enemy fighters, climbing to about 500 feet above the British bombers, came in to the attack on the outskirts of Wilhelmshaven. In that turning movement of the bombers, six of the Wellingtons were compelled to break formation in order to run up on the others and resume their places. Upon these the fighters pounced and gave them no chance at all. One after the other went down, after taking their toll of the enemy.

The air was filled with the thunder of machine guns. Messerschmitts whirled about. Charles Driver kept gazing all around him, getting in bursts whenever a fighter came within his sights. Ramshaw carried on imperturbably as though he were flying over Hyde Park instead of taking part in an air battle over Wilhelmshaven. Ten minutes after the battle began Lilley got his first 110 full in the sights. Within seconds the centre turret, which was manned by Conolly, was caught by a cannon shell that put it out of action, so he scrambled back to his wireless set and managed to fix the generator to give some power, although it was barely turning over. While Conolly was doing this, a constant stream of fighters kept diving on the tail of the aircraft in an attempt to shoot it down, but Lilley kept them at bay. By now the Wellington was becoming separated from the other bombers. The enemy fighters, determined to destroy it, kept diving to the attack. Waiting his opportunity, the rear-gunner blazed away at a fourth 110. (Though 12 German fighters were claimed shot down, just three were lost and a handful damaged.) A little later the intercom system was smashed. Then Lilley's guns jammed but he made no attempt to leave his exposed position in the tail where he was a target for every enemy aircraft that came along. Instead he tried to get his guns working again, knowing that by so doing he was giving his friends in front a chance to survive. While he was grappling with his guns the enemy fighters, who failed to drive him from his turret, simply riddled him. So died a young hero.

Meanwhile the Messerschmitts were making a fierce attack on the front turret in an effort to silence its guns. Driver, seeing one enemy aircraft firing at him from starboard, gave him a burst, which sent him smoking down to the sea. Immediately another Messerschmitt 110 appeared overhead and claimed the gunner's attention. Driver barely had time to see it go into a three-quarter turn when he found himself under the fire of another fighter on which he had to swing his guns. While he was fighting with this aircraft, the Messerschmitt (believed flown by *Oberleutnant* Gresens of 2./ZG76), which went into the turn came up beneath him and simply blew out the bottom and the side of the turret with cannon shell. 'The first thing I knew,' said Driver afterwards, 'was that I felt pretty cold around my feet and legs. I looked down and saw water below me.' He sat there in the top of the turret with his legs dangling over the North Sea and nothing between him and the sea but the little seat on which he sat. The air seemed to be full of fighters with others climbing to the attack.

'The next thing I knew,' he continued, 'was that my guns refused to fire. I looked to see what the matter was and saw they'd been blown in halves at the barrels.' The cannon shell had cut through the barrels half way down and sheared both of them clean off. 'Then a hail of cannon shell passed in front of me and blew the perspex off,' he went on. He sat there quite in the open, exposed to the full blast of the bomber flying at top speed, and the bitterness of the blast on that December day can be imagined. His guns were useless. There was nothing more he could do, so he decided that the time had come to retreat. As he swung on his seat, he saw that the turret was on fire behind him, where some of the woodwork had been ignited by the cannon shell or tracer. Whipping the glove off his right hand – he wore silk gloves under his thick flying gloves to keep his hands warm – he began to beat at the flames with it. Soon he was beating as hard as he could go with both hands as the few remaining rounds exploded. In about ten minutes he had completely smothered the fire, which threatened to endanger the whole aircraft and then he climbed out of the shattered turret to join the rest of the crew.

When Driver appeared Ramshaw sat at the controls whistling and looking perfectly happy. The front of the aircraft was shot off, the rear-gunner was dead, the middle turret knocked out, the intercommunication system wrecked and the wireless damaged; enemy fighters were attacking from all directions, bursts of bullets were passing in front of him into the control board, but Ramshaw went on whistling. 'Are you OK?' he said to Driver. The Aircraftman put up his thumbs. Directly Hewitt saw him, he put his arms round the front-gunner, being under the impression that when his guns ceased firing he had been shot. Without saying a word the second pilot gave a jerk with his thumb over his shoulder and a nod of his head and Driver knew that he had lost his best friend. They made their way aft and extricated the dead gunner with difficulty, laying him on the floor of the fuselage and covering him. At that moment Bob Hewitt was shot in the arm. 'It doesn't hurt,' he said and went forward to help the captain. Driver went to the astrodome and gazed around:

> As I looked out I saw all the fabric flapping on the wings. The insides were all exposed and you could see the way they were built up. It was as though someone had taken a great knife and carved all along the leading edge of the wings. The nose of the aircraft was sheared away, but I had closed the bulkhead doors to exclude the blast from the other part of the fuselage. The engines themselves looked as though someone had used a sledge hammer and chisel on

them, the metal was all ripped away. We wouldn't have got back but for the pilot. He was cheerful all the way, looking after us like a father, he was marvellous.

As he stood there and surveyed the damage, the last enemy fighter finished off his attack and turned away, to run into the guns of another Wellington, which shot him down. In the distance were Messerschmitts at varying heights flying towards the land. As if the Wellington were not damaged enough already, it was then discovered that the petrol tanks had been holed. 'We are running out of petrol,' said Ramshaw at last. They possessed an emergency supply, which it was necessary to pump by hand. The pump handle was placed at the foot of the camp bed in the fuselage. For half an hour Driver pumped the petrol to keep the aircraft in the air, until their petrol reserves were exhausted. 'We can't make it,' said Ramshaw. 'We'll have to land in the sea.'

They were then limping along at 10,000 feet. As the petrol failed, the engines cut out and Ramshaw told the crew to get ready to abandon the aircraft on hitting the water. Conolly tried desperately to send out an SOS and did not cease trying until the bomber came down. Towards the end of their glide, as they were bracing themselves against the impact, Ramshaw said very off-handedly: 'I've seen a ship and I'll try to make it.' He succeeded. By careful manoeuvring he came down about 400 yards away from the *Erillas*, a Grimsby trawler, 100 miles from The Wash. Ramshaw, who handled the controls so skilfully, received a heavy blow on the head, which left him very dazed; but although they were all shaken up, Driver got off lightly. He at once concentrated on releasing the rubber dinghy, which was stored in a small compartment in the port wing. He got it launched at last and helped the others in, after the wounded second pilot had done what he could. Driver and Conolly made their escape from the sinking bomber by the astrodome, while Hewitt and Ramshaw struggled out of the escape hatch in the top of the pilot's cabin. Ramshaw was so badly shaken by the shock that in climbing out he fell into the sea. But for the prompt assistance of Driver he might easily have been drowned, for the seas were rough and the shattered bomber was low in the water and in imminent danger of foundering. Driver, with the help of the others, managed to haul him into the dinghy just as the Wimpy put her nose straight down and sank.

For fifteen minutes they tossed about in the heavy seas and then they were picked up and transferred to the *Erillas*. The Skipper and crew did all they could for them, providing them with dry clothes and hot coffee. The seas, however, were too much for Driver, who was seasick all the way back to Grimsby, where they landed about 10 o'clock next morning amid the cheers of the crowds on the docks. They had already been posted as missing and aircraft of Coastal Command had been out searching for them all night. Four other Wimpys on the squadron had been shot down off Wilhelmshaven. Only two Wimpys had landed back at Honington.

The loss of 12 Wellingtons, 11 complete crews and several wounded (another two Wimpys were written off in crashes and three others were damaged in crash-landings in England) caused many a sad heart; but Mrs Driver in Stockton-on-Tees was filled with joy and pride when, on 21 December she showed her son, who was home on leave, a telegram announcing that Aircraftman Charles Ronald Driver had been granted the immediate award of the Distinguished Flying Medal, which he received on Boxing Day 1939. It was the second to be awarded in the war. How he escaped that hail of cannon shell, which cut off the barrels of his guns and shot away the greater part of his turret, is a mystery. He won high honour. His best friend willingly gave his life.[7]

The RAF post-mortem into the disastrous raid on Wilhelmshaven concluded that its Wellingtons and Hampdens could no longer cross German territory in daylight and be expected to survive against *Luftwaffe* opposition. From thenceforth Blenheims, whose losses had been lower, were despatched singly or in pairs, to overfly the German North Sea bases. However, a few daylight bomber sweeps were flown over the North Sea. On 2 January 1940 12 Bf 110s attacked three Wellingtons of 149 Squadron. Two of the bombers were shot down and a third had a lucky escape. Meanwhile, RAF ground crews at the Wellington and Hampden bases installed armour plate and applied self-sealing covering to fuel tanks.

In January 1940 the leaflet raids which took place between 7th and 14th afforded an opportunity of reconnoitring the area along the Dutch and Belgian frontiers. On the night of 12/13th the first leaflet raid on Prague and Vienna was made when three Whitleys took off shortly before five in the afternoon. They crossed the German frontier near Karlsruhe at 14,000 feet and their next main landmark was Munich, which was clearly visible. The Bavarian Alps were then crossed, 'their snow-clad peaks showing up magnificently in the starry night.' On reaching Vienna pamphlets were dropped and 'after circling the city, which was a mass of twinkling lights reflected from the black waters of the Danube,' the aircraft set a course for their base, which was reached safely in the early hours of the morning of the 13th. The average temperature throughout the flight was minus 20° centigrade.

Owing to very bad weather the raids were only on a small scale in January and up to 25 February. On that date and for five successive nights, leaflets were dropped in the Berlin area and in the Hamburg, Bremen, Kiel, Lübeck, Cologne and Rhineland areas. In the first few days of March leaflet raids were flown as far as the Posen area and to Czechoslovakia. A leaflet raid on 7 March over the Rhine and the Ruhr was of particular value. The glow of the blast-furnaces was easily seen and their whereabouts were noted. On the night of 15/16 March came the longest raid of all, to Poland. Two Whitleys went to Warsaw and dropped between six and seven million leaflets. On the return journey one aircraft landed in France, the other, flown by Flight Lieutenant Tomlin, behind the lines in Germany. The crew, thinking that they were safely over the border in friendly territory, left the Whitley, Tomlin having locked the controls. It was then near dawn. Locals, when asked at what place the aircraft had landed, greeted the crew with laughter when they discovered that the British airmen imagined that they were in France. By gestures the locals explained that France was a short distance away across the wooded hills. The atmosphere continued to be cordial, but a number of soldiers presently appeared on bicycles. Maintaining their friendly attitude towards the locals the crew of the Whitley gradually edged away and then made a bolt for it. The soldiers opened rifle fire upon them, but the crew reached their aircraft in safety, took off and on the few gallons of petrol remaining succeeded in reaching France.[8]

On 28 March, Flying Officer Trevor James Geach of 77 Squadron at Driffield, who was on a reconnaissance in a Whitley, was not so fortunate. He was shot down by a Dutch Air Force Fokker G1A. Sergeant James Emerson Miller, the Canadian air observer, jumped out of the aircraft at 60 feet and was killed. The Whitley crashed at Vondelingenweg Pernis and the crew were interned but soon released. Two months later, on 28/29 May, Geach crashed at Campineulles-les-Grandes on the bombing operation by Whitleys and Wellingtons on German positions at Hirson near the Dunkirk perimeter during the evacuation of the BEF. All the crew were killed.

On 27 March flight mechanics and duty ground crews at Feltwell had just seen 75 New Zealand Squadron aircrew off on an 'op' and 15 of the mechanics trooped off to the ante room connected to one of the hangars to await their return. Aircraftman Second Class Jimmy Morris was flight mechanic on Wellington Ic *G-George* and he got on very well with the aircrew and ground crew. When the war had started Jimmy was an apprentice engineer and, like most boys of his age, was keen to get into the conflict. He did not know what possessed him to take this attitude as he had a good home life in Liverpool with his mother, father and brother who was six years his junior. Mr Morris was in charge of a power station in Liverpool, so he and his brother were well cared for. For two years he had worked in a smithy heaving a 7lb sledgehammer for an eight and a half hour day. For this he was paid eight shillings per week of five and a half days. From the smithy he was transferred to the fitting shop. This was a world of nuts, bolts, rivets, welding and cutting gear along with general engineering. At the age of 18 he was getting a wage of 27 shillings a week. He enlisted in the RAF at the second attempt and was accepted as a tradesman under training at 3/6 a day. He was really pleased about it. He finished his 12 week course and when he passed out as a 1st class engine mechanic he felt that it was not bad as a first step up the ladder. Posted to Feltwell in the middle of the Norfolk fens, about three miles from Lakenheath railway station, he discovered that the squadron had Wellington Ic bombers and they had given a good account of themselves in the early part of the war:

> The Station was pre-war built and we had good billets but that was about all. I was billeted with about thirty chaps and attached to B Flight. We had a good few visits from German aircraft, both day and night. Sometimes we would go on to the hangar roof and watch Jerry over Lakenheath and feel very smug and safe, till this particular night. Some of the lads were asleep; some playing cards. One of the chaps came in from the toilet and said it sounded as if a German aircraft was flying around. He had hardly got the words out of his mouth when a great big explosion ripped through the room with glass flying all over the place. We did a head count and everybody was in one piece. On going out into the hangar we discovered a great hole in the hangar floor. It was five feet deep and about 15 feet from where we had been sitting in the anteroom. The result of all this was, for about six weeks, everybody was affected by deafness. Jerry paid us a lot of visits, sometimes two or three times a week, all low level stuff. One day I was towing a 500 gallon petrol bowser, having just been to the fuel dump to get it filled up so that I could top up the tanks on my kite. I was half-way back to *G-George* when all hell let loose. Four Jerry raiders flew across the field at about 50 feet, bullet and bombs flying everywhere and there was I sitting on top of 500 gallons of petrol. One bullet in the bowser and I would have been roasted!

In April 1940 Air Marshal Charles 'Peter' Portal CB DSO DFC took over from Air Chief Marshal Sir Edgar Ludlow-Hewitt as C-in-C Bomber Command. When the decision was taken in May to start strategic bombing of Germany by night, there was little the *Luftwaffe* could do to counter these early raids. The subject of night fighting was raised at a conference of German service chiefs just before the war. According to *Kommodore* Josef Kammhuber, who was present at the conference it was dismissed out of hand with the words, 'Night fighting! It will never come to that!'[9] An RAF officer who was captured by the Germans in France towards the end of May and who subsequently escaped, said that he had:

> an opportunity of inspecting a railway station and marshalling yard on the Somme shortly after it had been bombed and there is no doubt that that the damage was terrific. Trucks and engines had been lifted bodily off the track and thrown on their sides; many of

them had been set on fire, the permanent way had been torn up, railway lines buckled.... The general appearance was utter chaos and confusion and reminded one of the film: *The Shape of Things to Come* by H G Wells.

Bernard George 'Max' Meyer, who had been posted to 144 Squadron at RAF Hemswell in Lincolnshire at the beginning of October 1939, recalls:[10]

144 Squadron was equipped with the fairly new Handley Page Hampden, a twin engined medium to heavy bomber which, having taken part in several daylight sorties over the North Sea searching for enemy naval units, had suffered heavy losses in engagements with enemy fighters. I was one of several replacements and a fairly junior officer with about 500 flying hours, which was average for someone with my length of service in the RAF. From the pilot's point of view perhaps the Hampden's biggest drawback was the narrow fuselage. It was impossible to have side-by-side seating in the cockpit as in other aircraft, which meant that you sat there entirely alone and once strapped in on your seat type parachute, remained there for the duration of the flight. On one flight I sat there for 9½ hours and was so stiff when I got back that I had to be lifted out of the cockpit by the ground crew. However, despite these problems and until the really heavy bombers came into service later on, the Hampden proved to be a very efficient and successful bomber much liked by its crews for its responsiveness and versatility. It was also solidly constructed and capable of taking a lot of punishment. The engines were especially reliable and economical to run. One occasion later when we were hit by flak in one engine over Hannover, the other engine, working very hard, I must admit, brought us home safely.

After the Airspeed Oxford and the Avro Anson during training the Hampden was something quite different. The greater performance of the two Bristol Pegasus XVIII engines with propellers in fine pitch at full take-off boost was quite startling. You felt a massive punch in your back as you opened up the throttles. Once off the ground with wheels and flaps up, it handled beautifully. With its two 1,000hp engines, it became a fast, powerful and highly manoeuvrable flying machine. The pilot's field of view was excellent. From a high seating position the outlook forward and on both beams was much better than that of most other operational aircraft at that time, a most useful characteristic, particularly when low flying was to become very important for Hampden operations in the future. However, you certainly couldn't take liberties with the Hampden. As with most powerful aircraft on take-off, especially with a full bomb-load, it would, given the chance, swing viciously to starboard and if action was not taken immediately to correct the swing, you would find yourself hurtling along at right angles to your intended take-off path. Another rather more unpleasant trick of the Hampden could occur if you made a very flat turn, for example, on a bombing run up to the target. There was a tendency for the twin rudders to slam right over and lock in that position. I think it was called a stabilized yaw. Unless you took immediate corrective action, which was to push the nose down and build up a high speed, it was impossible to centralize the rudders and you would remain in a sort of flat spin until you hit the ground. If you had insufficient height in which to recover control, it was of course, usually fatal, as quite a number of Hampden pilots found to their cost.

It was decided that the losses suffered in daylight raids were becoming unacceptable and in future we would operate under cover of darkness. It was therefore rather a disappointment for me to be told by my Flight Commander that I would have to gain considerably more night flying experience before I could go on my first night operation over enemy territory. It was mid-April 1940 before I was considered to be sufficiently qualified to take part in operations at night. My first night operation [*on 20/21 April*] was a mine-laying sortie to the mouth of the River Elbe. You were usually detailed for several easy 'trips' to start with, until you had gained sufficient experience to undertake the more difficult ones later. Our flight to the mouth of the Elbe was fairly uneventful. We crossed the North Sea to Terschelling and then followed the Friesian Islands until we reached our target area. It was a moonlight night – we saw a few searchlights on the mainland and encountered some light flak in the target area. The round trip took just on five hours' flying time.

My next three operations were all on mine-laying, in the Baltic, necessitating flights of around seven hours' duration. During this period the weather was never very good and on one occasion I was diverted on return to an airfield in Scotland because the weather in Lincolnshire was unfit for landing. Mine-laying was carried out at low altitude and with great care, to ensure accurate positioning of the mine. Because the sophisticated navigational aids were not available in these early days of the war, we navigated by dead reckoning and map reading in the final stages. We usually had to spend quite some time flying around in the target area to establish our correct positioning of the mines. This made us extremely vulnerable to attack from ground defences and flak ships. A small parachute attached to the mine to retard its entry into the water separated on entry and floated on the top for a short time. The German navy used fast, armed boats to search for the parachutes and buoy the spot for sweeping later. In an attempt to stop the patrol boats doing this, we used to remain in the area as long as fuel permitted and shoot them up, if they appeared. I can well remember an occasion when we spotted a smallish vessel just ahead of us. It looked like one of these boats so I put the nose of the aircraft down and gave it a good long burst from my fixed forward firing gun and at the same time told my rear gunners to also have a go. However, the stream of tracer from my gun completely dazzled me and reduced my night vision to almost nil.

Unfortunately for me, the armourers who had prepared the aircraft had not changed the ammunition to that for night-time use, which has much less tracer in its make-up. Just as I pulled up and away from the boat I felt a distinct shudder run through our aircraft. At the same time I wished I had been less adventurous and given the vessel a wide berth because it suddenly replied to our attack in a very hostile manner with a barrage of multi pom-pom and cannon fire as we passed over it. Fortunately we were diving at high speed and quickly drew away down at sea level. We had, of course, picked on a flak-ship, which the Germans used to guard likely mine-laying areas. The following day my ground crew had to fit new bomb-bay doors to replace the old ones which were not only badly damaged but, also had lengths of aerial wire embedded in them, which we must have removed from the mast of that ship.

An ingenuity rivalling that of Heath Robinson was developed by 'Max' Meyer's Canadian navigator, Pilot Officer William Frank Tudhope DFC. Among other things which used to be served out to the crews who took part in long bombing raids were cold meat pies. These were palatable when hot, but not quite so appetising when cold. Bomber crews would get hungry after spending six or eight hours in the air, but even so Meyer and Tudhope found that the cold meat pies still left much to be desired. It was then that the navigator had his brilliant idea. Placing the meat pies in a paper bag, he tied the closed mouth of the bag against the side of the hot-air pipe which was used for heating the cabin, then he inserted the mouth of the hot-air pipe, with its bag of meat pies attached, into a bigger paper bag, the mouth of which was tied securely round the pipe to prevent the hot air from escaping. By the time they had reached Berlin, their pies were deliciously hot and after bombing their targets they would settle down and enjoy a good meal. Bill Tudhope was killed later, on the Homberg operation on the night of 10/11 August 1941, piloting a Hampden which crashed in the Ijsselmeer.

Meyer's crew used to sing all sorts of popular songs while they were flying over Germany. Sometimes they transmitted on their wireless to tell the Germans what they thought of them and if their language was a little strong they were perhaps to be excused. Of course the weather often played the most extraordinary tricks. Once over Hannover Meyer found that the port engine had frozen at 8,000 feet and so much snow came into the aircraft that he was able to scoop it off his sleeve to make a snowball for the navigator. Another time he ran into thick cumulus cloud at 15,000 feet and soon heard the buzzing on the intercom system which presaged an electrical storm:

> I noticed a little blue ball of fire on my front gun. It got larger until it was as big as a grape fruit and my navigator looked ghastly in the blue light. The propellers from boss to tip were one mass of blue flame and the whole of the leading edge of each wing was lit up; while a vivid blue flame, three feet long streamed out in front of each wing-tip. My wireless operator did not dare touch anything. He got shocks right and left and saw a trail of blue sparks flowing out of the aerial.[11]

On 3 April Germany mounted *Weserubung Nord* and supply ships sailed for the invasion of Norway. On the night of 6/7 April, during a reconnaissance patrol, a Whitley on 10 Squadron crashed at Scartho near Grimsby, and a Hampden on 83 Squadron was abandoned over Whitley Bay with the loss of all the crew. On 7 April a dozen Wellingtons on 9 and 115 Squadrons at Lossiemouth and Kinloss searched off the Danish coast for heavy German naval units. They did not find them, but on the way home, flying close to broken cloud, 115 Squadron were jumped by Bf 110s. Two of the Squadron's Wimpys were shot down and both crews were lost without trace.

At dawn on 9 April German forces invaded Denmark and Norway and Bomber Command was ordered to do what it could to slow the German advance in southern Norway. The Wellington, Whitley and Hampden squadrons (and Blenheim units in 2 Group) were not suited for the role. There was no fighter escort and the distance involved round trips of up to 1,000 miles entirely over water. Twenty-four Hampdens and Wellingtons searched for German warships off Bergen and 12 aircraft were recalled. Twelve Wellingtons on 9 and 115 Squadrons were dispatched against two cruisers, the *Köln* and the *Königsberg,* at Bergen. Their attack according to the enemy was 'vigorously pressed home' but it resulted in nothing more than some near misses and a few wounded German sailors. The *Köln* made good her escape that evening but the *Königsberg* had been damaged by Norwegian shore batteries during her approach and she was sunk next day by Fleet Air Arm Skuas. On the 11th six Hampdens were dispatched to search for shipping off Kristiansund but abandoned the task because the weather was too clear. Six Wellingtons on 115 Squadron were dispatched to bomb Sola airfield near Stavanger 450 miles from bomber airfields on England's east coast. Three aircraft got their bombs away. One of the remaining three was shot down by German fighters. On 11/12 April, 23 Whitleys and 20 Hampdens searched for shipping in the Skagerrak and Kattegat when four aircraft attacked ships at various locations between Kiel Bay and Oslo. A Whitley scored a direct hit on a ship which was believed to be an ammunition ship and which appeared to explode. One Whitley was lost.

In 5 Group, from the outbreak of the war in 1939 and again in 1940, 44 and 50 Squadrons were detached for short periods to Coastal Command. 50 Squadron's contingent included the famous 'Ye Olde Dingo Flyte' led by their quiet, unassuming Australian CO, Squadron Leader Duncan Charles Frederick Good, born in Adelaide in South Australia in 1916 and who received his commission in the RAF in 1937. 'Ye Olde Dingo Flyte' was originally founded in the First World War when 50 Squadron, then commanded by a Major Harris who later became Air Chief Marshal Sir Arthur Harris of Bomber Command, used the attack signal 'All Dingoes Run.' When the squadron re-formed a few years before the Second World War, 'A' Flight commemorated the historic past and the old signal used in the defence of London by painting 'Ye Olde Dingo Flyte' above the door of the flight office.

Wilfred John 'Mike' Lewis, a Canadian Hampden pilot on 44 Squadron at Waddington in Lincolnshire and who had joined the RAF on a short service commission in 1939, hoping later to have 'a very good shot at becoming an airline pilot' recalls:

> I did my first flight and first tour on Hampdens. I loved the Hampden, two tremendously reliable engines. A beautiful aeroplane to fly, terrible to fly in – cramped, no heat, no facilities where you could relieve yourself, you got in there and you were stuck there. The aeroplane was like a fighter. It was only 3 feet wide on the outside of the fuselage and the pilot was a very busy person. There were 111 items for the pilot to take care of because on the original aircraft he had not only to find the instruments, the engine and all that, but also he had all the bomb switches to hold the bombs. After the war broke out we were placed on standby to attack German naval units if they ventured out into the North Sea and that's as far as we could go. We could not drop bombs on land. Most times we didn't find anything at all. It heated up in the Norwegian campaign, which resulted in a disastrous attack on a cruiser and destroyers in Kristiansund on 12 April.

Early in the morning of the 12th the 26,000-ton battle cruisers *Scharnhorst* and *Gneisenau*, nicknamed by the RAF *Salmon & Glukstein* (a famous London department store), now joined by the *Hipper*, which had left Trondheim on the night of the 10/11th, were picked up by Hudsons of Coastal Command off the south-west coast of Norway. A striking force amounting to 83 aircraft – 36 Wellingtons, 24 Hampdens and 23 Blenheims

– was dispatched the same day but was once more frustrated by the weather. As a last resort 12 Hampdens on 44 and 50 Squadrons went out in sections of three to try to attack the warships in Kristiansund but were caught by German fighters. Having no defence against a beam attack, they were 'hacked down from the wing man inwards' until half their number had perished. Three Wellingtons were also shot down. 'It was an error in the Group operational headquarters in not transmitting Bomber Command's operational directive that we should not approach within 50 miles of the Norwegian coast unless we had cloud cover,' recalled 'Mike' Lewis:

We went in under an absolutely cloudless sky. We were literally over the harbour when the next thing people started reporting that fighters were climbing up. The German pilots had obviously been briefed on the ability of the Hampden to defend itself because we couldn't traverse our guns to reach them. They turned in and just sat blasting away at us and blowing us out of the sky until eventually they ran out of gas and had to go home themselves. If there had been more gasoline I think that none of us would have reached our home. We were sitting ducks. It was terrifying.

German radio admitted the loss of five fighters, one of which made a bad mistake by flying right over the top of the Hampden piloted by Squadron Leader Good, presenting a nice blue belly as a perfect target for Sergeant Smith the rear-gunner sitting in the 'tin,' with an angle of fire below the tail to deal with attackers who came up from below and Sergeant Wallace the wireless operator sitting in the turret above him with an angle of fire over the tail to cope with attacks from above, who promptly shot it down, amid much jubilation. The surviving Hampdens closed their ranks and another nine Messerschmitt 109s attacked and continued to attack until the Hampdens were 60 miles out at sea. Good, looking down on the North Sea, saw the seventh victim ditch 120 miles from Newcastle and watched Australian Pilot Officer John Bartlett Bull's crew launch their yellow dinghy. He circled round while his navigator marked the exact position so that help could be sent to pick them up. The four gallant men in the yellow dinghy laughed and waved cheerily. And that was the last ever seen of them, for they were never found. When Squadron Leader Good landed, his aircraft was very much shot about. But the unbelievable thing was that the petrol tank had been pierced and the petrol had caught fire. The tank itself was all blistered and there was an area of the wing five feet long by four feet wide all burned. Somehow, in some way the blazing petrol was put out. Everyone was amazed. It was considered to be impossible. That day it was surely a miracle which saved Squadron Leader Good and his crew.

After the debacle of 12 April 1940, Bomber Command quickly reverted to night operations against airfields and shipping in Norway. Almost 200 sorties were flown against the airfields in Norway and Denmark between 14 April and 21 April but the distance was considerable, the weather over the North Sea often unfavourable and the enemy defences too strong to allow RAF aircraft to operate except by night or under cover of cloud. On 17/18 April, when 20 Wellingtons and Whitleys set out to attack airfields at Stavanger, Trondheim and Oslo, only 11 Wimpys found their target and they bombed Stavanger airfield. One Wellington on 99 Squadron at Newmarket piloted by Flying Officer Abraham Frederick Smith, a South African, was lost without trace.

Nine Whitleys on 77 Squadron stationed at Driffield but temporarily deployed to Kinloss on the shores of the Moray Firth in Scotland for operations over Norway, took off the next night to attack shipping in the Oslo and Trondheim areas. The weather was bad and only three aircraft bombed the port which lies just south of the Arctic Circle. Thirty miles short of the target while the Whitleys were flying at 10,000 feet the Whitley flown by Flying Officer Ray Chance suffered a port engine failure and a flame started flickering from it. The Whitley quickly lost height and at 23.40 it hit the turbulent Arctic waters. Chance recalls:

Events seem to have belonged to another world. I remember a noise like a thousand panes of glass being shattered and that a steam roller had landed on my feet and working up, was crushing my head. I must have gone unconscious. I was aware later, that I was in heaven. A long dim corridor stretched before me and at the end, on the right, was a large double door, which led to a ballroom, the dazzling lights of which shone into the corridor. No one was about so I decided to make my way towards it.

Eventually, Chance, who had a smashed right foot, managed to get into the dinghy with the other survivors. Sergeant Tindall the bomb aimer was hanging on one side of the dinghy. Pilot Officer Ronald Hall the navigator was 50 yards away in the darkness crying for help. Then Chance heard him shouting but more faintly and he conceived the idea of going over the side and trying to drag the dinghy towards him. He got up on one elbow but fell back exhausted. He had the agony of listening to him drown. In the small hours leading Aircraftman O'Brien and Aircraftman First Class Douglas appeared to be on the verge of passing out, so sitting on the rim, Chance supported both with an arm around each neck. He thought that they would fall backwards into the sea, which was getting choppier now. To try to keep up their spirits and their warmth, Chance led the crew in singing *Roll Out The Barrel*. Finally, they were picked up by HMS *Basilisk* (which was sunk later off Dunkirk during the BEF evacuation). On the second day they reached Scapa Flow. Chance was in hospital for a long time after that. It was probably the first time in the war that a crew had survived a Whitley ditching in the sea.[12]

One of the functions of the RAF during the evacuation of Norway was to reduce the enemy's air activity by bombing his airfields. In accordance with this plan Bomber Command attacked Stavanger-Sola and Oslo-Fornebu airfields by day and by night throughout the entire period of the evacuation, besides directing a lesser number of sorties against the Danish airfields of Aalborg and Rye. On the night of 20/21 April, 36 Whitleys were detailed to bomb various airfields and shipping and 22 aircraft bombed targets, including airfields at Stavanger and Kristiansund and at Aalborg. No shipping was located. Twenty-three Hampdens meanwhile laid mines in the Elbe estuary and some then patrolled seaplane bases at Borkum and Sylt. There were no losses from any of these operations. A number of Wellingtons on 9 Squadron that flew from Honington to attack Stavanger airfield had strict orders not to attack without positive identification of the target. Sergeant Frank Petts, a pilot on the Squadron, recalls:

We had of course no aids to help in this identification. Our only *en route* navigation aid was Radio Luxemburg, which unlike Allied or enemy broadcasting stations was good for loop bearings, but we made our landfall a few miles north of Stavanger, having broken cloud well out to sea. We could not afford to overshoot before descending or we might have finished up in the mountains. At one point the coast was clear of cloud but southwards stretched a solid sheet of low stratus. We tried from several directions but could not find a break and the cloud base was too low for us to creep in beneath it so we brought our bombs back. Several other crews had the same experience but the last to arrive found a break and were able to bomb.[13]

The heaviest raid on the airfields in Norway and Denmark was on the night of 30 April/1 May when 50 aircraft – 24 Whitleys, 16 Wellingtons and 10 Hampdens – were dispatched to bomb Stavanger, Fornebu and Aalborg airfields. Thirty-five aircraft bombed these targets, and on the operation on Stavanger, two Wellingtons on 37 Squadron at Feltwell and a Whitley were lost off the coast of Norway. Three other aircraft crashed in England on return and a Wellington was lost over The Wash with all the crew killed. On 1/2 May, 12 Whitleys and six Hampdens bombed all three airfields again without loss. Eleven Hampdens carried out mine-laying in the Elbe estuary and in Helsingör harbour, Denmark, also with no losses. The night following, 12 Whitleys and a dozen Wellingtons returned to bomb Stavanger, Rye and Fornebu and 26 Hampdens laid mines in Oslo Fiord and Kiel Bay. Twenty-two bombers got their bombs away on the airfields and all except one aircraft, a Whitley on 51 Squadron at Dishforth, which crashed at Easingwold, Yorkshire, returned safely from the night's operations. On the night of 3/4 May, 10 Hampdens laid mines off the Norwegian and German coasts and two Wellingtons sent to patrol seaplane bases were recalled.

Squadron Leader Good sat on one of the bomb trolleys by his Hampden at Waddington waiting while the ground staff completed their preparations for the night's operations. It was just after 7 p.m. on Saturday, 4 May. The sky was red and the Squadron Leader felt decidedly uneasy. He and four other crews had been briefed to mine the port of Oslo and it was a long sea crossing from England to Norway and back again. Taking off at about 8 p.m., the pilot set course for Norway, to help to make Oslo as dangerous as possible for the German supply ships using the port. Throughout the long journey across the North Sea he remained uneasy, looking round for fighters all the time. It was as though he had a foreboding. About 23.30 the Norwegian coast came into sight. The pilot was by no means sure of his position after the long crossing. Flying at 8,000 feet, he saw above him a layer of stratocumulus clouds at 10,000 or 12,000 feet; below him the mountains of Norway were covered with snow. Changing course, he flew inland across Norway in search of his target. The crew of the bomber were quite undisturbed. No searchlights sought them, not a gun fired at them. Good scanned the land below him all the time to try to pick up Oslo Fiord. Pilot Officer Walter George Gardiner, the navigator/bomb-aimer seated in the front cockpit, was bent on the same task. 'Nothing could shake Gardiner,' Good once remarked. 'Finally, about 50 miles away, I saw a whole packet of searchlights and flak go up and decided that was the place, so I went across to have a look.' The Hampden was then about 20 miles away. Maintaining the same course, the pilot started to lose height until he was down to 2,000 feet. The tongue of land running up to Oslo and dividing the fiord into two was plainly visible. He decided to use that tongue of land to mask his approach to the port, dart from its cover at top speed, deposit his mine and do a steep turn away to head for home.

Good took the Hampden down until it was just below the level of the spit of land. Everything remained quiet and the pilot was convinced that the enemy had no idea of his approach or that the port was likely to be attacked. Boosting the speed, the pilot flew out from the cover of the point into the open fiord with bomb doors open. As he did so a searchlight from the opposite cliff caught the pilot and navigator and nearly blinded them. At once the defences came into action. 'The ack-ack was the heaviest I've ever seen. You would not think an aircraft could fly through it without being cut to pieces. There were a lot of light guns as well as machine guns firing tracer,' Gardiner stated after his return.

Good saw streams of pink shells like fireworks spraying out from the opposite sides of the fiord ahead. He observed the two streams of fire crossing each other in the centre and, knowing that no aircraft could possibly run that gauntlet of fire, decided on the instant to drop down almost to water level in order to run in underneath the fiery arch of shells and tracer. The Germans were firing directly across at each other and somebody must have suffered badly that night. Moving the stick forward, he dived under the barrage of fire. The masts of ships rushed past just above the level of his wing tips. Ahead was the spot where he was to lay his mine. Just as he was about to shout to Gardiner to drop it, there was a crash like the breaking of windows, an enormous flash of light which blinded him so that he could not see what he was doing and an acrid, sulphurous, burning smell. He knew he had been hit. The aircraft started to run away from him. Yet even at that moment the task he had come so far to perform overshadowed everything else. 'Let it go – I'm hit!' he shouted to advise Gardiner to deposit the mine and tell him that he was wounded. 'I'm hit! I'm hit!' he repeated. But no one could hear him. The wires of the intercom system were severed by the explosion. The Hampden ran on past the island where the mine was to be dropped and did a steep turn. The senses of the pilot were so clouded that he could never afterwards recall anything that happened from just after he was hit until he came out of the turn. He must have been flying the aircraft subconsciously according to the plan so firmly fixed in his mind. Coming out of the turn, he sought to climb, but when he tried to pull the wheel back he discovered that his arms were powerless. Wounds in the left wrist and right elbow rendered both arms useless.

The Hampden's nose dropped and pointed straight towards the sea. Unable to use his arms to pull back the wheel, in that desperate emergency he thought of the trimming wheel at the right hand side of his seat. The trimming wheel is a device which acts upon the elevator in order to take the physical strain off the pilot. Directly he has found the correct amount of control required to hold the aircraft on her course at the desired height, by turning the trimming wheels he can hold the rudder and elevators in position without having to endure the strain all the time on his arms and legs. Unable to use his arms, which hung down helplessly, he managed to hook one of his fingers in the trimming wheel and, by swaying his body, gradually moved it round and gained a little height. A gigantic effort was required to do this, but he managed it. Then he started to kick on the rudder, thinking that the noise made by the escape of the compressed air would attract the attention of other members of the crew. All this time the searchlights were flashing and the guns were doing their best to blow the Hampden out of the sky. He looked at the altimeter and saw that they were climbing. He knew something was wrong with his face. Dimly he saw the blood dripping out of his cuffs.

Although badly wounded, he still remained conscious. It must have been through sheer will-power that he clung to his senses. He kicked again on the rudder, but the crew merely thought that he was taking the usual evasive action.

Less than a minute earlier as the Hampden made its run up under the cover of the spit of land, Gardiner in the nose saw the ships slipping by. They were moored close inshore parallel with the cliffs, no doubt to protect them from air attack. How he regretted that they had no bombs with which to attack them, for there was no one on board and the ships were quite undefended. Dazzled by the searchlight as they ran out into the open fiord, amazed by the heaviness of the gunfire which greeted them, he waited patiently for the island to turn up where he had to drop his mine:

> I think it was a Bofors gun which hit us. It was the last shell of a burst of five – they fire in clips of about five. I could see them – bang! bang! bang! And the last got us. They must have had our range nicely. I thought it had hit the outer fuselage and did not worry very much.

The Hampden ran on its course as he expected. Although he received no order, he automatically dropped the mine on the right spot and reported that it was away. Then the bomber banked in a right-hand turn and began to sway and dive. Gardiner remained there quite cool, thinking the captain was just doing his best to dodge the shells. Not until the wing nearly hit the mast of a ship did he suddenly wonder if all was well. Quickly he switched on the light in his cockpit to have a look round. To his surprise there was a pool of blood in the tunnel under the pilot's seat and he saw the blood steadily dripping down. Instantly he realized that the pilot was wounded and he knew he would have to fly the Hampden back to its base. Gardiner had already worked out the two courses to take them back to Britain. Knowing these would be essential, he rapidly noted them on a piece of paper and then crawled through the tunnel and stood up behind the pilot. A glance revealed the serious face wounds of his captain and then his eye caught sight of the altimeter.

Swiftly he thrust his arm past the wounded pilot, caught hold of the control wheel and pulled it back. The aircraft was so low that he anticipated hitting the edge of the cliff at any moment. As soon as he pulled the stick back, the bomber started to climb, but not until he had taken the aircraft to a safe height and knew it was no longer in danger of hitting anything, could he attend to the pilot. With difficulty he unbuckled the captain's parachute harness; then he undid the straps which held him in his seat, after which he was able to pull down the back of the seat – for with the pilot strapped into his seat and his feet in the pedals the back cannot be let down.

Wriggling over the wounded man, the navigator grabbed the wheel to take the Hampden to a higher level. Eventually he attracted the attention of Sergeant Wallace, the wireless operator, who had no idea that anything was wrong. He heard the bang, as did Sergeant Smith, the rear-gunner who was also a trained navigator, but they were so busy firing at the searchlights and guns on the ground that they paid little attention to it.

In the pilot's cockpit blood was everywhere. 'Pull him out from under me,' Gardiner said. With considerable difficulty, Wallace succeeded in drawing the wounded man backwards until his head lay on the padded top of the main spar, on which the back of the pilot's seat rests when it is pulled down. After further efforts, he manipulated him so that the back of the pilot's seat could be raised again. The remarkable thing is that Squadron Leader Good had made his crew practise this exact manoeuvre in case something like this ever came to pass, in which event they would know exactly what to do. Somehow Wallace and Smith managed between them to lower Good down the well leading to the front cockpit. The wounded man was bleeding very badly from one arm and it was obvious that unless this was stopped quickly, his chances would be small. Obtaining the bandages and dressings from the first-aid kit, Smith improvised a tourniquet with a small bottle and succeeded in checking the loss of blood. Then he gave him an injection of morphia in his calf and covered him up with fur coats to make him as comfortable as possible. In spite of the morphia and the loss of blood, the wounded man did not lose consciousness. He was very weak and in a sorry condition. He had a hole in his cheek, his tongue was torn and part of his nose was nearly off; he had swallowed a tooth or two that was knocked out and a lot of blood, yet he still knew what was going on.

Meanwhile Gardiner had taken the bomber up to 8,000 feet to fly across the country to Stavanger. Asking the wireless operator to see if the tanks were holed, he was thankful to learn that they were intact. Sergeant Wallace did his best to repair the intercommunication system, but could only succeed in passing messages through to the pilot. Smith, who remained in the front cockpit to check the navigation, could not speak to the pilot, so he had to pass slips of paper up to him from the tunnel under the seat.

Leaving Stavanger behind, the bomber sped homeward across the North Sea. The wounded man lay with his back against the bulkhead listening to the hum of the engines. A sudden flapping disturbed him.

It's all right,' shouted the pilot down to him. 'We're on our way home.'

And they were. Advising the base that they were returning with a casualty on board, the wireless operator got a fix by which they checked their course and they duly touched down and taxied right up to the tarmac where an ambulance was waiting to take Squadron Leader Good to hospital Before he knew what was happening they were cutting his uniform off him – his Royal Australian Air Force uniform which was something he prized beyond anything. No words could express his gratitude to the surgeons whose skill left him almost unscarred. In ten days he was out of hospital. Pilot Officer Gardiner was awarded the DFC. It meant that another nicely engraved copper dingo could be added to the rows of dingoes, all running for their lives, on the blackboard in Squadron Leader Good's office at Waddington. Each copper dingo represented a decoration awarded to Australian members of the Squadron.[14]

Early on 10 May the long-awaited German offensive in the west began with German troops crossing the borders of Belgium and Holland with airborne landings in several places. At Honington Wing Commander Andrew 'Square' McKee, the thick-set New Zealander CO of 9 Squadron, who was about five foot five in both directions, could tell his crews little more than they had gleaned from their wireless sets. Twenty-year-old Sergeant Rupert Cooling, who was known as 'Tiny' because he was six foot seven, was second pilot on Sergeant Douglas' crew, one of two new crews who had arrived on the Station barely three days before. Cooling recalls:

> The mess was quiet at lunchtime. Serious groups gathered round the radiogram, listening silently to the news. A lot was said but little was learned: things did not seem to be going well. The murmur of voices stilled as 'Square' McKee walked briskly into the crew room, followed by his flight commanders. The target was the aerodrome at Waalhaven. It had been seized by German troops. Junkers Ju 52s were flying in men, munitions and supplies. Dutch troops were to attack at last light. The Wellingtons would crater the airfield, destroy the transports and soften up the defences. Each was to carry sixteen 250lb bombs, nose and tail fused for maximum fragmentation. Weather was forecast to be fine. Flak, said the intelligence officer, would be light stuff, mainly 20mm. The Germans had had no time to bring in heavy anti-aircraft weapons. Single engined fighters were unlikely but there were reports of Bf 110 activity. He did not mention that five out of six Blenheims had been shot down by 110s earlier in the day and over the same target.

At 17.30 hours 36 Wellingtons were dispatched. Douglas piloted *U-Uncle*, a Wellington Ia. 'Tiny' Cooling continues:

> Away to starboard, England was reduced to a dark shadow, separating sea from sky. With it strangely, went those last niggling doubts; those faint tremors of fear were swamped by a rising tide of excitement. 'Wireless operator to front turret. Second pilot to the astrodome.' Sergeant Douglas made his dispositions. We were 6,000 feet above the polders. In the distance I saw that the flickering

curtain of flak was hemmed with orange flame and rolling curls of dense black smoke. 'Bomb doors open. Target in sight. Right a little, right.' The last word was drawn out and then chopped, as the nose came round to the required heading. Now the lights were directly ahead. 'Left, left. Steady. Bombs gone.'

The Wellington jerked perceptively, as 4,000lb of metal and high explosive plunged from the gaping belly. There was a sharp 'twack' like some large and floppy fly swat striking the upper surface of the starboard wing. A triangle of the camouflage covering leapt up to dance upon the upper surface of the starboard wing. Surprised at his own calm and composure, Cooling said, 'Pilot, we've been hit. Starboard mainplane. There's a patch of fabric flapping just outboard of the engine.'

U-Uncle flew on past the Dutch coast. Out over the North Sea Sergeant Douglas handed over control to 'Tiny' Cooling before going aft to see the damage for himself:

It was dark when *U for Uncle* crossed the Suffolk coast. Electric blue flashes from Honington beckoned us to within sight of the flickering gooseneck flare path. With a gentle bump the wheels touched, the tail settled. Then the Wellington tugged determinedly to starboard. In the light of the downward recognition lamp the flattened starboard tyre was clearly visible. Still hot, the engine exhaust rings ticked and cracked above our heads in the cool night air as we examined the wing, the wheel and the undercarriage doors by the light of our torches. A ragged piece of torn fabric as big as a dinner plate dripped intermittently, exuding the sweet smell of high-octane petrol. One undercarriage door, perforated like the surface of a cheese grater, reflected a scatter of silver streaks on the matt black paint.

'Max' Meyer on 144 Squadron recalls:[15]

By now and having successfully carried out several quite difficult mine-laying operations, we as a crew were considered to be competent to attack targets on the mainland. So, on 11/12 May we were detailed to bomb the railway yards at Mönchengladbach in an attempt to slow up the German advance. [*This was the first raid of the war on a German town. 37 aircraft – 19 Hampdens and 18 Whitleys – were to attack road and rail communications.*] These were really pioneering days for the RAF. Few people had much experience of flying long distances at night, sometimes in appalling weather conditions let alone against highly efficient enemy defences. To find our way, we flew by dead-reckoning navigation and by map reading if we could see the ground. The sophisticated navigational aids did not become available until much later in the war.

Two Hampdens and a Whitley were lost. Four people including an Englishwoman living in Mönchengladbach were killed.[16] One of the Hampdens lost was a 144 Squadron aircraft at Hemswell piloted by Wing Commander Arthur Noble Luxmoore. He suffered a savage attack from the pom-poms of a mechanized column of German troops and suddenly felt the bomber get out of control as it shuddered from a direct hit, which destroyed part of the rudder controls. With a supreme physical effort, he regained control and held on his course to his target, where Pilot Officer R E Allitt, the second pilot and bomb-aimer, carried out his task and bombed the works. Turning to struggle home, the bomber was subjected to an intense barrage. The Hampden shuddered again as a shell blew away a large part of the main plane. Fighting to keep her in the air, Luxmoore carried on. Another hit put the starboard engine out of action. The crew felt the aircraft shudder again and yet again as two more shells struck home. The Hampden started to fly in circles owing to the loss of the rudder control. Luxmoore called Sergeant Herbert Watley the observer to enter the tunnel right under the pilot's seat and apply all his strength to the rudder bar to help to regain control and keep the bomber on the right course. Then it started to dive and only after a fierce fight could they get the Hampden on an even keel again. All the time the aircraft kept trying to spin or fly in circles and it took the utmost physical strength of Watley and the captain to counteract these movements. Once or twice when the unrelenting searchlights held them, Watley rushed to his guns and attacked them and succeeded in shooting two of them out. Corporal Ronald Jolly the wireless operator had the satisfaction of shooting another one out. By sheer physical strength the pilot and Watley fought to maintain the heavy bomber in the air while Jolly worked calmly at the wireless obtaining fixes to enable the navigator to give the pilot his course. Luxmoore was determined not to let his crew fall into enemy hands. Fighting all the time to counteract the erratic movements of the bomber, he flew safely across the Ardennes and arrived over France after a nightmare passage of a hundred miles. They were down now to less than 1,000 feet and he gave the crew the order to bail out. Allitt and Watley at once got clear. At that moment Jolly was getting a fix from Le Bourget and did not receive the order as he was not on the intercommunication system. When he got through to the captain again he heard his voice saying: 'Have you jumped?' Quickly destroying the aircraft papers and leaving the transmitter key switched on, Jolly bailed out at a low altitude and while he was floating down to safety, he saw the bomber fall out of control and burst into flames. Knowing that he alone would not be able to maintain control, Luxmoore had held on long enough to enable his crew to get out safely but by that time it was too late for him to save himself.

A further series of adventures befell the other members of the crew. As Allitt got up again after landing in a clearing in a wood he thought: 'If only I had my torch and maps I'd escape.' A second later he realized that he actually had his torch and maps in his hand – he had grabbed them and retained a grip on them all the way down. Making his way to the nearest village, he was at once challenged by a French soldier who held him up with his bayonet under the impression that he was a German parachutist and put him under arrest in the guard room. He explained that he was an English flying officer, but they were taking no chances until a French officer arrived and escorted him to his general.

Watley landed in a big tree down which he climbed with difficulty in the dark. Making his way laboriously, with many a stumble, through the undergrowth of the wood, he suddenly felt himself slipping and rolling downwards. When at last he came to a stop he found he was on the edge of water, so he wisely remained where he was until daylight. In the dawn he saw he was on the bank of a river, so he set off again to the west, falling in with two Belgian peasants whom he accompanied along the road. From time to time German aircraft flew over the road and machine gunned them, but each time they managed to escape. After tramping for eight miles Watley was challenged by some French soldiers who promptly arrested him, having no doubt that he also was a German parachutist. Marching him to headquarters, they handed over their prisoner.

Jolly landed on a steep slope, which happened to be the roof of a house, down which he slid. The lines of his parachute were entangled somewhere above and as he tried to make his way forward he felt something give and break at every step he took. Floundering along in the dark, he could not understand where he was or what was happening and at length he came to the conclusion that he was walking on ice. Not until he fell a few feet did he realise that he had walked the whole length of the roof of a greenhouse! He banged on the door of the house. There was no answer. Then he walked into the village where some people, as soon as they saw him, shouted 'Boche!' and bolted for their lives. At last he induced the village constable to take him in charge and eventually all three of the crew met as prisoners at headquarters about 15 miles away. They were properly identified and released, to be entertained most lavishly with wine, when it was food they needed. They would not soon forget the French general kissing them on both cheeks as he bade them adieu before they drove off in a British staff car to the nearest RAF aerodrome, where an aircraft arrived from Hemswell to pick them up next day. When His Majesty the King was decorating the three men for their coolness and courage at Hemswell, he listened keenly to their descriptions of what had happened and Jolly's account of how he stumbled along the roof of the greenhouse in the dark, thinking it was ice breaking under his feet, was so funny that the King could not help laughing. 'Too bad to laugh at them after what they have been through,' he said and continued to chuckle as he moved on.[17]

On the night of 14/15 May Wellingtons of 149 Squadron bombed Aachen. The following day the War Cabinet authorized attacks east of the Rhine. The industrial area of the Ruhr was the largest centre of heavy industry and coal-mining in Europe and the principal producing area of coke, iron and steel. It is no coincidence therefore that it was considered by the Ministry of Economic Warfare to be by far the most important centre of heavy industry in all Germany and was so densely built-up that a bomb dropped there at random had 'an even chance of hitting some work of man'. Bomber Command began its strategic air offensive against Germany on the night of 15/16 May when 99 bombers, 39 of them Wellingtons, bombed oil and steel plants and railway centres in the Ruhr. And then on the night of 17/18 May, 48 Hampdens and 24 Whitleys were dispatched to bomb oil refineries at Bremen on the banks of the River Weser and Wellingtons and Hampdens were sent to bomb railway yards at Cologne and German troop concentrations in Belgium. In Hamburg a fertilizer factory was destroyed and 34 people were killed and 72 injured in the Reeperbahn district. In Bremen a few fires were started. All 130 aircraft that were dispatched this night returned safely, although not everyone found the target. A second pilot of a Whitley on 51 Squadron recalled:

I shall not forget my first operational sortie. I was a sergeant pilot, but I had been flying since 1936 and had about 1,000 hours experience – a lot more than my flying officer captain. He immediately sent me down to the bomb aimer's position to help with the map reading – not the happiest position in a Whitley on take-off, but we eventually staggered off the ground and wallowed up to about 3,000 feet when he called me back and said it wouldn't climb any higher. I raised the flaps for him and then resumed my position in the nose – my confidence was not increasing at this stage. It was cloudy all the way out to the target and there was nothing to see, but eventually after about the right time by dead reckoning, we saw some searchlights well off to the left. We turned towards the lights, but it was still hazy and we couldn't identify the target (Bremen) and so in accordance with our instructions in those days we didn't bomb and turned for home.

After a short time, the captain called me back to the cockpit to give him a break. I settled down in the seat, but soon realised that although the gyro showed us heading west, as we should have been, the master compass had been set-up 180° out (red on black as it was called) and we were actually heading east. I reset the compass and gyro correctly and turned back onto west. But I then began to wonder just how long the compass had been synchronised incorrectly and a long and increasingly heated conversation ensued within the crew. It eventually appeared to me that the captain had not reset the compass since take-off – so every heading actually taken had been the reciprocal of the one intended. By my estimation this now put us somewhere out over the Atlantic rather than the North Sea. Fortunately my experience prevailed over the captain's seniority and we turned back towards the east and the long drag back towards land. But where were the searchlights that we had clearly seen when we thought we were over Bremen? We settled for Dublin, but I think we calculated later that they must have been Sligo. We let down below the cloud, still over the sea, but fortunately I recognised the Irish coast when we reached it and eventually landed at Aldergrove (Belfast) ten hours or so after take-off. I don't think we were the only crew to make this mistake.

A Whitley V on 10 Squadron at Dishforth, Yorkshire, returned earlier than it should have done after setting off for Bremen. The pilot, an officer named Warren, became lost in a thunderstorm off Flamborough Head and crossed and re-crossed the English Channel into enemy territory before finally returning over England where they picked up the Thames Estuary in place of the Rhine. Rattigan the second pilot called from the nose; 'That looks an airfield coming up now. Over to starboard. Hell, they just turned the lights off!' The Whitley lifted as its load of 250lb HE bombs fell away onto the Fighter Command airfield at Bassingbourn in Cambridgeshire.[18] Warren was demoted to second pilot and it is said that he was known in the mess for ever after as 'Baron von Warren'. The story goes that two Spitfires flew over Dishforth and dropped Iron Crosses![19]

Pilot Officer (later Squadron Leader) Geoff Rothwell's first tour of operations commenced at Newmarket in May 1940 on 99 Squadron on Wellingtons:

I was allotted as second pilot to Pilot Officer Paddy Thallon. At the time I joined the squadron the German *Wehrmacht* was advancing through the Low Countries and the allied armies were in retreat. The targets for our Whitley, Hampden and Wellington bombers were roads, bridges and railways by night, whilst Battles and Blenheims attacked the German armoured columns and troop concentrations by day. Our attacks were very primitive as we had limited navigational aids to establish our position and had to rely on wireless fixes, pinpoints on the ground and by dropping illuminating flares and dead reckoning. We had to cope with equipment failure frequently and there were always a number of aborted sorties on the squadron. Losses were fairly light but many aircraft were damaged from light flak because most of our operations were carried out at heights of 3,000–5,000 feet and, at times, as low as 1,000 feet. Despite the difficulties morale on the squadron was high and there was always a jolly atmosphere in the Mess. However, a very sobering occasion was when, after the evacuation of the Allied Forces from Dunkirk, we were ordered to parade late at night. Our CO addressed us in the moonlight. He sent cold shivers up our spines when he announced that a German invasion was anticipated and that we were to be prepared to fly at short notice to Northern Ireland for refuelling and then on to Canada from where the fight would continue. When it was apparent that there was no stopping the German army the offensive was directed against the *Fatherland* and strategic bomb-ing of oil refineries and storage depots in the Ruhr Valley began. A favourite target was the railway marshalling yards at Hamm. Schiphol airfield on the outskirts of Amsterdam was bombed on a number of occasions. Target identification was extremely difficult and it was often only the light flak and searchlights in the target area that led us to our objective. Throughout the summer Frankfurt-am-Main, Wilhelmshaven, Berlin and Kiel, Hamburg and Düsseldorf on the right bank of the Rhine and Munich and many towns in the Ruhr Valley, were attacked. The defences, which at the outset had been rather haphazard and not particularly effective, showed a marked improvement and our losses mounted.[20]

The Battle of France was clearly being lost. On 27/28 May when Whitleys, Hampdens and Wellingtons attacked communications behind the battle front, largely ineffective attacks were made on oil targets at Hamburg and Bremen again. Day and night attacks on German positions near the shrinking BEF perimeter at Dunkirk were resumed over the next few days. On the night of 31 May/1 June, for the fifth day in a row, 93 Blenheims of 2 Group by day and 33 Wellingtons by night attacked the German positions around Dunkirk. Two Wellingtons on 37 Squadron at Feltwell were shot down in the attack on Nieuwpoort. Flying Officer Robert Collin Simmons and crew were lost without trace. The other Wimpy crashed near Eringhem. Two of the crew survived and were taken prisoner. The Skipper, Pilot Officer Bill Gray DFM survived the crash but he died of his wounds on 9 June and was buried at Cambrai. Sergeant Jim Brown and 56-year-old Pilot Officer Sir Arnold Talbot Wilson the rear gunner were killed. Talbot Wilson KCIE CSI CMG DSO had served in the political department of the Indian Army throughout the Great War. He was awarded the DSO and further honours had followed but his two years in office as the British civil commissioner in Baghdad ended in 1920 amid scenes of revolt by the local populace, inflamed by his dictatorial style of administration. Nevertheless he then gained a senior position with the Anglo–Persian Oil Company, serving as their residential director in the Gulf until 1932 when he left the company and returned to England where he represented the good people of Hitchin from 1933 to 1940. But his opinionated style of debate in the House of Westminster aroused feelings of hostility towards him, particularly when sections of the press labelled him as an apologist for the likes of the Axis dictators. Even so he enlisted in the volunteer reserve and was commissioned.[21]

By early morning of 2 June the remaining troops of the BEF (British Expeditionary Force) had been evacuated from the shores around Dunkirk. Thousands of French troops had still to be evacuated and during the daylight hours of 3 June Wellingtons stood ready, bombed up, to attack German positions near Dunkirk. 'Tiny' Cooling on 9 Squadron recalls:

> We were to wait by the Wellingtons, prepared to take off at 15.30 hours. The target had yet to be decided. We lay on the grass at Honington by our allotted aircraft in the warm sunshine. A daylight operation was a daunting thought. Take-off was delayed by two hours; hopes rose. Take-off would be 20.00 hours; the target Bergues, German positions on the southern edge of the Dunkirk perimeter. 'For God's sake,' said Wing Commander McKee with uncharacteristic emotion 'make sure you drop your bombs over enemy occupied territory. Our troops have enough to cope with without the added burden of someone's misdirected aim. And keep well away from the Channel. The Navy will fire at anything overhead. In present circumstances, who can blame them?

Douglas decided that Cooling would carry out the take-off and approach to the target. 'It was still daylight when I took off. As the coast appeared at Orford Ness I looked to port. A few hundred feet ahead was another Wellington; beyond it a third.' The moment of pride to be in such company made Cooling recall Shakespeare's *Henry V* before another famous battle in France. 'We few, we happy few, we band of brothers', he thought. The navigator's voice sounded over the intercom. 'Set course one-seven-one from Orford Ness. ETA target 42 minutes.'

> The starboard wing dipped; the other aircraft were lost to sight. The turreted nose travelled round the horizon until, within the cockpit, the compass grid wires were aligned with the north-seeking needle. Level out, on course, the light is draining and darkness, like sediment, deepens in the Eastern Hemisphere. The sun has set and yet, due south beyond the bulbous nose, there is another sunset, a golden glowing arc resting upon the distant skyline. It is puzzling for a moment until we realize the glow is above Dunkirk; the light is from fires blazing ninety miles away.
> Douglas took over the controls; it was the second pilot's job to drop the bombs, whilst the navigator kept track of our wanderings as we sought out 'targets of opportunity.' From the bomb aimer's position the sight was awesome. Six thousand feet below, Dunkirk was a sea of flame glinting like a brightly spot lit plaque of beaten

copper. We turned and flew south, avoiding the coast; skirting the column of smoke like a deep grey stake into the heart of the town. A flare ignited and drifted above a pale grey sea of smoke. We might have been flying over a lake of milky water. Spot a gun flash in that sea of featureless mist; line up its imagined position to track down the aiming wires of the bombsight and then let go a stick of three or four. Did we deceive ourselves? Scatter enough bombs about and chance will ensure that something is hit. It was time we were buying, fragments of time to load another boat; to allow another ship to sail. We left the burning beacon behind and headed home.

Italy's decision, at midnight on 10 June, to declare war on Britain and France caused Bomber Command to re-direct its bombing strategy. Mussolini's intentions had already been anticipated and it was agreed that as soon as Italy joined the war Wellingtons and longer-range Whitleys would bomb her heavy industry in the north of the country. Accordingly, on 3 June preparations were begun to transform Salon in the Marseilles area into a refuelling and operational base. At 15.30 hours on 11 June, Wellingtons from 99 Squadron flew in from England and landed at the forward base. Behind the scenes chaos reigned as first one order to bomb Italy was given, then countermanded by the French. Finally, an exasperated Group Captain Field, the CO of *Haddock* force at Salon, ordered the Wellingtons off. The Wellingtons were prevented from taking off when at the last moment a procession of French lorries were driven directly into their path and left there! When the political shenanigans had been sorted out, more Wellingtons made the seven-hour flight from England to Salon.

Thirty-six Whitleys, meanwhile, having refuelled in the Channel Islands, were already en-route to Genoa and Turin, in north-west Italy, a distance of 1,350 miles there and back. W Jacobs, a Whitley WOp/AG on 77 Squadron recalls:

On 11 June about midday, still heavy with sleep, I was roused by someone obviously in great haste and told to report to the crew room immediately. It transpired that Italy had entered the conflict and we were to proceed to Jersey as a means of getting closer to Turin, where, that night we were to bomb the Fiat Works. What a glorious summer day it was as we left Driffield at 14.30 hours thinking somewhat disgruntled what we could have been doing at Bridlington on a well-deserved day off.

We left Jersey at 20.10 hours for Turin. About two and a half hours out, still climbing to clear the Alps, we entered cloud and soon encountered severe turbulence. Electrical disturbance was the worst I had experienced and the noise in my headphones was unbearable. Fearing for my equipment led me to disconnect the aerials and, in so doing, I suffered superficial burns to the fingers of my right hand. It became agonisingly cold and we soon felt the depth of its penetration. The cloud seemed solid and without top as we struggled laboriously for height. We now heard ominous bumps as of something striking the aircraft and soon deduced that ice was being flung off the propellers. The captain asked me to shine the Aldis Lamp along the leading edges of the wings and we could see the ice building up despite the action of the pulsating de-icer boots. The ice formed with great rapidity and soon we could see it building up thickly over the leading edges and we began to wallow very badly. We descended rapidly as low as we dared but there was no improvement in our situation, which was now of extreme hazard. The fear we all shared was aggravated by the effect of the arctic conditions and here was now ice inside the cabin – it was quite impossible to keep still. To me the navigator seemed to be performing the wildest gyrations and I have no doubt that I appeared the same to him. The pilot was fighting with the aeroplane to keep it airborne and what the poor sod in the tail was doing only God knows. We were obviously not going to make it this trip and reluctantly decided to abort. I believe we dropped our bombs safe before staggering round to return to Jersey. We found that most crews had experienced the same as ourselves and only a few had, miraculously, avoided it and found the target; seemingly Turin was clear and with no blackout. We were airborne for five hours and 55 minutes.

The leader of the raid wrote later:

We were warned that over Italy fighter opposition would probably be encountered. The Italian fighters – CR.42s, it was pointed out, were biplanes, with considerable powers of manoeuvre and probably better suited to the task of night interception than the Bf 109 or 110. We must be on the lookout for them. Nothing much happened till we were over France after refuelling in the Channel Islands. Then we ran into electrical storms of great severity. There was a good deal of lightning. When we emerged from these into a clear patch somewhere near Bourges the lightning continued. This time it was produced by French flak through which we flew till we ran into heavy weather again and began to climb in order to get over the Alps. I got my heavily laden Whitley to 17,500 feet flying blind on my instruments but before the climb started in earnest I got a perfect 'fix' of my position from Lac Léman. The town of Geneva at its western end showed bright with many lights. It was 10/10th cloud over the Alps but we knew we were crossing them because of the bumps, which the aircraft felt every time it crossed a peak. Down we went through the murk till I altered course 15° to starboard so as to find the River Po. I reached it in darkness but I could make it out by the patches of cultivation along its banks, which showed a deeper shade against the prevailing black. I could not see the waters of the river. On we went till I judged we were over Turin. Then I let go a flare, which lit up the middle of the city. I turned back at once and climbed to 5,000 feet. When I got to that height I loosed another flare into a cloud which began to glow and shed a soft light over the whole town including the target. I ran in, dropped two bombs, one of which burst on the Fiat building, the other in the railway sidings beside it.

The bursting of the bombs seemed to be the signal for the enemy to switch on his searchlights. These could not find us but innumerable flashes of light, constantly renewed appeared beneath us. It seemed as though the whole of Turin was firing at us. I have never seen anything like it before or since. But no shells could be seen bursting anywhere. We were still at 5,000 feet but the air about us remained unlit by anything except our flare, though the flashes below winked at us with unabated zeal. I did my second run and hit the north end of the works. There was a large green flash, which meant that the bombs had certainly fallen on the annealing plant. I knew that, if I hit that, the flash would be a green one. Having no more bombs I dropped more flares to guide other attacking aircraft and drew off a little to watch the show. The flares lit up everything. I climbed to 10,000 feet, keeping a smart look out for the CR.42s. I did not see any and no one else did; but we did run into a heavy A/A barrage. The shell-bursts made a squeaky, gritty noise. It was only then that I realized what had happened. The Italian gunners, who had been producing all those flashes I had seen below, had evidently decided that we were flying at 10,000 feet when we bombed. As we were only at 5,000, naturally we saw nothing of the bursts, which were about a mile above our heads.[22]

On 12/13 June, 29 Hampdens and 8 Whitleys were dispatched to military objectives in France but only 15 found suitable targets. A Hampden on 11 Squadron was lost when it hit a balloon cable at Harwich, crashing and setting fire to a flour mill on the docks. All the crew were killed. The night following, 163 bombers were detailed to bomb a wide range of communications targets in France, Belgium and Holland. A Wellington on 9 Squadron at Honington flown by Sergeant Bob Hewitt, who three weeks earlier had got his own crew after surviving the ditching off Cromer in December, was lost on the operation on Pont de l'Arche. In Glasgow Hewitt's wife Helen Annie waited for news but Hewitt and his five crew were dead. They were all laid to rest at Drosay Churchyard, Seine-Maritime.

At Honington, once he heard that Hewitt was missing, Sergeant C Naylor, a navigator, went to see 'Tiny' Cooling. Naylor broke down and cried like a baby. Cooling later wrote about the incident in a poem:

This muster of names,
This directory of faceless, formless beings
Suffocates the mind.

Is it solely a tabulation as on
pages of Smiths in volume S to Z?
Or a company of friends
Awaiting recognition
Amidst a legion of Strangers?

In the quest, shadows emerge,
Forgotten faces relive
Brief moments of shared experience
And call upon yet others to be identified. . .

Now what became of him? And him?
And their names too are
carved in the roster.

I dare not look for my own,
it should be there.

Our Flight Commander, Hinks,
Quiet Ronnie Frost (he joined with me),
Young Naylor who was lost in the North Sea. . .
Was he twenty when he came into my room
and cried like a baby the night Bob Hewitt died,
leaving a pregnant wife?
Three weeks later
I helped to clear his room,
And found his Bible by his bed.[23]

On 14/15 June, 43 Whitleys bombed targets in France in support of the land battle. Twenty-four Wellingtons and five Hampdens bombed targets in the Ruhr and in Southern Germany and 16 Wellingtons flew as far south as Basle and Konstanz on the Bodensee (Lake Constance). A Wellington on 38 Squadron at Marham failed to return from the sortie to the Black Forest. The pilot was killed. His five crew members survived to be taken into captivity.

On 15 June two Wellingtons on 99 Squadron and six on 149 Squadron took off from Salon for a raid on Genoa, Italy's largest port and capital of Liguria. Violent thunderstorms en route prevented all but one of the Wellington crews from finding their targets and seven bombers were forced to return to Salon with their bomb loads intact. On the night of 16/17 June nine Wellingtons made another attempt to bomb Italy but only five crews were able to find and attack the Caproni works at Milan. Crews returned to Salon to discover that the French had sued for an armistice and, effectively, all future operations were brought to an end. Valuable experience was gained from the raids and two months later, on the night of 13/14 August, 32 Whitleys, nearly all of which reached the target area, bombed objectives in the Plain of Lombardy. The Fiat aircraft factory at Turin was hit repeatedly, for by good chance a parachute flare fell on the roof, burning slowly and lighting up the target. Many fires and heavy explosions were caused, both at these works and at the Caproni works in Milan. The attack was repeated on the next night, in very unfavourable weather, by four Whitleys and a fortnight later Genoa and Alessandria, a town in Northern Italy on the River Tanaro, were amongst the objectives bombed.

On 18/19 June, 69 Whitleys, Wellingtons and Hampdens were dispatched to oil targets at Hamburg, Bremen and in the Ruhr and to railways at many other places. The following night 112 Hampdens, Wellingtons and Whitleys set off for 15 oil and railway targets between Hamburg and Mannheim. Nineteen of the Hampdens were detailed to bomb the Dortmund–Ems Canal. Ten of them were detailed to attack the eastern viaduct, which was the older one built of stone, and the other nine were told to attack the western viaduct, which was constructed of concrete. The crews studied their maps and the magnificent photographs which had been taken of the area, as well as a model made in plasticine of the two viaducts. At 09.30 the bombers began to follow each other into the sky at short intervals and set course for their target. It was rather misty to start with and there was considerable cloud over Holland, but as they flew inland the clouds dispersed and it developed into a beautiful moonlight night. The captains of the aircraft, who had been instructed to arrive independently over the target, had no difficulty in locating their position. The moon was almost full and from 1,000 feet visibility of the ground was quite good. The leader of the raiders, Squadron Leader Walter Charles Sheen DSO, recognized the canal about 10 miles from the target and flew straight along it, the reflections of the moon upon the water making an excellent guide. Now and again he saw the dark shapes of barges, while here and there the canal widened out to enable barges to be moored without interfering with the normal traffic. Dropping down to a height of 50 feet he raced along the canal and made his run over the viaduct. But flying too fast he was a little off his target so he circled to the east and away to the north again. This time he made no mistake but made a very steady and slow approach at 120 mph. He dropped down to 50 feet and even lower, until the wings of the bomber were almost level with the parapets of the viaduct. 'Bomb gone!' called out Sergeant Bartlett, the bomb-aimer. 'I've seen it splash into the water in the middle of the viaduct!' shouted the rear-gunner, as they climbed and set course for home.

Flight Lieutenant 'Max' Meyer DFC on 144 Squadron picked up the canal a few miles north of the viaducts, dropped down to a height of 250 feet and sped over the great barges. About a mile from the target he took the Hampden down to 50 feet. 'It was a grand sight to see the moonlight on the canal,' he recorded. 'As we singled out certain land-marks, we turned up on the western viaduct and dropped our bomb and the rear-gunner saw it splash into the water as it fell.'

One of the attackers, Sergeant Joseph Unsworth, captain of a 49 Squadron Hampden crew at Scampton, flew around for 20 minutes in order to see what damage he had done. 'It was a fine moonlight night and the water shone like silver,' he said later. 'We got a direct hit on the side of the aqueduct with a heavy bomb and twenty minutes afterwards we saw the water seeping out, so we came back highly delighted.'

The viaducts on the Dortmund–Ems Canal were then quite defence-less. There was not a gun, nor a searchlight to defend that target, which was so vital to the Germans. The British bombers had the viaducts at their mercy and they made a smashing attack on the safety gates and embankments and the beds of the aqueducts. From this attack every British bomber returned safely to its base. Photographs taken later by reconnaissance aircraft showed that the viaducts were badly damaged and that the canal had been rendered unusable, for the water had drained away from it and left barges sitting on the mud. Men were seen doing their best to unload some of them in a field alongside the canal. Air Vice-Marshal Arthur Harris, the Air Officer Commanding 5 Group said:

> Please accept and convey to all concerned my thanks and admiration for the outstanding skill and resolution displayed by the crews in last night's operations. The high standard of training and organization, which led to this unsurpassed success, reflects also the greatest credit on the personnel concerned. It is precisely by such operations, conceived with care of set purpose and carried out with such admirable courage, skill and intelligence that we shall in the end confound and bring to ruin the efforts of the enemy who relies upon numbers, in the belief, which we shall disprove, that they can prevail against quality.[24]

Harris, a compact, silent, bull-terrier of a man with one outstanding characteristic, a bitter hatred of the Hun and all that he stood for, was 48 years old, born in Cheltenham, Gloucestershire on 13 April 1892, the son of a member of the Public Works Department of the Indian Civil Service. At the outbreak of war in 1914 he had joined the Rhodesia Regiment as a boy bugler. After taking part in the German south-west African campaign in 1915 he left for England and enlisted in the Royal

Flying Corps and was posted to France. He ended the war as a major with an AFC. In the next 20 years Harris commanded bomber squadrons and from 1933 to 1937 served in staff positions at the Air Ministry. He took command of 4 Group in 1937 and was Head of the RAF Purchasing Mission in America in 1938 before taking command of 5 Group in 1939, a position he held until 1940 before acting as Deputy Chief of Air Staff at the Air Ministry.

On the night of 1/2 July, 73 aircraft set off to bomb Osnabrück and Kiel and carry out mine laying. Eight of the Hampdens dispatched were to attack the *Scharnhorst* in the floating dock at Kiel. Four Hampdens were to make a high level attack and circle around while the other four stole in to make a low level attack. The weather that night was terrible. Flying at 9,000 feet over Sylt, 20-year-old Pilot Officer Alexander Webster, a tall dark-eyed young Scottish pilot on 61 Squadron at Hemswell, found thick snow getting inside the cockpit and billowing round him. His instruments began to ice up, the engine cowlings glowed red with heat and the engines and propellers were encompassed in a blue light, which ran along the leading edge of the aircraft; the wireless crackled viciously and now and again blue sparks leapt out. Circling over Kiel, Webster saw the flashes of the heavy guns and watched the searchlights groping up for them. A cone of red, green and white searchlights seemed to be following the aircraft around. Clearing the throttles to stop most of the noise of the engines, he said to his crew: 'Let's go in for that ship. Let's have a crack at it.' Approaching from over the town, he glided down from 9,000 feet to 500 feet. Not a gun fired at them. There was absolute silence:

> When it is quiet like that you feel that they are waiting for you, watching for you, laughing at you. By that time we were all keyed up and tense, wondering what was going on and why they were not doing something about it. The climax came when the searchlights got us and the guns started. For about sixty seconds we roared over Kiel at nought feet. I was blinded by the searchlights, so I steered by my instruments while Bisset directed me on to the target. I'm sure the German shells and machine-gun bullets must have killed off their own people. [*Ten people were killed in Kiel on this night*]. They seemed to throw everything they'd got at us, except the gun mountings. Bisset saw the ship ahead and kept yelling directions to keep me on my course. I flew straight toward the side of the dock. 'Hold it!' he shouted and let it go. 'Bomb away!' he called and the rear-gunner saw it head for the right spot and splash in. By then we were depending on speed. Keeping very low, we screamed over the harbour and out to sea, where it was now quiet, so we circled and climbed, feeling as happy as sandboys.[25]

Another of the Hampdens was flown by Flying Officer Guy Gibson on 83 Squadron at Scampton, who dropped the first 2,000lb bomb of the war. Gibson released the bomb on the sixth shallow dive-bombing attempt but it overshot the *Scharnhorst* and exploded in the town of Kiel. A navigator on another Hampden who claimed to have hit the *Scharnhorst* said:

> I directed my line of sight on the floating dock which stood out sharply in the estuary. Searchlights caught us in the dive but we went under the beam. Then I put the captain into dive as we came on the target. I could quite clearly see tracers coming from the pom-pom on the deck of the *Scharnhorst*. AA fire damaged our aircraft, putting a hole two foot square in the tail-plane. We came down very low to make sure and when we were dead in line I released a stick of bombs. A vast shoot of reddish-yellow flame came from the deck.

The Hampden flown by Canadian Pilot Officer Douglas Redmayne on 83 Squadron crashed in the target area killing all four crew. A 58 Squadron Whitley at Linton-on-Ouse also crashed in the target area with the loss of all four members of Pilot Officer Cecil John Trevelyen Jones' crew. As for Webster, he was able to announce to his father, the Chief Constable of Gravesend, that he had been awarded the DFC.[26]

Wellington pilot Patrick S Foss was another of the RAF's peacetime professionals, having entered the service with a short-service commission. He and his crew on 38 Squadron flew their first and second operations from Marham in July. The second was on the night of 29/30 July when 76 Hampdens, Wimpys and Whitleys were dispatched to Homberg, Cologne and Hamm and barges in Dutch ports and mine laying. The target for the Wellingtons was a petrol plant at Wesseling near Cologne. It was a murky night with a layer of cloud at 12,000 feet, the Wimpy's operational height. As they approached the target, Foss saw a Whitley ahead and just below, coned in the searchlights which lit the bomber up 'like daylight'. Foss decided to glide in low just beneath the bomber in the hope that the defence would not pick him up while they concentrated on 'him':

> In no time after our flash bomb [*for the photograph of the target area*] had exploded very low, four of the five searchlights bracketed us at about 8,000 feet. Shells began bursting all around us. I twisted and turned to shake off the lights. At that moment our rear gunner shouted that he could see a light which he took to be a fighter approaching. Any second now could be our last. As I sweated at the controls I offered up a prayer that I might be shown what to do to take us out of danger. An extraordinary impression came over me.

I found myself outside the Wellington and away in the sky, from where I could see the aircraft lit up and surrounded by shell bursts, just as if I was a spectator. I saw then how I might throw off the defences if I did a highly dangerous manoeuvre. I had the feeling of confidence to execute it. Then I was back in the cockpit and at the controls again, bathed in cold sweat. I pulled the Wellington up into a vertical stall turn; fell out of it and into a spiral towards the earth. Almost at once the lights left me and we were falling in the darkness. I eased out of the spiral and levelled off as best I could with an invisible earth. A single searchlight now came on and was laid along the ground, lighting up our track and illuminating the hills immediately in front of us. We were only a few hundred feet up. We climbed over the hills and, as the light went out, we made our way back to Marham.[27]

On 3/4 August 1940 when the night was quite clear and starry, 71 Hampdens, Wellingtons and Whitleys set out to bomb oil targets in the Ruhr, to Kiel, to a seaplane base in Holland and mine-laying. Three aircraft failed to return. The 49 Squadron Hampden crew of Sergeant Joseph Unsworth at Scampton met with an unexpected, but happy, ending to an adventure which began with the bombing of Kiel docks. On arriving back in England after being up for over nine hours, they found such a thick ground fog with low cloud and rain over their base that Control would not permit them to run the risk of landing. They were accordingly diverted to another aerodrome where conditions were if anything slightly worse, so they were sent off elsewhere. They wandered round from one aerodrome to another, only to find that visibility on the ground was nil and it was impossible to get down. 'It was a strange sight to see a church spire sticking out through the top of the fog,' Unsworth reported.

About 6.30 in the morning they made their final attempt at an aerodrome on the east coast, but conditions were worse than ever. The pilot turned away into the driving rain that was associated with the fog. It was daylight, but he could see nothing. Visibility simply did not exist and the pilot, who was soon wet through, was obliged to fly with the hatch open in order to maintain control. For 20 minutes he flew in these conditions and then the port engine cut out. It did not even cough – there could not have been a drop of petrol left. Leading Aircraftman Ailwood, the rear-gunner, however, did not worry about their desperate plight. He slept as calmly in 'the tin' as though he had been in bed.

'Stand by,' ordered Unsworth. The wireless operator gave Ailwood a kick with his foot to awaken him, before tapping out: 'Going down in sea. Taking emergency action.' They were now 10 miles east of Skegness. Fifty feet from the surface of the sea the other engine cut out. The captain called the navigator up out of the front cockpit. Ailwood got the dinghy ready while the wireless operator still tapped away. Then the captain called to them to stand behind him. 'When I looked round it amazed me to see them all so unconcerned, although not many had escaped after a crash landing at sea,' the pilot said later. Occasionally a boat loomed up and vanished in the fog. The pilot tried to turn and skate back near a trawler whose crew thought they were Germans going to machine gun them. As they skimmed along nearly touching the surface, the pilot cut off the petrol and put the switches down. They blew up their Mae Wests. The astral hatch was opened for a speedy exit amidships. Then they hit at between 90 and 100 mph.

'I've never heard a noise like it in my life – like thunder,' remarked the pilot when it was all over. As the cowling touched, both engines shot out, the perspex nose was smashed in and a great wave of water gushed up through the tunnel, drenching the crew as they rushed out of the astral hatch. If the hatch had not been open to provide a vent, they might have been seriously injured by that great rush of water. For a moment the bomber dived under the surface and then came up again to stop about 30 yards ahead. The pilot and other members of the crew braced themselves when the shock came and none was injured. In three seconds the wireless operator, the rear-gunner and the navigator were in the dinghy; while the captain was swimming alongside. It was as much as the other three men could do to haul him in, owing to the weight of his sodden clothing. In ten minutes they saw the trawler appear out of the fog and rain and five minutes later they were on board. The Skipper was unshakeable as an oak. The airmen he had saved might have been paying him a formal call. 'It's turned out nice again,' he remarked casually to Unsworth, whose opinion of the weather can be guessed! The airmen quickly stripped and donned some spare clothes collected by the crew, while their own wet clothing was put to dry in the engine room and the Skipper served them all with a generous tot of rum, which soon warmed them up. On their way back they steamed right into a magnetic minefield laid by the enemy. A naval patrol hailed them through the megaphone. 'Do you know you're right on top of a minefield?' he called. 'Of course I do, but it doesn't bother us,' called the Skipper through his megaphone and they proceeded to port, where the bomber crew got a fine reception and in due course Sergeant Unsworth learned that he had been awarded the DFM.[28] On the night of 13/14 October 1941 Pilot Officer Joe Unsworth was killed flying a 207 Squadron Manchester on the raid on Cologne.

The Germans had not only worked hard to repair the damage to the Dortmund–Ems Canal after the raid on 19/20 June but they also defended the canal so well with searchlights and guns that they probably considered it impossible for any aircraft ever again to make a successful attack on the waterway. Nevertheless the RAF went back from time to time to do their worst. On one occasion Acting Flight Lieutenant Roderick Alastair Brook 'Babe' Learoyd on 49 Squadron acted as a decoy to draw the fire of the defences while other bombers slid down to attack; another time he made a high level attack. He was thus not unfamiliar with the Dortmund–Ems Canal when he started out to make his third attack upon it on 12/13 August, when two Hampden units, 49 and 83 Squadrons in 5 Group, carried out a low-level attack. It was a night of half moon which gave sufficient light in which to see the target. The Hampdens carefully timed their attack so as to drop their special charges at intervals of exactly two minutes, beginning at 01.30. At one point the canal was especially vulnerable. North of Münster two aqueducts, one on four arches, the other on two, carried the canal across the River Ems. The width of each channel was only a hundred feet at water level. To destroy both aqueducts meant cutting the canal entirely, while the destruction of one would greatly reduce the volume of traffic passing through it. The aqueduct was heavily protected by anti-aircraft guns disposed so as to form a lane down which an attacking aircraft must fly if it was to reach the target but it was decided to attack from a very low level in order to make certain that the aqueduct would be hit. One by one the 11 Hampdens went in from the north, the moon shining in the faces of their crews and throwing the objective into relief. The first aircraft was hit and the wireless operator wounded; the second was hit and destroyed. The third was set on fire but before the aircraft became uncontrollable, the pilot succeeded in gaining enough height to enable the crew and himself to bail out. They did so and were made prisoners. The fourth Hampden was hit in three places but got back to base. The fifth and last Hampden, piloted by Flight Lieutenant Learoyd, went down the anti-aircraft lane at 200 feet:

After a moment, three big holes appeared in the starboard wing. They were firing at point-blank range. The navigator continued to direct me on to the target. I could not see it because I was blinded by the glare of the searchlights and had to keep my head below the level of the cockpit top. At last I heard the navigator say 'Bombs gone'; I immediately did a steep turn to the right and got away, being fired at heavily for five minutes. The carrier pigeon we carried laid an egg during the attack.

The attack achieved an element of surprise and the damage to the canal restricted barge traffic on this important waterway for a number of weeks. Learoyd was awarded Bomber Command's first Victoria Cross of the war. His VC citation read:

This officer, as first pilot of a Hampden aircraft, has repeatedly shown the highest conception of his duty and complete indifference to personal danger in making attacks at the lowest altitude objective on the Dortmund–Ems Canal. He had attacked this objective on a previous occasion and was well aware of the risks entailed. To achieve success it was necessary to approach from a direction well known to the enemy, through a lane of especially disposed anti-aircraft defences and in the face of the most intense point blank fire from guns of all calibres. The reception of the preceding aircraft might well have deterred the stoutest heart, all being hit and two lost. Flight Lieutenant Learoyd nevertheless made his attack at 150 feet, his aircraft being repeatedly hit and large pieces of the main planes torn away. He was almost blinded by the glare of many search-lights at close range but pressed home this attack with the greatest resolution and skill. He subsequently brought his wrecked aircraft home and, as the landing flaps were inoperative and the under-carriage indicators out of action, waited for dawn in the vicinity of his aerodrome before landing, which he accomplished without causing injury to his crew or further damage to the aircraft. The high courage, skill and determination, which this officer has invariably displayed on many occasions in the face of the enemy, sets an example which is unsurpassed.[29]

Notes

1. And six squadrons of Bristol Blenheim IV light bombers in 2 Group.
2. *Gunner's Moon* by John Bushby (Futura 1972).
3. F/O Cogman and his crew were shot down on 19/20 May 1940 on the operation to Gelsenkirchen. The Whitley crashed at De Klef, ENE of Eindhoven. Cogman evaded and three of his crew were captured. One man was killed. Raphael and his crew ditched 60 miles off the Dutch coast on 18/19 May when they were hit by a Bf 110 when returning from the raid on Hannover. Raphael, who had a painful foot wound and the crew, all of whom were injured, were rescued after four hours afloat and taken to Great Yarmouth. *RAF Bomber Command Losses of the Second World War, Vol. 1* by W R Chorley (Midland).
4. F/Sgt Albert Heller DFM and Sgt Ernie Short MID were on P/O Ernest Ronald Peter Shackle Cooper's Halifax crew on 35 Squadron on the night of 25/26 July 1941 when the aircraft was shot down on the operation on Berlin and they were all killed.
5. Adapted from the 51 Squadron official history in *The Right of the Line: The Royal Air Force in the European War 1939–1945* by John Terraine (Hodder & Stoughton 1985) and *Bomber Command: The Air Ministry Account of Bomber Command's Offensive Against the Axis September 1939–July 1941* (HMSO 1941). W/O Tom Bowles MID was shot down on the operation to Jülich on the night of 21/22 May 1940 and was taken prisoner with his crew. He died of tuberculosis in captivity on

26 April 1941. F/L A A Emery DFM was KIA on the night of 4/5 April 1943 piloting a 51 Squadron Halifax on the operation on Kiel.

6. See *Bombs Away!* by Martin W Bowman (Pen & Sword 2010). Wellingtons were first-line equipment for: 9 Squadron at Honington, Suffolk; 37 Squadron at Feltwell, Norfolk; 99 and 149 Squadrons at Mildenhall and Newmarket, Suffolk respectively; 38 and 115 Squadrons at Marham, Norfolk; while 214 and 215 (at Methwold) were similarly equipped in Reserve.

7. Adapted from *So Few: The Immortal Record of the Royal Air Force* by David Masters (1941). LAC Conolly was mentioned in dispatches. Jack Ramshaw was awarded the DFM in May 1940.

8. Adapted from *Bomber Command: The Air Ministry Account of Bomber Command's Offensive Against the Axis September 1939–July 1941.* (HMSO 1941).

9. Up until May 1940 the night air defence of the *Reich* was almost entirely the province of the flak arm of the *Luftwaffe*. No specialized night fighting arm existed though one fighter *Gruppe* was undertaking experimental *Helle Nachtjagd* (illuminated night fighting) sorties with the aid of searchlights in northern Germany and in the Rhineland. The *Helle Nachtjagd* technique used in 1940 and early 1941 was entirely dependent on weather conditions and radar-guided searchlights simply could not penetrate thick layers of cloud or industrial haze over the Ruhr and other industrial centres. Kammhuber realised that *Helle Nachtjagd* was only a short-term solution and soon concentrated all his energies in developing an efficient radar-controlled air defence system. On 22 June 1940 Hauptmann Wolfgang Falck, *Kommandeur*, I/ZG1 who had some experience with radar-directed night-fighting sorties in the Bf 110 flying from Aalborg, Denmark during April 1940, was ordered to form the basis of a *Nachtjagd*, or night fighting arm, by establishing the first defence of the Ruhr with the aid of one flak searchlight regiment. In July Göring ordered Kammhuber to set up of a full-scale night fighting arm. Within three months, Kammhuber's organisation was remodelled into *Fliegerkorps XII* and by the end of 1940 the infant *Nachtjagd* had evolved into three searchlight batallions and five night fighter *Gruppen*.

10. Meyer joined the RAF in 1937 on a Short Service Commission for a period of 4 years' active service and for 6 years in the Reserve. He was posted to 76 Squadron in April 1939, then in the process of re-equipping with the Hampden to replace the obsolete Armstrong Whitworth Wellesley.

11. Adapted from *So Few: The Immortal Record of the Royal Air Force* by David Masters (1941).

12. See *Out of the Blue: The Role of Luck in Air Warfare 1917–1966* edited by Laddie Lucas (Hutchinson 1985). The first Bomber Command aircraft

to be shot down at night by a German fighter occurred on the night of 25/26 April when *Oberfeldwebel* Hermann Förster of IV./JG2 flying a Bf 109D shot down a 49 Squadron Hampden being flown on a mine-laying operation by P/O Arthur Herbert Benson. All the crew were killed. Förster was KIA in North Africa on 14 December 1941.

13. See *Wellington The Geodetic Giant* by Martin W Bowman (Airlife 1998).

14. Adapted from *So Few: The Immortal Record of the Royal Air Force* by David Masters (1941). On 28/29 April 1941 S/L Good DFC was lost with another crew on a *Gardening* (mine-laying) operation.

15. 'The verbal conventions when referring to squadrons numbers was, generally speaking, if the number were below 20 it was usually spoken of as the number, followed by the word "Squadron". Over the 20 and below the century one spoke merely the two digits of its number. Thus one spoke of having been on (you were always "on" a squadron unlike the Navy who were always "in" their ships) for example, "Five Squadron" but later served on "55". Over the hundred and it was the three digits, "One-five-six" or "Two-oh-one".' *Gunner's Moon* by John Bushby (Futura 1972).

16. *The Bomber Command War Diaries: An Operational Reference Book 1939–1945*. Martin Middlebrook and Chris Everitt. (Midland 1985).

17. Adapted from *So Few: The Immortal Record of the Royal Air Force* by David Masters (1941).

18. See *Out of the Blue: The Role of Luck in Air Warfare 1917–1966* edited by Laddie Lucas (Hutchinson 1985).

19. *Bomber Command* by Max Hastings (Pan 1979).

20. F/L W H Thallon and three of his crew of a 12 Squadron Wellington survived being shot down at Terschelling Island on 20/21 January 1942 by *Oberleutnant* Ludwig Becker of 6./NJG2 during the operation to Emden. Sgt Edmund G R Fowler, Thallon's second pilot and Sgt William Rutherford the rear gunner were KIA. (Becker went on to shoot down, within 40 minutes, two more Wimpys on 142 and 101 Squadrons into the North Sea). After completing 37 operations Rothwell was posted to an OTU to instruct pupils converting from Anson and Oxford trainers to Wellingtons. He had flown over 180 hours on operations. See *Battles With the Nachtjagd: The Night Airwar Over Europe 1939–1945* by Theo Boiten and Martin W Bowman (Schiffer 2006).

21. *RAF Bomber Command Losses of the Second World War. Vol. 9 Roll of Honour 1939–47*. W R Chorley (Midland 2007).

22. 23 aircraft were not able to reach Italy because of difficult weather over the Alps. Nine aircraft bombed Turin but not the designated factories; most bombed railway yards. Two other aircraft bombed Genoa. Both cities were fully lit up, as in peacetime, when the bombers arrived; Turin's lights were turned off during the raid but

Genoa's were not. Heavy anti-aircraft fire was encountered over Turin. A Whitley V from 77 Squadron crashed in flames near Lignieres-Orgeres, France on its return flight. All the crew were killed. *The Bomber Command War Diaries: An Operational Reference Book 1939–1945*. Martin Middlebrook and Chris Everitt (Midland 1985). During the operation to the Battle Area a Hampden and a Whitley crashed. Both crews were killed.

23. Sgt Naylor was KIA on the raid on Levekusen on 18/19 June 1940. Squadron Leader J O Hinks was KIA on the raid on Magdeburg on 14/15 October 1940. Rupert Cooling died in 2010 aged 90.

24. Adapted from *So Few: The Immortal Record of the Royal Air Force* by David Masters (1941).

25. Adapted from *So Few: The Immortal Record of the Royal Air Force* by David Masters (1941).

26. Gibson was awarded the DFC in July and in August he was posted to instruct at an OTU before joining 29 Squadron flying Beaufighter night fighters. In 99 operational sorties Gibson claimed three enemy aircraft destroyed and was promoted to squadron leader with a bar to his DFC on completion of his second tour in 1941. After a short spell of instructing he took command of 106 Squadron.

27. See *Out of the Blue: The Role of Luck in Air Warfare 1917–1966* edited by Laddie Lucas (Hutchinson 1985). There were no losses.

28. Adapted from *So Few: The Immortal Record of the Royal Air Force* by David Masters (1941).

29. Acting F/L Roderick Alastair Brook Learoyd, 49 Squadron, Hampden P4403. Awarded for action 12 August 1940, *London Gazette*, 20 August 1940.

CHAPTER 2

'Gentlemen of the shade, minions of the moon'

To sum up, those of us who came through those early days of the war, flying obsolescent aircraft with poor equipment and few navigational aids, pioneering long distance night flying under war conditions and in often extremely bad weather, were generally surprised that we survived. . . . I am sure I was.

Bernard 'Max' Meyer DFC

John 'Jim' Verran was born on 9 December 1915 at Wai Pawa in Hawks Bay District on New Zealand's North Island. His grandparents came from Cornwall, his father being born in Australia. Educated at Palmerston North Boys' High School, Jim's first job was with a law firm. Leaving after five years he then joined Dominion Motors at Auckland. In 1939 the Royal New Zealand Air Force was recruiting and along with many others, Jim applied for aircrew. As he wryly described the situation, 'They had filled their quota well before the letter V was reached.' Disgusted at not having the opportunity to join the RNZAF, Jim and 11 other hopeful young men each paid their own passage to England intent on joining the RAF. They successfully negotiated aircrew selection and Jim trained on Miles Magisters. After the outbreak of war he flew Tiger Moths. As Jim says, he had two first solos, one in the Magister and another in the Tiger Moth! Passing out, Jim was posted to initial training at Hastings, where, after the usual square bashing along the pier, administration and aircrew lectures, he was duly commissioned. At South Cerney Jim found no difficulty flying Airspeed Oxfords but then came the time to fly at night. 'I thought * * * *; how am I going to find my way around in the dark? I was on my own in a strange country with lots to think about.' He experienced engine failure for the first time when flying at 14,000 feet. His only passenger was an Aircraftman Bessant. 'The shock of the failure caused a blade tip to break off and enter the cockpit, hitting the compass and drenching me in alcohol.' The blade tip became one of Jim's treasured possessions.

At 10 OTU Abingdon, Verran was 'a bit shattered' to find that he was going to fly a Whitley. The early marks of Whitley were powered by the Armstrong Whitworth 920hp Tiger engines, which had a disconcerting habit of blowing off cylinder heads, even complete cylinders, punching holes in the long chord cowlings. Deliveries of Whitley V and the much more reliable Merlin IV and X engines only began in August 1939. Verran recalls:

> The Whitley was an interesting aeroplane. When you changed from fine to coarse pitch, the revs of the Tiger engine 'fell off the clock'. I learned to fly the Whitley 'on the step'. What you did was climb to a slightly higher altitude than intended and then gently trim out the aircraft thereby reducing the angle of attack of the wing. With care you could maintain height but fly at a faster speed than other aircraft. The Whitley was a bit traumatic but in the end we got used to it.

It was at the OTUs that forming up as crews and initial operational training took place. Jack Short was an air gunner who, after ground school, was posted to RAF Edgehill to find a crew and begin operational training in Wellington Ics. He recalls:

> 'Crewing-up' was itself an interesting process. All aircrew specializations on strength were put together in a large area, such as a gymnasium, and all milled around chatting and choosing at random a pilot, navigator, signaller, bomb-aimer and gunners until a crew was formed. Although a haphazard arrangement, it apparently worked! My Skipper, a F/Sgt, selected by chance, proved OK and our workup as a crew was straightforward – least I have no recollection of being too badly frightened by our early flying experience as a crew.

Jim Verran's first squadron was 102 at Driffield in Yorkshire:

> Reporting on 1 July, I flew a night check and then thirty minutes solo. On 15 August Driffield was heavily bombed. We had got rather blasé about raids and used to just sit tight. On this particular occasion, having been to Milan the night before, we were sitting in the Mess after lunch feeling pretty drowsy, when the air raid siren went off. Nobody moved. Then all of a sudden there was a bang, bang, bang and the whole place took off! [*The attack destroyed twelve Whitleys and put the Station out of action for most of the rest of the year*]. We had to get to the west wing of the mess and go across the road to get into an air raid shelter. In the process I got caught up in the blast of the bomb that hit the Mess. The blast was such that the loop on the

back of one of my uniform buttons actually chipped a piece of bone off my sternum. Amazingly, the skin was not broken but a lump the size of a pigeon's egg developed on my chest. That evening Pilot Officer Leonard Cheshire, my roommate, and I went to see a Bing Crosby film at the local cinema.

Born on 7 September 1917 in Chester, Geoffrey Leonard Cheshire was the son of Professor Geoffrey Cheshire, a barrister, academic and influential writer on English law. Leonard was brought up at his parents' home near Oxford and educated at the Dragon School, Oxford, then Stowe School and Merton College, Oxford, where, between 1937 and the outbreak of war in 1939, when he graduated with an Honours degree in Law, he was a member of the University Air Squadron. He was once bet half a pint of beer by a friend who said he could not reach Paris with just a few pennies in his pocket; Cheshire won his bet. While staying with German friends he witnessed a Hitler rally in Germany, causing great offence to his hosts by not giving the Nazi salute. On 12/13 November 1940 Cheshire was awarded the DSO for getting his very badly damaged Whitley home from a raid on Wesseling. On leave in New York while ferrying aircraft to England, Cheshire would meet and marry 41-year-old Constance Binney, a wealthy divorcee, once America's top silent movie star and successor to Mary Pickford in 1922. On his return to England and at age 25, Cheshire became the youngest group captain in the RAF. By then he liked a suite at the Ritz on leave and to bask in The Mayfair cocktail bar.[1] For now he and Verran had to rely on Bing Crosby at the local cinema for their entertainment.

Pilot Officer Jim Verran flew a tour on the Whitley, once bombing the Caproni aircraft factory in Milan. This raid, on the night of 13/14 August 1940, was the first one direct from the UK to an Italian target. For this operation the aircraft flew from Harwell. Jim described the raid as being 'quiet, very little flak except over the target and no sign of night fighters. Weather over the Alps was clear, the altitude being 17,000 feet. Losing height heading for the Plain of Lombardy, visibility became poorer, with clouds and ground haze.' The total flight time for the raid was 9 hours 5 minutes, one Whitley failing to return through lack of fuel and having to ditch in the sea off Dymchurch. Verran continues:

We came back up to Driffield on the 15th. We had lunch, we were in the anteroom. People were still pretty tired after the flight and the air raid siren went and we thought 'another bloody raid'. Then all of a sudden the bombs began to drop and there was a mass exodus out of the mess to the air raid shelter. We had to go along one of the wings of the mess to reach the shelter and one of the bombs hit the mess. One chap was blown down the entrance to the shelter with a window frame wrapped round him. Quite a number of aircraft were hit and there was a fair bit of damage to the Station. As a result we were taken off flying for Bomber Command and were sent to Prestwick flying Ansons on Atlantic patrols protecting shipping.

Later, when he completed his tour of 30 ops, Jim Verran was asked to undertake a further five, the reason being a shortage of crews due to the high loss rate. During the latter part of his tour he was also used as a training captain. His tour over, Verran was posted to 22 OTU at Wellesbourne Mountford near Stratford-upon-Avon in Warwickshire as an instructor flying Wellingtons. Needless to say, he had never flown a Wellington! The OTU trained mainly French Canadians.[2] With no course on instructional techniques, as Jim says, 'We picked it up as we went along. We had a card with all the drills and were flying seven days a week, day and night and had little time for breaks, so it was pretty exhausting. However, we did let off steam in the Mess; indeed, Doc Mogg our MO broke my nose!' Jim Verran was recommended for an AFC but with too few medals to go round, the toss of a coin led to a Mentioned in Dispatches instead. Tired of instructing, he formed a crew of like-minded aircrew and requested to go back on ops. This was accepted and after some crew training and a couple of cross country flights they were posted to 1654 HCU at Wigsley to train on the Avro Manchester. Jim recalls the Manchester as being a delight to fly and he had no problems with the notorious Vulture engines.[3]

Flight Lieutenant 'Mike' Lewis was one of the six original pilots to fly on 207, the first Manchester squadron. He recalls:

It was a disaster. The aircraft itself, the airframe, had many short-comings in the equipment in the beginning but as we found out, Avro were excellent in doing modifications and re-equipping the aeroplane. The engines never were and never did become reliable. They did not give enough power for the aeroplane, so we ended up with two extremely unreliable 1,750hp engines and having to haul a 50,000lb aircraft. We should really have had 2,500hp engines. If you felt that you'd lost one, that was it; you weren't coming home. It didn't matter if you feathered the propeller or not; there was only one way you went and that was down. I saw an aircraft doing a run up on the ground and had two pistons come right out through the side of the engine. The original bearings were made without any silver as an economy measure, so they weren't hard enough. The bearings would collapse the connecting rod and the piston would fling out through the side of the engine and bang! Your engine just destroyed itself. I finished my second tour on Manchesters except for one month in July 1941 when they had to ground them and put new engines in them.

On the night of 15/16 August just over 80 Blenheims, Hampdens and Wellingtons visited multiple targets in Germany, France and the Netherlands and four Whitleys flew to Italian targets. Two Blenheims and a Whitley failed to return. The night following, 150 Blenheims, Hampdens, Wellingtons and Whitleys were dispatched to bomb targets in the Ruhr and Frankfurt, to the distant targets of Leuna, Augsburg and the Zeiss Works at Jena and to airfields in the Netherlands. Squadron Leader Charles John French Kydd DFC led the attack on the immense oil plant at Leuna near Merseburg, just west of Leipzig. It was a glorious night with a bright moon when he dropped his load of bombs full on his target, which was the hydrogenation plant. He and his crew expected to see the whole plant go up in flames, but to their bitter disappointment nothing happened. For 20 minutes they cruised around, watching the buildings on which their bombs had fallen. Then all of a sudden they saw it burst into flames, which grew so intense that they could still see it when they were 50 miles away on their homeward journey. They enjoyed their sandwiches and hot drink from the thermos after that raid. On the way out they were only attacked at Hannover and Brunswick by the anti-aircraft defences. 'But on the way back the Germans went completely mad and seemed to be letting fly all over the place at nobody in particular they were swishing it all over the sky,' he remarked afterwards.

They noticed in several raids that a man used to wait for them at one particular spot and blaze away with a rifle, no matter how high they were flying. This sportsman always delighted them. Another laugh came when the rear-gunner requested his captain's permission to shoot a star out of the sky, under the impression that it was the light of an enemy aircraft. He was not the only gunner to be misled by a star, for some have tried to shoot out the light of Jupiter, under the impression that the planet was stalking them. One uncanny experience befell the captain and crew of a bomber who were haunted near their target by a weird light, which followed them around in the dark. The pilot tried all sorts of tactics to shake off the pursuer, but he could not get away. Wherever he went, whatever he did that menacing light maintained its position astern. The guns on the ground fired on them madly and every second they were expecting their pursuer to open fire. Then they discovered that one of their own flares had somehow become entangled by the parachute in the tail of the bomber![4]

On the night of 16/17 August six aircraft, three of them Whitleys, were lost and a 144 Squadron Hampden returning from the raid on Merseburg crashed on return to Hemswell with the loss of all the crew. One of the Whitley casualties was a 102 Squadron aircraft at Driffield flown by Pilot Officer Mark Hubbard Rogers, which crashed in the Walser Valley in Austria after the raid on Augsburg. All the crew were killed. Another was *G-George* on 10 Squadron at Leeming, 25 miles south-west of Middlesbrough, which was flown by Flying Officer W M Nixon, which failed to return from the attack on the Zeiss Works. Nixon force-landed near Zevenbergen and all the crew were taken into captivity. Pilot Officer W G 'Pete' Whitby, the second pilot, who had worked in the wool trade in Europe before joining the RAF aged 20, kept an old steeplechaser at Thirsk to ride in off duty moments in the occasional point-to-point race, and a mare named Myrtle Green at Catterick. After his release from PoW camp in 1945 Whitby found that Myrtle Green had bred him four foals and run up a bill for £600 for fodder.[5]

Just over 100 Blenheims, Hampdens and Wellingtons visited five targets in Germany and airfields in Holland, Belgium and France and carried out mine-laying in enemy waters on 17/18 August without loss. Two nights later attacks on another five targets in north Germany, as well as mine-laying and raids on an oil refinery at Ambes in France and airfield targets in Holland, France and Belgium, were carried out by 120 bombers. Two Blenheims and a Whitley failed to return. The following night 42 Hampdens were dispatched to widely spread targets including the Magdeburg ship lifts in the canal system of Germany. For some days previously the men detailed for the task studied a model of the lifts as well as very fine enlargements of photographs that were taken from all angles by RAF photo reconnaissance pilots. The two lifts were really huge troughs, each about 275 feet long by 50 or 60 feet wide and capable of carrying ships or barges up to about 1,000 tons. The biggest barges on the German canals equal in carrying capacity two train loads of 50 trucks each, so if important canals could be put out of action for a few days the matter would have been a grave one for the enemy. Each ship lift had lock gates which sealed the ends and enabled the ships to pass in and out and rise with the lift to the high-level canal or drop down to the canal at the low level.

The weather on the night of the operation was bad and of the Hampden pilots who started out, only Squadron Leader Kydd DFC and Pilot Officer Alexander Webster DFC on 61 Squadron found the target. The Squadron Leader and his crew made out the ship lifts quite clearly just as the defences opened up on them. The Germans had brought up so many anti-aircraft guns and searchlights that they regarded the area as a death trap for raiders. As soon as Kydd straightened out to make his run over the lifts, the full blast of the guns met him, the searchlights blinded him with their glare and the gunfire was so fierce that he was driven off his target. He circled into the clouds and dived down to make another run but the hell of fire turned him away before the bomb-aimer could get his sights properly on the target. Undeterred, for the third time he straightened out on his target, only to be deflected off it once more by the weight of the fire. For the fourth time he dived into the inferno and the German gunners again succeeded in putting him off his target but still he would not give up. For the fifth time, he dived down and straightened out to make his run over the target. The deadly guns and blinding searchlights blazed at him, but this time he kept his course through it all. Straight and true he held the Hampden along the canal and right over the centre of the lifts.

'Bombs away,' said the bomb-aimer over the intercom and Kydd swept into the clouds and flew home. Kydd recalls:

> There was low cloud from the Dutch coast all across Germany and visibility was only one mile. The clouds became a little more broken over the target and we flew low to identify the place. The first time we made our run the searchlights were so blinding and the anti-aircraft fire was so heavy that we were put off. I made another run and again the defences deflected us off our target; so I tried again, with the same result. The fourth time it was the same, but the fifth time the bomb-aimer got right on the target from 500 feet and let go our bombs. Strangely enough, we were not hit. We could hear everything exploding all round us and bumping us about, but we escaped damage.[6]

Squadron Leader Kydd's actions resulted in the award of the DSO. Pilot Officer Webster, who faced the concerted fire of 12 anti-aircraft guns with the same unshakeable determination as his CO, dived down until he was flying at only 50 feet and dropped a delayed action bomb in the great troughs. He received a Bar to his decoration. Squadron Leader Kydd died on 21 June 1941 when the 207 Squadron Manchester he was in crashed on take-off at Waddington at the start of an air test.

On the night of 23/24 August the *Luftwaffe* rained bombs on London, the first to fall on the capital since 1918. Bomber Command was quick to retaliate. On the night of 25/26 August about 50 Wellingtons, Hampdens and Whitleys attacked Berlin as a reprisal. The flight involved a round trip of eight hours and 1,200 miles. Seven aircraft aborted and of the remaining force, 29 bombers claimed to have bombed Berlin and a further 27 overflew the German capital but were unable to pinpoint their targets because of thick cloud. Five aircraft were lost to enemy action, including three that ditched in the North Sea. Bombing results had been un-impressive but the RAF had scored a great victory for morale. Berlin was bombed again on the night of 28/29 August when 79 Blenheims, Hampdens, Wellingtons and Whitleys took part in raids on the German capital and other targets. George Bury, Pilot Officer Barr's navigator on a 115 Squadron Wellington recalls:

> The target was Klingenberg Electric. Having been warned that the area was very heavily defended, we decided to fly at 15,000 feet. That was 5,000 feet higher than our normal height. At this height it was essential to use oxygen all the time but after a few hours the masks

became wet and uncomfortable to use. But, if taken off, frequent movement was very tiring. As it turned out the flight as far as we were concerned turned out to be fairly uneventful. Searchlights were very active. Although one did pick us up, he failed to keep us within his beam long enough for the others in the group to join in. When just ahead we saw a Wellington caught by two at the same time and quick as a flash many others concentrated on the same target and he was caught in a cone of at least ten searchlights. The whole area around the aircraft was as bright as day and no matter which way he turned and twisted, they easily held on to him. The last we saw of him he was in a steep dive with shells bursting all around. This was our eighth flight and the first time that we had seen another aircraft. We were beginning to think that we were fighting the whole war on our own.[7]

Twenty-year-old Flying Officer David Albert Alton Romans, a Canadian Hampden pilot on 44 Squadron at Waddington, born in Nova Scotia, was slightly less than six feet tall, with a slim figure, dark wavy hair, dark eyes and a small dark moustache. He had come to England to join the RAF about three months before the outbreak of war. When Berlin and Cologne and airfields in Holland and Belgium were attacked again on the last night of August by 77 Blenheims, Hampdens, Wellingtons and Whitleys, Romans' crew had the misfortune of coming down on the sea returning from the raid on Berlin. After ditching off Salthouse on the Norfolk coast they paddled ashore in a dinghy and were fortunate to walk through a minefield unscathed.

On the night of 5/6 September while returning from Stettin, Romans hit the water the second time, fortunately without injury, a quarter of a mile off Lowestoft. On this occasion they had to take to the dinghy, so two members of the crew sat in it, while the navigator and Romans swam behind pushing it... this was a trifle unorthodox but very effective. They were picked up by the trawler *Ben Hur* and landed at Lowestoft. After that, his friends promptly dubbed him 'Duckfeet'! The Hampden, although partly submerged, remained afloat for a time but when an attempt was made to tow it ashore it sank.

On the operation to Eschwage airfield on the night of 26/27 September David Romans flew as navigator-bomb aimer, carrying out his duties in the cramped front cockpit behind the pilot, Pilot Officer John Edgecombe Lowe. At the back of the pilot's seat was an opening perhaps four feet deep, just big enough for a man to get down, which continued in a sloping tunnel under the pilot's seat leading into the front cockpit. When the time came to make the bombing run the navigator had to crawl or slide through this tunnel to the nose of the aircraft. To make the drop he had to lay down flat on the floor to manipulate the bomb sight and bomb controls. In the centre section, behind the entrance to the front cockpit, was a small well in which the collapsible dinghy and other things were stored; then further back came a metal door, which completely cut off the wireless operator who sat with his wireless panel and two machine-guns facing aft in a turret with a sliding dome. Further aft, his head on a level with the wireless operator's feet, the rear-gunner sat with his legs stretched out on the padded floor of the fuselage in the rear turret.

Fair at the start, the weather worsened a bit over the sea, but this bad patch was gradually left behind them and by the time they reached the other side the weather had cleared and there was a good moon to aid them in their task. Flying at 4,000 feet, the Hampden approached its target. In the front cockpit, Romans, making his preparations to bomb, saw the searchlights feeling about for them. The anti-aircraft fire began to increase. Watching the sudden flashes of the guns below, he saw numerous shells bursting around him. As the ack-ack grew in intensity, the bomber began to swing about to evade it. Suddenly Romans felt two severe jolts on the aircraft, which at once began to stall and dive. Thinking that the pilot, who was his friend, was merely taking evasive action, he paid no attention for a second or two. All his faculties were alert. 'Watch your speed!' he called to Lowe on the intercom. There was no answer. He sensed that something was wrong. The aircraft was going down. There was silence instead of the voice he knew so well. Ripping off his helmet, he moved through the tunnel quicker than ever before as the aircraft continued to go down. Bobbing up behind the pilot's seat, he saw him slumped over the controls. In an instant Romans was up on the padded rest of the main spar tugging at the pilot's straps in order to let down the back of the seat. All the time he struggled to release the pilot, the Hampden dropped. Lowe made no movement. There was no sign of blood, nothing to tell what had happened. Romans got the back of the seat down at last. Kneeling upon it, he shifted the limp body of the pilot off the control column until he was lying flat on the lowered back of the seat. The needle of the altimeter gradually moved round. The speed had dropped to no more than 80mph and they were down to 2,000 feet. Romans clambered over his recumbent friend and sat on top of him while he grabbed the control column and, easing it back, pulled the bomber out of her dive. Then he managed to get the feet of the pilot out of the rudder controls and insert his own:

I managed to pull the aircraft up and got her under control again. During this time the wireless operator simply thought we were doing evasive action, but I succeeded after awhile in letting him know what was wrong. As I took the aircraft up to 6,000 feet, the wireless operator struggled to pull the pilot out from underneath me. It was an awful job in the cramped space, but he got him out, took off his parachute and helmet and saw that he was hit at the side of the head.

Romans estimated that from the instant he felt the shells bursting until he succeeded in pulling up the aircraft and saving it from crashing, a bare minute, or at most a minute and a half, elapsed. If he had hesitated for a few seconds longer, the BBC would probably have announced that 'one of our aircraft did not return.' The shells, which hit the aircraft between the starboard engine and the fuselage, had wrought havoc with the instruments. The gyroscope controlling the automatic compass was put out of action. A glance at the rev counter shocked him. It was not registering at all. Through his mind flashed the thought that the engines were stopped. Swiftly he looked out of the sides of the cockpit. The propellers were working! He breathed freely once more, knowing the engines were all right and that it was the revolution counter that had been smashed. Meanwhile the wireless operator, getting the first-aid kit, attended to the stricken pilot, who was quite unconscious. Giving him a dose of morphia, he found a tiny puncture behind the pilot's ear. It was hardly discernible. Very carefully he bandaged up the pilot's head and made him as comfortable as possible. Unhappily Lowe was mortally wounded. Through that tiny puncture a small fragment of shell had entered and pierced the brain.

'Get my map and instruments from down below,' said Romans to the wireless operator. The Canadian was anxious to find out his position to fix his course, and directly the wireless operator returned, he successfully took a sight while piloting the aircraft. Twice later he was able to check his position. After flying for three hours over the sea against a headwind of 25mph, Romans made his landfall on the east coast and landed safely at Waddington. Pilot Officer Romans was awarded the DFC.

There was another night when, flying on a long trip, Romans was suddenly perturbed. Speaking to the rear-gunner on the intercom he was unable to get any reply. Fearing the worst, feeling sure that he had been hit, he dived through the tunnel to his aid, striking his head a terrific bump on the way. Reaching the 'tin', he looked down. The rear-gunner lay there with eyes closed. Stooping over, Romans took the gunner's hand to feel his pulse and see if he was still alive. At his touch the gunner opened his eyes and looked up. 'Did you see any ack-ack?' asked Romans. 'No!' was the reply. The rear-gunner had calmly slept through it all.[8]

Romans later flew operations as a Flying Fortress pilot on 90 Squadron. On 8 September 1941 on an operation to bomb the *Admiral Scheer* in Oslo harbour, Romans and his crew were killed when their aircraft was attacked at 25,000 feet by two Bf 109s. One of the attackers was shot down but the Fortress crashed in mountainous terrain.

Max Meyer, who had carried out over 30 bombing operations on 144 Squadron and knew full well what it was to have his aircraft shot about, decided that he would do a spot of mine-laying for a change at Brest:

We thought it would be easy so we volunteered. But when we got quite close to the port we were met by a terrific barrage. As we went in to Brest, they drove me down to within 20 feet of the water. They were firing so hard that we could see the tracer splashing into the water in front of us. We have never had so much stuff so close before. It was just like turning hoses on us. We skated in about 20 feet off the water, then climbed up to drop our mine in the inner harbour, after which we dropped down and skated out again; but we didn't sing on that trip.

Meyer flew his final operation of his tour on 4 September 1940, another *Gardening* (mine-laying) trip, to Stettin in the Baltic this time. He recalled:

I was put down for another trip two nights later and was almost on my way out to my aircraft when my Squadron Commander came down to the Flights to say that my trip was cancelled. I was some-what taken aback, thinking I had done something wrong but he said I was not to go because I had done enough and my tour of operations was ended. I was surprised because up till then there had been no such thing as a set number of operations for a 'tour', which was a word none of us had heard of before. We obviously talked about this amongst ourselves and had assumed that we would just go on operating indefinitely. However, someone, somewhere had decided that bomber crews would have to be limited to a certain number of 'trips' and from now on this would be thirty operations or 200 hours of operational flying. One other crew was taken off that night, since we had both carried out thirty-seven operational sorties. So ended my first tour and after some very welcome leave, I was posted to the Hampden Operational Training Unit as an instructor engaged in training new crews.[9]

The bombing directive on 21 September released the Whitley Group from anti-invasion duties and gave a high place to electric power plants in Berlin. By the end of 1940 the 'Big City' as it was to become known to bomber crews, would have been bombed on ten occasions. On 23/24th September the German capital was selected for a special retaliatory effort, the first time that all the bombers would attack targets in one German city. The Whitleys were joined by all available Hampdens and Wellingtons and 129 aircraft took off for 18 separate targets, which included three gas-works and six power stations and subsidiary targets such as seven railway yards and the Tempelhof airfield. Weather and icing conditions proved unexpectedly severe but 84 of the bombers managed to reach Berlin. Most of the bombs probably fell in the Moabit area of the city where a power station was one of the selected targets. The only significant success was at Charlottenburg where incendiaries set fire to a gasometer. Many of the bombs failed to explode, including one that dropped in the garden of the Chancellery. Several houses were damaged in the Tiergarten district and 781 Germans lost their homes. Twenty-two Germans were killed. Three bombers failed to return. One of these was a Whitley on 77 Squadron at Linton-on-Ouse flown by Pilot Officer Andrew Woodrow Dunn DFC who had taken off at 20.00 hours with the intention of bombing the large aircraft factory at Spandau on the outskirts of Berlin. There were a few clouds about but conditions were not too bad as they sped across Germany. Sergeant Riley in the rear turret kept a sharp look-out in the darkness for enemy fighters. His four guns were ready to blaze away instantly but no enemy fighters troubled him on the long trip over. Directly the Whitley reached the outskirts of Spandau the searchlights began to move round. The bomber could not escape the beams. The vivid flashes of anti-aircraft guns lit up the ground like sheet lightning as the shells began to come up. Dropping their flares as they roared over Spandau, the Whitley crew had no difficulty in locating the aircraft factory. It was too immense to be missed.

As they turned and made their run over the target, the guns put up a fierce barrage. Now and again they felt bits of bursting shells jar the aircraft, but they held their course and dropped their full load of high explosives and incendiaries dead on the target. Riley watched the bombs strike home and the factory burst into flames. Unfortunately for the crew of the Whitley, a piece of shell holed one of the petrol tanks. Conserving his fuel as much as possible Dunn made his way back across Germany. He flew over Holland and then crossed the Dutch coast and headed over the North Sea. He watched the pointer of the altimeter sliding back inexorably as he slowly lost height. His eye from time to time glanced at the dwindling fuel reserves from the emergency tanks. There was too far to go and too little fuel. He must have thought, 'here we go again' for on 19/20 June, Dunn had been forced to ditch off Hastings Pier returning from the raid on Wanne-Eickel. Two of his crew were injured but they were all rescued. On the night of 20/21 May he had force landed near Abbeville on the raid on Cambrai. One of the crew was taken prisoner. On 6/7 June he had again forced landed at Finningley when returning from the raid on Bapune. One of the crew was injured. Three nights later Dunn crash landed at Abingdon returning from the battle area.

When the Whitley was 80 miles from the Dutch coast, the wireless operator got in touch with the home stations, fixed his position and advised them that they were in difficulties. They flew on, getting lower, looking eagerly for some ship which might assist them. There was nothing, only the empty seas heaving around them. It was so rough that some of the crew wondered whether they could make a safe landing. But on this point Riley was convinced. 'I knew we were going to do it,' he said afterwards.

The crew got ready to abandon the aircraft. They chopped off the escape door so that they could launch the rubber dinghy and get into it without delay. Meanwhile, the wireless operator transmitted their position so long as the power lasted to enable a ship to be sent to their rescue. The second pilot came up from the forward cockpit and crawled under the main spar into the fuselage where the other three members of the crew clustered round the escape door. All braced themselves for the shock. They were thrown about as the Whitley hit the water, but Dunn made a magnificent landing in the rough seas and soon joined his crew. The dinghy was safely launched. One of the men took the Very pistol for signalling purposes and another, a flask of water and another, a packet of biscuits. Quickly the five men got into the rubber dinghy and pushed away from the sinking Whitley. It was exactly 05.50 on 24 September, for Riley's wristwatch was stopped by the jolt of the Whitley hitting the sea. They had been flying for seven hours and fifty minutes and were then 100 miles away from the English coast. From that moment all the resources of the RAF and the Royal Navy were concentrated on their rescue. A Hudson was instructed to locate them, but failed to do so; but at 10.50, five hours after they took to the dinghy, another Hudson, detailed for the search, managed to come on the little boat amid the rough seas and at once signalled its position. The dinghy was then 100 miles to the east of Hartlepool. This Hudson flew around until relieved at 12.35 by another, which in its turn was relieved just before 14.00.

Seated in the flooded dinghy, the crew were wet through and very cold. They sought to warm themselves by taking their emergency spirit ration, but it made Riley rather sick. Waving to the first Hudson about 11.00, they wondered how long they would have to wait before they were rescued. Tired out by their long flight and exhausted by the incessant action of the rough seas, some of them started to doze. The little bunch of men in the dinghy was not easily seen in the high seas, off which a 30mph wind was whipping the tops. Approaching as closely as possible, a Hudson dropped a container of food and comforts for the men. It fell only ten yards away, but although Riley and his companions paddled hard to reach it, the seas were too much for them and they suffered the disappointment of seeing the parcel vanish. The continual pounding of the seas had its effect on the drifting men. Sergeant Bernard Savill DFM grew lightheaded and fell overboard, but his companions managed to get him back again. Shortly afterwards he dropped in again, but once more his companions dragged him out. They were growing weak and the struggle exhausted them, but they still mustered enough strength to haul him into the dinghy when he slipped in for the third time. All grew very quiet. Then they saw Savill fall in again and the seas closed on him for ever.

Just after 06.00 on 25 September, four Hudsons flew off in formation to try to find the dinghy. A search along the track where the dinghy was last sighted yielded no result. Below them two destroyers cast around to find the hapless airmen. One Hudson was cheered by the sight of the missing dinghy making for land and reported the news to base. 'It followed us for a long time,' stated Riley. 'We sighted a destroyer later in the afternoon and the Hudson seemed to direct it to us, but as soon as the Hudson went off we lost sight of the destroyer.' Night closed down on the tragic group of airmen drifting on the waves. Lack of food and the long exposure to the seas were telling on them. That night another man grew lightheaded and imagined he was back walking on the aerodrome. In his delusion he walked overboard and was lost.

For two days the RAF and the Royal Navy had been seeking them, sparing no resources and no effort. At dawn on the morning of 26 September five Hudsons took up the task. They were detailed to search an area off Flamborough Head 90 miles long by 59 miles wide – over 5,000 square miles. All morning they continued their search, fighting now and again with German aircraft that sought to interfere with them. Once a Hudson came on two Heinkel 115 seaplanes circling the two destroyers *Ashanti* and *Bedouin*, which were prosecuting the search down below and it promptly attacked the Heinkels and drove them into the clouds. A Blenheim went out to join in the hunt. A motor launch engaged on the same errand of mercy was so battered by the heavy seas that she sprang a leak and was obliged to return. Time and again during the morning the Hudsons fought short engagements with enemy aircraft, which always succeeded in escaping in the clouds. From dawn until the early afternoon they kept up a continuous search, but not a sight of the missing airmen cheered their eyes. A few minutes after 14.00 they were all obliged to return to their base because they were at the end of their fuel. In the afternoon four Ansons went out to resume the quest, but they, too, failed to locate the missing airmen. Hopeless though further search seemed, neither the RAF nor the Royal Navy would abandon it.

At dawn the next day, 27 September, five Hudsons and four Ansons flew off to quarter the seas and try to find and save the missing airmen. Visibility was poor, the seas were rough and as they swept down from time to time to look closer at the surface, their windows were coated with brine. At last a Hudson saw the missing dinghy, but it was able to keep it in sight for only five minutes. The position, however, was marked and at 11.15 another Hudson flew to the position and searched the seas around it. It found nothing. An hour later another aircraft went to the same spot, with the same result. Baffled and disappointed, they returned to base and three Ansons flew off to continue the search. These found the destroyers and escorted them to the spot where the missing dinghy was last seen – they saw nothing but the empty seas heaving in all directions.

A Hudson took off at 13.00 hours to resume the search. At 13.30 another Hudson followed. Just after 14.00 the missing dinghy was seen ahead by one of the Hudsons whose pilot, coming down very low, manoeuvred as close as possible and dropped a float and with it a watertight bag of comforts. Luckily they dropped just within the reach of Sergeant Riley who with an effort managed to secure the bag. Although very weak after all he had suffered and endured, Riley was still in fair condition and the first thing he did was to light up a cigarette. His two companions were far gone and remained in a comatose state. From the moment that the Hudson sighted the dinghy it started to circle round and would not let it out of sight for a second. An hour later the other Hudson came on the scene and for hour after hour the two aircraft followed each other round and round that pitiful little group on the sea below. Just after 16.00 they saw one of the airmen fall out of the dinghy and vanish. He had already fallen into the sea earlier in the day and been helped back by Riley. 'The last day aircraft were above all the time. We had seen so many of them that we took no notice. It was a boat we wanted,' he remarked, when he had recovered from his ordeal. So from 14.00 until 17.30 those Hudsons went round and round that little dinghy which the RAF and the Royal Navy had sought for more than three days. The crews of the Hudsons were determined not to lose it again. At last the destroyers *Ashanti* and *Bedouin* steamed up in answer to the signals and the Hudsons dropped flares by the dinghy and kept diving over it to lead them to the position. At 17.35 a boat was launched from one of the destroyers and Riley and his companion were tenderly lifted from the rubber dinghy and taken on board. The Hudsons waited awhile to learn the condition of the rescued men. 'One fair, one very ill,' signalled the destroyer.

Of those five men[10] who so bravely launched the little dinghy when their Whitley came down in the North Sea, only Sergeant Riley survived, and after being picked up the next thing he remembered was waking up in Rosyth hospital on the following day. Drifting for 84 hours, he was carried a distance of about 90 miles. As if the agony of that ordeal were not enough, Riley had barely recovered and gone on leave to his home when he was subjected to the terrible raid in Manchester which laid the heart of the city in ruins. Many died that night in the brutal attack, but Riley escaped. 'The Germans can't kill me!' the gallant young sergeant remarked when it was all over. Nor will they ever conquer those who show such courage.[11]

Recalled from three weeks' leave, his reward for flying 38 ops on many months of night operations against the enemy, Flight Sergeant Douglas Hayhurst DFM, a Hampden navigator on 83 Squadron, was put on a makeshift crew as navigator to Canadian Pilot Officer Clare Arthur Connor, pilot, 18-year-old Sergeant John Hannah the blue-eyed, fair haired Scottish wireless operator/air gunner and Sergeant George 'Buffy' James, rear gunner, who had flown nine ops. Hannah, born at Paisley in November 1921 had served as a salesman in a Glasgow shoe shop before he joined the RAF in 1939. Hayhurst recalls:

It was Sunday, 15 September 1940. England was in danger of invasion. The Spitfire and Hurricane boys had shot down 185 planes (sic) over London that day and we were detailed to bomb flat-bottomed invasion barges at Antwerp. Our Group Captain instructed us to make sure of our targets by flying low to lay our eggs. We had a good machine – Hampden P1355 *Betty* – and with bright moonlight aiding visibility, everything seemed to be on our side.[12] Airborne at 22.35, we crossed the English coast, climbing steadily and keeping our eyes skinned for lurking enemy fighters. Conversation between us was spasmodic and after an uneventful sea-crossing we reached the Belgian coast on time and track, at a height of about 5,000 feet. As planned, we began to lose height steadily from the coast to the target and very soon I could see the searchlights groping the skies above Antwerp. We must have been first there, because there was no flak. A few minutes later I saw the docks and then the basins in which were anchored hundreds of invasion barges. I excitedly announced the fact to the rest of the crew and gave Connor a course to steer, asking him to lose height steadily. Vulnerable though we would be, I wanted to be over the target at 2,000 feet to ensure good results.

Connor, the pilot, recalled:

We started to make our bombing run but found that we were not in line to make a good attack so we turned, circled round and got into a better position, as soon as we arrived we noticed that the anti-aircraft gun fire was fairly close to us. It wasn't long however, before they got our range and as we came round for the second attack we met a terrific barrage which we determined was not going to stop us. We were hit in the wing several times on the way down and the aircraft shook so much that it was not an easy matter to control it. However, we released our bombs and it was then that I saw flames reflected in my Perspex windscreen. I soon realized that something had happened but I was so busy taking violent evasive action that I did not at first give it any serious thought.

Hayhurst continues:

Every shell, pom-pom and bullet in the world seemed to hit us. I was standing up in the front cabin looking below through the Perspex when a lump of shrapnel burst right up through, between my legs, without harming me. I called up the boys through the intercom. They were OK and enjoying it by the sound of things. Hannah and James were firing their twin Vickers like merry hell. Connor was jinking about like a paper boat in an ocean swell. We were just about 2,000 feet and despite our vigorous evasive action I could still see the target down below, a little ahead. The flak was terrific... like heavy rain on an iron roof... I could see holes appearing along the inside of the fuselage. How the hell we were all still alive God only knew... I had my hand on the master bomb-switch... the target came into my swaying bomb-sight... I pulled the switch over.... 'Bombs gone!' I shouted. 'Keep going down,' thinking it better to go lower than to climb. I looked below and saw the results of our bombing. There was an explosion and fires were breaking out on the target. Not bad! The flak around us was still terrific but Hannah and James must have run out of ammunition... there was no more firing from the back. Little fires were burning all over the floor of my cabin. I stamped most of them out and then tried to contact the boys in the back... no answer... I called up Connor and told him. 'Go back and see what you can do,' he said.

A Hampden must be the worst aircraft in the world for crawling around in. Even the smallest person, lightly clothed, would find difficulty in crawling from one part of the aircraft to another. By the time I had edged myself under the pilot's seat and crawled up behind him, I was sweating, although inwardly I felt cool and resigned to whatever fate was in store for me. Behind the pilot several small fires had broken out and I stamped them out without difficulty. There was a larger fire however, which had gained a good hold. I tore my helmet off and tried to beat it out... no use... I reached for the small extinguisher... it was red-hot. I gave it up as a bad job. Through the glass of the communicating door I saw the lower part of a body, standing but leaning... the legs covered in leather flying trousers and boots... motionless... flames were licking around his boots but he wasn't even stirring... poor Hannah, I thought, he's stopped a packet... no bloody wonder. Beyond that I could see the gunner's cockpit ablaze. I hoped that Buffy had made good his escape. I crawled back to the front and connected up my intercom. I wanted to speak to Connor but it was useless. The flames had damaged my speaking apparatus. I crawled up behind Connor again and just managed to touch his arm through the big plate of armour which protected his back and head.

'We're on fire; Hannah's dead, James has gone; I'm going now!' He waved me to go. I got back to my own cabin again and clipped on my parachute. I lifted the emergency hatch and looked below at the roads, fields and houses... the altimeter registered 1,500 feet... I thought of home, of mother and father... I said a hurried prayer and plunged head-first through the hatch... I remember seeing the burning plane roar on above me. I was turning over and over, filled with such an ecstatic feeling that I felt loath to pull the rip-cord. But life was too dear and the ground too near... I pulled and waited for the jolt. It came and I looked above me at the billowing shrouds of silk. Presently I was lying sprawled in a ploughed field with a sprained ankle. I had landed at Malderen, four miles from Antwerp itself. I stayed that night with some Belgians who showered kindnesses upon me. Dressed in civilian clothes I tried to make my way to the coast next morning at about 07.30. At mid-day, tired, hungry and fed-up and not giving a damn, I was arrested by two red-hatted gendarmes who regarded me with suspicion as I limped through a small village. I was taken back to the Belgians' house and as I had not said anything about them to the gendarmes I could only think that neighbours, scared of German reprisals, had given me away. Having changed back to my flying clothes, I was taken to Brussels military prison by car. Here I met Buffy who was covered in bandages. We speculated upon what had happened to Connor and Hannah and gave them up as dead. At Brussels we were taken aboard a Junkers 52 and escorted to an aerodrome south of Berlin. Buffy had plans for overpowering our German guards and taking over control of the plane. He actually had an iron crowbar to help him achieve this object but weight of numbers against us decided him to abandon the idea. From Berlin we were taken aboard a train to Frankfurt-on-Main and so to *Dulag Luft*. A fortnight later I heard the news that Connor and Hannah had reached base! Apparently, by some superhuman effort, Hannah (whom I had thought dead!) had extinguished the fires. Hannah was awarded the VC and Connor the DFC.[13]

Hannah's citation, in part, read:

... A fire started which quickly enveloped the wireless operator's and rear gunner's cockpits and as both the port and starboard petrol tanks had been pierced, there was grave risk of the fire spreading. Sergeant Hannah forced his way through the fire to obtain two extinguishers and discovered that the rear gunner had had to leave the aircraft. He could have acted likewise, through the bottom escape hatch or forward through the navigator's hatch but he remained and fought the fire for ten minutes with the extinguishers, beating the flames with his log book when these were empty. During this time thousands of rounds of ammunition exploded in all directions and he was almost blinded by the intense heat and fumes but had the presence of mind to obtain relief by turning on his oxygen supply. Air admitted through the large holes caused by the projectile made the bomb compartment an inferno and all the aluminium sheet metal on the floor of this airman's cockpit was melted away, leaving only the cross bearers. Working under these conditions, which caused burns to his face and eyes Sergeant Hannah succeeded in extinguishing the fire. He then crawled forward, ascertained that the navigator had left the aircraft and passed the latter's log and maps to the pilot. This airman displayed courage, coolness and devotion to duty of the highest order and, by his action in remaining and successfully extinguishing the fire under conditions of the greatest danger and difficulty, enabled the pilot to bring the aircraft safely to its base.[14]

The vagaries of chance provided much conversation in the RAF messes. For instance, Flying Officer Francis Edwin Eustace DFC, a modest but brilliant New Zealand pilot who was born at Nelson, was returning over the North Sea when there was an unexpected crash from the nose of the aircraft. His startled crew suddenly saw the face and head of the pilot smothered with blood. It streamed down the back of his helmet while the cords from the intercom system and his oxygen supply were twisted tightly round his neck. He was a shocking sight and appeared to be desperately wounded. In fact a seagull had hit the perspex and smashed right through it, the remains of the bird crashing into the face of the pilot to simulate frightful injuries. When the pilot, who was knocked out for a moment, cleared the mess off his face, he learned that he had escaped with no more than a black eye. It might have been worse.[15]

Wellington observer Sergeant Albert E Robinson on 115 Squadron recalls that:

Bombing by night presented a formidable barrier to the young crews of Bomber Command in 1940–41. If groping blindly through the curtain of darkness that had descended over Europe was to be overcome, it was crystal clear that in the initial stages an awful lot was going to depend on the crews themselves. Trial and error mostly only resulted in a high casualty rate. Unfortunately, it was with little result for so great an effort, a pot-pourri of calculated risk, personal skills and circumstances that favoured the more success-ful crews. The 'X' factor, a quality difficult to define but one that enabled them to take advantage of more than a full share of luck lifted them high above average. Whatever the mixture, a fierce deter-mination to succeed in spite of the numerous setbacks was a common denominator and it united the crews almost without exception. With such resolution, the crews attempted to face up to their task. It was not made any easier by briefing officers who spoke at length about the necessity for precision bombing. It would not be too critical to suggest that some of these briefings were out of touch with reality. Truthful crews considered it a reasonable effort if the city itself was found, let alone a specific aiming point. There were many reasons for this but the principal culprit was night navigation. This was based almost entirely on the age-old theory of dead reckoning. There was no problem if all the links in the chain were known but if not, it could turn out to be a hit-or-miss affair, especially with little or no radio assistance to help with the calculations. The basic requirement for success was to establish the wind speed and direction but in order to assess these it was necessary at various times during the flight to define the position of the aircraft in relation to the ground – obtain a 'fix', as it was known to the navigator. Under variable conditions this was not always possible. The flight could be blown well off course, sometimes miles away if there were adverse winds and with it went little chance of finding out the true position of the aircraft. This in turn usually added up to wasted effort, with bombs being brought back or jettisoned in the sea.

Inexperienced crews could end up on the slopes of a mountain or in the grey wastes of the sea. The North Sea in particular was a big enemy to Bomber Command; a heaving predator, menacing in its vastness to any crippled bomber struggling to maintain height over its darkened wilderness. The enemy coast to the hoped-for landfall in England offered little hope if a crippled bomber had to force-land and most certainly so if contact had been lost with any listening post as a result of a damaged radio. A bomber aircraft then was a lonely and desolate figure, struggling against the odds and with the chilling thought that no matter how expertly the aircraft was set down on the sea – turbulent or calm – the bomber would sink within minutes. There was the rubber dinghy, of course. It could be paddled but when exhaustion came and effort faded it would just drift along with the wind and tide, aimlessly and without hope, to a tortured end, unless providence took a hand. God knows how long this would take. Perhaps better not to have taken the dinghy at all.

That's how it went. Such possibilities could only be accepted by crews with a philosophical shrug of the shoulders. It came with a host of other things but even so most crews were optimistic and they set their sights on completing the mandatory, magical, number of 30 operations before being taken off for a rest at some training squadron. In comparison to the numbers involved, very few managed to achieve this; the average could have been as low as five missions before the Grim Reaper called the tune. Given the conditions, the chances of survival on any one operation, whether it was the first or 30th were not good. Any discerning bookmaker would rate the betting odds low. All aircrew were volunteers to a man but in saying this they needed to be. Each raid was equivalent to 'going over the top' in the 1914–18 war. However, if one were to put the clock back to the briefing room in 1940–41 and peer through the haze of cigarette smoke that hung in swirling clouds no one would have guessed it. It was more like a gathering at any sports club. We were boisterous, outgoing and extrovert but underneath this cloak there was a quiet confidence and rugged determination. Such an outlook was essential. The effort needed to penetrate Germany, certainly with the out-dated aircraft at the crews' disposal in 1940–41 required a deep-seated motivation and a special quality.

The Wellington was probably the best of the bunch when compared to the other bombers. A good old war-horse, it was as loyal and forgiving as the crews were to the bomber. But the fact remains that it was outdated, unable to reach much height over the target, poorly armed, had no internal heat and when carrying a full bomb load of 4,000lb had a speed of less than half that of an enemy fighter. Freezing temperatures often coated surfaces with ice and frost, froze controls and radio sets and brought instant ice-burn should metal surfaces be touched without a glove. Often engines were suspect (they invariably coughed and spluttered) and the dials on the instrument panel were constantly watched with anxious eyes, hoping that the readings would not give reasons for concern. Should one engine fail, as they often did, it was a heart-stopping moment with the certain knowledge that the Wellington would not be able to maintain height over a sustainable period. Its flying range would then be determined by irreversible factors such as the state of the aircraft, height at the time, angle and speed of descent and the skill of the pilot to nurse the aircraft along. They were always apprehensive lest the extra workload would cause the remaining engine to overheat – not the least of the problems was the possibility that it too could fail.

If all this sounds gloomy, then add for good measure the fact that from take-off to return the Wellington would be flying in isolation. In many respects the raid would be one of individual effort and self-planning by the crews. Often the route to the target would be varied by crew preference. They normally took into account the known flak areas but defences could alter their tactics or geographical position, so even the most carefully thought-out plans could go astray and bring the sting of the serpent at an unexpected moment. Strict radio silence did not help but this was essential because of the enemy's rapidly increasing radar detection. To break this silence was to invite trouble, the equivalent to sending a telegram to the *Luftwaffe* notifying them of intent!

But all these shortcomings were shrugged off with an unflagging optimism. Metaphorically speaking we were all in the same boat and in any case anything bad happened to the other fellow – or at least so said the mind's defence mechanism. The more missions that were flown, the easier it became to believe this. It could also induce a state of mind dubbed by the crews as, 'flak happy'. This could loosely be interpreted as over-confidence, a mistake for which many usually paid dearly, joining the list of doomed aircraft. These unfortunate souls just took off and literally vanished, never to be seen again –

just like a conjuror's rabbit. The toll under this category became harder to stomach, as the casualty list mounted.[16]

On the night of 6/7 September, 68 Blenheims, Hampdens, Wellingtons and Whitleys were dispatched to many targets. One Hampden and a Whitley were lost. One of the crews who made the long trip to Pölitz and Stettin was a 44 Squadron Hampden captained by Pilot Officer John 'Jack' de Lacey Wooldridge DFM RAFVR. Born in Yokohama, Japan on 18 July 1919 and educated at St. Paul's School, London, he had joined the RAF in 1938 and would fly two tours (73 operations) on heavy bombers, including 32 ops on Manchesters and Lancasters on 207 Squadron before being given command of a Mosquito squadron. He and his crew on 44 Squadron did not take their bombing operations seriously, despite the risks they ran. Time and again the wireless operator, Sergeant Buck, played practical jokes on the Germans by tuning in to their wave-length. 'Hallo, hallo, this is *Jairmany* calling. This is station XYZ and here is the news in English.' Then all the members of that happy crew would take their turn in giving a fake news item in English. The red-headed rear-gunner, who was a bit of a wag, improved the programme on one occasion by announcing: 'We will now give you a selection from Gilbert and Sullivan.' And all the crew solemnly sang 'Tit-Willow'.

They were flying quite low when a whole concentration of searchlights suddenly blazed up and trapped them. Instantly the wireless operator switched over to the German wave-length. 'Put out those lights. This is Goering up here!' he called in a mock German accent. The disobliging Germans refused to put out the lights, so Wooldridge simply evaded them.

He and the crew had some exciting experiences when they went to bomb the oil refineries at Hannover. It was a perfect night, clear and starry with a full moon and they bombed the refineries good and well, but found to their chagrin that two of the bombs would not come off the racks. Wooldridge set course for home and cruised along, looking for anything he could find. To his joy he saw an enemy aerodrome with the flare path lit and three aircraft flying round with navigation lights on. The first thing the captain of the English bomber did was to run over the flare path and try to drop those two bombs. They were stubborn and refused to budge. Owing to the noise made by the three Heinkel 111s, the English bomber remained unnoticed, so Wooldridge calmly dived down to 1,000 feet, switched on his lights and joined the Heinkels that were circling the aerodrome. Flying round, he waited for a chance to shoot down one of the Heinkels. It came as the first Heinkel turned in to land. Cutting across the aerodrome, Wooldridge attacked the Heinkel head on, giving him a good burst with his own gun:

As I turned, both rear-gunners shot him up. All the flare path lights were switched off at the critical moment just when the Heinkel was about to land and we saw him crash and go up in flames. We sailed around once more, letting fly at the others as they appeared. The other two switched off their lights as soon as the flare path lights went out and the anti-aircraft fire, with nothing to shoot at, was very erratic. Then one of the Heinkels switched his lights on to show he was a friend and promptly got shot at by his own defences.

Wooldridge flew off to the aerodrome at Nordeney, which was only seven minutes away. 'We still had our two bombs to dispose of,' he added. Seeing that the hangar lights were on, he audaciously turned on his navigation lights, at which the Germans signalled with white flashes. Without delay he replied with a haphazard series of white flashes, just to see what would happen. The enemy, completely misled, gave him the green signal to land. They had no idea it was a British bomber they were signalling in. Wooldridge, doing a close approach right over the hangars with bomb doors open, started to shake the bomber up and down and did it so vigorously that he succeeded in shaking off the two recalcitrant bombs. One hit the edge of the hangar and the other hit the tarmac. The explosion shot the bomber up a hundred feet and nearly turned it upside down. 'Then I dived straight to sea level and pushed off home – calling it a day,' he remarked.

Most people would have called it a day *and* a night. The same crew were coming back from the Ruhr one night when the captain saw a light in the sky. Ten minutes later he saw the light still in the same position on their tail. Convinced that it was an enemy fighter, he told his crew to train all the guns they could upon the light. 'I'm going to throttle back to let the Jerry overtake us and we'll get a sitter,' he told them.

Now!' he added and jerked the throttles back and held up the nose, waiting expectantly for the pursuing aircraft to speed past in flames. Unable to understand why nothing happened, he glanced back again. The light was still in the same position.

It was Sirius.

How they laughed when the realized the way in which they had been caught![17]

On the night of 8/9 September, 49 Hampden bombers were dispatched to bomb the Blohm Und Voss shipyard at Hamburg and another 84 aircraft raided the ports of Bremen, Emden and Ostend and bombed barges at Boulogne. Five Blenheims and two Wimpys were lost. One of these was *W-William* on 149 Squadron, which ran into a severe electrical storm near its target at Boulogne. Squadron Leader Lionel Vincent Andrews climbed to get above the storm but he ran into even more turbulent conditions, which made the Wimpy uncontrollable for a few seconds. Ice quickly formed on the surfaces of the aircraft, obscuring the pilot's view and forcing him to lose height. With his compass hopelessly defective Andrews turned for home but within minutes the port engine failed and burst into flames. Eventually, the crew was forced to bail out but they opened their parachutes while they were still miles out to sea off Clacton. Only the second pilot, Pilot Officer Charles Woodbine Parish, survived from the crew of six, after he swam about seven miles in full flying kit whilst battling cramp and sea-sickness. Two and half years later, on 20/21 April 1943, Flight Lieutenant Parish was killed when he was shot down over Denmark by *Unteroffizier* Berg of 7./NJG3 (who claimed the 7 Squadron Stirling as a 'Boeing') on the operation to Stettin. It was the RAF pilot's 54th operation of the war.

Pilot Officer David Penman, pilot of a 44 Squadron Hampden at Waddington four miles south of Lincoln had peacetime experience to call upon too and the Station, which had been established before the First World War, offered better than average accommodation and facilities. 'Waddo' had more permanent buildings and fewer curved Nissen huts and less mud and slush than the airfields built quickly after 1939. The light on the central tower of Lincoln Cathedral just to the north was a welcome sight for crews returning. When the Cathedral light was sharp the weather on the flat lands of Lincolnshire was usually clear.[18] Penman recalls:

I was fortunate to have gained experience of the Hampden before the war started, including flights of up to six hours and as far as Bordeaux as well as a good deal of low and high level bombing with practice bombs. However, weather forecasts were far from accurate and on many occasions very badly out. On one occasion after a weather briefing giving good weather over the Channel we flew into severe storms and it was all I could do to keep the aircraft from turning upside down. When I questioned the forecaster back at Waddington he said that the Station Commander had rubbed out certain lines on the weather chart before the briefing as he thought it would be best if the aircrew were not worried about bad weather! Nevertheless there were times when the forecasts were well out and one of them was on my first trip to Berlin, on 24/25 September carrying four 500lb bombs. We got there more quickly than expected and the bombs were dropped on B56, an area of Berlin. Apart from heavy gunfire over Berlin and searchlights we had little opposition. However on heading home we found we were not making good progress and then realized that a very strong tail wind had helped us reach Berlin and now as a head wind was cutting our ground speed for home. We had no warning of strong winds against us on return from Berlin that night. I did my best to control the fuel consumption and when well out over the North Sea we threw out everything we could, including the machine guns and ammunition. Reducing height to get below the strongest winds saved us from landing in the sea.

We were unable to make radio contact but our selected course heading was good and with the dawn breaking we crossed the English coast at Cromer with engines spluttering from lack of fuel. We crept over the coast only to find all possible landing areas spiked with long poles against the threat of invasion. After nine hours 20 minutes in the air I had no option but to do my best with a small, unspiked area. We touched down alright but with brakes locking the wheels skidded into a mound at the end of the area and bounced over it breaking one leg of the undercarriage before coming to rest a bit lopsided but otherwise intact. The aircraft was not badly damaged and was soon flying again.[19]

On 1/2 October almost 100 Blenheims, Hampdens, Wellingtons and Whitleys attacked numerous targets in Germany and the Channel ports while mines were also dropped off the enemy coasts. A Hampden, one Whitley and *G-George,* a Wellington on 9 Squadron at Honington, Suffolk, were lost. A second Hampden crash landed at Brackley in Northampton-shire on return from the *Gardening* operations. The Wimpy was piloted by 25-year-old Flight Lieutenant Charles Douglas Fox of Berryville, Virginia who became one of the first American bomber pilots to die in the European War while the US was still neutral. Fox, who arrived on the squadron on 25 July and who flew his first operation as skipper a month later, had made only half a dozen trips. His wireless operator made contact with Cullercoates at 02.46 when it was reported that they were going down into the sea off Lowestoft owing to a shortage of petrol. No further communication was received. A search by nine Wellingtons of the quadron from 06.30 in the morning to 17.30 in the evening yielded nothing and no bodies were ever found. Fox and the names of his crew were added to those on the stone memorial to the Missing at Runnymede.[20]

On 5 October Air Marshal Sir Richard Peirse KCB DSO AFC, who as Vice-Chief of Air Staff had already been closely concerned with the British bombing policy and was a part of the 'enormous array of talent' on the Air Staff under Air Chief Marshal Sir Cyril Newall in 1939, was appointed C-in-C Bomber Command vice Air Chief Marshal Sir Charles Portal, who succeeded Newell now that he had reached retirement age. With the appointment of Portal as the new Chief of Air Staff a new 'winter' directive was issued on 30 October in which oil targets remained 'top priority' but they were to be attacked only in bright moonlight when there was some chance of hitting them. In the words of the directive 'regular concentrated attacks should be made on objectives on large towns and centres of industry with the primary aim of causing very heavy material destruction which would demonstrate to the enemy the power and severity of air bombardment'. The reality however was that the Order of Battle numbered only 532 aircraft – 217 Blenheims in 2 Group, 100 Wellingtons, 71 Hampdens, 59 Whitleys and 85 obsolete Battles, so only about 230 aircraft were suitable for night operations in winter. While mainly Hampdens, Wellingtons and Whitleys carried out night raids on targets in Germany and the occupied countries throughout the rest of October and into November numbers rarely totalled more than a few score unless other types – notably Blenheims – helped to swell the force.

On the night of 8/9 October, 108 Blenheims, Hampdens, Wellingtons and Whitleys were sent to bomb many targets and all except two aircraft returned safely. A Whitley crashed at Snape in Yorkshire with the loss of all five crew and a Blenheim IV crashed on return to base at Bodney. Sorties followed the same pattern the following night when 70 aircraft including Fairey Battles, Hampdens and Wellingtons were dispatched. One Wellington was lost without trace on a sortie to Herringen. The largest raid was by 20 Hampdens on the Krupps armament works in Essen but only three aircraft reached the target because of icing conditions. On 10/11 October, 157 aircraft of all types were dispatched to 13 targets in Germany. There were no losses. Attacks on oil and shipbuilding targets in Germany and on French Channel ports and minelaying operations were carried out by 86 aircraft of all types on 11/12 October without loss. The night following over 60 Hampdens and Wellingtons attacked five targets in Germany and carried out minelaying in enemy waters and 24 Blenheims and six Battles bombed the Channel ports in the last major raid on these targets in the invasion-threat period. Again there were no losses. On the night of 13/14 October, 125 were dispatched to several targets. Hampdens and Wellingtons visited the Ruhr, Wilhelmshaven and Kiel while Battles and Blenheims the Channel ports. The weather was bad and only 41 aircraft reported bombing primary targets. A Wellington was lost without trace on the raid on Wilhelmshaven and two Battles were lost in crashes on return.

On 14/15 October, 78 Hampdens, Wellingtons and Whitleys were dispatched to Berlin, Stettin, Böhlen, Magdeburg and Le Havre. Two Hampdens were lost on the operation against Berlin and a Wellington was lost on the operation to Magdeburg. A Whitley on 10 Squadron, which set out from Leeming for Le Havre, crashed after hitting a barrage-balloon cable at Weybridge in Surrey. All the crew were killed. Another two Whitleys on 10 Squadron, which were on sorties to Stettin, were lost when one was abandoned over Hexham in Northumberland and the other crashed near Thirsk, Yorkshire, killing two of the crew. A Whitley

19-year old AC1 Charles Ronald Driver on 9 Squadron at Honington who flew as a gunner on Sergeant Jack Ramshaw's Wimpy; one of nine Wellingtons in a force of twenty-four on 18 December 1939. The raid ended in tragic consequences for Ramshaw's crew. (*RAF*)

The Whitley was perhaps best known for its night leaflet-dropping flights over Germany and the occupied territories, which began on the first night of the war. A total of 123 'Nickelling' sorties were flown before Christmas 1939 at a cost of only four aircraft. In the New Year, operations were extended to include such distant targets as Prague and Vienna, which were reached from forward airfields in France. The long leaflet flights over Germany and further afield exposed crews to bitter cold, with frostbite a constant hazard.

The New Zealand High Commissioner Mr W. J. Jordan meets a Wellington crew of the New Zealand Flight at Feltwell on 20 March 1940. On 27/28 March they flew their first operational sortie when three Wellingtons were dispatched on leaflet raids over Germany. (*IWM*)

Bomber Command was asked to help Coastal Command in the war against the German forces that invaded Norway. On 12 April 1940 Wellington L4387/LG-L, borrowed from 215 Squadron and with extra fuel tanks in the bomb bay, was used by a crew from the recently formed 75 (New Zealand) Squadron to carry out a reconnaissance north of Narvik. With a nav officer joining the crew, Flight Lieutenant Breckon took off from Wick at 08.00 hours and reached the vicinity of the Lofoten Islands at 13.05 hours. A total overcast forced the reconnaissance to be made at between 500 and 800 feet. Several photographs were taken and though a Ju 88 appeared it did not intercept and the Wimp returned safely to Wick 14 hours and 30 minutes after leaving – a record for an operational sortie that was not surpassed for some time. A total of 933 Imperial gallons of fuel were consumed, averaging 2.14 mpg. The photograph shows Sergeant Hughes, who navigated the trip, using his sextant. The fold-down seat is for the observer's use

When Group Pool Squadrons in 6 Training Group were mostly disbanded from 8 April 1940, having been used to form Operational Training Units, 185 Squadron at Cottesmore changed its name to 14 OTU, finishing Hampden replacement crews for 5 Group. This view from the top gunner's position shows Hampdens of this OTU while on formation practice. RAF Bomber Command eventually had 24 OTUs. (IWM)

Blenheim IVs on 40 Squadron. Experience during the French campaign in the summer of 1940 revealed that the Blenheim could withstand a surprising amount of punishment. Nevertheless, losses in 2 Group were heavy. (*IWM*)

Formation of Handley Page Hampdens of 106 Squadron aircraft of 5 Group on 19 April 1940 wh the unit was non-operational in a training capacity at Finningley. Hampdens began dropping magnetic sea mines in enemy waters in April 1940. The Hampden was the only aircraft which co carry these weapons in its bomb bay at this time and remained this aircraft's task for some mont in addition to bombing operations. The 'Panhandle' or 'flying Suitcase' as it was known was not imbued with an altogether impressive performance and it appeared to have an inherent problem related to loss of control, identified as 'stabilised yaw'. Crew positions were cramped but there v a good under-fuselage defensive gun position. P1320/ZN-B was flown by Pilot Officer Page, L4182/ZN-K by Pilot Officer Hattersley and L4180/ZN-F by an unknown pilot. The squadron became operational in September 1940. L4180 went down in the sea near Spurn Head while returning from a mine laying sortie off Copenhagen on 29/30 October. P1320 spiralled into the ground at Tickencote, north-west of Stamford, Lincolnshire on 25 November during a training fl Sergeant Bagnall and the rear gunner were injured. The other two crew members were killed. (*IV*

Sergeant Rupert Cooling, who was known as 'Tiny' because he was 6 foot [inc]hes tall, a 20-year old second pilot on Wellingtons on 9 Squadron. (*Cooling*)

[fi]lling the four .303 calibre [Bro]wning machine guns in the rear [turre]t of a 58 Squadron Whitley at [Lint]on-on-Ouse. The four guns could [fire e]ighty-plus rounds a second but [their e]ffective range was around [600 y]ards and of little use against [armo]ur. (*IWM*)

Thumbs up for a Whitley rear gunner. (*IWM*)

A Fordson tractor pulls a train of practice bombs and armourers out to a waiting aircraft at 10 OTU. A Whitley can be seen in the background. At this time 10 OTU had an establishment of fifty-four Whitleys and eighteen Avro Ansons. At the end of July 1940 crews at the end of their training were despatched on short operational flights – usually leaflet raids over occupied France – to gain further experience before being sent to a front-line unit. Later OTU sorties would also include bombing and mine-laying trips to the enemy coast. (*IWM*)

Engine fitters overhaul one of the Bristol Pegasus XVIII radial engines of a 37 Squadron Wellington at Feltwell in July 1940. (*IWM*)

Maintenance work is carried out on a Whitley III at 10 OTU at Abingdon, Berkshire in July 1940. 10 OTU was formed in April 1940 by merging two training squadrons (97 and 166) in 6 Group. The front-line squadrons of 4 Group were by now flying the definitive Merlin-engined Whitley V, but earlier versions were still used for training, including these Mk.IIIs powered by Armstrong Siddeley Tiger radials. (*IWM*)

On the night of 12/13 August 1940 Flight Lieutenant Roderick Learoyd on 49 Squadron was the pilot of Hampden P4403/EA-M, one of eleven dispatched from Scampton to make a low-level attack on the aqueducts carrying the Dortmund-Ems Canal over the Rover Ems near Münster. Learoyd received the Victoria Cross. (*IWM*)

Verran, a New Zealander and
Whitley on 102 Squadron at
field in Yorkshire.
Verran via Ian Frimston)

A trainee wireless operator,
practising on a radio set in a
special cubicle known as the
'Harwell Box' to simulate its
sition in a bomber, at 10 OTU at
bingdon in August 1940. Above
he direction-finding (D/F) loop
hich was mounted on top of the
ircraft's fuselage. With the door
hut, the airman was given some
idea of operating in a darkened
aircraft interior. At this stage of
he war, wireless operators were
also trained as air gunners and
their total course lasted longer
than that of any other crew
member. (*IWM*)

The next award of Britain's highest decoration for bravery also went to a Hampden crew member and also to a Scampton-based airman. Sergeant John Hannah was the wireless operator/air gunner on Hampden P1355/OL-W on 83 Squadron, which took a direct hit from a small shell while attacking barge concentrations at Antwerp on 15/16 September 1940. A fire started in the rear of crew compartment and burned fiercely. The under-gunner and the navigator thought the aircraft doomed and bailed out. Sergeant Hannah stayed to fight the fire and, having exhausted the extinguishers, beat out the remaining flames. Hannah was badly burned about the hands and face and the heat was so intense that ammunition exploded and metal was melted and burnt through. Hannah's actions undoubtedly saved the aircraft and Pilot Officer C. A. Connor was able to fly it safely back to England. At the age of eighteen Sergeant Hannah was the youngest RAF recipient of the VC.

Some 1,386 Wellingtons were lost in Bomber Command service. These are Wellington ICs on 149 Squadron at Mildenhall; one of six operational Wellington squadrons in 3 Group. The aircraft nearest the camera is P9273 OJ-N which FTR from the operation on Ostend on 8/9 September 1940. P/O R. G. Furness and crew were lost without trace. 149 Squadron was in action from the first day of the war, taking part in searches for enemy warships off Germany's North Sea coast. These ineffectual sweeps continued without loss until the fateful 18 December, when two of its aircraft were among twelve Wellingtons shot down by enemy fighters off Wilhelmshaven.

The crew of a Wimpy at this time normally consisted of two pilots, observer (pictured) (who was also responsible for aiming the bombs), wireless operator/air gunner and rear gunner. Another gunner might also be carried to man the front turret.

Whitley V Z6462 is brought out from Armstrong Whitworth's final assembly hall at Baginton aerodrome, Coventry on 20 December 1940. Delivered to 58 Squadron at Linton-on-Ouse and coded GE-D this Whitley was shot down over the Netherlands during a raid on Wilhelmshaven on 16/17 January 1941 and crashed at Anna Paulowna. Sergeant A. E. Barlow the pilot and his crew survived and they were taken into captivity. (*IWM*)

Halifax I crews on 35 Squadron having a cuppa from the YMCA tea wagon. (*IWM*)

A Stirling crew are interrogated on their return from a raid on Berlin in April 1941. (*IWM*)

bomber crew studying a map before a raid in 1941. (*IWM*)

Aircrew on 149 Squadron at Mildenhall on 1 May 1941. On the night of 31 March/1 April during a raid on Emden, a specially modified Wellington flown by Pilot Officer John Henry Franks (centre, with moustache) dropped one of the first two 4,000lb high-capacity (HC) blast-bombs of the war. The other was dropped by a 9 Squadron aircraft on the same target. The 'Cookie' had a thin case and powerful explosive filling, and was intended to cause maximum damage to buildings. It was to become one of the most widely used and destructive devices in Bomber Command's armoury. Squadron Leader John Henry Franks DFC was piloting a Wellington of 57 Squadron when he was KIA on 20/21 July 1942.

Armourers on 75 Squadron ZAF with two 500lb bombs : Feltwell in May 1941 give the 'thumbs up' in front of the 'Wellington Devil'. The Wellington was the mainstay of Bomber Command, equipping a total of eighteen squadrons in 1 and 3 Groups. Wellingtons also equipped two new squadrons – 104 and 405 'Vancouver' RCAF, the latter being the first Canadian squadron in Bomber Command – which were formed in April in 4 Group. (IWM)

On the night of 7/8 July 1941 Wellington L7818 on 75 Squadron was flying over the Zuider Zee after attacking Münster when it was attacked from below by a Bf 110. Cannon shell strikes on the starboard wing caused a fire and feed from a fractured fuel line threatened to spread to the whole wing. After the crew had made strenuous efforts to douse the flames with extinguishers through a hole in the fuselage, Squadron Leader Reuben P. Widdowson alerted his crew to be prepared to abandon the aircraft. Sergeant James Ward the second pilot volunteered to climb out through the astro-hatch to try and put out the flames. With a rope tied round his waist he managed to make holes in the fabric and moved down the fuselage side and out across the wing where he managed to smother the fire in the wing fabric. Exhausted, he then returned to the inside of the aircraft. Ward received the VC for his action but he was to die on the night of 15/16 September when the Wellington in which he was flying was shot down over Hamburg. L7818 was gained, was sent to 15 OTU after repair. On 8 April 1942 it collided with a Spitfire in a rainstorm and crashed at Cold Ashton, Gloucestershire. (IWM)

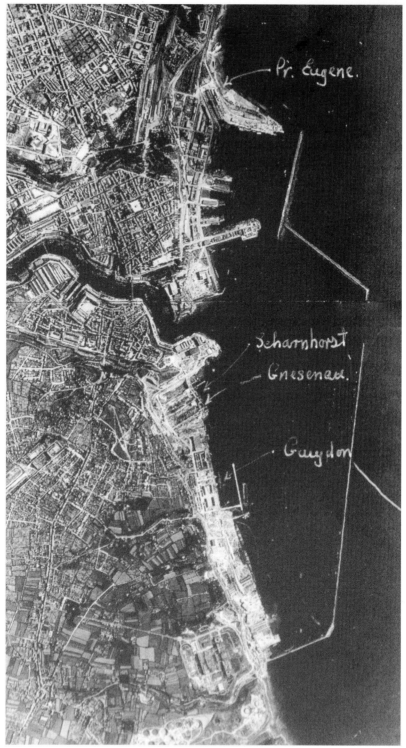

On 24 July 1941 a major daylight operation was mounted against the *Gneisenau* and *Prinz Eugen* at Brest and the *Scharnhorst* at La Pallice on the French Atlantic coast. A force of seventy-nine Wellingtons and eighteen Hampdens, with three Boeing Fortress Is of 2 Group went to Brest. Six hits were claimed, but the Wellingtons suffered from stronger than expected fighter opposition and lost ten of their number. The Hampdens, escorted by long-range Spitfires, fared better and all but two made it back. *(IWM)*

on 58 Squadron crash landed at Harpham in Yorkshire and a 77 Squadron Whitley crashed on return to its base at Topcliffe.

The next night 134 aircraft attempted to bomb many targets in Germany. A Hampden on 83 Squadron at Scampton, which force landed at Southwold in Suffolk, was the only loss. Included in the total number of bombers dispatched were nine Fairey Battles who attacked Calais and Boulogne. This was the last occasion that this aircraft operated with Bomber Command.

On 16/17 October, 73 Hampdens and Wellingtons attacked Bremen, Kiel, Merseburg and Bordeaux and six Hampdens laid mines in enemy waters. The Merseburg force also dropped incendiary devices into the Harz forests. One Hampden was shot down at Ambares-et-Lagrave during a *Gardening* sortie with the loss of all the crew and a second crashed at Abingdon airfield. Another Hampden went down in the sea north of Terschelling on the operation on Merseburg. A Wellington on 311 Squadron at East Wretham was lost on Bremen and three more of the Czechoslovak Squadron's Wimpys were lost in crashes in England when fog covered the bases on return. Another two Wellingtons and five other Hampdens also crashed in England.

The next major operation was on 20/21st October when 139 bombers went to many targets in the occupied countries, Italy and Germany. Berlin was the largest raid with a visit by 30 Hampdens. Turin, Milan, Bergamo, Savona and Aosta in Italy were all bombed and at Aosta a direct hit was scored on the steel works. A Hampden was shot down with the loss of all the crew on the raid on Berlin. Two other Hampdens force landed, at Colchester in Essex and near Veryan, Cornwall. A Whitley returning from Milan ditched in the River Mersey and all the crew were rescued. Two Whitleys returning from the raid on the Skoda Works at Pilzen in Czechoslovakia also ditched, one coming down in the River Humber, the other off Blakeney in Norfolk. Both crews were rescued. A third Whitley, *O-Orange* on 58 Squadron at Linton-on-Ouse, which crashed on fire, on the slopes of the Cleveland Hills near Ingleby Greenow in Yorkshire, was claimed shot down by *Hauptmann* Karl Hülshoff commanding I./NJG2, the specialist German intruder unit. Pilot Officer Ernest Henry Brown and two his crew were killed. Two were injured, one of whom died two days later. Hülshoff claimed the Whitley as a 'Hereford'. He destroyed four more aircraft over England during 1940–41, adding another seven victories before the end of the war.[21]

Hamburg, the second largest city of the *Reich*, with a population of just over a million and a half, was one of many targets bombed on 24/25 October, when 113 aircraft tried to reach many targets in the Reich. Hamburg contained within it 3,000 industrial establishments and 5,000 commercial, most of them engaged in the transport and shipping industries. All the major and most of the minor shipbuilding yards were employed on building submarines and were responsible for about

45 per cent of the total production of U-boats. Among them were the renowned Blohm and Voss shipyards. Targets of almost equal importance were the Europaische Tanklager and Transport AG, the Rhenania Ossag distillation plant, the Deutsche Petroleum AG refineries, Theodor Zeise at Altona, the second largest German manufacturer of ships' screws, and at Wilhelmsburg the Ernst Schliemann's works and the largest wool combing plant of the Hamburger Wollkammerai AG. Other important industries included those concerned with food processing and with the manufacture of machinery, electrical and precision instruments, chemicals and aircraft components. One Wellington was lost on the raid on Hamburg. At Linton-on-Ouse nine Whitley Vs on 102 Squadron were detailed to bomb the Air Ministry Building in the Leipzigstrasse in Berlin. Pilot Officer A G Davies took off at 22.02 hours and just six minutes later he was shot down in flames near Tholthorpe by 21-year-old Feldwebel Hans Hahn of III./NJG2 who claimed it as a 'Wellington' for his first victory. Davies was injured and the second pilot and the observer died in the aircraft. Sergeant Angus Stewart Wilson and Pilot Officer Terence Edward Lee died of their injuries on 2 November.

On 28 October *Leutnant* Heinz Völker flying a Ju 88C-4 attacked two Hampdens on 49 Squadron as they were returning from Hamburg to Lindholme. The first Hampden was damaged but was able to land safely. Völker then attacked a second, which went down in the North Sea half a mile off Skegness with the loss of all Pilot Officer John Raymond Bufton's crew.[22] Völker scored a total of 12 victories and was awarded the *Ritterkreuz*. He and his two crew were killed on 22 July 1941, when over Ashwell, Hertfordshire, their Ju 88C-4 collided with a Wellington of 11 OTU. All eight men on the Wimpy were killed.

Flight Officer Joan Morgan, who supervised and ensured the security of the Cipher officers and staff at 1 Group Headquarters at Hucknall, now travelled miles each month visiting the Cipher Officers at their respective stations, trying to deal with any problems and report to Headquarters:

> The stations were all operational, mostly flying Wellingtons and one almost became used to hearing that planes did not return from their sorties, sometimes friends that I had met the day before. It became a very lonely life at times, sitting in a car, being driven over the Yorkshire and Lincolnshire countryside, not allowed to give any-body a lift unless authorised and at one time I even had an airman 'riding shot-gun' next to the Driver, when there were scares of German parachutists being dropped. One day, while I was being driven by a new driver, it was wet and windy, when suddenly the car went into a violent skid across the road then back again to end upside down in a dyke. I must have been concussed because the next

thing I vaguely remember was a man helping to get us out. After treatment I was sent to a RAF Hospital and Convalescent Home in Torquay, formerly a large hotel with lovely grounds. After about ten days I was pronounced 'walking wounded' and advised to take exercise. I was referred to the resident PT coach, Dan Maskell of Wimbledon fame, and I played against him or others on the very good tennis courts there. As I walked too through the Rest Rooms and gardens, I could not fail to see countless young pilots and others, their faces, hands and legs mutilated by horrific burns and dreadful injuries still recovering as best they could. It made me realise the great price they was paying.

Imagine my shock, when one morning walking down the stairs to breakfast, I noticed some bandaged men being brought into the foyer. I suddenly recognised George Morgan, a bomber pilot and a friend of mine. Apparently they were on their way back from a sortie when they were hit by flak and crash-landed in England. Thankfully none was seriously. After a few days George was also a 'walking wounded'. It was as though Fate had brought us together briefly. We had time to talk as we walked through the gardens and the town. The war seemed to be far away. All too soon I had to return to duty. As I left, he asked me to marry him. Despite many misgivings, sometime later we got married. When George finished his two tours of bombing operations, he was posted as flying instructor at a Station in South Wales. Nine weeks before the end of the war in Europe and with a young baby, I received the telegram – George had been killed in a plane crash in the Azores. After so many bombing operations in the earlier days of the war, it was so unexpected and doubly heartbreaking.

When on the night of 16/17 November, 127 bombers were dispatched, all of them were given Hamburg as their target. Weather conditions were unfavourable and only 60 crews reported bombing the target area. Twenty-five other aircraft bombed alternative targets. Two Wellingtons and a Blenheim went missing in action and five more aircraft crashed in England on the return.

German intruders over England continued to pose a hazard to return- ing aircrew. During the early evening of 27 November 1940, 17 Dorniers made concentrated attacks on four East Anglian bomber aerodromes and 33 bombs fell on RAF Mildenhall. A hangar was damaged and a barrack block received a direct hit. Casualties amounted to two killed, two seriously wounded and three slightly injured. The Newmarket satellite was also attacked that day.[23] Hitler personally put a stop to these highly efficient intruder operations. He told Kammhuber 'if the long-range night-fighting really had results, the British would have copied it a long time ago, as they imitate anything good that I do.' 'And,' he added, 'the

German citizen, whose house has been destroyed by a British bomber, would prefer it if the British aircraft were shot down by a German night fighter to crash next to his burning house.'[24] This decision allowed Bomber Command (and later the 8th Air Force) to build a strategic bombing offensive against Germany virtually undisturbed and it undoubtedly was a decisive factor in the outcome of the war.

On 4/5 December, Turin, a distance of 1,350 miles there and back and Düsseldorf on the River Rhine, the capital of North Rhine-Westphalia, were targeted, but only 30 bombers of 83 dispatched reached their objectives. One Wellington failed to return. Returning from Düsseldorf, Flying Officer F H Vivian put down at Lille-Nord and he and his crew were taken into captivity. Two more raids on Düsseldorf followed and then it was the turn of German ports and other cities.

On 16/17 December in Operation *Abigail Rachel*, 134 aircraft set out to raid the centre of Mannheim in retaliation for the German bombing of English cities, notably Coventry on 14/15 November and Southampton. The intention of *Abigail* was to cause the maximum possible destruction in a selected German town. The towns selected were Bremen (*Abigail Jezebel*), Düsseldorf (*Abigail Delilah*) and Mannheim. The original selection was *Delilah* and crews booked a date at 10.15 on the morning of the 16th, only to have it changed three hours later after adverse weather reports brought a late change of plan. Mannheim was selected instead. Good weather was reasonably certain for the first part of the night but not for the early hours of the following morning. The aiming point was officially 1,500 yards south of the Motorenwerke-Mannheim, a works engaged in the production of diesel engines for U-boats, but the moon was bright with good weather conditions and good visibility and all the later sorties had no difficulty in recognizing the town from the flak and the fires. Fourteen Wellingtons of 3 Group carrying their maximum load of 4lb incendiary bombs opened the attack, their fires providing a beacon for the following waves. Forty-seven out of 61 Wellingtons, 33 out of 35 Whitleys, 20 out of 29 Hampdens and three out of nine Blenheims succeeded in finding and bombing Mannheim. Eighty-nine tons of HE and nearly 14,000 incendiaries, including a number of special 250-pounders, were dropped in the six hours of attack. Bombs were clearly seen to fall all over the target area and countless fires and many large explosions were referred to in all reports. In the southern part of the target area dense black smoke was observed as though from an oil fire. Aircraft arriving late in the night reported than many blocks of buildings in the western and south-eastern areas of the target were ablaze and at Neckerstadt there was a continuous series of explosions thought to be from a munitions dump. Losses in aircraft and crews were slight. A Wellington crashed on take-off killing three members of the crew. A Hampden and a Blenheim were lost without trace while a second Hampden crashed in the English Channel with the loss of the crew. Four more aircraft crashed in England on return, at Rye and Hastings in Sussex and at Plympton and Norwich, and a Wellington overshot the runway at Mildenhall. Pilot Officer Brant on 10 Squadron brought his Whitley back from south-west Germany to Bircham Newton on one engine, jettisoning guns, ammunition and all loose objects to maintain a height of 2,000 feet over the sea.

Though results reported by all successful crews were 'satisfactory', on 21 December a PR Spitfire photographed Mannheim in daylight and the photographs clearly showed 'a wide dispersal' of the attack. From the mosaic, it was immediately apparent to Sir Richard Peirse, the C-in-C, that the operation had 'failed in its primary object'. Most of the damage occurred in the residential area of Mannheim but several bombs fell across the river at Ludwigshafen. Many aircraft were reported to have bombed from a great height without aiming, owing to the strength of the anti-aircraft defences. Sixteen large and 75 medium and small fires were caused, fire-fighting being made difficult by bomb damage to the main water system and by the freezing of water brought from the Rhine. A sugar and a refrigerator factory were put out of action, the Mannheim-Rheinau power station was damaged and output of armoured fighting vehicles and tank components from the Lanz works was cut by a quarter. Four other industrial plants were also hit. Twenty-three Germans were killed and 80 injured.

On the 18/19th nine Whitleys set out for Mannheim and 17 Wellingtons were detailed to bomb the Pirelli factory at Milan. On 99 Squadron at Newmarket one Wimpy crashed on take-off and another was ditched off Thorney Island. Five Wellingtons that went to Milan claimed to have caused a 'terrific blaze' there. In all, three raids were made on Italy in December, the most important being the attack on the Porto Marghera oil refinery and storage depot in Venice. This was one of the longest flights made by the RAF carrying bombs, not leaflets. It took about nine and a half hours. The aircraft took off from England soon after six in the evening and crossed the North Sea in darkness, for the moon had not risen. Presently the ground beneath was seen to be covered with snow. The temperature fell until at 15,000 feet, minus 25° was registered. About half-past nine the aircraft began to climb and reached 15,000 feet for their passage over the Alps. By then the night was clear, though the moon was still not up. Little was seen of the mountain barrier and when the Wellingtons began to descend on the other side it became difficult to find landmarks, for the ground was no longer snow-covered. One navigator eventually picked up Venice, whose towers and palaces seemed to float upon the lagoon like one of its own once famous fleet of galleys. His aircraft went lower, turning in towards the target, which was on the mainland, just west of a bridge near the docks. It was clearly visible; but, to make quite sure, flares were dropped. The Wellington made a run-up along the bridge and discharged its load of incendiaries and high explosives, which hit the target fair and square. It remained over the objective for 20 minutes:

> Then we turned for home and as we approached the foothills of the Alps on the way back, the navigator, who was in the astro hatch, said it looked as if the moon were sitting on the top of a peak... the Alps seemed a little more friendly now. That may have been due to the moon, but probably the fact that we were on the homeward journey had something to do with it too. Frankly, we were none of us sorry to see the last of the mountains.

Notes

1. *The Dam Busters* by Paul Brickhill (Evans Bros London 1951).
2. G/C (later Air Commodore) Henry Illiffe Cozens AFC was the highest ranking pupil to pass from the unit. He took delivery of the first Spitfire when CO of 19 Squadron at Duxford and he converted Guy Gibson on the Mosquito.
3. The prototype Manchester twin-engined bomber flew on 25 July 1939 and was initially fitted with twin fins, later increased to three. The Manchester I entered service on 207 Squadron at Waddington in November 1940 and the first operational flight took place on the night of 24/25 February 1941 when six Manchesters were part of a force of 57 aircraft that attacked Brest. One Manchester crashed in England.
4. Adapted from *So Few: The Immortal Record of the Royal Air Force* by David Masters (1941).
5. See *Bomber Command* by Max Hastings (Pan 1979).
6. Adapted from *So Few: The Immortal Record of the Royal Air Force* by David Masters (1941).
7. *RAF Marham* by Ken Delve. (PSL 1995).
8. Adapted from *So Few: The Immortal Record of the Royal Air Force* by David Masters (1941).
9. *Nachtjagd: The Night Fighter versus Bomber War over the Third Reich 1939–45* by Theo Boiten (Crowood 1997).
10. Dunn and Sergeants G H Riley, Derek Albert Gibbons, Bernard Leonard Savill DFM and Dudley Brooking Allen.
11. Adapted from *So Few: The Immortal Record of the Royal Air Force* by David Masters (1941).
12. The Hampden was named *Betty* by its former pilot, S/L J Collier, who had flown it as one of the diversion aircraft on 12 August 1940, when F/L R A B Learoyd on 49 Squadron had earned the award of the VC.
13. Adapted from *We Bombed the Barges* by Douglas A E Hayhurst DFM in *70 True Stories of the Second World War* (Odhams Press).

14. Sgt John Hannah, 83 Squadron, Hampden P1355. Awarded for action 15/16 September 1940, *London Gazette,* 1 October 1940. Hannah, who was the youngest member of the RAF to receive the VC, was invalided out of the service in 1942. He died of TB on 9 June 1947, leaving a widow, Janet, and three daughters. On 1 October 1940 Hayhurst was awarded the DFM. Connor, who received the DFC the same day was KIA on 3/4 November 1940 returning in a Hampden from a raid on Norway. See *For Valour: The Air VCs* by Chaz Bowyer (Grub Street 1992).

15. Adapted from *So Few: The Immortal Record of the Royal Air Force* by David Masters (1941).

16. As he recalls Robinson and the crew of W/O J W B Snowden in Wellington X9873/P joined the toll on 31 October/1 November 1941 when they FTR from a raid on Bremen (X9873 was the only a/c lost while 4 Whitleys FTR from the raid on Hamburg). 'A Bf 110 [*piloted by Oberfeldwebel Paul Gildner of 4./NJG1*] operating from Leeuwarden made a copybook attack from astern and below on our Wellington at 19.30 hours. We never saw him until it was too late. We were never in with the chance of a shot. He just loomed up out of the murk with a startling suddenness and opened up with a prolonged and devastating burst of cannon fire. It was all over in a matter of seconds. No time to consider. One minute we were happily on course and the next we were plunging down and about to crash, ironically, on Schiermonnikoog itself. [*It was Gildner's 20th victory and he added a 21st, a Whitley, later that same night*]. Fate decreed that I should survive this, plus some enlightening even if somewhat dreary years in German prison camps before liberation by Russian troops in May 1945.'

17. Adapted from *So Few: The Immortal Record of the Royal Air Force* by David Masters (1941).

18. *Chased By The Sun; The Australians in Bomber Command in WWII* by Hank Nelson (ABC Books 2002).

19. One Blenheim and one Whitley were lost this night.

20. See *Bombers First And Last* by Gordon Thorburn (Robson Books, 2006).

21. Boiten. Hülshoff was awarded the *Deutscheskreuz in Gold.* He was taken prisoner on 10 March 1941. After the war he entered the *BundesLuftwaffe* and from 1958 to 1964 was *Oberst* American Tactical Air Force at Ramstein AFB.

22. *Intruders over Britain: The Luftwaffe Night Fighter Offensive 1940 to 1945* by Simon W Parry (ARP 2003).

23. Apart from organising an effective short-range defensive *Nachtjagd,* Kammhuber also appreciated the value and effectiveness of long-range night intruding (*Fernachtjagd*) over Britain but the intruder force was never raised beyond one single *Gruppe* (I./NJG2) which

operated the Ju 88C-6 and Do 17 from Gilze-Rijen in the Netherlands. It never exceeded 21 aircraft but despite this and severe operational losses (21 aircraft alone during 1940) *Fernachtjagd* made a promising start. I./NJG2's first intruder victories were two Wellingtons destroyed by *Feldwebel* Otto Wiese 100 kilometres west of Texel and *Feldwebel* Georg Schramm over the North Sea on the night of 22/23 July, and by December claims for another 16 bombers followed. By October 1941 the handful of crews had claimed more aircraft destroyed than all other *Nachtjagd* units combined.

24. At least 19 Bomber Command aircraft were destroyed from July to December 1940 in the 'Kammhuber Line', as the continuous belt of searchlights and radar positions between Schleswig–Holstein and northern France was christened by the British bomber crews. About 30 bombers were brought down by flak during the same period.

CHAPTER 3

The Moon Period

The plant lies on the northern bank of the Emscher Kanal, which at this point runs parallel and very close to the Rhein–Herne Kanal. The main town of Gelsenkirchen is on the south bank but to the west of the target is an industrial residential area. Get right up to your target and do your stuff. Note carefully and report the position of any outstanding landmarks for future reference, also the position of flak and searchlights. There is a strong concentration of lights reported just north of the town. Get us some good pictures. The leaflets are to be dropped in the target area. The approach to the target is suggested but not laid down in a hard and fast manner. Captains of bombing aircraft are allowed considerable latitude in the choice of routes to the target, once the area in which it is located has been entered. This is natural, for it is impossible to foresee the exact circumstances in which they will be called upon to make the attack....

NIGHT RAID, Briefing the crew. Bomber Command:
The Air Ministry Account of Bomber Command's Offensive
Against the Axis September 1939–July, 1941.

'It is better to keep your mouth shut and let people think you're a fool than to open it and remove all doubt' said the notice that could be found on walls in many rooms at all of the bomber stations. The 135 Wellington, Blenheim, Hampden and Whitley crews, who had a preliminary warning that they would be wanted that night, 9/10 January, were assembled in the Briefing Rooms some hours before the start of the raid. They sat facing a dais behind which was a blackboard. Once seated, the crews were told what they had to do that night – it was the January moon period. The intelligence officers told them that their target was the Gelsenberg–Benzin AG synthetic-oil plant at Gelsenkirchen, an industrial city in the Ruhr, 15 miles west of Dortmund. The intelligence officers went on:

The plant consists of two atmospheric distillation units producing petrol from coal. The development and extension of these works was undertaken in 1938. Their output capacity is 325,000 metric tons per annum. The most vital section of this plant and also the most vulnerable is the hydrogenation plant itself. It lies in the top half of the target running from the narrow-neck in a north-westerly direction and covers most of that part of the target. This section of the plant consists of a Compressor house, Hydrogenation stalls, Water-gas units, CO^2 conversion plant and Sulphur purification. A direct hit with a large bomb on the compressor house, where the low pressure hydrogen lines lead to the compressors, will cause a real explosion, which is always likely to lead to severe damage in a building containing a large amount of moving machinery. Damage to the compressors will put the whole plant out of action and since they are most difficult to replace, the compressor house would be a very profitable aiming point. A hit here may cause damage out of all proportion to the size of the bomb.

A Whitley V on 78 Squadron at Dishforth flown by Sergeant C A Smith was lost on the way home when it was shot down on the Dutch–German border by *Oberleutnant* Reinhold Eckardt of 6./NJG1. All five crew were killed. A Vickers Wellington on 103 Squadron at Newton, Nottinghamshire, flown by Sergeants W R Crich DFM and Arthur Farley did not return to its base. Heavy and accurate flak was reported around the target area and they were hit after dropping five 500lb HE bombs and bundles of *Nickels* on the target from 13,000 feet. F Waern the observer pinpointed their position over the Dutch Coast, as 20 miles off course. Short of fuel and without radio communications after an hour, Crich realised that the position was hopeless and was left with the choice of abandoning the aircraft or attempting a forced landing. When they looked for a place to land Norman 'Jock' Cameron, the 23-year-old rear gunner saw mountains and snow and thought that they must have been flying the reciprocal of what they had plotted and were over Switzerland. On the ground in a field near 'White House Farm' Llanover, near Abergavenny, a searchlight unit stood to. Orders had been given to treat all aircraft in the vicinity as 'hostile' and any assistance in landing that the searchlight unit could have given was therefore withheld. Crich lowered the undercarriage and selected a field in which to land. The snow camouflaged the slope of the field down to the river Usk. Not allowing for the unseen slope he burst a tyre on landing and came to a halt, feet from electric wires slung across the field. Had they been hit the aircraft would have burst into flames. The six crew – all sergeants – suffered cuts and bruises and one a broken arm. When they got out of the Wimpy, 'men speaking a funny language' and pointing guns at them seemed to confirm the theory that they had landed in Switzerland. In 'pidgin French and Franglais' they tried to tell their adversaries that they were British airmen. This, of course, convinced the men with guns –

who were Welsh – that they were not English as they were speaking 'in such a strange way.' A guard was mounted to keep the gathering crowd at bay. After being patched up, the crew enjoyed the hospitality of Major D Berrington's cellar at Pant Y Goitre House. Major Berrington's son was killed 18 months later, near Ross on Wye, piloting a Halifax. The crumpled Wellington in the field now strewn with leaflets, was dismantled, loaded onto lorries, reassembled and put back into service. This was 'Jock' Cameron's third major air crash, having suffered severe head and leg injuries in two previous crashes while serving in the Auxiliary Air Force. Crews always wanted him as their WOp/AG as he was considered to have a charmed life.

Only 56 aircraft reported bombing the designated targets and the Germans reported bombs dropping not only in Gelsenkirchen but also in adjacent towns of Buer, Horst and Hessler. This was the story that was pieced together at debriefings. When the crews landed they were taken in lorries from the dispersal point to the Briefing Room or to the Operations Room – the procedure varied with stations – where they were interrogated by an intelligence officer who had been present at the briefing and taken part in it. To ensure a certain uniformity in the reports, intelligence officers made use of a questionnaire. The crews were interrogated one by one as they arrived and the interrogation was thorough, even when they reported ten-tenths cloud which had made it impossible for them to see the target. Two or three intelligence officers might be employed on this if there had been a large number of crews out on the operation. The rooms were soon full of pilots, navigators, wireless operators and air gunners, sipping tea or coffee and answering questions. '...fires looked like a heath fire to me... I couldn't see the explosions because of the searchlights... there were so many that they lit up the ack-ack bursts... two rows of very vivid bright fires... we did one of those horribly steady run-ups and I saw the bomb flashes... there was a wee spot of light flak here... when I dropped the bomb the whole aircraft shivered as though a shell had burst near it... absolutely screeching round the sky... the moon was wizard.' Then, the dawn very near, they went to breakfast and so to bed.[1]

January 1941 saw minor operational raids on Italy. It was also marked the start of 'the milk run' to Brest, the French dockyard where large German warships sheltered from the Royal Navy until February 1942.[2] On the night of 11/12 January, 11 Wellingtons crossed the snow-clad Alps and attacked the royal arsenal at Turin. It was a bitterly cold flight, so cold in the only long-distance bombers then in operation that while crossing the Alps one crew had their bomb-release mechanism frozen solid. The pilot arrived over the arsenal only to find that the bombs were very undesirable frozen assets, for the flak curtain was thickest over the target area. He had to get rid of them some way, as he depended on a lighter aircraft to make the long flight back to base. So he went on to the Fiat factory. Again the bombs would not go down. He flew on to another war factory and tried again. This third time he was lucky. The mechanism worked and the bombs went down where they would do some good. He saw the bombs burst in the centre of the factory building and the four fires started by his incendiaries. Five minutes later, while he was still stooging around, there followed a large explosion and a series of smaller ones. Most of the aircraft that night swept across the silver streak of the River Po, picking out the darkened streets and squares of the city to pin-point their target without much difficulty. As attacks went in those days, it was highly successful. The 'bomphleteers' who had brought supplies of a four-page pamphlet of Mr Churchill's recent address to the Italian people sent them drifting over the city like a fall of giant snowflakes.

The next night, when 26 Hampdens and Wellingtons raided Brest, in the last of a series of 'experience raids' designed to blood new aircrew, nine Wellingtons on 149 Squadron led by the CO, Wing Commander (later Group Captain) 'Speedy' Powell OBE DSO attacked the Porto Marghera oil refinery and storage depot in Venice. A secondary target was the oil-storage installation used by the Italian navy on a small island in the Venice lagoon. (Three other Wimpys flew to Regensburg on the Danube, a port for Rumanian oil distribution). Powell arrived over the Adriatic shortly before 2 o'clock on a bright, frosty morning, with the starry sky clear and visibility good. The last of the attackers left an hour later, when the target area was well ablaze and a pall of fire-drenched smoke rose 500 feet. They also smashed the *Duce's* oil-storage tanks, and the fires of Porto Marghera were still plainly discernable when the bombers were climbing over the French Alps. Regensburg received its visit between 02.30 and 04.30. There conditions were not so good. Cloud formations concealed the target, but diving through the various rifts the pilots levelled off at about 1,000 feet and enabled bomb-aimers to sight accurately as the bombs were released When the crews got back to Britain they were thrilled and excited. The long pull over the Alps in winter held no terrors for them, although icing conditions had been rather bad. The round trip involved 1,500 miles and crossing the Swiss Alps twice in the moonlight. Pilot Officer 'Ken' Wilson, a 20-year-old Rhodesian and the observer in Sergeant Richard Hodgson's crew looked to portside over the Alps. 'Suddenly the most fantastic sight took our breaths away. Towering about 4,000 feet above us were the Jungfrau and the Eiger, the full moon shining on them in the clear, crisp night, turning them into giant stacks of millions of glistening, polished diamonds.'

Dick Hodgson's crew attacked the secondary target, which blew up. Then they carried out a low-level run across Venice, dropping bundles of propaganda leaflets. It was then that the Wellington was hit. Wilson felt the Wimpy shudder violently 'as if had hit a cattle grid'. Bullets burst all around him and 'Lofty' Harding the wireless operator. Hodgson yelled over the intercom, 'We're on fire!' They had flown right over the only armed naval patrol ship in the lagoon. Wilson reckoned that the Wimpy must have been doing 200 mph as they hit the water. The front-gunner, Sergeant 'Charlie' Pummery, was still in his turret. Incredibly he and Les Hatherly the navigator, 'Lofty' Harding, Wilson, Hodgson and 'Mac' McAnally, the rear gunner, all survived without injury. They were rescued by the Royal Italian Navy and taken to an island south of Venice for interrogation and were later sent to PoW camps. Their Wellington was the only loss of the night.[3]

Speedy' Powell gave a graphic picture of how he took his men in:

There was fog over the foothills on the other side. It looked like a great sea of ice, with the high ground standing up like islands. The plains of Lombardy were also completely covered by fog. Then, as we neared the Adriatic coast, the fog disappeared and when we got to Venice, flying 'up moon,' it was like day. I had more or less made up my mind all along to go down low and the moment we got over the Alps I started losing height. Over Venice we circled round to draw their fire and see how much there was. They had quite a lot of light stuff. Some of it was getting pretty accurate towards the end. Having seen how much there was, I decided to go right down. We flew over Mestre, whistling among the chimneys. There was a sort of fort or citadel outside Mestre and two sentries standing on the ramparts had a crack at us. We could see them standing up with levelled rifles. I had given orders to the front and rear gunners that they were to fire back at anybody who fired at us and they opened up on the sentries.

The time was now round about 2am yet it was so light that one could see people in the street. I heaved the aircraft over a couple of factory chimney stacks. Then we started to climb to do the bombing. We went up to 700 feet. We were carrying a 1,000lb bomb and when it burst it nearly blew us out of the air. The bomb landed either on or beside a large building with a lot of pipes all round it. There was a colossal belt of smoke and flame, which shot up almost level with the aircraft. The smoke died away but the flames persisted. Then there were a couple of great explosions. We went round again and dropped the other bomb in the middle of the flame, adding to it by half as much again. I knew of an aerodrome about 20 miles away at Padua so we went whistling along the railway tracks at about 'nought' feet to find it. We passed three trains on the way. We were flying right alongside them. We flew over Padua itself, again doing tight turns round the chimneys and church spires and having dropped leaflets there, flew on to Padua aerodrome, where the front and rear gunners let fly, left, right and centre, at the hangars. We streaked across the aerodrome at 20 feet. We could see that there were no aircraft dispersed around the aerodrome, so we assumed that they were in the hangars. Immediately we came on to the scene the aerodrome defences opened up on us. Tracer was flying alongside almost parallel with us. I was behind the trees to get cover. I had wanted to have a crack at another aerodrome but there was not much time and we'd got the Alps to cross again, so we left it at that and came away.

HQ Bomber Command sent messages of congratulations to the squadrons involved in the raid on Venice and HM King George VI congratulated crews when he visited RAF Mildenhall on 18 January to decorate a large number of airmen and officers, including 'Speedy' Powell. The Royal party inspected the operations room and the photographic section and made a tour of the aerodrome, lunching in the Officers' Mess. When visiting the Airmen's Mess the King and Queen saw that the men were being entertained by a string orchestra as they ate! An enemy aircraft appeared overhead and was engaged by the Station defences whilst the Royal party was still at the Station. No bombs were dropped.[4]

Further raids followed, to Wilhelmshaven and Brest and the other ports on the French Atlantic coast while Dunkirk and Boulogne were visited by small numbers of Whitleys and Wellingtons respectively. On 13/14 January, 24 Wellingtons and Whitleys visited Wilhelmshaven, Dunkirk and Boulogne. Pilot Officer Halley, who started out to bomb aerodromes in Norway, got into a gigantic cumulus cloud, which towered up for about 16,000 feet. He saw a purplish glow develop on the right wing-tip and then it seemed that the wing-tip was on fire, but instead of the fire streaming back, as one would expect, it vibrated in front of the wing-tip. He dodged out of that cloud as quickly as possible and thereafter went round the massive cloud peaks or navigated between them so far as was possible. Nevertheless, he got caught in another disturbance which lit up the leading edges of the wings and the wing-tips in blue light, while the propellers became arcs of blue flame. Suddenly from the starboard wing-tip a great jagged spark of a bright purple colour shot out like forked lightning – it was huge, about 30 feet long. There was an explosion followed by a bright flash inside the cockpit and all the luminous dials and instruments stood out brighter than ever before. At the same time the wireless blew up and a bit just missed the face of the wireless operator, who was temporarily blinded by the flash. The bomber crew were lucky, inasmuch as they had only just received a wireless bearing from their base which enabled them to navigate safely back to Scotland.[5]

Flight Lieutenant de Villiers Leach was caught in similar electrical storms. Flying at the two mile level to escape the lower cloud, he saw the cumulonimbus clouds reaching up and up to 20,000 feet, two miles above him:

They were lit up by the moon and looked like giant peaks. They got higher and higher and surrounded me and it was getting so cold that I thought it better not to go over them and came down through a gap to 4,000 feet where we flew in cloud. A bluish flame, two or three inches wide, appeared at the tip of the propeller arc and gradually increased to about a foot in depth. When I looked out to port, I saw the whole wing fringed with the flame which looked like a bluish-white aura. Suddenly there was a terrific flash. I was absolutely blinded for a moment and when I looked again the aura had vanished.[6]

There were no losses from any of the raids that night, which included 12 Hampdens mine-laying off the Brittany ports.

On the night of 6/7 February, 24 Whitleys set out for Dunkirk where less than a year earlier large numbers of soldiers of the BEF had been rescued by the Royal Navy. An equal number of Wellingtons set out to bomb Boulogne. A PRU Wimpy accompanied the Wellingtons on the Boulogne raid but its cameras failed. All the Whitleys returned but one Wellington of 311 Czech Squadron was lost. Pilot Officer Cigos, the pilot, and his wife lodged with other RAF couples at the Red House in the isolated Suffolk village of Livermere, three miles from RAF Honington and six miles from Bury St. Edmunds. One of the RAF couples was another Wimpy pilot, Flight Lieutenant 'Ken' Batchelor on 9 Squadron and his wife Doris who was always known as 'Mickey'. Batchelor had bombed Cologne on 27/28 November, which was ironic as he had lived in Cologne for a time after the First World War when his father was serving in the Army of Occupation. When a reconnaissance photo later that month revealed a Wellington half-submerged in Boulogne harbour 'Mickey' worried about the Czech pilot and his crew. She knew that unfortunately the Germans seldom took Czechs prisoner but shot them as traitors, so she thought that there was little hope for him. She also knew that Mrs Cigos was extraordinarily brave and she would not believe that her husband was dead. She was right. Cigos had force-landed and all the crew were captured. Among them was Pilot Officer Arnost 'Wally' Valenta, who was later incarcerated in *Stalag Luft III* at Sagan in Silesia. Mickey Batchelor need not have worried. None of the crew were shot, for now.[7]

On 15 January 1941 Sir Richard Peirse was instructed that the primary aim of the bombing offensive, until further orders, should be the destruction of the German synthetic oil plants. The secondary aim of the bombing offensive when the weather was unfavourable for the major plan would be to harass industrial towns and communications. This priority was based on an official assessment that 'the latest reports and analysis on Germany's oil position revealed that the Axis Powers would be passing through the most critical period as regards their oil resources during the next six months'. There were 17 locations where oil was being produced from nearby deposits of cheaply mined brown coal (lignite) and it was calculated that a reduction of 80 per cent in Germany's internal production of oil could be achieved if the first nine of these plants could be destroyed. The Directive went on to assert that , 'On the assumption that our present scale of air attack on the enemy's oil plants is maintained, their oil position may be causing them grave anxiety by the spring of 1941.' However, during January and February the bomber force operated exclusively against oil targets on only three nights and only one attempt was made by over 200 aircraft. This was during the new moon on 10/11 February when Peirse committed a record total of 222 aircraft to oil targets at Hannover.

Three Stirling Is on 7 Squadron, led by Acting Squadron Leader John Martin Griffith-Jones DFC,[8] were included for the first time, as part of the force of 43 aircraft detailed to attack oil storage tanks at Rotterdam. The Squadron had been the first in the RAF to receive the four-engined bomber, in August 1940. An enormous aircraft, its wingspan was nine feet less than the original design. This was by special request to Short Brothers, the makers, to allow it to pass through the doors of the standard RAF hangar! This was an important requirement if it were to be serviced away from the elements but this fundamental change caused problems. It had to have a huge undercarriage, which meant that the cockpit window was 20 feet from the ground. The Stirling could take off and land in very short distances – as short as a Wimpy – but it was not the easiest aeroplane to fly and it had a tendency to swing on takeoff and landing. But once airborne it was 'well behaved' and very strong. The first of the four-engined bombers was slower and had a much lower ceiling than the Lancaster or the Halifax, both of which came later and replaced the Stirling towards the end of 1943. However, New Zealand bomb aimer Huia Russell on joining 149 Squadron in 1942 'felt sympathy' for the Wellington crews way below them:

We reached on flying at 17,000/18,000 feet at about 170 mph IAS (Indicated Air Speed), which gave us a TAS of over 200 mph. There were occasional exceptions. There was *G-George* flown by a Canadian WO which had difficulty in attaining 9,000 feet on a couple of occasions. This was rapidly dumped on an HCU, probably Waterbeach. It was later reported to have been discovered as some fault in the basic trim of the aircraft. Mine-laying was then carried out at 600 feet which gave crews the opportunity of belting across Denmark at about 200 feet when going to the Baltic. This had its hazards and one night we lost three out of nine aircraft. Many years later I heard from one of the pilots who had survived that his altimeter was misreading and he had hit the ground. Presumably the barometric pressure over Denmark was vastly different from that at base. On one occasion an aircraft returned with telephone wires wrapped around its loop aerial thereafter the crew all wore a piece of the wire attached to their battledress as a lucky charm. This seemed to work as they survived their first tour. I do not know if the pilot was wearing his mascot on his second tour when he was shot down and taken prisoner.[9]

The raid on Hannover was described by HQ 3 Group as 'by far their most ambitious as yet undertaken'. It represented the first time the Group had dispatched more than 100 aircraft, as the bulk of the force was made up once again of Wellingtons. *H-Harry,* one of the 112 Wimpys that took part, was skippered by Sergeant-pilot Bill Garrioch on XV Squadron at RAF Wyton near Huntingdon and whose crew were flying their 16th operation of the war. Garrioch recalls:

The briefing officer announced the target, the route in and out and the bomb load – 4,000lb made up of seven 500lb bombs and the balance in incendiaries. The Met Office forecast clear skies, strong westerly winds, a full moon and very cold. Group Captain Forster said that this was to be the biggest show of the war to date, wished us all the usual good luck and told us to beware of moving stars (night fighters)! This great man, a First World War pilot, still wore a steel brace on his back caused by spinal injuries received in a crash. Even so, he flew with us occasionally. Take-off was timed for 17.30 hours and the flight duration expected to be about seven hours. The usual pre-flight planning between pilot, navigator and crews then followed. We then went to the mess for our tea of bacon and eggs, back to our quarters to change into warmer clothing and of course to empty our pockets. The ritual of this act always gave me a momentary feeling of apprehension until I put some small change back into my pocket in case we had to land away from base on return. The funny thing is I had only half a crown in small change, which I put into my pocket; that being the only article carried on my person.

We boarded the Bedford crew bus for the six-mile journey to Alconbury, our satellite airfield. Generally during these bus journeys there was the usual chatter, pocket chess or cards but on this occasion everyone seemed quiet and preoccupied with their thoughts, so much so that our navigator Sergeant Bob Beioley remarked on it. Bob and Sergeant Glyndwr 'Taffy' Rearden the WOp/AG had completed twelve operations with me on Blenheims before converting to the Wimpy. Prior to air test in the morning Taffy expressed the wish to be the front gunner that night as a change from being cooped up inside the cabin. I agreed, as WOp/AG Sergeant George Hedge RNZAF was also a fully qualified WOp/AG. Soon we arrived at our dispersal. I signed the Form 700 and as I climbed the ladder into the aircraft 'Chiefy' Wright said to me, 'If you break this one; don't bring it back!' (*H-Harry* was Flight Lieutenant Morris's aircraft but my *D-Dog* was being repaired after I had accidentally hit my wingtip on the control caravan during a previous take-off). I laughed and said that I would be a good boy and nurse his precious Wimpy. I glanced at my watch and at the other aircraft around the dispersal area.

Time to start up. Fuel on, first port and the starboard engines coughed, burst into life and warmed up at 1,000 rpm. Soon we ran each engine up to take-off rpm (2,650), tested the magnetos, oil pressure and temperature and cylinder head temperature and checked and set the gyro, cooling gills, flaps, etc. All the crew reported ready. The time was now 17.25 hours. I gave the signal and with a final wave to our much-appreciated ground crew, we moved out towards our take-off position near the end of the runway. We were No. 2 to go. At precisely 17.30 hours No. 1 started his take-off run and as he reached the end of the runway I lined up and got my green light from the caravan. Brakes off, I opened the throttle slowly to maximum power as we started rolling. As we gathered speed the noise was deafening and seemed to reach a crescendo that vibrated throughout the loaded aircraft. I kept the nose down until the last bit of the all-too-short runway loomed up, then, pulling up; she lifted clear, a light kiss on the concrete and off. Wheels up and nose kept down to increase flying speed. I throttled back to climbing rpm to reach operating height and the engine noise now changed to a welcome hum. All was well.

Bob gave me the course, which I confirmed from my kneepad. As the snow-covered countryside receded far below in the darkness, Sergeant Bill Jordan, the 2nd pilot who was on his second trip with me for familiarization, flew the aircraft and the gunners entered their turrets while I visited each member of the crew to ensure that all was in order. Soon we reached the coast at Orford Ness and levelled off at 11,000 feet. The navigator and the wireless operator were at their stations and the lighting was very subdued, creating an eerie yet efficient atmosphere tinged with the smell of dope and fuel, amid the roar of the smooth-sounding Pegasus engines. When we were over the sea Taffy and Sergeant Jock Hall, rear gunner, a Scotsman with many trips in Coastal Command, test-fired their guns. From now on we were on the alert for night fighters. It was cold and clear. The patches of white cumulus would make us an easily identified target seen from above. I took over before we reached the Dutch coast, which we crossed at 18.50 hours – another 213 miles and 65 minutes to the target. We had a very strong tail wind and ground speed was nearly 200 mph. Bob got a pinpoint. We were almost dead on track – a slight course alteration and all was well. We were lucky so far.

It was unbelievably quiet. We flew towards the target and still there was no flak. We were very much alert but it was the easiest run-in so far and the ground was easily identifiable. Only five minutes to the target. Then we saw it. Bob was a good navigator – we were almost spot-on. On the eastern horizon the rising moon assisted target identification. With bomb doors opened and bombs fused Bob went down to the bombsights. He saw the target nestled in the crook of the 'Y-section' of a big road junction. We had a following wind so I throttled back a little and kept the aircraft steady. Right a little... I did not see any activity at all, not even a little flak. The first Wimpys' bombs burst. Then suddenly there was a series of flashes close to Gilmore's aircraft. Bob called, 'Left... left... left... a bit more... steady now... steady.' Flak now curled lazily up towards us and then there was heavy ack-ack to our left. It was accurate for height but was not near us: must be the other aircraft in trouble. Bob called 'Bombs gone!' and I immediately turned steeply to port. Jock in the rear turret watched our bombs burst. There were only six flashes. Where was the seventh? Gilmore's aircraft started a fire and our incendiaries were well alight. Ack-ack was almost non-existent with us but as we flew away we saw other aircraft getting a hot reception and the sky was full of flak. All this time the fires seemed to grow in intensity – Hannover was visible 40 miles away. The moon was up and it was like daylight. We watched for enemy fighters but all was quiet and we could not even see other aircraft.

Against a strong head wind our ground speed was now only 85 knots; it was going to be a long haul home. Large white cumulus clouds were building up below. As we crossed the eastern coast of the Zuider Zee at Kempen, Jock suddenly called out, 'Fighter below and behind!' I put the engines to cruising revs and steep turned to starboard to face him. As I turned I saw a Me 110, which was turning to meet me. I turned violently to port to avoid him. Jock gave him a long burst but he still attacked, hitting the aircraft in the fuselage and port engine. I put the flaps down and soon the shooting stopped. He had overshot.

I heard the cannon fire hit the aircraft somewhere behind me. Jock said that he had been hit. Could we get him out of the turret? The port engine was on fire. I turned off the fuel and full throttle. Bob called, 'Are we on fire?' Bob's sudden announcement on the intercom must have paralyzed my senses if only for a fleeting instant because as I was looking through the cockpit window, super-imposed in space, just outside the windscreen was a very clear picture of my grandfather and a great uncle looking directly at me. It was so clear that I even recognized my uncle's old tweed jacket!

Then it was gone and I was back to reality. It frightened me because these two much-loved relatives had been dead for about seven years. Much later George told me that cannon shells came through the fuselage and exploded in his radio equipment. How he and Bob were not hit I'll never know. I was saved by the armour plate behind my head. At that moment I knew we had to survive and I seemed to find added strength and courage to risk anything that would bring us out of this alive. I looked back and the fuselage was full of smoke. I could not see anyone. Perhaps a flare was burning. Taffy moaned faintly saying, 'Get me out' and I saw the fighter turn to port over our port wingtip. Bill Jordan went forward to open the escape hatch and to get Taffy out of the turret. I told the crew to prepare to bail out and raised the flaps.

We were diving now. The fighter came in again and once more I put the flaps down and the aircraft yawed violently to port while I throttled back and side slipped to almost stalling speed. Cannon and machine gun tracer went just over the top of us but miraculously we were not hit. This time, as the fighter went over the top of us I raised the flaps and control was easier. I think only the starboard flap worked. I told Taffy to shoot the fighter down, position 10 o'clock. He did not answer. Bill Jordan tried desperately to operate the turret door release and get him out. George Hedge was standing beside me ready to help when Bill opened the floor escape hatch. Bob and Jock were still back in the smoke-filled fuselage. Were they alive? I did not know. I decided that unless we bailed out or landed quickly we would all die. We were blazing very badly now. I signalled to George not to jump as I had not given the order and I dived for the ground in the hope that a crash landing might save some of us. The aircraft persisted in turning to port. We were diving very steeply and fast, over 300 knots. Through the cockpit window I saw the port engine and that the inner wing was now on fire. Off all fuel and full throttle starboard engine. The frozen expanse of the Zuider Zee was hurtling towards us. I tried to level off but the elevators were sluggish and we hit the ice slightly nose down and skidded for what seemed to be miles. Then, suddenly, she broke through the ice and the nose filled up with water and ice through the open escape hatch. Then the aircraft stopped. We must have crashed at about 22.30.[10]

In all, 183 aircraft claimed to have bombed their primary objectives in Hannover (32 aircraft bombed alternative targets) but clouds caused the bombing to drift off target, although large explosions and many fires were started. All the aircraft that visited Rotterdam, including the three Stirlings which bombed oil storage tanks beside the Waal at Rotterdam in a separate operation, returned safely.[11]

Four aircraft were shot down on the operation on Hannover and four more were brought down over eastern England by Dornier Do 17Z and Ju 88C-2 Intruders of NJG2. One of two Blenheims on 21 Squadron that was attacked was shot down in flames over Bodney airfield in Norfolk and the other force landed at the same airfield after being attacked and damaged off the Norfolk coast. Two Hampdens were claimed shot down by *Oberleutnant* Kurt Herrmann and his *Bordfunker*, *Unteroffizier* Englebert Böttner. Their first victim was a 49 Squadron Hampden returning to Scampton. A burst of fire set the aircraft on fire. Two of the crew bailed out safely while the other two perished in the aircraft which crashed at Langworth, Lincolnshire. A few minutes later Herrmann attacked a 144 Squadron Hampden piloted by Sergeant William Alexander McVie who was flying with his navigation lights on. Herrmann's fire hit the aircraft's hydraulics, undercarriage and flaps. The lights went out and the Hampden dived away to land safely at Hemswell.[12] In another 144 Squadron Hampden Sergeant E Dainty orbited Hemswell but was refused permission to land because of the intruder activity and eventually, low on fuel, the crew abandoned the aircraft, which crashed at Snettisham, Norfolk. After attacking three airfields with incendiary bombs and chasing an unidentified aircraft without result, *Hauptmann* Rolf Jung, the *Staffelkapitän* of 2./NJG2, saw a Wellington with its navigation lights on. It was a 115 Squadron Wellington returning to Marham and flown by Sergeant Harold Humphrey Rogers. He had narrowly missed colliding with two other aircraft and was intent on avoiding a similar situation. Rogers had attacked Rotterdam as strong winds had prevented him reaching his target at Hannover. He had also machine gunned two airfields in Holland on the return. Near a flashing landmark beacon at Swaffham, Rogers switched on the Wellington's navigation lights. Almost immediately the port engine was hit and Sergeant Hill the rear gunner was wounded in his left arm. The aircraft began to lose height rapidly but Rogers was able to make a successful forced landing on a railway cutting at Narborough.[13]

Another Wimpy crew that ditched in the North Sea was captained by Sergeant W R Crich DFM on 103 Squadron at RAF Newton who a month earlier had crash-landed in Wales returning from Düsseldorf. They were hit by flak and had an engine failure and could not gain height, so the captain decided to ditch in the sea when 30–35 miles off Aldburgh. At 75mph the aircraft stalled and at 10 feet 'pancaked' into the water. The gunners were ordered to leave their turrets and the flotation gear was prepared. There was no time to jettison 250 gallons of fuel or guns and ammunition. 'Jock' Cameron the tail gunner was last to leave, by which time he was up to his waist in water; and he was a non-swimmer. Sergeant Farley the 2nd pilot, despite a broken collar bone, pulled him clear and he only sustained muscular injuries to his arm at this stage. Neither injured man had been properly braced for the crash. The dinghy was released automatically by an immersion switch. At first it was found to be only partially inflated and turned over. The two mooring lines, the wireless, the wireless aerial and sundry other lines were all entangled but eventually cut loose. The ration container, distress signals and paddles were lost at this time. The crew mustered three water bottles, each three quarters full, drogue, fluorescent dye and nine dinghy leak stoppers. Otherwise they had nothing. The crew sat on the narrow inflated rim. They crossed and re-crossed their own sickly green fluorescent wake all night. The following morning, at 07.00 hours two Blenheims were sighted twice within a mile or two of the dinghy at about 1,000 feet. The crew, each man wearing his yellow hat, waved a large white scarf but failed to attract attention. A Wellington appeared making a square search and passed at less than 1,000 feet and only 300 yards away, but did not see them despite attempts to attract it using a mirror as a heliograph. The motion of the swell made members of the crew so sea-sick, as well as cold and wet, that one of the crew wanted to let himself slip over the side into the waves.

On the second day a strong easterly wind sprang up. By using a white scarf as a sail and their flying boots as paddles and bailers they advanced towards the coast. At 22.00 hours that night three ships were seen within hailing distance. Each ship answered and the last one stopped. It was the SS *Tovelli*. The airmen were exhausted and suffering from exposure and severe frost bite of the feet. Too weak, from lack of food, to help themselves they had to be hauled up the sheer side of the ship with the help of sailors. (This experience was allegedly the catalyst for canopies being added to the dinghies.)

Meanwhile at a pub near Newton a wake had been held for them and quite a reception awaited them. Survivors' leave did not apply and seven days later, with the exception of Jock Cameron and Arthur Farley, the others were flying again. Bone and muscle mended but the frost bitten foot injuries persisted. On 29 May 1941 Jock Cameron was declared fit for non-operational flying and sent to Harrowbeer for Air Sea Rescue as 'a rest'. Some rest! He felt very vulnerable and a 'sitting duck' in the lumbering sea planes. Picking decaying bodies out of the sea when searching for newly ditched airmen was to give him horrific nightmares for the rest of his life.[14]

On the night of 11/12 February 1941, when Hannover and Bremen were the targets for 108 aircraft, airfields in East Anglia became enveloped in dense fog, and 18 aircraft – nine Wellingtons, seven Whitleys (including four on 51 Squadron at Dishforth) and two Hampdens – were lost in crashes. Another Hampden crashed in the Irish Sea returning from Bremen. Three nights later, on 14/15 February, 44 Wellingtons were detailed to bomb the Nordstern oil plant at Gelsenkirchen, one of the leading nine synthetic oil plants on Peirse's list of 17 primary plants, but only nine crews claimed to have bombed the target. Another 22 Blenheims and 22 Wellingtons were detailed to bomb the Meerbeck oil plant near Homberg, a spa town at the foot of the Taunus Mountains. Sixteen claimed to have hit the target. There were no losses and all aircraft returned safely.

Flying Officer David Penman on 44 Squadron at Waddington flew his final operation of his first tour in Hampdens on 15/16 February when 33 Hampdens and 37 Blenheims were detailed to attack the Meerbeck oil plant near Homberg again. Another 73 Wellingtons and 27 Whitleys visited the Holten oil plant at Sterkrade. A Whitley on 77 Squadron at Topcliffe and a Wellington on XV Squadron at Wyton flown by Pilot Officer Cyril Bertie Dove were lost. The Wimpy was shot down by *Feldwebel* Ernst Kalinowski of 6./NJG1 at Barchem between Apeldoorn and Enschede. Bertie Dove and two of his crew were killed and two others were taken prisoner. The crew of the Whitley, which crashed at Malden in Germany, were taken into captivity. At Homberg the oil plant was difficult to identify because of searchlight glare and cloud, and ground haze made aiming very difficult. Only 40 aircraft, including Penman's, which dropped four 500lb and two 250lb bombs, got their bomb loads away. They were then held by searchlights and no results could be observed. All of the Homberg force returned without loss but Penman's crew was in for a shock when they flew back in the dark over Lincolnshire:

We were given permission to land and with all airfield and aircraft lights on we were flying up the grass landing area, marked with burning goose neck flares at 1,000 feet prior to making our left hand circuit for landing. There was a sudden rattle of cannon fire as tracer bullets streamed into our starboard wing and engine. As I swung the aircraft violently in a diving turn to the left the faint shape of a Me 110 went past us. I switched off all lights and broadcast a warning of 'Intruder in the circuit'. All lights on the airfield went out. My considerable knowledge of Waddington enabled me to continue the circuit, land the aircraft, swing off the landing area and shut off the engines. We got out of the aircraft; no one had been hit but petrol was pouring out of the starboard side.

Looking up he saw another Hampden with lights on joining the circuit with the Bf 110 following him and opening fire. The Hampden was hit and the pilot, Squadron Leader Smalies was lucky that a bullet which came his way hit the large metal box holding his parachute straps together and did not damage him. Fortunately his aircraft was not badly damaged and after the Bf 110 left he landed safely.[15]

The crew had just walked away from their aircraft when another Hampden crashed into it in the darkness.

By now the situation in the Atlantic was desperate. Since the fall of France the previous summer, 900 British, Allied and neutral merchant ships had been sunk, mainly by *U-boats*, and the situation was critical. On 9 March Winston Churchill issued a directive which gave absolute priority to the Battle of the Atlantic. The Air Staff instructed Peirse that 'the Prime Minister has ruled that for the next four months we should devote our energies to defeating the attempt of the enemy to strangle our food supplies and our connection with the United States.' For the next seven weeks, Bomber Command would operate mainly against *U-boat* bases on the French Atlantic coast and the German ports and ship-building yards and towns and cities that supplied the *U-boat* fleet with diesel engines and other equipment. Only a proportion of the operational effort could be used to bomb oil targets.

On the night of 10/11 March, 19 Hampdens were given Cologne as their target and eight Blenheims and six Handley Page Halifaxes of 35 Squadron at Linton-on-Ouse led by Wing Commander R W P Collings AFC attacked Le Havre. The Halifax was the second four-engined bomber to be introduced into operational service and this was the first Halifax operation of the war. The weather was excellent to the French coast where 8/10ths cloud was encountered. Crews located Le Havre first by searchlights and flak and then the target was seen through a good break in the cloud, the dock area being clearly visible. The bombers delivered a level attack from 13,000 feet and Collings dropped one stick of twelve 500lb SAP bombs, which were seen to burst along the edge of the main docks. Only slight heavy flak and scattered searchlights were encountered and one aircraft that was damaged by flak returned safely on three engines. *F-Freddie*, the Halifax flown by Squadron Leader P A Gilchrist DFC of Weyburn, Saskatchewan, was shot down near Aldershot, over Normandy in Hampshire by an RAF fighter. Gilchrist and Sergeant R Aedy the flight engineer, who was injured, were the only crewmembers to survive the encounter. One Hampden was lost on the operation on Cologne when it crashed near Venlo and another crashed at Bishop's Norton in Lincolnshire on the return with the loss of all the crew.

On 12/13 March the Blohm und Voss *U-boat* yards and other industry sites in Hamburg were the targets for the force of 88 aircraft – mainly Hampdens, Whitleys and Wellingtons – and some Avro Manchesters and Halifaxes, which were attacking a German territorial target for the first time. All four Manchesters and the three Halifaxes dispatched returned safely, as did the rest of the force. They roared in, banking into the funnel of the runway at each station and over the hawthorn hedges before touching down. With flaps lowered the Halifax had the appearance of a monstrous fan tailed pigeon. There was nothing soft or weak about the undercarriage that jutted from its belly; solid and big it accentuated the great strength of the airframe.[16] Twenty HE and 300–400 incendiary bombs fell in the Blohm und Voss yards causing damage to the main office block and other parts of the base, including two slipways on which *U-boats* were being built. Other targets this night were the Focke-Wulf aircraft factory in Bremen, which was visited by 86 Wellingtons and Blenheims, and two targets in Berlin, which were bombed by 72 Hampdens, Wellingtons and Whitleys. Twelve HE bombs hit the Focke-Wulf factory and two Wellingtons and a Blenheim failed to return. At Berlin the bombing was very scattered with more bombs in the southern districts of the capital than elsewhere, though a goods station suffered severely, a chemical factory was damaged beyond repair and an *SS* barracks in the Grossluchtenfeld was destroyed. Three bombers failed to return. A solitary Hampden, groping its way back in thick weather from Berlin where it had failed to find its primary target, dropped its bombs on a railway junction, which just happened to be at the precise moment the night express from The Hague to Berlin was travelling. The train received a direct hit and casualties were heavy.

Hamburg was again the target on 13/14 March for 139 aircraft who took off in bright moonlight to bomb the Blohm und Voss *U-boat* yards. A Manchester on 207 Squadron piloted by Flying Officer Hugh Vernon Matthews DFC was shot down by *Feldwebel* Hans Hahn of III./NJG2 soon after take-off from Waddington. As the Manchester hit the ground at Wisby its bomb load exploded, killing all but two of the crew. Sergeant W A Cox was thrown clear and he survived but lost a leg. Sergeant Joeseph Marsden died later in hospital. This was the first Manchester lost on operations although Hahn claimed it as a 'Hudson'.[17] Six other aircraft were shot down on the raid on Hamburg. The Blohm und Voss shipyard was again hit and there was much other damage including a large fire in a timber yard and a direct hit on the main fire station, which damaged the reserve fire-hose store. A total of 119 fires, 31 of them large, were started. Over 50 people were killed and 139 injured. It was the heaviest death toll in Hamburg so far in the war.[18]

Sergeant Douglas Mourton, a Whitley wireless operator on 102 Squadron at Topcliffe, on Sergeant 'Ricky' Rix's crew, thought initially that Hamburg was a comparatively easy trip. But the 24-year-old WOp/ AG knew that he would be lucky to complete a tour of operations. One night late in 1940, just before a trip to the Ruhr, he had written a 'final' letter to Maisie his wife of less than a year saying that if she ever received the letter he would 'be beyond the reach of any written correspondence'. As the target approached Mourton, a wallpaper salesman before the war, could see another Whitley flying a parallel course. 'Suddenly it exploded. What had an aircraft been a few seconds before was now a mass of debris, flying through the air. It had apparently been hit by an anti-aircraft shell; most likely in the bomb bay.' Later he learned that the

Whitley was *S-Sugar* and the second pilot had been Sergeant Alec Elliott, his best friend on the squadron with whom he had passed many nights in the pub and played innumerable games of crib while waiting in the crew room.[19] Five other bombers also failed to return.

The following night it was the turn of oil plants at Gelsenkirchen to be attacked by 101 aircraft, including 61 Wellingtons, one of which was shot down with the loss of all the crew. Much damage was caused to the Hydriewerk Scholven oil plant after hits by an estimated 16 bomb loads, and the workers' housing estate nearby was also bombed. In each of these raids on German territory the anti-aircraft and searchlight defences were superb and caused much consternation among the aircrews – incredulous of their accuracy – and no doubt were responsible for many bombs being scattered.

Small numbers of aircraft attacked on moonless nights in marginal weather conditions, such as 15/16 March when the naval port at Lorient in Brittany and Düsseldorf were raided. Bremen, Wilhelmshaven and Kiel were attacked the following nights. On the night of the 23/24 March a few score Wimpys and Whitleys set out to bomb Berlin and in equal measure, raids were carried out against Kiel and Hannover. No major damage was caused to any of these targets but these types of operation persisted.

Four nights later 38 Wellingtons and a Short Stirling I set out to attack Cologne, and 35 Hampdens and Whitleys, and four Manchesters on 207 Squadron at Waddington headed for Düsseldorf. One of the Manchesters was *P-Peter* piloted by 23-year-old Flight Lieutenant Johnnie Aloysius Siebert RAAF who had recently recommenced operations following a tour with 44 Squadron on Hampdens and had already visited Cologne, Brest, Lorient and La Rochelle. As the crews climbed into the lorry which took them to their dispersed aircraft at around 19.30 hours, they were seen off by Group Captain Boothman, the Station CO.[20] The former Schneider Trophy winner's parting words were to Siebert's navigator, Sergeant George Fominson, who was wryly advised to be sure to 'pick out a nice, fat maternity hospital' in Düsseldorf as his aiming-point. This was a sarcastic jibe at 'Lord Haw Haw' who was claiming in propaganda broadcasts at that time that the RAF only bombed hospitals and non-military targets. Their route took them over Holland again. In Eindhoven, on the River Dommel in North Brabant province and on the bombers' route to and from the Ruhr, Kees Rijken, who was 12 when the Germans attacked his country and thus about 14 when the air war really started, was an avid watcher:

> Almost every day and night the allied bombers came over Eindhoven, Most nights my father and I stood in the garden, watching, listening and sometimes sheltering from the shell splinters of the German ack-ack with a pan on our heads. When the ack-ack stopped we

knew that the German fighters were airborne. From our house we could see the sky in the direction of Germany start to light up and eventually turn red. When we were standing in the garden my father had the habit of signalling the *V for Victory* sign to the overflying aircraft with his pocket lantern. The impact of the great numbers of bombs that were dropped upon targets in the Ruhr was so great that sometimes the doors in our house started clattering.

Düsseldorf was bombed at around 22.30 hours in two approaches, the aircraft dropping eight bombs of 500lbs on each run over the target area. Intense flak was encountered and one shell burst beneath *P-Peter* and buffeted the starboard wing up in the air. Level flight was resumed and as they set course for England the crew speculated as to whether they had experienced a near miss or whether any damage had occurred on the starboard side. Approaching the searchlight belt on the Dutch border the flak died down and fighter attacks were expected. At this moment the starboard engine began to smoke, lost power and had to be stopped. Immediately the Manchester began to lose height and then the port engine started to lose power too. Siebert called that he couldn't hold them up any longer and the aircraft fell into a sideslip to port, nose down but still under some semblance of control. Sergeant Jim Taylor in the wireless operator's position slammed the switch of his W/T set over to transmit and without waiting for the 15 seconds necessary for the set to warm up began transmitting their position to base. As he did this he suddenly noticed tracer passing on their port side. The Manchester had been intercepted by a Bf 110 night fighter piloted by *Oberleutnant* Walter Fenske of I./NJG1.

Taylor was temporarily cut off from the intercom as he transmitted and missed the captain's first order to abandon the aircraft. The starboard engine had by now caught fire and a hydraulic failure was experienced in the aircraft. Neither of these were unusual experiences in Manchesters at this time and it is not absolutely certain that Fenske's fire actually hit the crippled Manchester but he was later credited with the kill. Taylor was then slapped firmly on the shoulder as Sergeant W W J McDougall, 2nd WOp/AG in the mid-upper-turret hastened forward to the escape hatch beneath the nose, struggling into his parachute as he went. Taylor slipped the clip over his Morse key to clamp it on 'transmit', ripped out his intercom lead and oxygen tube and followed McDougall. By this time the aircraft was side slipping viciously, diving steeply and the remaining engine was racing. The hydraulic failure had severed power to the rear turret and the main undercarriage had flopped down. As Taylor dived through the hatch Pete Gurnell the rear gunner, who had been unable to rotate his turret by hand, closely followed him. The starboard main wheel narrowly missed Taylor and Gurnell as the aircraft side slipped over them. They and Sergeant P C Robson, the second pilot, were the last crew members out alive. Siebert's body was located next day some distance from the wreckage of his aircraft. His parachute had not fully opened and he might have been stunned as he left the aircraft or did not get out soon enough.

Fenske had attacked the Manchester from below and as he broke away he observed the parachutes of the five remaining aircrew in the glow of the searchlights. The aircraft dived away beneath them, an engine still racing, and crashed on a farmhouse at Bakel, northeast of Helmond, near Eindhoven, killing some cows. None of the family of nine was killed or injured. Fenske then dropped a flare, which burst beneath the descending airmen. In its glow they could see that they were falling into an area of open water. Taylor and Gurnell were feverishly blowing up their Mae Wests when they splashed down into four inches of water overlying a further two feet of mud. Taylor sprained an ankle in the landing and after disposing of his 'chute waded for about an hour before reaching firm ground and discovering a bar in the village. He was given first aid and fed, before being sent on his way with the 'name' of a contact in the underground movement in Eindhoven. Early next morning he was spotted and arrested by a German patrol who took him to the airfield of Eindhoven, where he was reunited with the survivors of his own crew and that of a Wellington crew that had been shot down.[21] By a strange coincidence one of the two pigeons carried in *P-Peter* arrived back in its loft in the early hours of 28 March in the very street in Lincoln, where Taylor's girlfriend of the time, later his wife, then lived. How the pigeon managed to escape will never be known. Taylor and Gurnell had the tragic task of identifying the body of their pilot, brought in by the Germans, and were later kept in solitary confinement, deprived of cigarettes and interrogated for almost three days. Kees Rijken concludes:

On 29 March 1941 a staff member of the *Ortskommandantur* asked my father to see that a grave be dug in the *Ehrenfriedhof* (military part) of the municipal cemetery. An RAF flight lieutenant would be buried at 15.00 hours. The German official showed my father the identity disc of the fallen airman, who appeared to be John Sieberr RAAF and RC, No. 36155. At the town hall the officials did not know what the second 'A' in RAAF meant but the letters 'RC' were understood. Though the Germans had forbidden any public gathering the rumour that an 'English' airman would be buried that afternoon had spread quickly and thousands of inhabitants assembled around the cemetery. A German chaplain, a military band, a guard of honour and a Roman Catholic Dutch priest were present. *Luftwaffe* personnel carried the coffin, covered with the British flag, to the grave. The German military band played 'Ich hatte einen Kameradan' (I had a comrade) and a salute of honour was fired. After the funeral the Dutch people crowded round the grave and clearly showed their sympathy with the fallen airman and their antipathy to the Germans by wearing red, white and blue or orange knots. Many flowers were laid on John Siebert's grave.

On 28 March meanwhile, a photo-reconnaissance of the docks at Brest on the French coast confirmed the presence of the two 26,000-ton battle cruisers, *Scharnhorst* and *Gneisenau*. These warships had destroyed 115,622 tons during the cruise which finished at Brest on 22 March and if they were allowed to join forces with the Bismarck all three warships would wreak unprecedented havoc on the British trade routes. They at once became a target of real importance not only for Coastal but also for Bomber Command, but during the next three days weather conditions were unfavourable. Finally, on the night of 30/31 March, 109 aircraft including 50 Wellingtons were ordered to attack the battle cruisers, in what was the first of 63 raids to be launched against Brest during 1941. All the aircraft returned safely. No hits were achieved.

On 31 March/1 April six Wimpys on 149 Squadron at Mildenhall were dispatched on the raid on Emden and 28 Wellingtons attacked Bremen. At Mildenhall on 3 March, 149 Squadron had received two of the new Wellington Mk. II bombers which, with their powerful Rolls-Royce Merlin engines, were capable of carrying a 4,000lb high-capacity (HC) light-case bomb commonly called a 'Cookie' that was being brought into service. This bomb somewhat resembled a giant dustbin. On the night of 31 March one was first dropped in anger when two aircraft on 149 Squadron acted as cover for the Mk. II Wellingtons carrying the 'Cookies'. *X-X-ray* piloted by Pilot Officer John Henry Franks[22] successfully completed the operation but the second failed to get airborne and slid to a halt in a barley field at the edge of Mr Norman's small-holding at West Row – the *Wizard of Oz* painted on the bomber had failed to work its magic. The Wellington flown by Sergeant G J P Morhen landed heavily on return, stalled and crashed. One gunner died of his injuries later. A second 'Cookie' was dropped by a 9 Squadron Wellington. Cookies had no ballistic characteristics. Once released, they could land anywhere within a five-mile radius of the aiming point. One of the Cookies fell in the east part of the town near the Post office and telephone exchange, causing severe dislocation to these services. The other fell in the old part of the town. When it exploded, 'masses of debris' said the official communiqué, 'flying through the air were outlined against the glow of fires and the results appeared to be devastating.' 'Houses took to the air' said the pilot who dropped it. These 'high capacity' bombs soon came to be called *Luftminen* by the Germans.

The weather in April improved steadily permitting operations to be flown on most nights, and on 3/4 April, 90 aircraft attempted to bomb the warships at Brest again. One Blenheim was lost without trace and a Whitley was shot down. Two Whitleys on 77 Squadron were lost, one in a crash landing at Waddington, which killed four of the crew, and the other in a crash at Eartham near Chichester, which claimed three more crew members. Shortly after midnight *H-Harry*, a Wellington on 115 Squadron, was returning to Marham after the raid but when over The Wash the Wimpy was hit by a burst of fire and rapidly lost height. Sergeant C M Thompson the pilot and Sergeant Humphrey Yule Chard succeeded in holding *Harry* on an even keel until it eventually hit the mud flats at Ongar Hill, Terrington St Clement near King's Lynn. Sergeant Russell the rear gunner was the only man to get out alive and he was finally reached by rescuers several hours later suffering from exposure.

Fifty-four aircraft returned to Brest the night following when a Hampden on 106 Squadron at Coningsby, flown by Wing Commander Patrick Julyan Polglase MID, was shot down by flak and crashed at St-Renan with no survivors. Some bombs hit the Continental Hotel in the port just as the evening meal was being served and several German naval officers, including some from the *Scharnhorst* and the *Gneisenau*, were believed to have been killed. A direct hit was claimed on the *Gneisenau*, which was in dry dock, but the 250lb bomb did not explode. It did however cause the *Gneisenau* to be removed on 5 April to the outer harbour. Ten Hampdens set out for Brest but only one of the bombers bombed the objective because of cloud and a 50 Squadron aircraft exploded off the Isles of Scilly killing all four crew. On 6 April a Coastal Command Beaufort torpedo bomber flown by Flying Officer Kenneth Campbell, the only one of four aircraft to locate the target in the haze, scored a direct hit on the *Gneisenau*, which had been moored at a buoy in the inner harbour alongside one of the shore quays. To her seaward was a long stone mole; behind her was sharply rising ground; in dominating positions all around were 270 anti-aircraft guns. Three flak ships moored in the outer harbour and the *Gneisenau's* own formidable armament added to the strength of the defences. Campbell flew in below mast height and launched his torpedo from a range of 500 yards before he was instantly shot down with the loss of all the crew, but the torpedo ran true and pierced the *Gneisenau's* stern beneath the water line. The battle cruiser was so badly damaged that eight months later the starboard propeller shaft was still under repair. Campbell was awarded a posthumous Victoria Cross.[23]

That night Brest was bombed again but Bomber Command could not emulate Campbell's supreme effort. In bad weather only 47 out of 71 aircraft dispatched got their bombs away, all aircraft returning safely. Twenty-four Hampdens carried out minelaying operations off Brittany and the Frisians and a Hampden on 83 Squadron at Scampton was lost without trace.

Two heavy raids were carried out on the naval base and industrial area at Kiel on consecutive nights. The first, by 229 aircraft on 7/8 April, was the largest raid to one target so far in the war. Visibility was perfect and the attacked lasted for five hours. Numerous fires were started and widespread damage was caused. Four aircraft failed to return. On the night following, 160 aircraft were dispatched. Crews claimed another successful raid and 8,000 civilians and 300 naval personnel were bombed out. Four aircraft were lost. Nine more crashed in England. One of these was Wellington *C-Charlie* on 218 'Gold Coast' Squadron at Marham near King's Lynn. Squadron Leader G D Lambert DFC AFC, the pilot, who was flying his 12th op, recalls:

We crossed the English coast north of Great Yarmouth and set course for the target in NW Germany. It was necessary to avoid friendly coast wise shipping convoys whose positions were known to us. They would open fire without warning if they felt threatened. Flying into North Germany we always avoided the heavily armed Island of Heligoland. We made towards the target without much opposition from flak or searchlights. Approaching the target area it was more exciting; on our bombing run we were caught and held in a cone of searchlights and much flak. The noise of anti aircraft shells exploding became audible over the engine noise of our Wellington. After bombing the aiming mark I dived away to get out of trouble. We had been at about 11,000 feet. We set course for our Marham base nearly 500 miles away over the North Sea. It soon became apparent our port engine had been badly damaged and was out of action. It was difficult or impossible to maintain height. We were flying off the coast of Holland and very near the surface of the North Sea. We threw everything portable out of the aeroplane; guns, ammunition, all equipment, even the Elsan lavatory was hacked off with the axe went out and the axe after it. I judged we were going to make a forced landing and turned on course for nearby Dutch coast as home was nearly a hundred miles distant. The rear gunner reported a night fighter on our tail and reminded me we had neither guns nor ammunition. I signalled SOS using the navigation lights normally extinguished and waggled the wings by rolling the aircraft to indicate distress. The German fighter drew alongside, he waggled his wings to indicate he understood and made off on other duties. He must have been a gentleman! We were down to about 200 feet or less from the sea but I found, probably due to using up of fuel, I was able to maintain height and even climb a little at times. I decided to turn around 180° and make once again for home 80–100 miles away. We limped over the coast north of Great Yarmouth. I made an emergency landing with little or no fuel left in the badly damaged

Wellington at RAF Horsham St Faith, Norwich after 8 hours 10 minutes. This was compared to 6.35 the previous night.[24]

On 9/10 April, 80 aircraft – most of them Wellingtons and Hampdens, as well as 17 Whitleys and three Stirlings of 7 Squadron – visited Berlin in perfect visibility and nearly a full moon. Other aircraft attacked Vegesack and Emden and also dropped mines in the East Frisians. The operation on Vegesack cost two Wellingtons. *D-Dog* flown by Wing Commander Vyvian Blackden, CO of 12 Squadron, which was flying its first operation on Wellingtons, failed to return from Emden. Another three Wellingtons, a Whitley and a Stirling on 7 Squadron flown by Flight Lieutenant 'Farmer' Pike DFC and his 7 Squadron crew, who were shot down by *Feldwebel* Karl-Heinz Scherfling of 7./NJG1 were lost on the Berlin operation.[25] Another Stirling had returned early to Newmarket with engine overheating. During March–April 7 Squadron operated from the famous Rowley Mile strip because Oakington's grass runways had many soft patches and were unsuitable for the operation of heavy aircraft. The famous racecourse had been used as a landing ground for aircraft in the First World War. HRH the Prince of Wales landed at the strip in 1935 before travelling by road to attend the Jubilee Review at Mildenhall. After the Munich Crisis, in 1938, the Air Ministry took an interest in the area as a satellite for bombers at RAF Mildenhall. The Rowley Mile course in about 300 acres north of the Beacon Course and Cambridge Hill offered one of the largest grass landing and take-off runs – 2,500 yards – in an east-west direction. A Wellington Ia filled with 1,500lb of bombs and 720 gallons of fuel required a 1,080-yard run to become airborne which left little margin for error. The Rowley Mile strip was the longest of its kind in Britain where a Wellington Ia could operate carrying 2,000lb of bombs. Although long and flat, crews had to remember to hurdle the 20-foot high Devil's Dyke running along one boundary. Accommodation for air and ground crews was in the racecourse administration buildings, the grandstand and requisitioned housing locally until new huts could be built.

Flight Lieutenant Ken Batchelor on 9 Squadron at Honington, Suffolk was flying *S-Sugar*, one of the 36 Wellingtons that made up the Berlin force:

Just after crossing the Dutch frontier we could see the searchlight barrier running right down from Emden. As we got closer we could see also that they were coning one or two of our chaps with about thirty searchlights. We saw five aircraft downed in about ten minutes.[26] Later, another crew reported having seen six parachutes from one. On and on we went on track, over the huge lakes and on to the north of Hannover, which was very busy pasting someone. We came in south and saw plenty of activity over Brandenburg. We stooged on, fairly unmolested, picking up a railway line to follow it to the target. Over the centre of Berlin, with the Wilhelmstrasse plainly visible, suddenly – ching! A wandering master searchlight found us and immediately thirty more coned and caught us perfectly. It was as bright as daylight in the cockpit and we were completely blinded. We bombed and then began weaving round and round and up and down to lose them but still they stuck fast and then the apex, with us in it, was filled with all the heavy flak that they could put up. We could see the yellow bursts everywhere with red-hot shrapnel, the puffs lit up by searchlights and the concussions bumping us all around as the close ones crumped and cracked in our ears, above the roar of the engines. We could not get out. After what seemed like hours we cleared and got out south. We had been thoroughly pasted and it scared all of us more than any of us had been scared before![27]

After the raid on Brest on the night of 10/11 April, when the port was attacked by 53 aircraft, it was determined that four bombs had hit the *Gneisenau* and there were two near-misses. Extensive damage was done to the gunnery and damage-control rooms and to the living quarters, and 50 Germans were killed and 90 injured. The *Scharnhorst* was not hit but her refitting was delayed by the damage to dock facilities. One Wellington crashed off Brest and the crew were lost. Five Hampdens failed to return from an operation on Düsseldorf by 29 Hampdens and 24 Whitleys and one Wellington was lost from the 11 Wimpys that attacked Bordeaux-Mérignac airfield. It was Brest again on 12/13 April, when 60 aircraft were dispatched but conditions were poor and only 37 aircraft bombed. Most of the others dropped their bombs on Lorient as an alternative. Ninety-four aircraft were sent to Brest two nights' later but again bombing was poor because of cloud. All the bombers returned safely.

On the night of 15/16 April when 96 aircraft were detailed to bomb Kiel again, just over half the number was made up of Wellingtons, with 21 Whitleys and 19 Hampdens and five Halifaxes on 35 Squadron and two Stirlings completing the rest of the attacking force. Five Hampdens laid mines off Brest without loss and 23 neophyte crews flying Whitleys were given the docks at Boulogne in a separate operation. One of the Whitleys failed to return when it was shot down and crashed at Bourthes with the loss of all five crew. Cloud prevented accurate bombing at Kiel, which reported only light damage compared to recent raids. One Wellington was shot down at Kiel-Holtenau with all six crew killed. Flight Sergeant (later Squadron Leader) Wallace Ivor 'Wally' Lashbrook on 35 Squadron, piloting Halifax *G-George* lost his hydraulics over Hamburg. He recalled:

The starboard undercarriage fell down on of its own accord and so we were late back to Linton-on-Ouse and very short of fuel. Thankful to be home, I was not best pleased therefore when they switched off the runway lights just as we made our approach, thinking that we were an enemy intruder. We overshot the approach but ran out of fuel before we could line-up with the runway again. I was therefore committed to landing straight ahead. It was very dark, but when it got really black I just pulled back on the stick and hoped for the best. We were doing all right until we hit a tree, which brought us to a very abrupt stop. I scrambled out of the top hatch, but immediately fell ten feet to the ground as I hadn't realised that the fuselage had broken off right behind the cockpit. In fact the aircraft had broken into five pieces, most of it wrapped around this large tree. The rest of the crew were alive, but two were not in very good shape so I set off to look for help. It was still pitch black and almost straight away I walked into a large drainage ditch – up to my neck. I eventually reached a cottage, but had considerable difficulty persuading the owner that I was not a German (probably my Scots accent). I managed to convince him however to ring the Station for help. It later transpired that the ambulance had turned over on the way to the scene of the crash! Still soaking wet, all I could borrow from Sick Quarters when I eventually got there was a plain airman's blue uniform with no wings or rank badges, but it was at least dry and warm. But my warm feeling was soon shattered when I got home where my wife, seeing the plain uniform, simply wouldn't believe that I hadn't been stripped of rank and wings for some dreadful and degrading misdemeanour. It was not my best day in the war.

The aircraft had come down near Tollerton village. The navigator and the tail gunner were slightly injured with the rest of the crew escaping relatively unharmed.

A follow-up raid on Berlin by 118 aircraft on 17/18 April was largely thwarted by haze over the two aiming points. Eight aircraft failed to return from the Berlin operation and two Wellingtons were lost from the ten that set out to bomb Cologne. Five of the aircraft that were lost were Whitleys, three of them on 77 Squadron at Topcliffe, one of whose crew ditched 60 miles off Blyth in Northumberland. They and a 58 Squadron crew that also came down in the North Sea were both rescued. A Wellington crashed near Combe Martin in Devon returning from Berlin.

This was the largest total lost on night operations so far in the war but raids on the German capital and other cities were having an effect. In Berlin deep shelters away from buildings and water mains were being hastily constructed. The Unter-den-Linden district in the heart of the German capital was suffering severe damage and the Opera House, the War Museum (which contained the death mask of Hindenburg) and the old Royal Stables had been hit.

Repeated attacks were made on the *Scharnhorst* and *Gneisenau* throughout April. On 10/11 April, 53 bombers – 36 Wellingtons, 12 Blenheims and five Manchesters, headed for Brest to try and finish off the *Gneisenau* which had been recently damaged by a Coastal Command torpedo bomber. Four hits were claimed on the *Gneisenau*. Returning crews joked that 'the *Scharnhorst* doesn't look so *Gneisenau*'... but the ships were undamaged. Twenty-nine Hampdens and 24 Whitleys went to bomb Düsseldorf and minor operations were flown to Bordeaux/Mérignac airfield and to Rotterdam. One Wellington failed to return from Brest and five Hampdens were lost on the raid on Düsseldorf.[28] On 12/13 April, 66 aircraft including 35 Wellingtons returned to Brest. Only 37 aircraft bombed in poor cloud conditions and most other aircraft bombed Lorient as an alternative target. There were no losses. Two nights later 94 aircraft including 46 Wellingtons returned to Brest but bombing was again thwarted by cloud and the results were poor. Cloud also interfered with the bombing of Kiel on 15/16 April which was raided by 96 aircraft, 49 of them Wimpys.

The Wellington was carrying the lion's share of raids and 75 New Zealand Squadron at Feltwell was one that was often in the thick of things.[29] It took a lot to keep the New Zealanders down. 'Joe' Lawton, an observer, had been in one of the crews trained in the use of mustard gas in the event of an invasion of Britain. Then in September 1940 his Wimpy was hit by a Ju 88 over Boulogne and he was so badly wounded by a 20mm cannon shell that he was totally incapacitated and not expected to live. In April 1941, after hospitalization at the RAF Hospital Ely, Lawton was back again on 'ops' and was 'lucky enough' to be crewed with Squadron Leader Reuben Widdowson, a Canadian RAF pilot who had served on the North West Frontier of India pre-war. Lawton believed that his Skipper's experience was a factor that was to save them all:

> On the Hamburg raid on 10/11 May the sky was still quite light as we set out, avoiding the Friesian Islands and Heligoland and then heading for the Elbe and the target. We were attacked and hit by what we thought to be a Ju 88. An armour-piercing shell penetrated the armour plate in the turret and critically wounded the gunner, Peter Cannaway, from Hawks Bay, in the stomach. The co-pilot, Tony Saunders and I managed to lift him from his turret and lay him on the floor. He was still quite conscious. We gave him an injection of morphine to help him. He died before we could get him back to base.

Three Wellingtons and a Whitley failed to return from the Hamburg raid. One of the Wimpys that was lost on the operation was *B-Beer* on

115 Squadron at Marham, which was piloted by 26-year-old Sergeant
John Anderson. The Australian second pilot, 20-year-old Sergeant Alex
Kerr recalls:

We'd been briefed to attack an aircraft works. We bombed from
about 9,000 feet and were on our way back when some flak hit the
rear turret. Twenty-year-old Sergeant David Fraser the rear gunner
was trying to extinguish the fire but couldn't put it out. The flames
became obvious from the ground and we were caught in score of
searchlights. About 20 lights homed in on us and it was like daylight.
Though we got the turret fire out, a night fighter [*a Bf 110 piloted by
22-year-old* Leutnant *Eckart-Wilhelm 'Hugo' von Bonin of 6./NJG1*] had
come in and lined itself up. He polished us off and some of the
bullets he fired set off the flares inside the aircraft and set the aircraft
on fire. I'd been hit several times, as had my observer Sergeant Bill
Legg and we were both lying on the floor of the aircraft. We were
lucky. The fire had put out the hydraulics on the rear turret and
when the order was given to abandon the aircraft by the captain the
rear gunner was not able to go out sideways as you would normally
do but crawled back inside the aircraft to get out of the hatch. Fraser
saw me lying on the aircraft floor and picked me up, sat me on the
edge of the hatch, put my parachute on, put my hand on the rip-
cord, said 'For God's sake pull it!' and chucked me out. I came
to consciousness enough to pull the cord. We came down by parachute [*Anderson landed in the River Elbe and drowned*] and I was taken
to the nearest PoW hospital, which was staffed entirely by French
prisoners. No one could speak English but there was a Professor of
Surgery there from Strasbourg University, one of the few surgeons
in Europe who was skilled enough to save my life.
    Bill Legg was left inside the aircraft. He came to, looked around,
saw that there was no one else there [*Sergeants Geoff Hogg and Bernard
Morgan the WOp and front gunner respectively, had bailed out safely*],
got up to clip on his parachute, had a dizzy spell and dropped it
through the escape hatch. He was in an aircraft that was on fire with
no parachute. He walked up to the front, saw that there was no pilot
there either and got into the pilot's seat. He decided to end it quickly
and dive straight into the ground but then he had second thoughts
and ended up bringing the aircraft down and landing it in a field
near Tönning in Schleswig–Holstein at about 1 o'clock in the morning,
pitch black, with great skill. He ended up in the same hospital as I
did a month later. He was badly wounded.[30] After nine months in
hospital I was sent to a regular prison camp near Berlin. There were
about 200 prisoners in the camp and I was number 182. When I got
there some of the boys had started on a tunnel. We worked on it for
several months and we got out exactly a year to the day I was shot

down, 10 May 1942. Fifty of us got out – 40 including me – were recaptured and one was shot.

The 10/11 May raid on Hamburg was one of six attacks on the port by Bomber Command that month. The next night three more Wellingtons were lost when Hamburg was attacked by just over 90 aircraft. A separate force of just over 80 Hampdens attacked Bremen and Squadron Leader C G C Rawlins DFC and crew on 144 Squadron at Hemswell fell to *Oberleutnant* Helmut Woltersdorf of 4./NJG1 and crashed at Medemblik on the west shore of the Ijsselmeer. Rawlins and one of his four crew survived.

Throughout that spring, summer and autumn Bomber Command operated mainly against Bremen, Cologne, Kiel, Münster and Mannheim. Flight Sergeant George P Dove, an air gunner on 10 Squadron recalls:

> We were at RAF Leeming in 1941 with Whitley Vs and were briefed that if our primary or secondary targets could not be found, any target of opportunity could be bombed. Despite the good met forecast, we found ourselves in 10/10ths cloud and any hope of finding either target was soon dashed. After sniffing around for an hour looking for a break, the Skipper called up and said 'that's it; we'll head North West over Holland and home'. The thick cloud persisted until we were well over Holland when it suddenly cleared and there, right ahead of us, was an airfield fully lit-up, with aircraft circling with nav lights on. The navigator said it was Schiphol and it was the *Luftwaffe* doing circuits and bumps. It was at this point that our pilot, who was a pre-war regular and very much a press-on type, decided to switch on our nav lights and join the circuit. Picture a Whitley in the circuit with assorted *Luftwaffe* aircraft over a German airfield. We must have arrived towards the end of the night's exercise because one by one the aircraft landed until we were the only one left in the circuit. The runway controller was flashing us a persistent green to come in. The pilot called on the intercom, 'I am going to do a long downwind leg, then come back over the hangars low and fast. Navigator, drop the bombs on the hangars and rear gunner spray the airfield as we pass.' As we sped out to sea, I gave a running commentary on what was happening. All the lights went out at once, bursts of flak, searchlights and red flares – all too late, we were well on our way home.

On the night of 2/3 June the target was Düsseldorf. Cloud conditions prevented accurate bombing and only 107 aircraft out of the 150 bombers dispatched claimed to have bombed. Two Hampdens and a Whitley were lost. Squadron Leader Fred J 'Popeye' Lucas from South Otago, a

Wellington pilot and 'A Flight' commander on 75 New Zealand Squadron, did not remember feeling 'superstitious' about the start of a second operational tour but there were times in the trip when he thought that they were going to provide another statistic. It was probably one of the worst he experienced in over 81 night operations over Germany. He had completed his first tour of operations, having done 37, on 23/24 September 1940 on the operation to Berlin and had then been posted to an OTU at Hampstead Norris. His facial resemblance to the famous cartoon character 'Popeye' became even more pronounced when he removed his false teeth. His gumminess was the legacy of his determination to become a pilot after being turned down by the RNZAF because of his poor educational background. Undaunted, 'Popeye' Lucas had sailed to England as a deck hand and the RAF accepted him on condition that he had his teeth fixed.[31]

After his return from Düsseldorf, to his log-book entry he added the words:

'Thirty-four holes in aircraft – a write off.' At the target, all hell was let loose on our first run in. We were thrown all over the place and my navigator, Dave Florence, said, 'It's a dummy run – go round again.' The second run was just as bad but we got our bombs away before something hit us with a terrific 'whammm' followed by a further 'whumff, whumpp' after which we couldn't close the bomb doors. It was like an inferno; the Wellington was taking hits from all sides, with shell flashes and tracer zipping by and searchlights probing everywhere. The port motor was struck and started a fire, which luckily, went out. Our hydraulics were shot away and the red light showed the undercarriage was down. I leaned forward to adjust the gyro compass and at the same instant heard an eerie 'sw-i-i-sh' behind my neck, followed by a rush of cold air. A lump of shrapnel the size of a fist, sliced through where my neck had lately been and exited through the other window. Something plucked at my sleeve and I turned to see what my second pilot, Tim Williams, of Hawkes Bay, otherwise known as 'Scruffy', wanted but it was more shrapnel passing through the sleeve on my overall.

The Wellington made it across the Dutch coast and to England where Lucas was told to divert to Newmarket because Feltwell had just been bombed. The port engine was virtually seized up and fuel critically low. With the fuel gauges reading zero 'Popeye' Lucas prepared to run straight in for a landing on the long grass runway at Newmarket Heath but control told him to go round again because they had a Stirling coming in on three engines and it had priority. 'Lucky bastard' Lucas retorted; 'We've only got one.' It fell on deaf ears. Fortunately 'Popeye' Lucas was familiar with the airfield and could find a place in the dark, well away from the flare path where he could get down – quickly. His Wellington floated interminably until at last, as their remaining engine finally cut, he touched down. A few minutes later Control came on again: 'You are free to land now.'

> As we lounged on our parachutes under the wing of the aircraft, waiting for transport, 'Scruffy' Williams whose first trip this had been, was lying relaxed on the damp grass, his head on his parachute, chewing a blade of grass. 'Gee' he mused. 'If all the trips are like this one, it won't be so bad...'

On the 10/11 June the first major operation for more than a week was mounted when 100 aircraft set out to attack the *Scharnhorst* and the *Gneisenau* at Brest where they had now been joined by the 10,000-ton heavy cruiser *Prinz Eugen*. Many bombs fell in the dock area but there were no hits on the warships. No aircraft were lost. A return visit was made to Düsseldorf the next night by 92 Wellingtons and six Stirlings, when six Wellingtons were lost and attacks were also made on Duisburg and Boulogne. On the night of 12/13 June, 227 Wellingtons and Whitleys were dispatched to bomb railway yards at Schwerte, Hamm and Osnabrück. Included in the attack on Schwerte were four Wellingtons of 405 'Vancouver' Squadron, the first of the Canadian squadrons in Bomber Command. Ninety-one Hampdens were to bomb the railway yards at Soest and eleven Halifaxes and seven Stirlings the Chemische Werke, a chemical and synthetic rubber plant at Hüls on the edge of the Ruhr. This plant west of Duisburg near Recklinghausen accounted for approximately 29 per cent of Germany's synthetic rubber and 18 per cent of its total rubber supply. Fires were started in the target area and all the aircraft returned, though a 35 Squadron Halifax overshot the runway landing back at Linton-on-Ouse. At Soest and Schwerte only about 40 aircraft in each raid actually bombed the primary targets. Five aircraft were lost and a Whitley on 102 Squadron crashed at Topcliffe on the return. At Hamm the bombing was better and there were no losses, though a Wellington on 115 Squadron crashed on the approach to Marham. Another Wellington crashed returning from the operation on Osnabrück where 'good' bombing was also claimed and one Wimpy was shot down over Holland.

The following night it was the turn of 36 Whitleys and six Wellingtons to set out for the railway yards at Schwerte but they could not locate the target so the town was bombed instead. A Whitley on 102 Squadron was shot down and all the crew were killed. Another 110 aircraft that were detailed to bomb the *Scharnhorst*, *Gneisenau* and *Prinz Eugen* at Brest again were thwarted by haze and smoke-screens and no hits were observed. Twenty-nine Hampdens bombed Cologne on the night of

14/15 June. The target was cloud-covered and only light damage was reported. The following night Hannover and railway targets in Cologne and Düsseldorf were attacked. Only about four bomb loads were reported to have hit the target at Cologne, which was poor reward for the 90 aircraft dispatched. A Hampden failed to return and two Whitleys were shot down on the raid on Hannover. The night following it was Cologne and Düsseldorf again and Duisburg and Boulogne were also attacked by small numbers of Wellingtons. Just 55 high-explosive bombs and 300 incendiaries fell on Cologne and damage was scattered. Only 58 aircraft claimed to have bombed Düsseldorf. For 223 total sorties, four aircraft including a Wellington that failed to return from a raid on Duisburg, were lost.

On 18/19 June, 100 aircraft went to Bremen and 57 Wellingtons and eight Stirlings went to Brest where haze and smoke-screens prevented identification of warship targets. Low cloud hindered the attack at Bremen and three Whitleys and three Wellingtons failed to return. Pilot Officer Forman on 149 Squadron had to nurse his Wimpy back with the hydraulics badly damaged. He then decided to circle until daylight. When fuel was low he decided to land but two other aircraft turned onto approach ahead of him. He had to belly land at RAF Lakenheath, which was not yet in operation. 149 Squadron continued to play a full part in the bombing campaign throughout 1941 and it was also chosen to participate in the making of *Target for Tonight* by Harry Watts, which was filmed by the Crown Film Unit. It featured the Wellington *F-Freddie* flown by Flight Lieutenant Percy Pickard who took the 'leading roles', and for a short time Mildenhall was like a film set.[32] The *F-Freddie* that appeared in the film had never actually taken part in an operation against the enemy. The original Wimpy had been wrecked when it ran into the earth bank of the bomb dump at Mildenhall when returning from a raid.

On 26/27 June when Bomber Command raided Cologne, Kiel and Düsseldorf weather conditions were appalling and prevented good bombing. Two Wellingtons and two Manchesters were lost. One of the Manchesters was a 97 Squadron aircraft at Coningsby piloted by Flying Officer Frank Eustace DFC, the New Zealand pilot who in the autumn of 1940 had been hit in the head by a seagull that had smashed through the cockpit window. He and his crew were killed when the Manchester crashed off Westerhever. Everyone on board the other Manchester, a 61 Squadron aircraft from Hemswell piloted by Flying Officer Kenneth Gordon Webb, was killed when their aircraft crashed near Brünsbuttel. Flight Lieutenant John Price, Wellington tail gunner on 150 Squadron recalls:

On this raid the weather closed in completely; cloud cover was 10/10ths. The cumulonimbus (thunderclouds) where winds inside the turbulence can easily exceed 200mph towered to over 35,000 feet.

To me it was unbelievable, the terrible turbulence encountered in those storm centres can only be seen by an airman and I have actually been through them. You see the lightning (in close contact) it envelopes your aircraft with a sheet of blinding white light, millions of volts of electricity. If you are lucky the riggers have welded all your weak spots together, the metal is bonded together and (hopefully) it is earthed. The next step for the unfortunate pilot is how to control an aircraft that is thrown about like a butterfly in a high wind. We weighed about ten tons but no pilot on earth could fly in these conditions. We were turned upside down and thrown about like a leaf in a winter storm, leaving it all to fate and destiny. Our pilot managed to obtain a lower altitude. Then by rotating my turret 180° I saw ice forming quickly on the wings. I spoke to the captain, warning him of the danger. Even at a lower altitude our de-icers were not good enough to avoid an eventual ditching into the North Sea. At about 7,000 feet and out of those terrible cumulus towers of hail, ice and winds I sighed with relief as great chunks of ice broke off from the wings and blown away by our airspeed sailed past my rear turret. It was far worse than facing the flak and German night fighters. Nature can throw better weapons at you than the enemy! We still had bombs on board, had used up most of our fuel and having escaped by a sheer miracle the terror of electrical storms and the icing etc, we decided to go home, cruising at about 7,000 feet above the cold grey North Sea. Our first priority now was to get rid of the bombs, so we dropped them on or near Texel. We knew that German night fighters were nearby. Going home was a very strange and frightening experience to me.

On 27/28 June when 73 Wellingtons and 35 Whitleys set out for Bremen they encountered storms, icing conditions and intense night fighter activity. Sergeant Brian Booth, rear gunner on a Whitley V on 102 Squadron, recalled:

We set off from Topcliffe with the 'met' officer forecasting good weather conditions on the way. As it turned out we ran into an unpleasant front as we approached the enemy coast. This gave icing conditions at about 8,000 feet, which meant that we were unable to climb above or into cloud and were 'stooging' along, beautifully silhouetted against the cloud – a sitting duck. It was not long before we were caught in the cones of searchlights and a fighter came straight in. That was the end; smoke and the smell of cordite and the old Whitley flying at all angles, even upside down! Fortunately, Jimmy Cullen our pilot was an experienced Skipper and he did a great job getting the old kite to fly straight and level long enough for us all to get out by parachute. There were no serious injuries apart from poor old Mike Featherstone, the second pilot, who got a bullet in his bum.[33]

Their attacker was 23-year-old *Oberleutnant* Helmut *'Bubi'* ('Nipper') Lent, *Staffelkapitän* 6./NJG1. Lent, who had entered the *Luftwaffe* in 1936 as an officer cadet and trainee pilot, was born into a Prussian family of profound religious faith and believed that his God protected him in combat. It was said that he mouthed a prayer for his victims each time a bomber fell to his guns.[34] He had become a national hero after the air battle of 18 December 1939 when, flying a Bf 110C-1 *Zerstörer* in 3./ZG76, he had claimed three Wellingtons destroyed. His seven *Zerstörer* victories marked him out as an outstanding pilot and Lent scored his first night victories on 11/12 May when he destroyed two Wellington Ics on 40 Squadron during the raid by 92 aircraft on Hamburg. Lent was destined to rise to command of NJG3 and to score an incredible final total of 113 victories, including 105 Bomber Command aircraft. Another *Experten*, *Oberleutnant* Reinhold Eckardt of 6./NJG1, destroyed four bombers in 46 minutes, including Whitley V Z6647 of 77 Squadron, which crashed at Dollern, during a *Helle Nachtjagd* sortie in the Hamburg area where five bombers fell to night fighters. A total of 11 Whitleys, including four on 10 Squadron at Leeming, were lost and three Wellingtons also failed to return; the heaviest night loss of the war so far. One of the three Whitleys on 77 Squadron that were lost ditched in the sea 10 miles east of Flamborough Head and the crew was rescued although the pilot died later, on 29 June. Many of the bombers that had won through to the target bombed Hamburg 50 miles away by mistake. Twenty-eight Hampdens that attacked the *U-boat* construction yards at Vegesack returned with no losses.

Next day cloud cover was forecast over the North Sea and Germany so sneak daylight attacks on Comines and Bremen by Blenheims and a raid on Bremerhaven by six Stirlings of 7 and XV Squadrons were briefed. Neither the Bremen and Bremerhaven raiders reached their targets and a Stirling of 7 Squadron was shot down into the sea, 20 miles off Flamborough Head, by Bf 109s of I./JG52. There were no survivors. On 29/30 June, 106 aircraft returned to Bremen and another 28 aircraft – 13 Stirlings, six Manchesters, two Halifaxes and seven Wellingtons – went to Hamburg where they caused considerable damage. Sixty-nine aircraft claimed to have bombed Bremen with good results. Five bombers were shot down, three of them Wellingtons. A fourth Wellington was ditched in the North Sea 40 miles off Grimsby by its Polish crew who were rescued. At Hamburg three of the six bombers that failed to return were shot down over the target by night fighters,[35] and a Wellington crash-landed at Manby airfield in Lincolnshire on the return.

Further raids were made on the Ruhr, Brest, Bremen, Cologne, Duisburg and Essen. Münster, an important railway junction and garrison town, which had not been attacked for five months, was bombed five nights running from 6 to 10 July. It was twice set on fire from end to end and the Germans called it 'the unhappy town'. On the 5/6 July raid 65 Wellingtons and 29 Whitleys were dispatched. Crews reported a successful raid in good visibility and only light defences at the target. One Whitley was lost. Sergeant Hanlon on 149 Squadron was on his bomb run when *F-Freddie*'s port engine became troublesome. He had almost reached base when the propeller began to wobble and then fell off. That same night, three Hampdens failed to return from the 39 that set out for Osnabrück where good bombing was reported. All 33 Wellingtons that went to Bielefeld returned safely and they also returned with reports of good bombing.

On 6/7 July, 88 Hampdens and 21 Wellingtons returned to Brest where smoke screens concealed the warships. A Hampden and a Wellington were shot down. Forty-seven Wellingtons returned to Münster, where crews claimed many fires in the target area. A 40 Squadron Wellington from Alconbury, flown by Pilot Officer John Edwin MacKenzie Steeds, a New Zealander, crashed off Texel with the loss of all the crew, while a 115 Squadron Wimpy piloted by Sergeant Oswald Arthur Matthews RNZAF crashed in the North Sea. All six crew perished. Two Whitleys failed to return from the raid on Dortmund by 31 Whitleys and 15 Wellingtons. Haze was present over the target but fires were claimed.

At Waterbeach, six miles northeast of Cambridge, Flight Lieutenant Eric Masters, a Wellington pilot on 99 Squadron, had completed 29 ops. On 7 July his 30th and final operation of his tour would be a sortie to Cologne. Masters was philosophical about it. 'Our losses were running at approximately five per cent so one believed one was living on luck after the 20th trip. One was just as likely to "buy it" on the first as on the 30th.' Just over 100 Wellingtons were dispatched to Cologne, 50 Wimpys to Münster and 40 Hampdens were given Mönchengladbach as their target. At Osnabrück 54 Whitleys and 18 Wellingtons attacked the railway yards and claimed 'good' results. Three Whitleys, including one which crashed off Flamborough Head with the loss of all the crew, failed to return. Two Hampdens failed to return from the raid on Mönchengladbach. Three Wellingtons were lost on the operation on Münster and a Halifax was shot down on the minor operation on Frankfurt by 14 Halifaxes and three Stirlings. At Cologne, Wellington crews reported perfect weather and good bombing. A 9 Squadron Wellington flown by 26-year-old New Zealander, Pilot Officer Douglas James Jamieson, crashed near Maastricht killing all six crew. Flying Officer Reginald Maurice Peter Jenkyns and his crew on 214 Squadron at Stradishall also died, their Wellington crashing at Genk-Boden in Belgium.

All had gone well aboard Masters' Wellington crew until they approached the Rhine:

Pilot Officer Don Elliott, my Canadian navigator, came to stand beside me. There were two areas of AA activity ahead and I decided to head between them so that Elliott could pick out the river reflecting the moonlight from the south and from his map would be able to place us exactly. We discovered we were just south of Cologne. I wanted to get a really good run at the target and needed to get north of the city. There was no need for navigation now and having passed over the river I turned north and flew past Cologne on its eastern side watching the flak exploding, flares dropping, flash bombs illuminating huge areas and bombs bursting. I felt remote from it all. North of Cologne I turned over the river and headed south. Elliott was now in the prone bomb aiming position, just below and in front of me, getting a very clear view of the river and giving me course corrections to keep us in line with the target. The activity over the target had practically ceased and it became very peaceful. One of the gunners remarked 'Everyone else seems to have gone home Skipper.'

In these last minutes I had kept straight and level and at the same speed for much too long. The Germans must have wondered about this crazy lone raider. We were caught in the bluish-white beam of a master searchlight. Six more standard searchlights coned us. Now the whole fury of the Cologne defences concentrated on us. I increased speed, still heading for the target. The flak followed us expertly, throwing the aircraft about. Pilot Officer Johnny Agrell the second pilot, who was watching it all at the astrodome ready to deal with the flash-bomb, called out that we had been hit. I had felt a judder in the control column and then found it rigid in the fore and aft direction (elevator control). As I had been holding it in the dive I was now unable to bring the nose up.

The flak was still after us. I told Don to jettison the bombs (live) in a last hope to get the nose up but when this failed I realised we were virtually out of control at 10,000 feet and losing height rapidly. I had no alternative but to give the order, 'Bail out!' I was thankful my chest parachute pack was in its storage position. At times I had been known to forget to take it on a trip and I had delegated Don Elliott to make sure it was always on the 'tumbril'. I was glad that on this occasion he had not let me down.

Eric Masters and his crew bailed out, were captured and marched off into captivity.

Squadron Leader Reuben Widdowson, one of the 75 Squadron RNZAF crews that attacked Münster was fortunate to return. Joe Lawton, his observer, recalls. 'Tony Saunders had by now left our crew and been replaced by Sergeant Jim Ward who came from Wanganui.[36] He was thus the co-pilot with Ben Widdowson on this trip. The attack was successful and I was able to take good photographs of the target area.'

Crossing the Zuider Zee on the way home a Bf 110 night fighter attacked from dead astern and hit the starboard engine and put the hydraulic system out of action, with the result that the undercarriage fell half down. The bomb doors fell open too, the wireless sets were put out of action and the front gunner was wounded in the foot. Alan Box, rear gunner, hit the attacker, who according to *Luftwaffe* records, force-landed on the island of Texel in the Frisians. Worst of all a fire started burning up through the upper surface of the Wellington's starboard wing where a petrol feed pipe had been split open. The fire became intense and the crew put on their parachutes and prepared to bail out. Some got going with the fire extinguisher, bursting a hole in the side of the fuselage so that they could get at the wing but the fire was too far out along the wing for them to do any good. They tried throwing coffee from their flasks at it but that did not work either. By this time the Wellington had reached the Dutch coast and was flying along parallel with it, the crew waiting to see how the fire was going to develop. Finally Sergeant Ward thought there was a sporting chance of reaching the fire by getting out through the astrodome, then down the side of the fuselage and out on to the wing. He planned to take a canvas cockpit cover, cram it in the hole in the wing and perhaps block the fuel spilling out of the feed pipe. His courage was to earn the VC.

Ward recalls:

Joe said he thought it was crazy. There was a rope there; just the normal length of rope attached to the rubber dinghy to stop it drifting away from the aircraft when it's released on the water. We tied that round my chest and I climbed up through the astrodome. I still had my parachute on. I wanted to take it off because I thought it would get in the way but they wouldn't let me. I sat on the edge of the astrodome for a bit with my legs still inside, working out how I was going to do it. Then I reached out with one foot and kicked a hole in the fabric so that I could get my foot into the framework of the plane. I punched another hole through the fabric in front of me to get a handhold, after which I made further holes and went down the side of the fuselage on to the wing. Joe was holding on to the rope so that I wouldn't sort of drop straight off.

I went out three or four feet along the wing. The fire was burning up through the wing rather like a big gas jet and it was blowing back just past my shoulder. I had only one hand to work with getting out, because I was holding on with the other to the cockpit cover. I never realized before how bulky a cockpit cover was. The wind kept catching it and several times nearly blew it away and me with it. I kept bunching it under my arm. Then out it would blow again. All the time, of course, I was lying as flat as I could on the wing but I couldn't get right down close because of the parachute in front of me on my chest. The wind kept lifting me off the wing. Once it slapped me back on to the fuselage again but I managed to hang on. The slipstream from the engine made things worse. It was like being in a terrific gale, only much worse than any gale I've ever known in my life. I can't explain it but there was no sort of real sensation of danger out there at all. It was just a matter of doing one thing after another and that's about all there was to it. I tried stuffing the cockpit cover down through the hole in the wing on to the pipe where the fire was starting from but as soon as I took my hand away, the terrific draught blew it out again and finally it blew away altogether. The rear gunner told me afterwards that he saw it go sailing past his turret. I just couldn't hold on to it any longer. After that there was nothing to do but to get back again. I worked my way back along the wing and managed to haul myself up on to the top of the fuselage and got to sitting on the edge of the astrodome again. Joe kept the dinghy rope taut all the time and that helped. By the time I got back I was absolutely done in. I got partly back into the astro hatch but I just couldn't get my right foot inside. I just sort of sat there looking at it until Joe reached out and pulled it in for me. After that, when I got inside, I just fell straight on to the bunk and stayed there for a time.

Just when they were within reach of the English coast the fire on the wing suddenly blazed up again. Some petrol that had formed a pool inside the lower surface of the wing had caught fire. However, after this final flare-up the fire died right out much to the relief of all the crew. As Joe Lawton had given Widdowson a magnetic course to steer back to base before going to help Ward he had not had another chance to confirm their position. However, they were soon able to obtain a visual as they approached the English coast. By this time the wireless operator had contacted Feltwell and had been given a course to steer. Because of the damage they were instructed to go directly to Newmarket Heath where the grass runway was long enough to land the aircraft without flaps or brakes. The crew pumped the wheels down with the emergency gear and Widdowson decided that instead of going to Feltwell he would try to land at Newmarket, which had a far greater landing space. As he circled before landing he called up the control and said, 'We've been badly shot up. I hope we shan't mess up your flare-path too badly when we land.' He put the aircraft down beautifully but the Wellington ended up running into a barbed-wire entanglement. Fortunately nobody was hurt.[37]

Squadron Leader Ray Glass DFC a pilot on 214 Squadron was one of 57 Wellington crews dispatched to Osnabrück on 9/10 July, in a Merlin engined Wellington II:

We carried a 4,000lb 'Dustbin' bomb. In a Wimpy the bomb doors and floor were removed and the bomb attached by a 1-inch wire hawser and toggle to a metal beam introduced under the main spar. An axe was supplied to cut the hawser in case it hung up. So much for technology! We reached the Zuider Zee but with a full moon silhouetting us from above and below we were a sitting target. We were attacked by a Me 109 and 110, which were beaten off by the rear gunner who claimed the 110 as a 'probable'. Our port engine was hit so we bombed Bergen airfield and observed a huge smoke ring of debris and the runway lights went out.[38]

In the summer of 1941 ground trials of the new radar navigational aid *Gee*[39] were in progress at Marham, Norfolk. Twelve pilots and a dozen observers on 115 and 218 Squadrons were involved in the trials. They were informed that they would be off operational flying until these were completed but on Sunday 13 July they were notified of briefing for a 'maximum' effort attack by 69 Wellingtons, 47 of which were targeted on Bremen, 20 on Vegesack and two on Emden. Sixteen aircraft would claim to have bombed Bremen, from which two Wellingtons would fail to return.[40] On 115 Squadron the all-sergeant crew on the Wellington Ic captained by W J Reid were short of their regular second pilot, who had been sent to London to attend a Commission Board, and 27-year-old Sergeant-pilot Frederick Birkett Tipper, who was regarded as a jinx on the Squadron, took his place. The crew that he had flown with on his first sortie had suffered a very 'shaky do'. On his second operation the aircraft had crashed on take-off, fortunately with no fatal result. Bremen would be Tipper's third operational flight. When he boarded the aircraft Geoff Buckingham, observer, found to his intense annoyance that the floor tracks for his observer's chair, which allowed it to move backwards and forwards, were broken, leaving it free to slide all over the place in the event of violent evasive action. Furthermore, the chair cushion was missing. Instead of throwing his parachute pack on the bed as he usually did he would have to sit on it in lieu of the cushion. Little did he realize that before the night was out the object of his annoyance would save his life.

The sky was clear in England but over the North Sea thick cloud and icing was encountered. As they approached the enemy coastline there was a partial thinning of the cloud and Tipper was able to pass a pinpoint on the Dutch Coast to Buckingham. Buckingham then left the cockpit and made his way aft to the astrodome where he would keep a constant vigil for night fighters. The Wellington was now at 9,000 feet.

Buckingham had just spotted Texel Beacon and was returning to this station from the cockpit when Sergeant T W Oliver in the rear turret yelled over the intercom, 'Fighter!' Simultaneously he opened up with his guns, racking the fuselage with vibration and filling it with cordite fumes. *Oberleutnant* Egmont Prinz zur Lippe-Weissenfeld, the Austrian Prince and *Staffelkapitän*, IV./NJG1 had just made his initial strike, setting the starboard engine of the bomber on fire. He was now somewhere out in the darkness manoeuvring for a second attack. Buckingham rushed forward to the cockpit and pressed the starboard engine fire extinguisher button. This put out the fire. Next he jettisoned the bombs and gave Tipper a reciprocal course to fly. He then returned to the cabin to check his log. At this moment the second attack occurred and it was far more devastating than the first. Cannon fire from beneath the bomber raked the whole length of the fuselage wounding all members of the crew, some more seriously than the others. Buckingham blacked out. When he came round he was lying across the step, adjacent to the forward escape hatch. As the aircraft had gone into a dive, the loose seat, which he had cursed so roundly at the beginning of the flight, had slid to the nose and deposited him on the floor by the escape hatch. His parachute pack, which he had used as a cushion, was lying on top of him.

Buckingham took stock of the situation. The bomber was on fire and he was wounded in face and arm with cannon shrapnel. There was a hole in the back of his leg, which was bleeding profusely. The door to the front turret was wide open. There was no sign of the pilot. Fastening his parachute pack to the harness he found that one J-clip had been smashed by the cannon fire. He used the remaining clip then heaved on the edge of the escape hatch. In an instant he was out and away into the night. Hanging awkwardly beneath his parachute, suspended at an angle by one clip only, he made a bad landing injuring his anklebone. Tipper's body was recovered from the wreckage. It was assumed that the pilot had been killed by the second burst of fire from the night fighter. Later zur Lippe visited the crew in hospital and expressed his regret that a member of the crew had died. He said he was after the bomber not the crew.[41]

Notes

1. On 14/15 March, 101 aircraft returned to Gelsenkirchen and caused much damage to the Hydriewerk Scholven, which was hit by an estimated 16 aircraft bomb loads. Production stopped completely.
2. In RAF terminology the 'milk run' was a regular series of operations to a particular target (like Berlin) and it should not be confused with the American phrase, which signified 'an easy mission'. Brest would be attacked by Bomber Command 34 times from 1 August 1941 to 12 February 1942.

3. See *Out of the Blue: The Role of Luck in Air Warfare 1917–1966* edited by Laddie Lucas (Hutchinson 1985).

4. Airfields in East Anglia became regular targets for German intruders. A Dornier Do 215 made exceptionally low-level attacks on Mildenhall on 30 January 1941 and again on 1/2 February, causing considerable damage to aircraft and buildings. A Dornier returned on 2 February, dropping ten bombs in a shallow dive but no serious damage was done. A Dornier Do 17 flying at 2,500ft attacked the Newmarket satellite again on 3 February. Ten bombs were dropped and two aircraft were damaged in addition to several buildings. Mildenhall's AA guns engaged an intruder on 18 February. No bombs were dropped and the gunners claimed a direct hit. The 24th February saw a further bombing raid and then on 27 February three separate attacks were made by a single Do 215. No bombs were dropped on the first two approaches but 11 were dropped on the third, causing only crater damage. The Mildenhall 'K' site at Cavenham was also attacked on 27 February. 'K' sites were dummy airfields designed to lure enemy aircraft away from their true targets, the flares on the landing paths being positioned closer than usual to give an illusion of greater height. At first obsolete or unserviceable aircraft were left on these fields as decoys but later realistic dummies were specially made for this purpose at the Shepperton Film Studios. The 'K' site at Euston was so realistic that Wellington *U-Uncle* on 149 Squadron once landed there, on a totally unprepared field, when returning short of fuel from a raid. Such sites had served their purpose by 1942 and were then either abandoned or converted to genuine operational stations. The Cavenham site was abandoned but a new airfield, RAF Tuddenham, was opened in 1943 only a few hundred yards from the original dummy site. *Mildenhall: Bombers, Blackbirds and The Boom Years* by Martin W Bowman (Tempus 2007).

5. Adapted from *So Few: The Immortal Record of the Royal Air Force* by David Masters (1941).

6. Adapted from *So Few: The Immortal Record of the Royal Air Force* by David Masters (1941).

7. See *Bomber Crew: Taking on the Reich* by John Sweetman (Little, Brown 2004).

8. KIA 3/4 March 1941.

9. 218 Gold Coast Squadron Assoc Newsletter No. 37 November 2005.

10. 'Taffy' Rearden died trapped in his front turret, which sank beneath the ice on the frozen Ijsselmeer about 17km W of Kempen. Jock Hall was badly injured with his foot almost severed and he had bullet holes in his burned clothing, but surgery at the Queen Wilhelmina hospital in Amsterdam was successful and he survived. Wellington T2702 *H-Harry* was credited to *Hauptmann* Walter Ehle of *Stab* II./NJG1 at Middenmeer, north of Schiphol, for his 5th victory. Ehle

poured 560 rounds of 7mm machine gun and 100 rounds of 20mm cannon into the Wellington. Ehle was KIA on 17/18 November 1943 in a crash at Horpmoel near St-Trond airfield. He had 35 night and four day victories.

11. Each Stirling carried 16 500lb bombs and they dropped a total of 46 500lb bombs (2 hung up).

12. McVie was KIA on the night of 15/16 May 1941 on the operation on Hannover. One other crew member was killed and two were taken prisoner.

13. *Intruders over Britain: The Luftwaffe Night Fighter Offensive 1940 to 1945* by Simon W Parry (ARP 2003). F/O Harold Rogers DFM was KIA on 8/9 April 1943 on 76 Squadron on the operation on Duisburg when he was flying as 2nd dickey to F/O Maurice Alec Stanley Elliott. All 8 crew died.

14. In April 1943 when he was a wireless operator on Walrus sea planes, they rescued a Spitfire pilot who had bailed out 75 miles out to sea. The Walrus could not take off again in the very rough seas and the crew spent 13 hours taxiing until they had to be towed back to land. In 1944 another Spitfire pilot bailed out just off The Hague and Cameron's Walrus was sent to the rescue. Despite very rough sea they landed within 400 yards. To the crew's dismay the 10ft waves made it impossible to reach the dinghy and after repeated efforts they tried to take off to get more help. In the meantime the German shore batteries had opened up so the pilot started to taxi out to sea and smoother water; the crew were afraid that the plane would break up. Spitfires of their own squadron were circling the Walrus but they could do nothing about the shore guns constantly firing at them. A Catalina came out to them and they signalled not to land but the American did. The Walrus crew got into their dinghy and boarded the Catalina and one of the fighters set fire to the Walrus to prevent it falling into enemy hands. The huge seas broke the Perspex panelling of the Catalina as it dipped a float under the sea, half flooding the aircraft. With no food and wet through, the two crews spent a miserable night bailing water. After a seemingly endless night, two naval motor launches arrived from England at 9am, and took most of the crew off. The 'Cat' then taxied to smooth water and took off. They had been at sea 21 hours – mostly under fire. There was so much water in the bottom of the aircraft that there were fish swimming in it. For someone who could not swim, had frost-bitten feet and was on 'non-operational duties' he had the misfortune to spend quite a few hours in and on the water. He was awarded membership of the exclusive Goldfish Club which was for those who had survived by ditching in the sea. Jock Cameron later bailed out of a burning Wellington over Pocklington on 5 November 1949, which also earned him membership of the exclusive Caterpillar Club.

15. *Nachtjagd: The Night Fighter versus Bomber War over the Third Reich 1939–45* by Theo Boiten (Crowood 1997). The Hampden was claimed as destroyed by *Oberleutnant* Herbert Bönsch of I./NJG2 who was flying a Ju 88 and not a Bf 110. Bönsch misidentified the Hampden as a Blenheim.

16. *Maximum Effort* by James Campbell (Futura 1957).

17. Born in Rheydt, the only child of the family, Hahn was killed the following October when, near Grantham, he collided with an Oxford after firing at it. Both pilots in the Oxford also died.

18. *The Bomber Command War Diaries: An Operational reference book 1939–1945.* Martin Middlebrook and Chris Everitt. (Midland 1985).

19. *Night Airwar: Personal recollections of the conflict over Europe, 1939–45* by Theo Boiten (Crowood 1999). *S-Sugar* crashed at Kampstrasse with the loss of all five of Sgt Anthony Leonard Roger Cook's crew.

20. In 1931 F/L J N Boothman, flying Supermarine S.6B S1595, won the Schneider Trophy outright for Britain, setting an average speed of 340.08 mph.

21. A 9 Squadron Wimpy on the Cologne operation crashed at Heusden, Belgium and all six crew were taken into captivity. A 78 Squadron Whitley on the operation on Düsseldorf crashed at Helenaveen, Holland with no survivors. A second Whitley crashed at Cottesmore and a Wellington on 57 Squadron at Feltwell crashed landing at East Wretham on the return from Cologne.

22. S/L John Henry Franks DFC was pilot of a Wellington on 57 Squadron when he was KIA on 29/30 June 1942.

23. RAF 1939–45 Vol. 1 *The Fight At Odds* by Denis Richards. HMSO 1953.

24. 218 Gold Coast Squadron Association Newsletter No. 58, edited by Margery Griffiths.

25. All six on W/C Vyvian Quentery Blackden's crew were killed. F/L Victor Fernley Baker Pike and five of the crew were killed. The Stirling crashed near Lingen, Germany. The sole survivor was taken prisoner.

26. Three Wellingtons – including a 9 Squadron aircraft – one Stirling and a Whitley were lost.

27. See *Out of the Blue: The Role of Luck in Air Warfare 1917–1966* edited by Laddie Lucas (Hutchinson 1985). Three months later, on 8/9 July 1941 WS-S T2973 was lost with Sgt Bernard George Pitt and all crew on the raid on Münster. The Wimpy had completed 35 operations.

28. Two were shot down by *Hauptmann* Werner Streib of *Stab* I./NJG1 and 1 by *Oberfeldwebel* Gerhard Herzog of 2./NJG1. *Leutnant* Hermann Reese of 2./NJG1 and *Leutnant* Hans-Dieter Frank of *Stab* I./NJG1 claimed the other 2. Frank had joined the *Luftwaffe* in 1937 and was introduced to night fighting in the spring of 1941. By mid-1942 he was a *Hauptmann* and *Staffelkapitän* 2 *Staffel* NJG1 flying He 219s.

Awarded *Ritterkreuz* on 20 June 1943, two nights later (21/22 June) he claimed six bombers destroyed. On 1 July 1943 he became *Kommandeur* I./NJG1.

29. On 1 June 1939, 1 RNZAF Unit had begun forming at Marham to fly Wellingtons. A decision had been taken early in 1937 that the New Zealanders would have a complement of 30 Wellingtons, six of which would be ready to leave for the antipodes in August 1939. When war clouds gathered the New Zealanders were put at the disposal of the RAF and the unit moved to RAF Harwell where it became 15 OTU.

30. Bill Legg was operated on several times by a fellow prisoner, Dr Chatenay, a young French doctor who had access to only limited medical supplies. Legg was repatriated in October 1943 under an exchange of PoWs with the Germans. In August 1944 he recommenced flying duties as an instructor.

31. *3 Group Bomber Command: An Operational Record* by Chris Ward & Steve Smith. (Pen & Sword 2008).

32. Pickard and his crew of Wellington Ic R3200 LN-O were hit by flak over the area of the Ruhr on the night of 19/20 June 1940 and they were forced to ditch 30 miles off Great Yarmouth. The crew were eventually rescued after 13 hours in their dinghy, which at one stage drifted into a coastal minefield.

33. From *It's Suicide but it's Fun* by Chris Goss. All the crew were taken prisoner.

34. *The Lent Papers* by Peter Hinchliffe (Cerberus 2003).

35. Four Stirlings and two Wellingtons were lost. *Oberleutnant* Helmut Lent destroyed Stirling Is N3664 and N6001 of 7 Squadron with the loss of all 14 crew. Apart from these two Stirling claims by Lent, *Nachtjäger* destroyed eight other bombers on the continent on 29/30 June. On 1 July Lent took command of the *4th Staffel* at Leeuwarden and during the month he claimed seven kills to take his score to 20 victories.

36. Ward, who was born of English parents, had arrived at Feltwell on 13 June and had flown a number of operations with experienced crews.

37. Ben Widdowson received an immediate DFC. Lawton says that it was fair to say that but for his great experience, the Wellington would probably have crashed on landing and very likely killed them all. Alan Box got a DFM for his part in shooting down the night fighter. Jim Ward was KIA on 15/16 September 1941, shot down in a 75 Squadron Wellington over Hamburg on his second trip.

38. 2 FTR. 82 a/c bombed Aachen, 1 Hampden and 1 Whitley FTR. Three crews of NJG1 claimed 3 of these losses.

39. A navigational and blind-bombing device, which was introduced into RAF service during August 1941. It consisted of the reception by

equipment in the aircraft of transmission from a 'master' (A) and two 'slave' stations (B & C) situated on a base line about 200 miles long. The difference in the time taken by the 'A' & 'B' and 'A' & 'C' signals to reach the aircraft were measured and displayed on a CRT on the navigator's table in the aircraft. From then on the aircraft could be located on two position lines known as *Gee* co-ordinates. Accuracy of a *Gee* fix varied from less than 0.5 miles to about 5 miles, depending on the skill of the navigator and the strength of the signal. *Gee* range varied with the conditions from 300–400 miles.

40. The starboard engine of a Wellington Ic of 75 Squadron flown by Sgt F T Minikin cut as the bomber crossed the coast at 6,000ft and the aircraft crashed in the sea near Corton, 2 miles N of Lowestoft. Both pilots, who were injured, were picked up. The others were KIA.

41. R1502 had crashed at Onderdijk, 5km south of Medemblik. Reid, M B Wallis, wireless operator and M G Dunne, the front gunner, survived.

CHAPTER 4

Fighting Fire With Fire

At the end of the runway
The WAAF corporal lingers,
Nervously threading
A scarf through her fingers

Husband? Or lover?
Or friend for a night?
Her face doesn't tell
In the dim evening light.

The Squadron is airborne,
But still the WAAF lingers,
Nervously threading
A scarf through her fingers.

Ronald A M Ransom

'You will direct the main effort of the bomber force, until further instructions, towards dislocating the German transportation system and to destroying the morale of the civil population as a whole and of the industrial workers in particular.' In these words Air Marshal Sir Richard Peirse, Commander-in-Chief of Bomber Command, was instructed on 9 July 1941 to open a new phase of the air offensive against Germany. Peirse was the son of an admiral and had fought with conspicuous gallantry in the First World War. He had held several colonial commands during the inter-war years before heading up the intelligence section of the RAF and becoming Deputy Chief of the Air Staff in 1938. The choice of German transportation as the main objective of the bomber force and German morale as the secondary was a confession of failure. In January 1941 Peirse had been instructed that the primary aim of the bombing offensive should be the destruction of the German synthetic oil plants. The only diversions contemplated from this strict programme were such operations as might be necessary against invasion ports and

142

enemy naval forces. At the outset the oil campaign was curtailed by the weather and then it was discarded, temporarily at least, when in March, Prime Minister Winston Churchill had given absolute priority to the Battle of the Atlantic. By July 1941, Peirse had a nominal strength of 49 squadrons or almost 1,000 aircraft on paper but eight of these squadrons were equipped with Blenheim light bombers. Although there were eight squadrons of the new 'heavies', four were not yet operational. Only 37 of the 49 squadrons were thus available for the assault against German transportation and morale and even these could not play a full part as less than two-thirds of their crews were fully trained and ready for operations. This had arisen mainly because of the drain of experienced crews to the Middle East, together with a shortening of the courses in the OTUs in an attempt to gain a greater output of aircrews. So for the time being at least, Peirse had to rely heavily on the Wellington squadrons, for so long the backbone of Bomber Command operations.

Sergeant Jack Saich, 20 years old, from Dunmow, Essex shouldered an enormous responsibility. He was captain of a young all-sergeant crew of Wellington *T-Tommy* on 9 Squadron at Honington. Robert Douglas 'Bob' Telling from Epsom, Surrey was the second pilot. The navigator was Smitten, a Canadian from Edmonton, Alberta. The three remaining members were an Englishman, 20-year-old Sergeant Eric Trott from Sheffield and two more Canadians – Hooper the front gunner from Vancouver and Sergeant English the rear gunner, who was from Picton, Nova Scotia. On 14/15 July *T-Tommy* was one of 78 Wellington Ics, which with 19 Whitleys, were dispatched to Bremen where they were given three aiming points; the shipyards, the goods station and the *Alstadt* or 'Old Town'. Another 85 aircraft – 44 Hampdens, 21 Wellingtons, 14 Halifaxes and six Stirlings on 7 Squadron at Oakington – were detailed to bomb a rubber factory and the city centre at Hannover. Six more Wellingtons were to bomb Rotterdam and ten Hampdens would lay mines in the Frisians and the Elbe.

T-Tommy took off from Honington at 23.30 on 14 July with seven 500lb bombs on board. It seemed at first that Bremen would prove hard to find for the weather was very thick. Just before *T-Tommy* reached the city, however, it came out of the clouds into a clear sky carved by the sharp blades of searchlights. Crews would report later that the 'whole town was ablaze'. There was a slight haze over the rooftops 11,000 feet below, but Smitten found the target and Saich began his bombing run. It was just twenty minutes to two in the morning. One bomb was released, when the wheeling searchlights caught and held *T-Tommy* in a cone of light which grew in size and intensity as more and more beams concentrated upon the aircraft. Two heavy anti-aircraft shells burst just behind and below the rear turret and inside the fuselage itself, level with the leading edge of the tail plane. The first shell wounded English in the shoulder and hand and cut the hydraulic controls to the turret so that it could no longer be turned except by the slow process of cranking it. Fragments of the other shell riddled the rear part of the fuselage and set on fire the fabric covering it and the tail fin. Saich said, 'The flames seemed to be the signal for every anti-aircraft gun in the target area to give full and uninterrupted attention to us.'

And all this time, be it remembered the rear gunner was in the blazing end of the torch. Saich took violent evasive action and succeeded in throwing the German gunners momentarily off their aim. While he was doing so Smitten went to the help of English in the rear turret. He made his way down the rocking, shell-torn fuselage till he was brought up short by the fierce fire separating him from the turret. Here for the moment he could go no further. He crawled back a little way, snatched a fire extinguisher and returned to the fire in the fuselage, which he presently subdued. Above him the fin still flamed. He sprayed it with all that remained of the methyl bromide in the extinguisher, thrusting it through the hot framework of the fuselage from which the fabric had burnt away. He was able at last to reach the turret.

English was still there but he had made preparations to abandon the aircraft by swinging the turret round into the beam position and opened the doors to throw himself out backwards. The doors now refused to close. Back went Smitten and returned with a light axe. He leant out through a hole beneath the fin, which he had just saved from burning, the wind of the slipstream tearing at him, and hacked away at the doors till they fell off. English was then able to rotate his turret by means of the hand gear and as soon as the gaping hole, where once the doors had been, coincided with the end of the fuselage, he extricated himself and entered the aircraft. While this was going on astern more trouble broke out forward. The Wellington was hit again and a shell splinter set light to the flares carried in the port wing. These were for use in an emergency, when a forced landing had to be made in darkness. They burned brightly – so brightly that Saich thought the port engine was on fire. He promptly turned off its petrol, opened the throttle fully and switched off. Soon, however, the flames died down, for the flares had burnt their way through the fabric of the main-plane and fallen from the aircraft. Realising what had happened, Jack Saich turned on the petrol again and restarted the engine. At his orders Bob Telling was crouched beside the main spar behind the wireless cabin pumping all the oil which could be extracted from a riddled auxiliary tank. *T-Tommy* was still under intense anti-aircraft fire and the shell splinters, one of which wounded him, were described by Telling as, 'angry hail tearing through the aircraft.'

One further misfortune had befallen the Wellington. At the moment when the Germans scored their first hit, the bomb doors were open, for the aircraft was completing its first bombing run-up and one of the bombs had just been released. The damage caused by the anti-aircraft shell made it impossible either to close the bomb doors or to release the remaining six bombs, since the hydraulic pipes had been punctured and the electrical wiring to the slips had been severed. As well as this and the damage to the fuselage, the rear turret, the rudder and the fin, there was a large hole knocked by a shell in the starboard wing. It had just missed the petrol tanks. In this condition *T-Tommy* was headed for base. The chances of making it did not appear bright. The aircraft with bomb doors open and a heavy load still on board was very hard to control, and Saich's task was not made easier by the hole in the wing through which the draught rushed, blanketing the starboard aileron, which was for all intents and purposes useless. Nevertheless be held sternly to the home-ward course given him by Smitten and at 05.35 hours on 15 July *T-Tommy* crossed the North Norfolk coast dead on track. Its speed had been much reduced and the petrol gauges had been registering zero gallons for two hours out of the four on the return journey from Bremen, over nearly 300 miles of sea. With dry land beneath him once more Saich determined to make a forced landing, for he thought that at any moment the engines would stop for lack of fuel.

The sky was now 'pale as water before dawn' and he picked out a barley field where it seemed to him that a successful landing might be made. In the half-light he did not see the obstruction poles set up in the field to hinder an airborne invasion. He set about making his perilous descent. The flaps would not work and when he came to pump the undercarriage down with the emergency hydraulic hand pump he found that, owing to loss of oil, it would only push the tail wheel and one of the main wheels into their positions. *T-Tommy* came in to land at High Barn Farm, Somerton near Caister, lop-sided a little to take full advantage of the one sound wheel. On touching down, the aircraft swung round but its motion was violently arrested by an obstruction pole. It shuddered and then came abruptly to rest on its belly with its back broken. All the crew except for Sergeant English, who was taken to the Norfolk and Norwich Hospital, returned to Honington. *T-Tommy* was little more than a wreck. It had flown to that East Anglian barley field with a huge hole in its starboard wing, with uncounted smaller holes in its fuselage, with nine feet of fabric burnt entirely away forward from the rear turret, with half the fin and half the rudder in the same condition. Yet it flew home. The operative word is 'flew.' Saich and Smitten were awarded the DFM.[1]

A Whitley and three Wellingtons were shot down on the operation on Bremen; one more Wimpy ditched in the North Sea and the crew was rescued. A 305 Polish Squadron Wellington crashed at Stiffkey on the Norfolk coast without injury to the crew. One Wimpy, which crashed near Veendam with the loss of all the crew, failed to return from the raid on Hannover where many fires were observed. A Wellington on 405 'Vancouver' Squadron at Pocklington was shot down and the entire crew was taken prisoner. Two of the six Stirlings dispatched by 7 Squadron crashed on return to England. *D-Dog* ran out of petrol near the Norfolk coast and crashed at Shotesham Park at Newton Flotman without injury to the crew. A second Stirling, which crashed in the centre of Northampton 'much to the disgust of the Chief Constable', resulted in the death of the pilot and several injuries to the crew who bailed out. Two of the other Stirlings sustained damage in landing away from Oakington.

Three German warships – *Scharnhorst*, *Gneisenau* and *Prinz Eugen* – had not been hit during recent bombing as they sheltered in Brest harbour, and the enemy decided it was time to move the *Scharnhorst* more than 200 miles further south to La Pallice. A large tanker covered with camouflage netting was left in the *Scharnhorst's* former berth at Brest after the battle cruiser had slipped her moorings and sailed south. The warship was spotted by reconnaissance aircraft at La Pallice on 23 July. That same evening a formation of six Stirlings – three on 7 Squadron and three on XV Squadron – were immediately dispatched to bomb the warship. As far as XV Squadron were concerned the operation was a failure. Flying Officer Robert Balmain Campbell RAAF bombed the target but was forced to ditch 50 miles from Milford Haven on the homeward trip. All the crew perished in the sea. Sergeant Jones bombed a ship at Fromontine instead of La Pallice and Pilot Officer Frank James Needham, unable to raise his undercarriage of his aircraft, was forced to jettison his bombs and fuel and return to Wyton.[2]

Next day Wellington, Hampden and Fortresses crews just could not believe it when they were told that they would make daylight attacks on the *Gneisenau* and *Prinz Eugen* at Brest while Halifaxes attacked the *Scharnhorst* at La Pallice. The German fighter opposition was stronger and more prolonged than anticipated by Group HQ and 16 bombers – 10 of them Wellingtons (12.5 per cent of the total force) – failed to return. Two other aircraft were lost when they ditched on the way home. The Wellingtons on 405 'Vancouver' Squadron at Pocklington in Yorkshire now received their first real test. All nine of the Wimpys succeeded in getting over the target, severely pasting the docks and surrounding area. One crew estimated a direct hit on the *Prinz Eugen*. On their way back five of the bombers were intercepted by Bf 109s. Two, including *U-Uncle* flown by the CO, Wing Commander P A Gilchrist DFC, whose Halifax on 35 Squadron had been downed returning from Le Havre four months earlier, were shot down. Gilchrist and two of his crew evaded capture.[3] Another, badly mauled by the fighters, crash landed at Plymouth. *V-Victor*, after having fought off four fighters, flew on, though rapidly losing height, with its fabric on fire, the rear turret out of action and extensive damage to the whole aircraft. Nevertheless the pilot, Sergeant Craig, brought the stricken Wimpy within 300 yards of home shore for a successful ditching off Torpoint.

Six hits were claimed on the *Gneisenau* and five direct hits were registered on the *Scharnhorst*, putting her out of action for four months.

Of the 15 Halifaxes attacking La Pallice, five were shot down and all the remainder damaged. Two of the 18 Hampdens were lost to fighter attacks. Despite the losses it was considered a highly successful operation. There were more losses that night when 34 Wellingtons and 30 Hampdens visited Kiel and 31 Whitleys and 16 Wellingtons went to Emden. One Hampden and one Wellington were lost on the Kiel raid. Two Wellingtons, which failed to return from Emden, were shot down by *Oberleutnant* Prinz Egmont zur Lippe-Weissenfeld and *Oberleutnant* Helmut Lent of 4./NJG1.

The following night, 30 Hampdens and 25 Whitleys were dispatched to Hannover while 43 Wellingtons visited Hamburg. Bombing results at Hannover were not observed and four Whitleys and a Hampden were shot down.[4] At Hamburg fires in the city and shipyards were claimed and two aircraft were lost. Bomber losses for the night reached ten when two Stirlings and a Halifax were lost from the nine bombers that went to Berlin. Altogether, during July, 63 Bomber Command aircraft were claimed shot down. Increasing the long-range bomber forces in the face of such losses was a policy advocated by none other than Lord Trenchard,[5] who in a memorandum to the War Cabinet in 1941 said:

> Such a policy may necessarily involve fairly heavy casualties but the counting of such losses has nothing to do with the soundness of the plan once you accept the view that the nation can stand the casualties. The pilots in the last war stood it and the pilots of this war are even better and, I feel, would welcome a policy of this description.... It is quite possible to lose as many as 70 per cent of your machines in a month, though these will not be all completely written off, as some can be required to fly again after crashes and accidents in England.... In the last war, casualties of pilots were sometimes as high as 30 per cent a month or more but now, owing to the universal use of parachutes, the percentage of those killed or wounded will be greatly reduced.

Reaction from the Chiefs of Staff was mixed but the Chief of Air Staff, Marshal of the RAF Sir Charles Portal, agreed with the Trenchard doctrine. 'The most vulnerable point in the German Nation at war is the morale of her civil population under air attack and that until this morale has been broken it will not be possible to launch an army on the mainland of Europe with any prospect of success.' He added 'we can depend on the superior staying power of our own people compared with the Germans.' It was Portal who later issued a memorandum stating that 'statistical information relating to the chances of survival of aircrews should be confined to the smallest number of people. The information can be so easily distorted and is then so dangerous to morale.' The bombing of German cities would continue despite the mounting cost in aircrew losses.[6]

In August a record 67 RAF bombers were shot down by flak and fighters. On 12/13 August, 65 Wellingtons and 13 Hampdens attacked Hannover and 70 aircraft visited Berlin. Four Wellingtons failed to return from the Hannover raid and only 32 aircraft reached the *Reich* capital, losing nine aircraft. *F-Freddie* on 142 Squadron, flown by Flight Lieutenant 'Doug' Gosman who had flown Fairey Battles in the disastrous air campaign in France in May 1940, was one of three Wimpys that failed to return. Sergeant Les Frith, his wireless operator, who was another survivor from the Fairey Battle period, was almost at the end of his tour. Born in Bradford, Les had joined the RAF as a regular in 1938. When the German armies began their attack on Holland and the Low Countries in May 1940, his squadron had been at Berry-au-Bac near Rheims. Sixty per cent of the squadron did not return to England and the demoralized survivors were sent to Binbrook, 11 miles south-south-west of Grimsby, to re-equip with Wellingtons. 'It was like flying in a bus after the Battle' recalled Frith. 'It was also a totally different bombing concept for us. We had been trained in dive bombing and low level attacks and we found ourselves as part of a strategic bomber force in 1 Group.' Les met and married a girl from Grimsby and they had settled into a pleasant cottage in Stainton-le-Vale, just a short cycle ride from RAF Binbrook. Now, over Berlin, he had swapped the delightful vale for the valley of death. 'The flak was terrible', Frith says. 'We had never seen anything like it. We managed to drop our bombs and had just turned for home when we saw another bomber hit by flak and blow up. Then we were coned in the searchlights. The port engine was hit and we began to lose height. We tried everything we could do to keep her flying but it was useless and the pilot gave the order to bail out.' Les Frith remained at his wireless set relaying to Binbrook what had happened until, with the aircraft at 1,500 feet, he bailed out, landed in a cabbage field and within a few hours was captured, so beginning almost four years of imprisonment. The rest of the crew were also taken into captivity.

Just over 150 aircraft returned to Hannover on 14/15 August when railway stations were used as aiming points. Nine aircraft were lost. Brunswick and Magdeburg were also hit but visibility at the latter was poor and no bombing results were observed. One of the 83 Hampdens dispatched to Brunswick was lost and four bombers failed to return from the raid on Magdeburg. On 16/17 August it was Cologne's turn when 72 aircraft were dispatched to bomb rail centres in the city but haze and smoke obscured the targets. Seven Whitleys and a Wellington were lost and a second Wellington crashed at Melton Constable in Norfolk returning to Binbrook. Three men were killed. Fifty-two Hampdens and six Manchesters were given rail targets at Düsseldorf where many fires were seen. Three Hampdens and two Manchesters were lost. Fifty-four

Wellingtons also attacked rail targets at Duisburg where several fires were seen by crews. One aircraft was lost.

Rail targets at Duisburg were attacked again on 17/18 August, and at Bremen the Focke-Wulf factory and the railway goods station were the aiming points for 39 Hampdens and 20 Whitleys. Hits were claimed on the factory. Two Hampdens were lost. The weather at Duisburg was bad and the bombing results were poor. The following night, 62 aircraft returned to rail targets in Cologne with the West Station as the aiming point, while 41 Wellingtons attacked the railway yards at Duisburg where the weather was clear and the bombing results were good. Five Whitleys and a Wellington failed to return from the raid on Cologne and a sixth Whitley crashed at Laxfield in Suffolk, with the loss of the whole crew. This one took 51 Squadron's losses at Dishforth for the night to four. A Hampden on 106 Squadron at Coningsby force landed at Lincoln injuring all the crew. A Wimpy on 149 Squadron at Mildenhall was lost on the operation on Duisburg and *A-Apple,* the Wellington Ic flown by Pilot Officer Gregory, was coned by searchlights near Venlo and then attacked by a Ju 88 and severely damaged. The rear of the Wimpy caught fire but Sergeant Billington the rear gunner extinguished the flames with his hands. Gregory brought his aircraft back safely to Mildenhall despite the elevators being put out of action and with large areas of fabric missing. Gregory was awarded the DFC and Billington the DFM.

Raids were mounted on Kiel and Mannheim, and on the night of 24/25 August, 44 aircraft were detailed for a raid on Düsseldorf and six Hampdens on 83 Squadron taxied out at Scampton for searchlight suppression operations in the German searchlight belt at Wesel. Their brief was to attack any searchlight which was holding another bomber in its searchlight beam. *V-Victor* taxied out at 20.30 hours and exploded, killing all four crew and four personnel on the ground. The bombs did not explode and 19-year-old Sergeant Roy Thomas, who was in charge of the bomb store, was given the unenviable job of locating the unexploded bombs in the darkness and rendering them harmless by defusing them. 'Some of them were quite warm,' he said with typical British under-statement. But despite his youth Roy Thomas had endured much. As a 17-year-old lad in South Wales in Neath in 1939 there was very little work and his father had just started back in the pit after 12 years on the dole. Roy had been told 'don't go down the mine', so he enlisted at 17 in the RAF in June 1939. By spring 1940 he was an armourer in France as part of the AASF, working in the Armoury and manning a gun pit with Lewis machine guns. One weekend in April in Paris he watched the BEF football team beat France 2-1. But this was soon followed by many German air raids and on 26 May he was in the back of a lorry heading for Dunkirk:

We were cut off very early and headed for Brest. After many days travelling with very little food – just biscuits and Ideal milk – we reached Brest on Sunday 16 June. I was the last to board a ship that sailed at 20.10 hours in semi darkness, avoiding Stuka bombers. At 5 a.m. next day we sighted Eddystone Lighthouse. It was a welcome sight. We reached Plymouth at 10.50 a.m. and received a marvellous reception. By the end of 1940 I had been promoted to Corporal when still just 18. As the year ended there was a terrible explosion at the bomb store and many men were killed. The Bomb Store was soon repaired and my job was to reorganise it, prepare the bomb loads and fuse the bombs on bomb trolleys before they were taken out to each individual aircraft on 49 and 83 Squadrons.

On 25/26 August, Karlsruhe was the target for 37 Wimpys and 12 Stirlings. Storms and thick cloud prevented accurate bombing and two Wellingtons and a Stirling were lost. Thirty-eight Hampdens and seven Manchesters attacked the city centre in Mannheim for the loss of three Hampdens. Almost 100 aircraft attacked Cologne on 26/27 August and the following night it was Mannheim again. On 28/29 August, rail targets at Duisburg were once again the objective of Bomber Command. The force this time was made up of 60 Wellingtons, 30 Hampdens, 13 Stirlings, nine Halifaxes and six Manchesters. Furthermore, six Hampdens on 49 and 106 Squadrons made searchlight suppression sorties near the target, as Sergeant George Luke, WOp/AG on Sergeant Eric Robert Holmes Lyon's crew, one of the three Hampdens on 106 Squadron used in the operation, explains:

> The apprehension felt at the possible danger involved was counter-acted to a degree by the feeling of pride, rather like being chosen for the first eleven at school. We 'intruders' were to take off early and reach the target 15 minutes ahead of the main force. We carried a small load of incendiary bombs to release at 14,000 feet and additional ammunition for the machine guns, which, after diving to low level, we would use against the searchlights on the target route. We were to continue to harass the searchlights, hopefully keeping them out of action for one hour allowing the main force to bomb, leave the target area and be well on route for home and then they would regain height and return to their bases. This would enable the main bomber force to avoid the searchlight cones and the resulting attention of the German fighter and flak concentrations.
>
> We released the incendiary bombs, surprisingly meeting little opposition *en route*, then dived to low altitude and commenced our attack on the searchlights. I felt great exhilaration during the low level attacks, the sense of speed being much greater and in my position as under gunner in the Hampden I was kept extremely busy firing away left and right at searchlights as they were switched on. They were extinguished immediately, whether by our marks-manship or intentionally by the Germans, we were not sure. We

continued our attack with the wireless operator firing from the upper gun position. I felt that we were successfully achieving our purpose, although in the hectic activity taking place I caught sight of one of the main force bombers, which was caught in a cone of searchlights, receiving a pasting from the flak batteries. We were meeting only light flak and machine gun fire from the searchlight defences. At low level and in the dark you are upon your target and gone almost before they can react. The pace of events was so fast that the hour-long attack seemed to last but a few minutes. Then we regained height and set course for base. We had crossed the Dutch coast at about 10,000 feet and were approximately 40 miles NW of Texel when because of a technical inability to switch fuel tanks we lost both engines and we were forced to ditch. We all survived but after drifting in a dinghy for three days we were in such poor physical condition that when we were found by a Dutch fishing boat they had no choice but to hand us over to the German Naval authorities in the small harbour of Zoutkamp.[7]

Berlin was attacked five times before the end of 1941. In Bomber slang Berlin was the 'Big City'. It was 'big' in the length of the flight, which meant flying 1,200 miles there and back, mostly over hostile territory, and 'big' in the strength of its defences, in spectacle, in significance in the war and in the imagination of those who learnt that it was their target.[8]

On the night of 7/8 September, 197 bombers went to three aiming points in Berlin while another 51 bombers headed for Kiel. The Berlin force comprised 103 Wellingtons, 43 Hampdens, 31 Whitleys, six Halifaxes and four Manchesters on 207 Squadron. Nowhere were searchlights more concentrated than at Berlin and the flak was always very heavy. 'There seemed to be about 50 searchlights in one bunch alone,' said the navigator of a Halifax. 'Shells burst close, some of them sending out clouds of smoke which, in the night sky, looked almost like barrage balloons.' Fifty out of 65 postal wagons were destroyed in the Potsdamer railway station, which was severely damaged. The railway lines leading to the Anhalter and Friedrichstrasse stations were hit in many places and traffic was dislocated or brought to a standstill for some time. Warehouses were burnt to the ground near the Ost Kreuz station. A 4,000lb bomb completely demolished five large buildings in the Pariser Platz at one end of the Unter-den-Linden and killed more than 100 people. Two hundred more were reported to have been scalded to death by the hot water system, which burst and flooded the basement in which they were sheltering.

Flight Lieutenant 'Mike' Lewis DFC, who was piloting *W-William*, one of the four Manchester Is on the raid, had finished his second tour and had returned after a week's leave expecting to be posted to 44 Squadron, but his old squadron commander had asked him to do one last trip (his 61st) because they did not have a captain to fly *William*. Sergeant Charles Hall, his WOp/AG recalls:

> The outward flight was uneventful until about midnight when at about 13,000 feet over the sea near Tönning in Schleswig-Holstein, Sergeant 'Dusty' Miller the rear gunner shouted, 'Night fighter astern!' This was accompanied by a stutter of machine gun fire, which hit our aircraft in the area of the port engine. As Miller opened fire the night fighter continued over the top of the Manchester enabling me, from my mid-upper gunner's position, to fire into the belly of the enemy aircraft at very short range. Flight Lieutenant Lewis had immediately dived our aircraft and sought cover of thick cloud and contact was lost with the enemy fighter. There were no casualties but we had a serious fuel leak so after dropping our 4,000lb bomb and incendiaries on a searchlight concentration at Wilhelmshaven (which had given us much trouble in previous operations) we set course for Waddington. The port engine cowling began to glow red-hot and then white hot in turn. Lewis shut down the engine, feathered the airscrew and activated the fire extinguisher within the engine cowling. This seemed to extinguish the fire but thereafter twelve very anxious eyes were focused on the port engine for signs of further trouble! It soon became apparent that we were not capable of maintaining height on the one remaining Vulture engine so we gradually lost height. With the gunners keeping a sharp lookout we descended through cloud emerging at 1,500 feet over Holland with the inhospitable grey-black waters of the North Sea clearly visible. At this point Lewis decided that we were not going to make the English coast and turned south aiming to reach the Friesian Islands. The Friesians eventually came into view and turning westward again Lewis kept the aircraft parallel to the shore. We took up our crash positions. Amidst noise, water and mayhem we hit, bouncing several times before settling in what turned out to be the surf of the north coast of Ameland.

Mike Lewis adds:

> The only evidence of anger was a lot of holes in the engine cowling and the wing and a great stream of gasoline coming out of the main port gas tank. None of the crew was damaged; no shot actually entered the fuselage. Probably one bullet went through the radiator and shortly thereafter the engine temperature suddenly started to go and bang! It ceased and that was it. We feathered the engine and started back home but we were just slowly losing height. I crash-landed the aircraft on the beach of the Dutch Friesian island of Ameland about 01.00 hours. I was fortunate: the whole crew

Boeing Fortress I AN530 on 90 Squadron at Polebrook, which flew the first high-altitude sortie against German warships at Brest on 24 July 1941. Persistent engine problems and equipment failures frustrated operations and only fifty-two sorties, many of them aborted early, were flown between 8 July and 25 September before Bomber Command's Fortress experiment was abandoned. *(IWM)*

Sergeant Beckett the rear gunner (left) and his pilot, P/O Gregory on 149 Squadron, safely back at Mildenhall, examine the damage caused to Wellington X9746 *A-Apple* by a German night-fighter during the raid on Duisburg on 18/19 August 1941. During the attack, the fabric covering the rear fuselage caught fire and Beckett had to use his parachute pack to beat out the flames. The Wellington's unique geodetic construction made repairs a relatively easy operation. (*IWM*)

A member of the ground crew in the narrow 'fighter-type' cockpit one of 44 'Rhodesia' Squadron's Hampdens at Waddington in September 1941. The aircraft's lo bomb bay enabled the Hampden carry a sea mine and later, to be used as a torpedo bomber by Coastal Command. At this time bomb tally painted on the fusela shows that the aircraft had carrie out five bombing raids and a mir laying operation – the 'Gardenin sortie being indicated by a painte parachute mine. 44 Squadron fle 2,043 sorties for the loss of forty-three Hampdens, before converti to Lancasters at the beginning of 1942. (*IWM*)

Halifax I L9530/MP-L on 76 Squadron at Middleton St George flown by Flight Lieutenant Christopher Cheshire. His aircraft was lost, shot down on the operation on Berlin on 12/13 August 1941. Cheshire survived and spent the rest of the war in a prison camp while his brother, Flying Officer Geoffrey Leonard Cheshire – then serving on 35 Squadron – went on to become one of Bomber Command's most celebrated pilots.

Stirlings on 7 Squadron at Oakington on 10 October 1941.

Avro Manchester B1A L7515/FM-S on 207 Squadron in November 1941. On 1 November 1940 the Squadron, previously a training unit, re-formed at Waddington in 5 Group for the purpose of bringing the new bomber into service. On 24/25 February 1942 the squadron carried out its first bombing raid, against German naval units at Brest. Six aircraft were dispatched. (*Avro*)

(*Facing page*) Manchester cockpit. The Manchester suffered unsuccessful sixteen-month operational career in Bomber Command, due mainly to problems with the untried and dangerously unreliable Rolls-Royce Vulture engines. 207 Squadron operated the type for most of this time, flying total of 360 sorties with the loss of twenty-five aircraft. (*Avro*)

An all-sergeant Whitley crew preparing for a night raid in November 1941. (*IWM*)

crew of *Sri Guroh,* a Merlin-engined Wellington II on 214 (Federated Malay States) Squadron at
dishall, Suffolk in front of their aircraft before setting out for Essen on 4 November 1941.
442/BU-V was one of several Wellingtons paid for by funds raised in the Malay States, in
ordance with the 'Gift Squadrons' scheme. All were named after towns in Malaya and bore a
r's head motif. The trip to Essen that night was mounted by just twenty-eight Wellingtons, all of
ch returned safely.

Halifax on 10 Squadron (previously on 76 Squadron – note the painted-out fuselage codes) being
uelled at Leeming, Yorkshire on 12 December 1941 soon after replacement of the squadron's
itleys. Almost immediately the squadron began intensive training for Operation *Veracity*; a major
light operation against the *Scharnhorst* and *Gneisenau* at Brest, which finally went ahead with
ty-seven Halifaxes, Stirlings and Manchesters on 18 December. Bombing from 16,000 feet, some
s were claimed on the sterns of both vessels but six bombers were shot down, mostly by fighters.
30 December, in the last raid of the year, sixteen Halifaxes tried again to cripple the warships
ring a second daylight operation, but the results could not be accurately assessed and the
ences shot down three of the attacking bombers. *(IWM)*

'Pip' Brimson of the WAAF who served at Waddington in 1942. (*Pip Brimson*)

When Air Marshal Arthur Harris became Commander-in-Chief of Bomber Command on 22 February 1942, he inherited a policy of area bombing which had evolved as a result of the failure of night precision attacks. (*IWM*)

Ops Room at Bomber Command Headquarters at Naphill, near High Wycombe with ACM Richard Pierse and AVM Saundby the Senior Staff Officer. (*IWM*)

Armourers on 149 Squadron at Mildenhall on 10 March 1942 fit bomb carriers to a pair of 1,000-pounders, while behind Stirling *N-Nuts* runs up its engines. That night was the third of three raids against Essen which were carried out during a seventy-two hour period by 126 aircraft – including twelve Stirlings. Two Stirlings from 149 failed to return. The bombing results on the three raids were disappointing even though, for the first time, the lead aircraft were equipped with the new radio navigation device, *Gee*. *(IWM)*

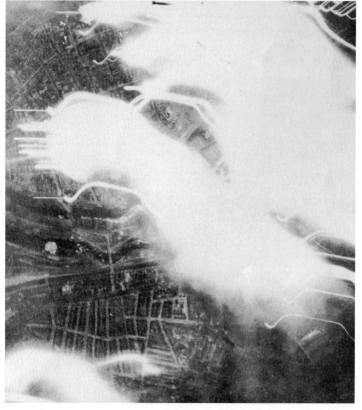

The raid on Lübeck on the Baltic Coast on the night of 28/29 March 1942 was a concentrated attack by 234 bombers carrying mostly incendiary loads which burned out 200 acres of the city, part which can be seen in this reconnaissance photo taken on the morning after the raid. Twelve RAF aircraft were lost and 320 Germans died, the highest casualty total so far for a single raid on a German town. *(IWM)*

...eir sortie successfully completed, the
...w settle down to the traditional post-
...eration breakfast of bacon and eggs and
...ge amounts of bread. (*IWM*)

Acting Squadron Leader John Dering
Nettleton of 44 'Rhodesia' Squadron, a
South African, who led the daring
daylight raid by Lancasters against the
*Maschinenfabrik Augsburg-Nürnberg
Aktiengesellschaft* (MAN) diesel engine
factory at Augsburg on 17 April 1942.
Nettleton survived and was awarded the
Victoria Cross. Promoted wing
commander and becoming CO of
44 Squadron, he FTR from a raid on
Turin on 12/13 July 1943. (*IWM*)

Cologne suffered further devastation throughout the war.

Flight Lieutenant Robert Horsley from York with his wife and mother after receiving the DFC at Buckingham Palace. He initially flew on 50 Squadron as a WOp/AG and his pilot was Leslie Manser. On the Cologne raid on 30/31 May Robert Horsley managed to bail out and he evaded capture. He was back in England only two months later. He later became a pilot on 617 Squadron and survived the war. His brother Hugh was also a Lancaster pilot but he was

ing Officer Leslie Manser, who was
osthumously awarded the VC after
crew was shot down on the raid on
Cologne on 30/31 May 1942.

Sergeant Leslie 'Beve' Baveystock
DFM, the second pilot on Manser's
crew who also survived the raid on
Cologne on 30/31 May 1942. The
award of the DFC followed on
25 January 1944 and he received a bar
to his DFC on 25 August.
F/L Baveystock DSO DFC DFM later
served on 201 Squadron in Coastal
Command as a Sunderland pilot. On
7 June 1944 he sank *U-955* in the Bay
of Biscay north of Spain and on
18 August he sank *U-107* in the Bay
of Biscay SW of St-Nazaire.
Baveystock was awarded the DSO on
13 October 1944.

Wing Commander Guy Gibson DFC* (centre, with moustache), the CO of 106 Squadron in 5 Group, with members of his Squadron at Coningsby on 31 May 1942 after the 'Thousand Bomber' raid to Cologne. Note the Manchesters parked in the background. The squadron began conversion to Lancasters in May, with the Manchesters flying their last 'ops' in June. Gibson had taken over 106 in April and during his tenure the squadron's enjoyed low loss and survived. No injuries other than a broken bone in one hand of the tail gunner and one who hit the windshield and had concussion. Very short, nothing dramatic except for that ten seconds and it's all over.

After Lewis put *W-William* down safely on the beach in about five feet of water the crew took to their dinghy and got ashore. As they had previously agreed not to compromise any Dutch civilians, they were taken prisoner. Their attacker was *Feldwebel* Siegfried Ney of 4./NJG1 who successfully claimed his fifth *Abschuss*.

Sergeant L D Izzard, the wireless operator-air gunner on Sergeant R A Norman RAAF's Halifax crew on 35 Squadron at Linton-on-Ouse recalls:

We were detailed to attack Berlin. Take-off was at 12.10 hours and due to the late despatch we proceeded to the secondary target, Kiel. Somewhere over Germany at 18,000 feet the aircraft became uncontrollable and the order was given to prepare to abandon aircraft. Height was lost and the bombs jettisoned (one hung up). At 10,000 feet the captain managed to regain control and level off. He called all crew members on intercom but got no response from the rear gunner. I went down the fuselage only to find the turret rotated through 90° and the gunner gone. It was his first operation with us and he obviously misunderstood or did not hear the advisory order correctly. Eventually we landed back at base at 03.20 hours and, upon closing down, a 1,000-pounder fell from the bomb bay.

A claim to fame mentioned upon another occasion. A piece of shrapnel hit my starboard buttock. Whilst it did not penetrate far it cut the skin and caused extensive bruising. 'Watty' Watts our navigator got me down on the floor and proceeded to remove my flying suit, battledress trousers and long-johns. My leg was numb. He fixed a field dressing with surgical tape and although I suffered no lasting harm other than having to eat my meals off the mantle-piece for a few days, the real pain came with the removal of the tape which had a near lethal grip on my body hairs. I think, upon reflection, that I am probably the only airman to have flown over Essex without any trousers.[9]

In all, 137 crews claimed to have bombed their allotted targets in Berlin. Fifteen bombers were MIA and at least 10, including two Wellingtons on 115 Squadron are thought to have been shot down by night fighters.[10] One by one the returning bombers landed back at their stations in eastern England. Pilot Officer Mike Evans and crew of a 149 Squadron[11] Wellington returned to Mildenhall after what was an eventful trip, as Sergeant Jim Coman the WOp recalls.

All went fairly well until we were making our bombing run, straight and level, when we were coned in searchlights and received numerous hits by flak. After releasing the bombs at 9,500 feet we took evasive action but were unable to get out of the searchlights so we dived to roof top level and moved out of the target area as quickly as possible. The AA gunners were actually shooting bits off their own buildings trying to hit us. We gained height as soon as possible to regain our bearings and arrived back at the Dutch coast short of fuel. All the main tanks were empty so we had approximately twenty minutes flying time on the engine nacelle tanks. We were attacked by a Ju 88 over the Dutch coast south of the Friesian Islands and north of Rotterdam, which our rear gunner engaged and the fighter broke off trailing smoke from one of its engines. We made an emergency landing at the nearest airfield on the English coast, at Martlesham Heath, a fighter 'drome. As we landed the engines cut out. They had been running for nine hours after take-off. We counted 150 holes in the aircraft before we left for Mildenhall but we failed to spot the most serious damage, which must have happened over the target when a shell must have penetrated the main spar when the bomb doors were open.

On the night of 10/11 September 1941, 76 Stirlings, Halifaxes and Wellingtons[12] bombed the royal arsenal and other targets in Turin. The interval of eight months had been well employed in the aircraft factories of Britain. The four-engined giants were coming out of the assembly shops and a new age of bombing was about to dawn in the Mediterranean skies. That night, for the first time, Bomber Command 'heavies' made the 1,200-mile out-and-in crossing and re-crossing the Alps. Some of the crews taking part in the flight to Italy had only the previous night flown to Berlin. They were getting to know their way around Europe.

One of the Stirling pilots described the passage over France:

It was as quiet as the grave. One of two searchlights poked into the clouds. We could see the splashes of light on the clouds below us but they were ineffective and soon gave up. We started climbing well before we got to the Alps. As we made the crossing we were flying at one time at over 20,000 feet. We could see the snow on the tops of the higher mountains and down in the valleys the mountain villages. The moon was up and it was a really beautiful night. We could see very far; we picked out Mont Blanc high among the other peaks. We didn't stay at 20,000 feet for long because there was no need to go as high but I had never been over the Alps before and I wanted to make sure of getting well up. As soon as we had crossed the Alps we lost height again and came down to Turin. We were about the third bomber over and already there were three large blocks of fire in a row. We went on and the navigator found the railway station. We dropped one stick of bombs across it. We went round again and came back to drop a second stick. After we had bombed we climbed again and as we turned towards the Alps we saw the attack getting under way. There were lots of bombs being dropped. Smoke and haze affected bombing but good results were claimed in the centre of the city and on the Fiat steelworks.

A few minutes after we had left Turin my rear gunner told me that three fighters were coming up very fast astern in close formation. At first they were nearly 2,000 feet below us. I think they must have seen us against the moon. I told the rear-gunner to get rid of them because there would not be much room for evasive action over the mountains. He opened up on them at once and they split formation. One of them disappeared into cloud and the other two joined some friends of theirs who had come up. They made no attack and soon made off. One solitary gun in the foot of the hills on the Italian side of the Alps took a pop at us. It just fired once for luck. We crossed the Alps lower this time and later I left it to 'George', the automatic pilot, to take us a good part of the way home. We came home very nicely.

Another pilot reported:

As we neared the Alps the clouds began to build up. We skirted a terrific electric storm going on over Mont Blanc. We could see great zigzag flashes of lightning. There were two layers of cloud over Genoa and a high bank of cloud had come up over the moon. Our bomb-aimer decided to drop a few incendiaries. A cautious Scotsman, he would not put all his bombs down at once. The incendiaries went with a rush right in the factory and soon you could see the flames coming out of the roofs and the windows. The whole of one end of the factory – it was an enormous place – was lit up. We went round again and dropped our next stick. We gave them a bit of both this time: high explosives as well as incendiaries. This time we put a high explosive right on the doorstep of one of the factory buildings. We went round a third time and saw that the fires were still going strong. Then we dropped a stick of bombs along the docks. The fires in the factory were still burning when we left. We saw nothing of the Alps on the return journey. We crossed in pitch-black darkness and cloud. Until we got back to base we had only one glimpse of the ground.[13]

On 29/30 September, when Bomber Command sent 139 aircraft to Stettin northeast of Berlin, 95 aircraft claimed good bombing in conditions of slight haze. Eight aircraft were lost and five crashed in England. Another 93 bombers, mostly Hampdens and Wellingtons, attacked Hamburg but searchlight glare prevented accurate bombing and two Wellingtons and two Hampdens were lost. Hamburg was the target the next night when 82 aircraft were despatched. Cloud prevented accurate bombing and one Wellington failed to return. After this it was visits to Karlsruhe, Stuttgart, Essen, Cologne and Emden. Of all the towns of the Ruhr, the chief was Essen with the great Krupps works, the most notorious firm of armament manufacturers the world has ever known, sprawling heavily across it. Krupps not only produced armaments of every kind but iron, steel, coal and coke, and locomotives, tractors and mining machinery. On the night of 10/11 October when 78 aircraft were sent to bomb the Krupp Works, because of bad weather only 13 crews claimed to have bombed in the Essen area. Sixty-nine aircraft went to Cologne where five Wellingtons failed to return. In a series of minor operations five Hampdens carried out searchlight-suppression flights in support of the two main raids and 23 Hampdens were despatched to Dunkirk where one of the aircraft was lost. Thirteen Wellingtons went to Rotterdam and 22 Wellingtons and Whitleys went to Ostend, while 22 Wellingtons visited Bordeaux where two Wimpys on 218 Squadron failed to return. Wellington R1511 was piloted by Sergeant Haley who recalled: 'We took off from Marham at 20.00 hours on 10 October to bomb oil tanks slightly North of Bordeaux. We reached our objective but shortly after we turned for home the starboard propeller fell off. I turned the aircraft towards the unoccupied zone and gave the order to bail out at approximately 04.00 hours.' Haley evaded capture and crossed the Pyrenees without a guide, arriving in Gibraltar on 4 March 1942. As for the rest of his crew, one man was killed and the other four were taken prisoner.

On the night of 12/13 October, 152 aircraft, mostly Wellingtons and Whitleys, were despatched to Nurnberg in the first large raid to the city. Only a few bombs fell in Nuremburg, many more bombs falling ten miles south of the city. That same night 99 aircraft, mostly Wellingtons and Hampdens, visited Bremen, and 79 Hampdens and 11 Manchesters went to Hüls and the chemical and synthetic rubber plant, the most heavily defended target in the *Reich* at this time. At Bremen 65 aircraft bombed in cloudy conditions and three aircraft failed to return. Hüls was completely cloud-covered and bombing was scattered. Two aircraft failed to return. Following raids on Düsseldorf and Cologne, on the night of 13/14 October, 80 aircraft were sent once more to Nuremburg but conditions *en route* were very bad, with icing and thick cloud, and 51 aircraft bombed alternative targets. Fourteen claimed to have bombed the Nuremburg area. Only one of these, a Whitley of 78 Squadron flown by Squadron Leader Albert John Drake Snow, which dropped six HEs, claimed to have identified and bombed its allocated target in Nuremburg. Snow was killed in a raid on Hamburg on 3/4 May 1942, just after the squadron converted to Halifaxes. Four Wellingtons were lost on the Nuremburg raid. One Wellington flew 600 miles back to base on its port engine – a remarkable feat, creditable to pilot, crew and the engineers who made the engine.

The night following, 27 Wellingtons and seven Stirlings went to Cologne and again bombing was inaccurate. Three Wellingtons were lost. On 16/17 October the target for 87 aircraft, 47 of them Wellingtons, was Duisburg. The rest of the force was made up of 26 Hampdens and 14 Whitleys. Eight further Hampdens carried out searchlight-suppression flights. The target was cloud covered and estimated positions were bombed. The only aircraft that failed to return was a Wellington on 40 Squadron piloted by Squadron Leader Thomas Gresham Kirby-Green, 'a big, black-haired Englishman who looked like an overgrown Spaniard,'[14] the son of a colonial governor who had grown up in Nyasaland (now Malawi) and educated in England. All of his crew, including Flying Officer Peter Campbell-Martin MC, the 44-year-old rear gunner, were killed when they were attacked by a night fighter on the way home. With the Wimpy spinning out of control Tom Kirby-Green gave the order to bail out. His parachute opened only moments before he hit the ground, injuring his spine so badly that he could not move. A few seconds later, 30 yards away, his Wimpy crashed. The rest of the crew had got out slightly before their Skipper, which put them above higher ground, and though their parachutes opened, with much less height to fall they were all killed instantly. After interrogation at *Dulag Luft*, Kirby-Green was incarcerated in *Stalag Luft I* at Barth, where he wore brightly striped kaftans and bedroom slippers, had a pair of bongo drums and played gramophone records of Latin music. And he would often receive exotic food packages from home.[15] Later he was moved to *Stalag Luft III* at Sagan in Silesia where he became a part of the famous 'X' Organisation, being put in charge of security. In the same camp 'Wally' Valenta, the Czech who had come down in a Wimpy in February 1941, trained men who spoke German for the Intelligence Branch. It was every officer's duty to escape and at *Stalag Luft III* three tunnels – 'Tom', 'Dick' and 'Harry' – were started from under barracks in the north compound, although when one was discovered it was decided to put all energies into 'Harry'. On the night of 24 March 1944 in what has since gone down in history as 'The Great Escape', no less than 76 Allied air force officers used 'Harry' to flee the supposedly 'escape proof' camp before their flight was discovered. Squadron Leader Kirby-Green was the 21st man out of the tunnel. 'Wally' Valenta intended catching a train down through Hirschberg to Czechoslovakia where he had friends, but he and a fellow escaper were caught near a Breslau autobahn. Kirby-Green and a fellow escaper were caught trying to cross the frontier into Czechoslovakia. Only three of the escapers made 'home runs'. The rest were captured and Hitler ordered that 50 were to be shot in cold blood. Kirby-Green and Wally Valenta were among them.[16]

Raids in late October 1941 continued with visits to Bremen, Wilhelms-haven, Manheim, Kiel, Frankfurt and Bremerhaven. Flight Sergeant 'Dick' Lord, a Canadian Whitley pilot on 77 Squadron, describes the raid on Bremerhaven on the night of 26/27 October:

My navigator said: 'Dick, if we are going to prang this place properly, it is about time we started looking for a gap in these bloody fog banks.' I said, 'Right!' and stooged the plane to where the clouds appeared to be less thick. We found a hole in the black mass of tiny water particles. The Hun found it too with about 30 of his searchlights. The light from them seemed to penetrate the very floor of the Whitley. I made no attempt to evade them... the navigator wanted a landfall. How he took it, glaring into those millions of candlepower, I cannot attempt to explain but he did so. He gave me fresh directions and we began our first run. An orange-coloured searchlight followed our course, shining through the clouds as if such things never existed. Then the flak came and the tracers and the bomb flashes. Some of the other boys were already on the job. We were flying at 16,000 feet; the remainder of the boys were lower. The shells were exploding at varying heights, mostly, I thought, at about 10,000 feet. I was wrong. We had just finished a tight turn when it happened. There was a terrific explosion somewhere at the back of my head... everything went black and then red, punctured with little green and yellow dots. I heard my radioman say 'My God!' Then everything was silent. In the silence I could feel myself thinking 'This is it! This is the end of your run... you have not done so badly... what's this? The seventh raid? You've been lucky – some chaps don't last seven trips....

Something spoke in my ear... I say something because it sounded like a very weak loudspeaker... 'For Christ's sake, Dick, pull your-self together... we're not done yet!' A light flashed by my eyes... it must have been a searchlight. It brought me to my senses with a jerk. I was sprawled over the steering column and the second pilot was puffing at me. I struggled into a sitting position. We were diving madly at the ground, spinning as we did so. The altimeter read 2,550 feet and was fast slipping back to 2,000. Too late to bail out.... If only I could have died with the explosion! My head was thumping and my right arm felt as heavy as lead. It was still resting on the joystick.

Two thousand feet. The cloud had gone but the searchlights played on us. Shells burst around us still. In a flash I saw all these things and in the same flash realized that unless we did something very drastic quickly we were going to pile in. The second pilot and I pulled on the stick. After what seemed an age there was a response from the controls. We stopped spinning and flattened out. The navigator down in the front turret shouted something but I couldn't make out what it was. The aircraft bucketed and I thought we had been hit again. Somehow we kept control of the old Whitley and climbed slowly into the shelter of the clouds. Someone said 'Are you OK Dick?' I replied that I was and was anyone hurt? The second pilot said 'No.' 'We'd better stooge back and get rid of our eggs,' I suggested.

The navigator laughed... 'We dropped them from approximately 1,200 feet, you ass!'

'Oh!' I said and asked for directions home. Over the North Sea we discussed the dive. 'We were only over Bremerhaven seven minutes,' said the wireless-operator, 'but what a seven minutes!'

'What did we hit with the bombs?' I asked.

'God knows,' said the navigator. 'We were diving straight on to a portion of the docks just before you pulled out!'

The Canadian rear gunner called over the intercom from his turret, 'The docks ain't where they used to be, Dick! We've gotta small portion in the fuselage right behind me. What the hell d'ya want to dive-bomb the place for? Jeez, we could ha' made just as good a show from 15,000!'[17]

On 39 nights between 30 July and 31 December 1941, RAF bombers operated in weather variously described as 'bad,' 'extremely bad,' 'very poor visibility,' 'thick cloud,' 'icing and ten-tenths cloud.' The noon weather forecast on 7 November showed that there would be a large area of bad weather with storms, thick cloud, icing and hail over the North Sea routes by which, the bombers that night would need to fly to Berlin, Cologne and Mannheim and back.[18] Even so, the aircraft were allowed to take off. It was an important milestone for Bomber Command, Sir Richard Peirse, having ordered a major effort with Berlin the main target. Air Vice-Marshal John Slessor of 5 Group objected to Peirse's plan and he telephoned the C-in-C that afternoon to plead his case. Slessor stated that his Hampdens lacked the range to fly to Berlin and back given the forecasted strong westerly winds. No doubt frustrated by the recent long run of bad weather and poor bombing results, Peirse wanted to mount a major effort against Berlin but he allowed Slessor to withdraw his 61 Hampdens and 14 Manchesters from the Berlin force and send them to Cologne instead. The target for 53 Wellingtons and two Stirlings of 1 and 3 Groups was Mannheim, which left 169 aircraft, just over a hundred of them Wellingtons, to raid Berlin. The raid was a disaster from start to finish. The forecast winds were even stronger than predicted and only 73 aircraft reached the general area of the German capital, where bombing was scattered. The Spandau Power Station was hit and damage was caused to a considerable area of Moabit, one of the working-class quarters of Berlin. On the return, crews had to contend with very strong head winds and severe icing conditions. Twenty-one Wellingtons and Whitleys and Stirlings failed to return.

A Wellington crew on 214 Squadron, flown by Pilot Officer Lucian Ercolani, reached England 60 hours after their aircraft was hit. Their high explosives had fallen but the target was obscured by cloud before the incendiaries could be dropped. On the way home Ercolani was looking for a suitable target for them when the Wellington was hit by AA fire. The incendiaries began to burn and soon the bomber was ablaze along the whole length of the bomb racks. The bomb release gear had been smashed and the incendiaries could not, therefore, be released. They burned strongly and set light to the fuselage; the fire resisted all attempts made by the crew to put it out, first with the extinguishers and then with coffee from their thermos flasks. The wireless operator took ten minutes to fight his way through the smoke and flames to reach the rear of the Wellington, whence he could let out his trailing aerial. This would give him a greater range and increase the chances of maintaining contact with base. The pilot remained at the controls but could speak to none of the crew, as the intercom was broken. The blazing bomber flew on. Eventually the fire in the fuselage was subdued but the incendiaries still burned. All this time flak was bursting round the aircraft and Ercolani decided to close the bomb doors in order to show as little light as possible to the German gunners. With fire in its belly the Wellington made out to sea, away from the coasts of the enemy but it was now down to 1,000 feet. Twenty-five minutes later the petrol gave out and the pilot ditched in the English Channel south of the Isle of Wight. The crew got safely into the dingy in which they remained for 57 hours until they reached shore near Ventnor.

As for the two other major attacks on 7/8 November, few bombs fell on Cologne also but all 61 Hampdens and 14 Manchesters returned safely. Forty-three aircraft claimed to have bombed Mannheim as ordered. Seven Wellingtons including two Wimpys on 300 (Masovian) Squadron failed to return from this raid. One of the Polish Squadron's Wellingtons lost was R1705, flown by Sergeant K Budzynski, who took off from Hemswell at around 17.20 hours. After leaving the target he found that they were short of petrol. The starboard wing tank was leaking and may have been hit by flak splinters. North of Lille at about 03.00, finding he could not get home, the Polish pilot ordered the crew to bail out. He was first out and came down near Quesnay. The aircraft dived uncontrolled and came down south of Lille. Budzynski and Pilot Officer Groyccki, the rear gunner, escaped, the others being taken prisoner.

Losses on the Berlin raid were high at 12.4 per cent (21 aircraft). Total losses for the 392 sorties flown were 37 aircraft (9.4 per cent); more than

double the previous highest for a single night. The loss rate, which was
no doubt a result of many aircraft suffering from icing or fuel starvation
over the North Sea, led to a disagreement between Bomber Command
and the Air Ministry and resulted in a conservation policy directive. For
the foreseeable future, generally only weakly defended targets would
be bombed. This would be the last major raid on the Big City until
January 1943.

It was while all able-bodied men and women were doing fire-watch duty
at home and at work; 8pm to midnight or midnight to 4am, that Peter
Bone began to think seriously for the first time about the part that
he would be expected to play in the war. The papers had announced
that his age group would register for military service in November 1941,
three months after his 19th birthday. Conscription was for the duration
of the war, however long it might last. No more talk of career plans now!
He passed his medical without any trouble, as he knew he would for he
and his friend had kept themselves fit after work and at weekend by
swimming and cycling. They both opted for the RAF and volunteered for
flying duties; one couldn't be forced to fly or serve in submarines. But
there was a waiting list, for thousands of other young men had, like
them, been stirred by the prowess of the RAF fighter pilots in the Battle of
Britain. So they were given a service number, a day's pay and an RAF
Volunteer Reserve badge and told, in effect, 'don't call us, we'll call you'.
Peter Bone recalls:

> So I returned home and to my work on the newspaper, writing up
> stories about local men and women serving at home and overseas.
> The home front was no longer under constant threat of bombard-
> ment but *U-boats* were still sinking over one and a half million tons
> of our merchant shipping a year in the North Atlantic. The desert
> war in North Africa was not going at all well, while the bombing war
> against Hitler's armament production was, it turned out, as yet
> ineffectual. The home front settled down to the relative tedium of
> preparing to become an armed fortress and a springboard for the
> liberation of Europe in 1943? 1944? 1945? No-one knew, of course,
> we lived just one day at a time. But as the weeks and months went
> by with no word from the RAF I felt increasingly uncomfortable at
> still being in 'Civvy Street', as we called it.

Early in December 1941, two more Canadian Wellington squadrons joined
5 Group operating from airfields from Scampton in central Lincolnshire
to Woodall Spa in the south. On 15 December, 419 Squadron formed at
RAF Mildenhall and four days later, 420 'Snowy Owl' Squadron RCAF
also formed in 5 Group. 420 Squadron flew 535 Hampden sorties from
Waddington, losing 19 aircraft, until it moved to 4 Group in August 1942.

Sharing Waddington was 44 Squadron, which would remain at the Lincolnshire Station until June 1943, when it moved to Dunholme Lodge, four miles north of Lincoln.

At Waddington Pip Brimson found that 'TOT' (Time for take-off) was 'time for tension' and time for touching wood:

Flying Control became the central viewing position when ops were due to take-off; it was a spacious room overlooking the airfield, with a front wall composed almost entirely of folding windows which in good weather could be pushed back to allow spectators to step out on to the balcony. Side doors also gave access to it. Part of the rear wall was taken up by a floor-to-ceiling blackboard with painted headings thus: Aircraft Letter, Pilot, ETO, ATO, ETA and ATA. The aircraft letter and pilot's name (and squadron) had already been filled in, as had the estimated times. The actual times had yet to be entered and these were the important ones. It was for ATA that one touched wood and 'arrival' was the operative word.

This, however, was take-off and 44 (Rhodesia) Squadron and 420 'Snowy Owl' Squadron RCAF were about to operate from Waddington RAF Station. The Commanding Officers of both squadrons were already in the Control Office, as was the MO, the Engineering Officer and the Officer in charge of Night Flying, the Senior Flying Control Officer and anyone else who could find a good excuse for being there. The Station Commander would arrive shortly. The duty staff in the office was made up of the Flying Control Officer, an elderly civilian Recorder, Jimmy, a grounded sergeant-observer and one of the floating population of 'odd bods' who peopled Control awhile and passed on; and myself – an R/T operator. At this time there was little for me to do as I sat at the bench, my headphones round my neck; my time would come later. No aircraft used R/T on take-off – all wireless equipment had been tested on the ground and in the air earlier in the day, as had engines and instruments, by the ground crew out on the Flights and aircrew on NFTs.

Surprisingly, there were also three dogs busily engaged in chasing each other round the office! Two were spaniels, belonging respectively to Wing Commander 'Babe' Learoyd vc and a colleague; the other, a large English sheep-dog, owned by a small, dapper Flight Lieutenant. The dogs found an ancient deflated Met balloon under a desk and proceeded to have a three-cornered tug-of-war with it, giving yelps and barks of delight when they could bear to let go for a moment. This came to a very full stop when the door of Flying Control opened and the Station Commander entered, almost stumbling over the scrum of dogs. They were rapidly separated and quietened.

Engines could be heard revving up in dispersals; serious business was about to commence and expectancy hung in the air. Aircraft began taxiing from their dispersals to the perimeter track, nose-to-tail: 44's Lancasters, 420's Hampdens. The first Lanc' turned on to the runway in use marked out by the Flare Party across the grassy plain. The Airfield Control Pilot's chequered caravan stood at the beginning of the runway and it was he who gave a green on the Aldis lamp: the signal to take-off. His assistant immediately rang Control giving the aircraft letter and time of becoming airborne. The 'kites' laden with bombs seemed reluctant to leave the ground. 'Up-up!' came an urgent mutter from someone nearby. Lanc' after Lanc' thundered past, the engine noise reaching a crescendo as each passed the Watch Office. Interspersed with them were graceful, triangular-winged Hampdens – sixteen aircraft were to operate from Waddington this night.

The sky was darkening and the runway lights glowed. Navigation lights gleamed red and green and the ACP now needed a white beam from the Aldis to establish the aircraft letter before giving a green. In Control, the regular ringing of his field telephone was punctuated by the FCO informing the Recorder, which aircraft was airborne and this information was then chalked up on the Ops board. On the bench at which the FCO and I sat and next to my loud-speaker, was a squared board with sections in which to show the disposition of each aircraft – represented by a button with the aircraft letter on it, a different colour for each squadron. The appropriate button was now transferred to the 'airborne' section. The loud-speaker in front of me remained silent except for atmospheric crackles and occasional bursts of Morse interference. There was little talk as take-off proceeded; each kite circling the 'drome before setting course for the first leg of the flight to the target. At last, all were away and a musical hum was all that remained of the noise that had echoed so deafeningly round the airfield – then that too faded. A feeling of relief that all had gone well pervaded Control and after a few words with the duty FCO, the spectators drifted away. The Control room staff settled down to wait patiently through the next five or six hours, until 'ops' returned.

We lived through those hours in a kind of limbo. On the surface we appeared relaxed, occupied with routine jobs – the FCO writing up the log, the Recorder jotting down changing QFEs and other meteorological information, brought up by a WAAF assistant from the Met Office below. I, with an ear to the loudspeaker, wrote letters, read, knitted and made tea. Our mouths became stale with the end-less cups of tea and the air, stale with cigarette smoke. There was always the possibility of an early return – an aircraft with engine trouble, or some other problem; this was not a frequent occurrence but it necessitated being poised for action.

The hours wore on until within half an hour of the first ETA; this was the time to prepare. The Flare Party, Crash Crew and fire-tender were alerted. Sick Quarters stood by and the ambulance was at the ready. The airfield lighting was switched on and the chance-light positioned at the end of the runway in case of emergency. The blackout curtains round Control's extensive windows were drawn and overhead lights switched off. Low wattage, screened strip-lights along the top of the bench were all the illumination we had – or needed. My watch-partner had arrived by this time and would do the logging whilst I dealt with the R/T; the log-book could be a vital record at this time and it was one person's full-time job in the hour or so that ops were landing to keep it up – we all took our turn at this on the duty roster. Once more the room began to fill with people – those anxious to know the fate of their crews, the success or other-wise of the raid, the number of casualties to be treated.

I wore my earphones now, to be sure of catching the first, faint call from one of our aircraft. I lived completely in the world of sound between my ears, my senses stretching out into the ether, register-ing and rejecting calls from other aircraft to neighbouring stations, noting foreign accents – the Poles, from Hemswell – Canadian and Australian voices; atmospherics and foreign station interference; distant Morse code, intermittently threading through my wave-band. Then, 'Hello Jetty' far away but clear – and our first returning aircraft was in contact. I gave him 'Pancake' and almost immedi-ately, up came a 420 kite. 'Airfield 1,000', I said. And another: 'Airfield 1,500'. By this time the first 'plane had called 'Funnels' as he approached the runway and the second told 'Prepare to land.' I had a stack of aircraft up to 3,500 feet, circling the airfield and as the lowest was given 'Pancake', each was brought down 500 feet. More were calling up at frequent intervals. There was no time to think of anything except the R/T and it required every ounce of concen-tration. Our 'button-board' was invaluable at this time – the FCO changed the aircraft 'buttons' as each fresh order was given, so the position of every aircraft could be seen at a glance. (In the early days, we jotted it all down on scraps of paper, until Flight Lieutenant Button, an ex-RFC pilot, invented the board and thus dispelled the attacks of blind panic if anyone inadvertently covered up or moved our list!)

I was glad to note that the 'Landed' section of the board was filling up, as each aircraft called 'Switching-off' and briefly hoped this would be a good night, with no-one missing. If any aircraft reported damage or casualties, they were given priority to land and approach instructions and all services drove out to the runway at top speed.

Tense and anxious moments followed, until the aircraft was safely down. We had all witnessed crashes and heard the sickening, tearing sound of a belly landing, which could end safely with the kite slewing to a stop on the slippery grass, or tragically in flames. 'This *was* a 'good' night. No one was missing. We could sit back and relax, letting the tension drain away; the last aircraft in dispersal, the airfield lights switched off. I said 'Goodnight' to Pat, my relief, at midnight. All was well.

Further abortive attempts were made to sink the German warships holed up in Brest and though black smoke was reported rising from the *Gneisenau,* the ships remained afloat. On 18 December, during a raid on Brest by 47 aircraft, Wing Commander Basil Vernon Robinson DSO DFC was forced to ditch 60 miles off the coast of England. The Halifax floated for 20 minutes and the 35 Squadron CO twice re-entered the aircraft, the second time to look for his favourite pipe![19] The crew was picked up that same evening. Five other crews – four of them Stirlings – failed to return. One of the Stirling crews was captured and there were no survivors from the other three bombers. A fifth Stirling returned damaged and a 97 Squadron Manchester crashed at Coningsby on return to take the Squadron's losses to two. The night following, 19 Whitleys tried without success to hit the warships at anchor in Brest harbour.

Further raids followed on Wilhelmshaven and Cologne and Brest again and Düsseldorf was attacked on 27/28 December when five Whitleys and two Wellingtons were lost. A third Wellington crashed on Dartmoor on return and a Whitley also crashed at Foxholes in Yorkshire. On 28/29 December, 86 Wellingtons attacked Wilhelmshaven, and 61 Hampdens of the 81 detailed reached their target, the Chemische Werke synthetic rubber plant at Hüls. At Wilhelmshaven the visibility was excellent and crews claimed good results. The one Wellington lost was flown by Sergeant Alois Siska on 311 Czech Squadron, who had been shot down twice before. His aircraft was hit over the docks and caught fire. Eventually, it became uncontrollable and crashed into the North Sea off Petten in the Netherlands. The rear gunner perished but somehow the remaining members of the crew managed to climb into the dinghy. They were adrift for four days and the freezing cold and high seas tested their resolve to the limits. Hallucinations then affected the second pilot and later he died on Siska's shoulder. Before daybreak on the fifth day the navigator also died and the wireless operator lapsed into unconsciousness. Siska and the front gunner discussed their chances of rescue, which seemed remote. Neither of them wanted to be alone with their two dead crew-members and one unconscious comrade and so they decided to end their lives using drugs from the first-aid box washed down with sea water. The drugs were ineffective and on the sixth day they were awakened by the sound of splashing water. The dinghy was sinking.

In desperation they decided to tip their dead comrades into the sea to reduce weight. They managed to get the second pilot overboard but they had no strength left to get the dead navigator out of the dinghy. Suddenly, the front gunner cried out that he could see land. After what seemed eternity, they were washed up on the Dutch coast where they were taken prisoner by German troops. They were taken to a naval hospital in Alkmaar and then to a military hospital in Amsterdam where German doctors decided to amputate Siska's legs because they were frostbitten and infected with gangrene. As they put the Czech pilot on the operating table he had a heart attack and the operation to remove his legs was abandoned. Different methods of healing his gangrenous legs were used and they responded in some measure to this treatment. Alois Siska spent the next two years in PoW camps before being moved by the *Gestapo* to Prague in July 1944.[20]

Hüls was clearly identified in the moonlight and the factory was thoroughly bombed, fired and photographed. Four Hampdens were lost. Pilot Officer Stuart Bruce Keith Brackenbury on 408 'Goose' Squadron RCAF at Balderton was on his eighth trip. He reached the target and bombed it. The flare they could have used to illuminate the target had not been needed so they were still carrying it when *Oberleutnant* Helmut Woltersdorf of 7./NJG1 in a Bf 110 night fighter attacked the Hampden[21] while at 15,000 feet. The flare was hit and ignited. Brackenbury bailed out.[22] He was free for four hours before being found by some Dutchmen who led him down back streets to the police station, which was manned by Germans. He was taken to meet *Major* Wolfgang Falck, *Kommandeur* NJG1 at Twente. Falck apologized and treated him well before he was taken to a prisoner of war camp.

Attacks were made on the *Scharnhorst* and *Gneisenau* at Brest again on 9/10 January 1942 in a night sortie. All told, 82 aircraft were despatched. Take off originally was to be at 03.20 hours on the 10th but it was brought forward to 00.04 hours because of weather. Crews had previously been briefed twice for this trip but each time it was cancelled. At take-off it was dark and there was no horizon, with cloud at 1,500 feet. They kept to 1,000–1,500 feet to Upper Heyford when the cloud thinned and they went up through it to 7,000 feet. Twenty minutes were spent over the target. *Nickels* (propaganda leaflets) were dropped but as the target could not be identified they brought their bombs back. Flak was heavy but inaccurate.

On the night of 10/11 January a Wellington was hit over Wilhelmshaven and a flare it carried was set alight. This in turn ignited the wooden catwalk that ran down the length of the fuselage and the fabric covering the geodetic framework. The fumes thus generated were such that the wireless operator was unable to get close enough to the seat of the fire to put it out. Dense quantities of smoke blotted out the control board. The Wellington, caught in the beams of 35 searchlights – they were counted by the rear gunner of another aircraft close by – began rapidly to lose height. Its captain gave the order to abandon aircraft.

> Through the cloud of smoke somebody grabbed my hand. I heard the crew leaving. I thought it would soon be time for me to go too. I got up to see that everybody was out. The smoke seemed a little better. In the fuselage I saw my second pilot at work on the fire. He was wearing his portable oxygen set, for he could not breathe properly in the fumes.

The second pilot eventually put out the fire with an extinguisher and his gloved hands and the pilot got the Wellington under control again. He and his one companion brought it back in safety.

Three other Wimpys and two Hampdens failed to return from the raid on Wilhelmshaven and another crashed in England. *Gardening* and Intruder operations cost two other aircraft.

Wimpy crews were 'tough'; a Wellington that iced-up over Münster on 28 January fell from 19,500 feet to 2,500 before control was regained. Hampden crews too had to be made of stern stuff. On 21/22 January a Hampden, one of 38 aircraft despatched, bombed Emden. The trip was uneventful save for the cold. The heating failed soon after the take-off but the pilot did not turn back. Here is what happened to the rear gunner. He had brought with him a few extra incendiaries intending to open the window of the 'scuttle' and drop them. The scuttle is made of perspex and is curved. In order to open it a catch must be pulled and the window pushed up:

> Well, I got it open all right. That brought a blast of air at 65° of frost in at me. Then I had to fuse my incendiaries. It's rather a niggling little job – pulling out a pin and getting your fingers into a little wire loop. My big outside gloves had to come off, of course. But I pulled the thin ones off too, to try and get the job done quickly. This was a mistake. The moment my fingers touched the metal they went dead and powerless. It's a nasty sensation. I couldn't even begin to fuse those bombs. Then I realised I couldn't possibly work my guns either. I guessed the wireless operator was in the same boat – and he was, too. So I knew that if a night fighter came for us we were helpless. There was nothing to be done about it, though. So I tried to get my gloves on again but I found I couldn't. I must say I thought that meant that my hands would be gone. Then I realised that the perspex was still open: that was why I was freezing up so quickly. I began to fumble with the catch to get it shut.
>
> For a long time I couldn't get any kind of grip on it. Then I knelt on my guns to get more purchase. The movement must have stirred me

up enough to realise that if I didn't get the Perspex shut I was done for: no one could stand it open for hours. I got one of my bent fingers round the catch and it came out. Now the curved perspex should push down shut. I heaved at it. It stuck. I heaved again. It was frozen fast. But the exertion was waking me up. I went on fighting it. You know how maddening it is when some gadget won't work. My life may have depended on my making this one work. I just kept on heaving: then I tried to jerk it. Nothing happened. I couldn't think of anything else to do. I just went on at it. Then suddenly it shut.[23]

On 12 February – a cold day, overcast, 10/10ths cloud – news arrived at Bomber Command Headquarters soon after 11am that the battle cruisers *Scharnhorst* and the *Gneisenau* and the heavy cruiser *Prinz Eugen*, accompanied by a strong escort of destroyers, R- and E-boats, fighter and bomber aircraft, had sailed from Brest and were moving up the Channel, right under the noses of the British in bad weather and low cloud. The German naval force was obviously making for their home ports. The German warships were not discovered until late that morning when a Spitfire flown by Squadron Leader 'Bobby' Oxspring spotted them off Le Touquet. All available Royal Navy and RAF units were ordered to attack the ships before darkness closed in. Most of Bomber Command was 'stood down' for the day and only 5 Group was at four hours' notice. In the largest Bomber Command daylight operation of the war to date 242 bombers[24] and aircraft of Coastal and Fighter Commands and of the Fleet Air Arm made frantic efforts to sink the ships. The attacks were kept up from a little before 3 o'clock in the afternoon to a quarter-past six in the evening, by which time it was almost dark. Icing at times very severe, and rain and hail were met with by most of the crews. All the attacks were in vain. Most of the aircraft were unable to find the German ships and of those aircraft which did bomb, no hits were registered. None of the attacks by other forces caused any serious damage to the German ships, though the *Scharnhorst* and the *Gneisenau* were both slowed down after striking three mines previously laid by 5 Group Hampdens or Manchesters in the Frisian Islands. Operation *Donnerkeil-Cerberus* had been a complete success.

One of the aircraft that took part in the 'Channel Dash' operation was a 12 Squadron Wellington at Binbrook flown by Pilot Officer 'Pat' Richardson DFC RAAF. The crew sighted the *Scharnhorst* through a break in the cloud. Richardson manoeuvred to carry out an attack, put the Wellington into a steep dive and prepared to dive bomb the battleship. Sparklets of fire flickered from the *Scharnhorst*'s pom-poms and other AA armament and tracer tore past the bomber's wings and fuselage as the Germans concentrated their full defences on the audacious attacker. A shell shattered the Wellington's Perspex, severely wounding Richardson in the left arm. Despite the shock of the wounds he continued to attack.

Taking over the observer's bomb controls, Richardson waited, then pressed the master switch and released a stick of bombs from 400 feet across the *Scharnhorst*'s bows.[25]

Another Australian in the Wellington attack was Pilot Officer H W Johnstone, whose section became separated from its formation and made an independent attack on the *Prinz Eugen* and the *Scharnhorst*. Low, dense cloud all over the sea had made it difficult to find the ships. Flak was coming up through the clouds as Johnstone's aircraft dived and a fragment of shell hit his arm. The Wellington went on down and the crew saw the *Gneisenau* and *Prinz Eugen* about a mile and a half apart, with all their guns seemingly turned on them. The Wellington was hit again and the top of the cockpit above Johnstone's head was knocked off. An oil pipe was cut out and oil spurted over the navigator. The Wellington did not break cloud suitably for aiming. It rose and was hit in the tail as it did so. Johnstone made one more dummy dive and then tore down at well over 300 mph. The *Prinz Eugen*'s deck seemed to shoot up to meet them, growing larger every second, with her guns firing steadily. The front gunner said later he found himself leaning to one side of his turret but then he said to himself: 'You silly blighter; they'll get you there just as easily.' He raked the decks of the warship with his gun during the dive and at 400 feet they let the bombs go. Then Johnstone tried to pull out of the dive but the aircraft did not answer at once. He tugged at the stick with both arms and with his feet braced on the instrument panel. The Wellington was only a foot or so from the water when it answered and shot up into the cloud.

A 214 Squadron Wimpy flown by Wing Commander Richard Denis Barry McFadden DFC took off from Stradishall with a seven-man crew and 500lb armour-piercing bombs intended to break through the battle-ships' armour-plated decks. Ten-tenths snow-bearing cloud from 900 feet to 9,000 feet prevented any sightings so McFadden bombed on estimated time of arrival (ETA). When the Wellington turned back to fly home it started to ice up very badly. The port engine packed up and after about twenty minutes, part of the propeller broke away and went through the side of the aircraft, damaging the hydraulics. The Wimpy eventually came down in the North Sea at about a quarter to five in the evening. Sergeant Robin Murray, one of the two wireless operators on the crew, recalled:

When we hit, the Perspex area behind the front turret broke and the wave took me right back up against the main spar. I came to, underwater, pulled myself along on the geodetics and came up by the pilot's controls. There were four of them already in the dinghy, which was still attached to the wing. I was the last one in. We'd lost Flight Lieutenant [Patrick Frederick] Hughes DFC and George Taylor. We paddled around with our hands looking for them, and Sergeant

Andy Everett the other wireless operator, swam round to the turret which was under water, because the plane had broken its back just behind the main spar – but it was no good. I had swallowed a lot of salt water and was very sick. We were all sopping wet. We made ourselves as comfortable as we could. There were five of us in the dinghy – McFadden, Stephens [*Squadron Leader Martin Tyringham Stephens DFC who had occupied the tail turret*], Pilot Officer Jimmy Wood [*the second pilot*], Everett and myself.

For the first few hours there was nothing around – just the sea. It was quite choppy and that was uncomfortable. Unfortunately, whoever had put the rations in the dinghy had forgotten the tin opener, so we couldn't open the tins. Then the knife fell overboard, so we didn't have that either. So all we had was Horlicks Malted Milk tablets. It was cold – the coldest winter for nearly a century. We were hoping that someone would come out and pick us up, because the wireless operator had sent out a Mayday signal – but what none of us realised was that the navigator must have got his co-ordinates wrong. We had done a 180° turn and we were heading out to sea again, so we landed off the Frisian Islands instead of, as we thought, 20 miles off Orford Ness. I had read about how you mustn't go into a deep sleep when you're cold, because you get hypothermia and that's it – you die. So I suggested that we always had two people awake so that we didn't all go right off into a deep sleep – and that's what we tried to do.

Everyone survived the first night. We thought that any moment somebody was going to pick us up. We saw quite a few aircraft flying very high – unrecognisable, of course. There were flares on the dinghy, but we didn't see any aircraft that was low enough to have seen us. Once we thought we saw a ship – that was on the second day. We set off a flare, but nothing happened and we tried to send off another. But it wouldn't work – it was damp. None of the flares worked at all after that. We saw quite a few aircraft that evening, just before dusk, flying very high. We came to the conclusion they were probably German. We hadn't got a paddle on board – we were just sitting there. It was very strange, because people just went into a coma. They just sort of lost themselves. Stephens went first, on the second day at 4 o'clock. That second night was very cold. We just talked about various things. There was no despondency – we never thought we weren't going to be picked up.

At dawn of that morning, Wing Commander McFadden died. There were no visible signs of injury. McFadden was firmly under the impression in his last hours that he was in his car, driving from the hangars back to the mess. He was the only one who got delirious in that way. People sort of went into a coma. They would be talking quite normally – and they would gradually drowse off. You'd shake them to try to keep them awake, but they'd gone. You could feel that they were going. But it was peaceful – there was no suffering at all. They weren't in pain – they just quietly died. Jimmy Wood died about three hours after Wing Commander McFadden. He was very quiet. Finally, Sergeant Everett died at dawn. I was disappointed that he had gone so quickly. He went while he was talking – just drifted off. I kept them all on the dinghy and was able to keep my legs out of the water by resting them on them. It sounds terrible, but by this time they were beyond help.

The final morning was the worst time, because we drifted in towards land. The water was as calm as a millpond and the cliffs were about 150 yards away, with a gun emplacement on the top. It was about 11 o'clock, I suppose, by the time I drifted into the shore. I got a tin lid and caught the sun and somebody came out of the gun emplacement. Then the tide started to go out. I was starting to drift out to sea. That was a bad moment. Then a German Marine Police boat with a Red Cross came out and they hauled me aboard. I was able to stand up and they got me on to the deck. They tied the dinghy on the back with the bodies of my crew and came slowly back. They took me into Flushing dock. I'll never forget that moment – the deck was above the quay and they put a ramp down and as I walked down the ramp to the ambulance, there were five or six German sailors there and they all came to attention and saluted me.

Robin Murray was taken to a hospital in Flushing where he was treated for severe frostbite in his legs and feet and his hands before he was sent to a PoW camp.

Bombing operations at night were now made on Cologne, Aachen and Mannheim and the French Atlantic ports while aircraft laid mines in enemy waters. On the night of 18/19 February, 25 Hampdens set out to lay mines in the Frisians and off Wilhelmshaven and Heligoland. The only aircraft that failed to return was flown by Pilot Officer Robert Kee on 420 Squadron at Waddington. Kee was a history undergraduate at Oxford and was in France with his tutor, A J P Taylor, when was war was declared and he had rushed back to join the RAF. His trip to waters off the Friesians was exactly the same as he had done on his first operation, as a second dickey (a junior pilot on his first op, flying with a more experienced pilot to gain operational experience), about six months earlier. This time he was the first pilot:

On the whole, mine-laying was regarded as a piece of cake. You then had to lay mines from a very low height, about 400 feet with the magnetic mines. We came down to 400 feet and the navigator said, 'I can't understand what's happening. We should be there but the sea has stopped and I can't see a coastline shape at all.' We flew around a bit, no one firing at us. We realised what had happened. The sea had frozen over – it was very cold in February – so that the outlines for the land were indecipherable anyway. Whether we were over the right island we couldn't tell. Finally it turned out that we were over the next-door one, so we were in the right lane for laying the mines. We thought we would lay them there because it was obviously an island and obviously a bit of sea. And then I can't really say what happened. I remember suddenly searchlights were on us and a total feeling of chaos. I remember seeing some tracer but I don't remember any feeling of being hit. I do remember very strongly the feeling that the engine had no power. We were in a spin at 400 feet. I had been told by my instructor that the only hope in a Hampden in a spin is to push the nose down as hard as you can, which I did even though the ground was very close. The next thing that I remembered was the shattering of everything and thinking, 'This is it!'

The navigator [Sergeant W H J Rutledge] and I were saved by the fact that the aircraft must have been just regaining flying speed. We slithered along the ice with minimum friction. We were in the forward, up-tilted part of the aircraft and survived. The two gunners [Sergeants Horace Baker and James Richard Branston Adams] were both killed in the crash. They were smashed to bits at the back of the aircraft. After the crash I was able to pull the navigator, who was unconscious, some of the way away from the wreckage in case the 2,000lb magnetic mine went off. I then made off over the dunes, just trying to get away from the possibility of capture. Eventually a rather frightened German soldier appeared over the dunes shouting at me. I said what I had learned to say from films of the First World War. When you were taken prisoner you said *Kamerad*. He took me into his dugout where there was a very polite and friendly naval officer – it was a naval flak unit – who spoke excellent English and had been at Oxford in the 'twenties. It became very unreal: I heard him reporting over the telephone: 'We shot one down by flak!'

I spent the night there and the next morning a small Fieseler *Storch* aircraft came over from Holland. I remember thinking – a slightly romantic notion one had of being an RAF pilot – that now I must try and escape. There had been one case of a Hampden pilot who had managed to get control of what was probably a *Storch* and killed the German pilot and flown it back to Britain. I thought that I would get into the aircraft and hit the pilot over the head and try to fly it. Now it seems absolutely ludicrous, because actually when we got into the thing there was another *Luftwaffe* officer with us who immediately produced a revolver and sat facing me. It was a tiny little aircraft and I was squashed in the back and he sat facing me throughout. I had to drop that romantic notion. At the same time I was by then beginning to feel extremely relieved to be still alive. Then I heard the phrase that I was to hear over and over again for the next few days: 'For you the war is over'. And indeed it was.

By the middle of February 1942 it was announced that the steel works at Essen, Duisburg and Düsseldorf had been frequently hit; so had the I G Farben chemical works near Cologne, the E Merck works at Darmstadt and eleven power stations in Germany. Severe damage had been caused to three tyre factories at Hannover and the synthetic rubber factory at Hüls; the boot-leather factory at Worms had been burnt out and the output of lorries at Antwerp seriously held up. Raids like this alone would not result in victory but at the beginning of 1942 a new and dynamic leader and the arrival of a new aircraft, which was to prove the most successful bomber of the war, were about to usher in a new era in RAF Bomber Command.

On 22 February, having been recalled from the USA, where he was head of the RAF Delegation, Air Marshal Arthur Travers Harris CB OBE arrived at High Wycombe, Buckinghamshire, to take over as commander-in-Chief of RAF Bomber Command from Air Vice-Marshal John Eustace Arthur 'Jackie' Baldwin DSO OBE, who since 8 January been standing in for Sir Richard Peirse, who had become AOC-in-C India on 6 March 1942. On 16 November 1943 Peirse was appointed Allied C-in-C, Air South-East Asia Command. While serving in this capacity he eloped with the wife of General Sir Claude Auchinleck, C-in-C India, an act which was universally condemned and effectively ended his career.[26]

From mid-1941, Harris had been head of the permanent RAF delegation in the United States in Washington DC, and one evening in December during the first great Washington conference between the leaders of the British and US war efforts, Marshal of the RAF Sir Charles Portal, Chief of the Air Staff sought out Harris and asked him to take over RAF Bomber Command. Harris was directed by Portal to break the German spirit by the use of night area rather than precision bombing and the targets would be civilian, not just military. The famous 'area bombing' directive, which had gained support from the Air Ministry and Prime Minister Winston Churchill, had been sent to Bomber Command on St Valentine's Day, 14 February, eight days before Harris assumed command. Immediately upon taking over his post, Harris stated that the only international convention that he and his command would feel obliged to honour, was an agreement going back to the Franco–Prussian War of 1870–71 that prohibited the release of explosive devices from gas-filled airships.

Bombing German cities to destruction was not an entirely new concept. Ever since October 1940 crews were instructed to drop their bombs on German cities, though only if their primary targets were ruled out because of bad weather. During 1941 more and more bombs began falling on built-up areas, mainly because pinpoint bombing of industrial targets was rendered impractical by the lack of navigational and bombing-aids. Harris saw the need to deprive the German factories of its workers and therefore its ability to manufacture weapons for war. From 1942 onward mass raids would be the order of the day, or rather the night, with little attention paid to precision raids on military targets. Flight Lieutenant John Price, an air gunner on 104 and 150 Squadrons, comments on the area bombing strategy:

> There have been many arguments for and against the indiscriminate bombing of civilian targets. For what it is worth, I have reason to believe that the High Command on either side knew that this course of events was inevitable even before the war started. Germany commenced this 'terror' tactic as long ago as the Spanish Civil War with the wholesale bombing of civilians in Guernica.[27] Both the *Luftwaffe* and the RAF avoided this during the early war years. In my year of bombing (1941) we were briefed in the Ops room to hit military targets only. In 1942 no Army was ready to invade the continent; the Royal Navy dare not put to sea in view of the *Scharnhorst, Gneisenau, Graf Spee* and *Tirpitz* etc, being more concerned with the protection of convoys with food and ammunition from America. Therefore, in logical terms, the only weapon we had to retaliate was our own Bomber Command. In other words, the Germans were hitting us badly with their raids so we had no recourse except to fight with the only weapon we had – the bomber.

However, 'Bomber' Harris did not possess the numbers of aircraft necessary for immediate mass raids.[28] On taking up his position he found that only 380 aircraft were serviceable and only 68 of these were heavy bombers, while 257 were medium bombers. Another of the new generation RAF bombers, the Manchester, had been suffering from a plague of engine failures and was proving a big disappointment. At Waddington a 44 Squadron Manchester lost a complete leading edge from one wing on take-off half way along the runway. Losing all lift and out of control it had charged across the grass and piled into another aircraft at dispersal, causing an almighty crash but fortunately without any serious injury to anyone. During March, 97 Squadron moved the short distance from Coningsby to Woodhall Spa, south-east of Lincoln where wealthy Victorians and Edwardians once went to take the waters to become the second squadron to begin conversion from the Manchester to the Avro Lancaster. On 36 raids with Manchesters, 97 Squadron had lost eight aircraft from 151 sorties.

Re-equipment would take time and the first Lancasters, a heavy bomber in every sense of the word, gave some trouble. In September 1941 they had been supplied to 44 (Rhodesia) Squadron at Waddington for Service trials. In early 1942 deliveries began to trickle through to 44 Squadron and on the night of 3/4 March four aircraft flew the first Lancaster operation when they dropped mines in the Heligoland Bight. That same night Harris selected the Renault factory at Billancourt near Paris, which had been earmarked for attack for some time, as his first target. A full moon was predicted so the C-in-C decided to send a mixed force of 235 aircraft led by the most experienced crews in Bomber Command to bomb the French factory in three waves. *Gee* coverage was not yet available over the southern areas of Britain and down into France and so the bomber force had to be dependent upon good weather and good visibility but the principle of using a flare-dropping force to illuminate the target and a liberal load of incendiaries mixed with high explosive, including a maximum quantity of 4,000 pounders was to be employed. All but twelve aircraft reached the target, approximately 121 aircraft an hour being concentrated over the factory, which was devastated by 461 tons of bombs. Of 14,746 machine tools in the factory, 721 were destroyed and 2,387 damaged and many others rendered unusable because of the destruction of buildings. Some 722 vehicles ready for delivery were wrecked. Out of 3,000 workmen on duty, only five had been killed but 367 French people were killed, 341 were badly injured and 9,250 people lost their homes.[29]

During March the first *Gee* navigational and target identification sets were installed in operational bombers and these greatly assisted aircraft in finding their targets on the nights of 8/9 and 9/10 March in attacks on Essen, which without *Gee* had been a difficult target to hit accurately. On the first raid the weather was good, apart from the inevitable industrial haze, and 211 bombers, of which 82 were equipped with *Gee*, took off for the great attack. The pathfinder/fire-raiser technique began when the first wave, relying entirely on *Gee*, dropped flares for 15 minutes. Two minutes after the first flares went down, other aircraft started bombing with incendiaries, taking as their aiming point the big square in the *Alstadt* or 'Old Town'. Many of the incendiaries were dropped after the flares had burnt out, and scattered fires therefore sprang up, seriously misleading the main force. Although 168 aircraft claimed to have bombed the target area, the brunt of the attack fell on the southern outskirts and many bombs struck also the neighbouring towns of Hamborn, Duisburg and Oberhausen. Of the 3,000 incendiaries and 127 high explosive bombs that fell on the Essen area, appreciable damage to engineering works, railways and houses was reported. Krupps was virtually untouched. Eight aircraft were lost.

On the night following, 187 bombers, again largely made up of Wellingtons and with just over 50 Stirlings, Hampdens, Manchesters and Halifaxes, attacked Essen again. Once more much of the attack went astray. A Stirling, hit by flak, jettisoned its incendiaries over Hamborn. Fires at once sprang up and these were bombed by the following crews, who were unable to see their objective through the smoke and haze. Hamborn received the main weight of bombs and the great Thyssen steel works attracted what was intended for Krupps. Two Wellingtons and a 35 Squadron Halifax, which crashed in the sea off Mablethorpe, were lost and two Wimpys crash-landed on their return, at Oakington and Driffield.

Another Wellington, a Mk III on 9 Squadron, which took off from Honington, was piloted by 26-year-old Sergeant James Cartwright, who was from Stockport. Shortly after taking off a radio message was received stating that the Wellington was returning to base with engine trouble.[30] Near Harleston, Suffolk, an eye witness saw the bomber circle once with the engines spluttering then saw an engine on fire and flames streaming behind it. Cartwright went around for a second time. The note of the engines then rose to a high-pitched whine as the aircraft dived to earth. None of the six crew bailed out before the Wellington crashed in a ball of flame in a meadow, scattering a number of propaganda leaflets about the area. One of those who died was the WOp/AG, 21-year-old Sergeant Albert Singerton whose brother Reg was a radio technician at Honington. The two brothers often conversed on the radio on the Wellington's return flight to base. Reg had been best man at Albert and Gladys' wedding in May 1941.

On 10/11 March when two of 44 Squadron's aircraft took part in another raid on Essen, it was the first Lancaster night-bombing operation on a German target. Only 62 of the 126 Main Force crews dispatched claimed to have bombed the city, which was obscured by unforecast cloud and industrial haze. Two other efforts on Essen before the end of the month were little more successful. On 25/26 March, 254 aircraft were dispatched making it the largest force sent to one target so far. Over 180 crews claimed to have bombed Essen but the flare dropping was too scattered and a good part of the Main Force was led astray by an unsuspected decoy near Rheinburg, 18 miles west of Essen. Only nine HE bombs and 700 incendiaries fell on target. On the second raid the following night many of the 115 aircraft that were dispatched were dazzled by the brilliance of their own flares. (This problem was solved later by the use of 'hooded' flares). Only 22 HE bombs fell on Essen. Ten Wellingtons and a Stirling were lost, adding to nine aircraft, five of them Manchesters, lost the night before.

The Manchester was known to be underpowered and it was an understatement to say that crews had little confidence in them. Just before he and his crew were killed on 25/26 March when they crashed through ice on the Ijsselmeer, Flight Lieutenant Robert Dunlop Mackenzie a New Zealander on 103 Squadron had said. 'These Manchesters, they're awful. The kite's all right but it's the engine. They're fine when they keep turning but they don't often do so.'

E W 'Bill' Anderson was a schoolmaster in peacetime and joined the RAF in 1940 as a Pilot Officer in administration. The death of an air crew friend led him to volunteer for flying and, despite 'advancing age' and a suspect right eye, he managed to pass on to training in Canada and then on to bomber operations on 9 Squadron at Honington. He soon discovered another inherent 'weakness' – he was air-sick every time he flew:

> The battle of the Ruhr in 1942 cost many good crews.[31] The squadron lost steadily like most of the squadrons nearby and the faces in the mess were continually changed. Lunch time was a simple affair; apart from the glass of milk which all air crew got, they had the same rations as the men and served themselves from a large hot-plate. Looking round the room Anderson was struck by the fact that 'the youngest faces were those of the flight lieutenants and squadron leaders, for they were the regulars who joined the Air Force straight from school just before the war. The rest of the air crew were generally older, while the oldest men in the room, those with last war medals, seemed invariably to be pilot officers. The talk was of many things, chiefly frivolous. Of last night's 'party' and the sheep that was put to bed with old 'so-and-so' who was 'out to the world.' And how odd it looked with its head on the pillow and its eyes staring glassily up at the ceiling. Of 'Joe's' awful efforts at 'circuits and bumps'. Of the CO's dog and its shameless behaviour. Of 'Jane'. In fact, of everything except the one thing that is on everybody's mind – what is the target for tonight?

On the afternoon of Palm Sunday, 28 March, when crews went to briefing they found that that the target was a new one; the Hanseatic port of Lübeck. 'It was a stroke of genius on the part of the authorities to give us a complete change of target, a complete change of method and a complete change of tactics' wrote Anderson. 'Nobody had been there before and the plan was simple and full of possibilities: The first arrivals were to drop flares, then aircraft carrying incendiaries were to get the heart of the target well alight and finally high explosive would complete the destruction.'

The night of 28/29 March was almost a full moon. At this time the Baltic ice was beginning to break up and the port would soon come into full use for supplying the military requirements of the German armies in north Russia and in Scandinavia. Also it would be open for import of iron ore and other strategic materials from Sweden, a major supplier to Germany. Lübeck was an historic city, which offered an ideal target for a mass raid by RAF bombers carrying incendiary bombs. Founded in the 12th century, its five Gothic Churches and a cathedral dating from 1173 and once been head of the powerful Hanseatic League, Lübeck later lost much of its trade to Hamburg and Bremen but improved canal and port facilities helped it to retain its position as a centre of Baltic trade. The name Lübeck is of Wendish origin and means 'lovely one'.

Bomber Command was to hit the city in three waves. Although Lübeck was beyond the range of *Gee* the experienced crews of the leading wave used the equipment to aid navigation over the major portion of the route. The aiming point for the attack was the *Alstadt* on the River Trave, which consisted of centuries old narrow streets lined with thousands of half-timbered houses, which was in Harris's words 'built more like a fire-lighter than a human habitation'. Once the fires took hold the city dwellings would burn like matchwood. Of 234 bombers dispatched, two-thirds of them carried incendiaries. Crews were briefed that there were only light defences so they could make their attacks from a low level, even coming down to 2,000 feet if necessary. Harris had ordered a half an hour interval between the two waves in order to allow the fires to get a good hold before the second wave arrived, the main object being to learn to what extent a first wave of aircraft could guide a second wave to the aiming point by starting a conflagration.

This raid would always stick in Bill Anderson's mind:

To begin with, it was perhaps the first really scientific attempt to blot out an industrial target covering a large area. It was a finger pointing to what was to come. And it was brilliantly successful. The night was clear with thousands of stars above and no cloud below to cover the nakedness of the land. We had to keep a careful watch for fighters. Just as we flew past the island fortress of Heligoland, we saw tracer in the sky and an aircraft caught fire and fell blazing into the sea and burnt for a while on the water. Soon we had crossed the enemy coast and passed safely through the Kiel Canal defences. Ahead of us lay the target but we were early, so we flew into the Baltic to use up the few minutes we had to spare. It was frozen over and there were lines along it as if the Germans had been having skating races. Then we turned and ran into the target. As we came in, a few flares went down in front of us and we saw the target and let our incendiaries go. We were not quite the first, for as I was watching them falling below like a shower of little silvery fish, a load went down, a smear of twinkling lights. A few moments later and our 'stick' splashed across the target and there blazing on the ground was a vivid white V for Victory. And then loads began to fall thick and fast. Five minutes later when we set course for home, the centre of the target was an inferno. Deep, glowing, red fires were burning and we all felt some of the horrors that must have been going on down there.[32]

There was good visibility during the attack and just over 190 aircraft claimed to have hit the target, 304 tons of bombs being dropped in 180 minutes. Soon after the attack began at 10.30 p.m. one crew reported that there were a few small fires. Twenty minutes later others reported that the fires seemed to have spread right across the island on which the old part of the town was situated. The greater part of it was burnt to the ground. Great quantities of stores accumulated during the winter for use in the Russian campaign were destroyed. A photo-reconnaissance a few days later revealed that about half the city, 200 acres, had been obliterated, mostly by fire; with just over 3,400 buildings including the Town Hall and municipal buildings, the gas works, electricity works and tram depot, being classed as destroyed or seriously damaged. About 1,500 of these were residential dwellings. Southwest of the island city in the suburb of St Lorenz, 65 acres of built-up area had been completely destroyed. Northeast of the island in the suburb of Marli a 4,000 pounder had destroyed ten large houses and partially destroyed 45 others over an area of five and a half acres. The Drager Works, which manufactured oxygen equipment for *U-boats* and aircraft, had been obliterated as had numerous other industrial concerns. But the greatest devastation was in the old town and the docks. It was so extensive that no goods could be sent through the town or the port for more than three weeks and the effectiveness of the port was reduced for many months longer.[33] Casualties totalled about 1,100 dead and injured: the greatest toll in a German raid so far in the war. All of this had been achieved for the loss of just eight bombers.

Bill Anderson concludes:

Back at base we discovered that we must have flown alongside one of the other crews in the squadron all the way, though we had not seen them. For the aircraft we had seen falling in flames by Heligoland was a fighter that they had shot down into the North Sea on the way out and it was their stick which had first gone down across the target. The operation was a wonderful tonic to the squadron and to our crew.[34]

In Berlin Dr. Josef Goebbels, Hitler's Propaganda Minister, whose Sunday had 'been thoroughly spoiled by an exceptionally heavy air raid by the RAF on Lübeck' could hardly contain his anger. He wrote:

In the morning I received a very alarming report from our propaganda office there, which I at first assumed to be exaggerated. In the course of the evening however, I was informed of the seriousness of the situation by a long distance call from Kaufmann. He believes that no German city has ever before been attacked so severely from the air. Conditions in parts of Lübeck are chaotic.

On 4 April, Goebbels wrote that:

> The damage is really enormous. I have been shown a newsreel of the destruction. It is horrible. One can well imagine how such an awful bombardment affects the population. Thank God it is a North German population, which on the whole is much tougher than the Germans in the south or the south-east. Nevertheless we can't get away from the fact that the English air raids have increased in scope and importance; if they can be continued for weeks on these lines, they might conceivably have a demoralizing effect on the population.

At High Wycombe, Harris and his staff were ecstatic when the results were known, and more fire raids would soon follow.

The increase in RAF night bombing in the more favourable spring weather met with a rapid rise in *Nachtjagd* victories. In March 1942, 41 bombers and in April, 46 bombers, were brought down by German night fighters. All approaches to occupied Europe and Germany were divided into circular and partly overlapping areas, which took full advantage of Bomber Command's tactic in sending bombers singly and on a broad front and not in concentrated streams. Each *Himmelbett Räume* ('four poster bed boxes') was about 20 miles square, with names like *Hamster*, *Eisbär* ('Polar Bear') and *Tiger*, was a theoretical spot in the sky, in which one to three fighters orbited a radio beacon waiting for bombers to appear. Each box was a killing-zone in the path of hundreds of incoming prey. Victories were mainly achieved on the return journey when the bomber stream had been more dispersed than on the way in. It was easier too for the *Jägerleitoffiziers* (JLOs or GCI-controllers) in their 'Battle Opera Houses' to orchestrate *Nachtjäger* movements and pinpoint individual target aircraft in the *Himmelbett Räume*. Though the JLOs were far removed from the actual battles, high tiered rows of *Leuchtspukers* or 'Light Spitter girls' projected information onto a huge screen for them, and operators moved the plots on the *Seeburg* plotting tables.

On 5/6 April, Harris dispatched just over 260 aircraft, mostly Wellingtons, to Cologne; another new record for a force sent to a single target. Primarily, the raid was aimed at the Humboldt works in the Deutz area of the city. Over 200 aircraft claimed good bombing results but the nearest bombs fell about five miles away from the Humboldt works. Five bombers failed to return. The following night 157 bombers went to Essen but the crews encountered severe storms and icing and there was complete cloud cover at the target. Only 49 aircraft claimed to have reached the target area and there was virtually no damage to the city. Again five aircraft were lost.[35] It could have been more. Pilot Officer Mike Evans and the crew of *G-George*, a Wellington on 149 Squadron at Lakenheath, had a narrow escape, as Sergeant Jim Coman the WOp/ AG, recalls:

> We were returning from Essen when we were attacked by a Messerschmitt 110 over the Dutch coast just south of the Friesian Islands at about 18,000 feet. The 110 hit us in our port wing, holing one petrol tank and causing us to lose about 400 gallons of fuel. The gunners returned fire and it broke off the attack and dived back through the clouds trailing smoke. Before landing at base we lowered the undercarriage to examine the port wheel for damage but nothing appeared amiss. However, the pilot decided to keep the weight off the wheel for as long as possible and landed port wing up but on reaching stalling speed and the wheel touching the ground, it collapsed. The wing hit the ground and swung us round 180° and the wing broke across one of the fuel tanks. We all evacuated the aircraft quickly, as we could hear the engine sizzling in the petrol spillage. Fortunately, it did not catch fire.

On the night of 8/9 April when the main Bomber Command operation was to Hamburg, 272 aircraft were dispatched, yet another record raid for aircraft numbers to one target. Over 170 Wellingtons and 41 Hampdens made up the bulk of the force and smaller numbers of four-engined Stirlings, Halifaxes and Lancasters. Thirteen Manchesters also took part. One was *Q-Queenie* on 'B' Flight on 83 Squadron piloted by Pilot Officer Jack Heathcote Morphett. His American rear gunner, Sergeant Charles Dewitt 'Tex' Gellatly RCAF was a soldier of fortune who was popularly reputed to have taken part in all kinds of odd events along the Mexican border and in South America before crossing the 49th parallel to join the Royal Canadian Air Force. Tall, thin and, of course, a Texan, 'Tex' generally presided over a flourishing poker school at Scampton on days when flying was 'scrubbed' and the flight commander had not devised some ground training. The weather on the day of the Hamburg operation was bad but the raid went ahead that night and the poker school finished early. Icing and electrical storms were again encountered and bomb aimers were hampered by cloud at the target and forced to make a guess estimate of the aiming point. Although 188 aircraft reported bombing in the target area the raid was a failure. Four Wellingtons and two of the Manchesters of 83 Squadron were lost. Pilot Officer M A Sproule was forced to ditch after his aircraft was hit by flak; he was rescued but the rest of his crew perished.[36] *Q-Queenie* and Morphett's crew failed to return to Scampton. Only Pilot Officer Lovegrove survived to be taken prisoner of war. 'Tex' Gellatly had played his last hand too.

Like everyone else, 83 Squadron could not wait to begin conversion to the Lancaster also. 'F......Manchesters!' was the terse and comprehensive comment from 'Chiefy' Whittaker, the grizzled, technical boss of B Flight whose job it was to keep them serviceable.[37]

It was on 8/9 April that 97 Squadron operations finally recommenced in earnest when 24 Lancasters carried out a mine-laying operation in the Heligoland Bight. Up to the beginning of 1942, mines had been laid almost entirely by Hampdens; but other and heavier types were adapted to carry these unseen and deadly weapons. From 1 January 1942 up to the end of May, as many mines were laid by Bomber Command as had been laid from April 1940 to 31 December 1941. The sowing of much frequented enemy waters with sea mines dropped from aircraft was one of the quietest and also one of the most effective of the operations of Bomber Command. Here is the account of an eye-witness:

> You set off in the dusk, climb through a murky sky over the flat East coast of England. You climb through cloud; on the top is a brighter, clearer evening. You fly straight on your course by compass, with the navigator getting 'fixes' from the wireless operator to check his position every now and then. Night falls when you are half-way across the sea. Nothing happens until the rear gunner speaks into your ears on the intercom, pointing out a splotch of light on the starboard beam. This is a searchlight shining up from below the cloud layer. You are nearing the enemy coast. That is either one of his flak ships, or a searchlight position on an island, or on the coast itself. Soon you begin to see more lights and then a barrage in the distance. The old hands who know their way about these parts can soon say exactly where they are from the shape of a familiar barrage, without any need for their scientific means of plotting their position. However, nothing is left to chance. You carefully check your position, going down to get, if possible, a sight of the actual enemy coastline. Now, usually, is the only point of danger in the whole business. You may be shot up as you come down through cloud or, if the cloud goes down to sea or ground level, an in-experienced pilot may fail to pull out his aircraft in time. She may stall, heavily laden as she is and flop on her tail into the sea.
> When you have fixed your position exactly, which is the most difficult and most important part of the operation, you hear the pilot say 'Bomb doors open.' 'Bomb doors open,' repeats the bomb aimer. 'Over target now,' you hear the navigator's voice saying, 'Mines gone,' says the bomb-aimer. 'Bomb doors closed,' from the pilot. 'Bomb doors closed' from the bomb aimer.
> Up through cloud you go again, the searchlights groping for you. You may circle over an island or a flak ship and a barrage prods its red fingers at you. But you will have to be very unlucky if anything

comes uncomfortably near. 'Set course for home,' says the navigator. 'On course,' says the pilot. The job is done and there is nothing more except to seek for your base across the sea.

On 11 April, 44 Squadron were ordered to fly long distance flights in formation to obtain endurance data on the Lancaster. At the same time 97 Squadron began flying low in groups of three in 'vee' formation to Selsey Bill, then up to Lanark, across to Falkirk and up to Inverness to a point just outside the town, where they feigned an attack and then back to Woodhall Spa. Crews knew that the real reason was that they were training for a special daylight operation and speculation as to the target was rife. Squadron Leader John Dering Nettleton, the South African CO of 44 Squadron, who had already completed two tours, was chosen to lead the operation. Born in Nongoma, Natal in South Africa on 28 June 1917, Nettleton went into the Merchant Marine for 18 months after he left school in the 1930s and then decided that he wanted to be a civil engineer. During his engineering apprenticeship he worked in various parts of South Africa for three years and joined the RNVR. He was described as a tough 'Botha Boy' and served as a naval cadet on the same sail training ship, *General Botha,* as his fellow South African and future Spitfire ace 'Sailor' Malan. Nettleton was commissioned into the RAF in 1938. Nettleton and Squadron Leader John Sherwood DFC*, the 97 Squadron CO, and selected officers were briefed that the objective, on 17 April, was the diesel engine manufacturing workshop at the MAN (*Maschinenfabrik Augsburg-Nurnberg Aktiengesellschaft*) factory at Augsburg. No one believed that the RAF would be so stupid as to send 12 of its newest four-engined bombers all that distance inside Germany in daylight but that is exactly what 5 Group did. The raid that followed was suicidal in the extreme, losses were high and damage to the factory as minimal but the official line in the following communiqué was that 'No life was lost in vain':

> Bomber Command is still taking a share in the Battle of the Atlantic and will continue to do so as long as the battle lasts. It has bombed units of the German Navy at Brest, it has pursued them to Kiel and Wilhelmshaven; and when one of them, the *Prinz Eugen*, joined the *Tirpitz* at Trondheim, both were attacked two nights running on 28th and 29th April last, the attacks being pressed home with great determination in spite of bad weather and heavy defences. It has not confined its activities only to ships and their bases but has used the long range of its striking power to go far into Germany and deliver a blow at the production of submarines.

The MAN factory manufactured many of the diesel engines which drove the *U-boats* on the surface. It was situated on the outskirts of

Augsburg in Southern Bavaria. In the late afternoon of 17 April, a force of 12 Lancasters flying in two formations of six, set out to attack it. Very careful preparations had been made for this operation, which involved flying hundreds of miles in daylight over hostile territory. The factory covered a large area and the crews of the Lancasters were instructed to drop their bombs on the main engine shops where they would do most damage. They were shown a pencil sketch of the factory from which they had no difficulty in recognising their objective. They did so, in fact, when still three miles away from it. Moreover, the situation of the factory in a fork made by the River Wertach and an *Autobahn* made it easy to identify. The Lancasters flew very low. Accurate map reading, notably by Flight Lieutenant McClure (Nettleton's Rhodesian navigator[38]) and Pilot Officer Sands, in the first flight, and Flying Officer Donald Stuart Reddy Hepburn (Squadron Leader Sherwood's Australian navigator) in the second brought them to their destination.

The first flight, led by Squadron Leader Nettleton, ran into German fighters when well into France. In the battle which ensued, fought only 50 feet above the surface of the earth, four of the Lancasters were shot down. Nettleton recalled:

> I saw two or three fighters about 1,000 feet above us. The next thing I knew, there were German fighters all round us. The first casualty I saw was Sergeant Rhodes' aircraft. Smoke poured from his cockpit and his port wing caught fire. He came straight for me out of control and I thought we were going to collide. We missed by a matter of feet and he crashed beneath me.[39] Two others went down almost at once and I saw a fourth on fire. At the time I was too much occupied to feel very much. I remember a bullet chipped a piece of perspex, which hit my second pilot in the back of the neck. I could hear him say 'What the hell.' I laughed at that.

The combat lasted about a quarter of an hour. When it was over Squadron Leader Nettleton, undeterred by the loss of all but one of his companions, flew on towards Augsburg. Over France he noticed people working in the fields and cows and sheep grazing and a fat woman wearing a blue blouse and a white skirt and horses bolting at the roar of his engines, with the ploughs to which they were attached bumping behind them. But once in Germany nothing was to be seen.

> The fields appeared untenanted by man or beast and there was no traffic on the roads. But when we got near the target they started to shoot at us but the heavy flak soon stopped – I think because the gunners could not depress their guns low enough to hit us. The light

flak, however, was terrific. We could see the target so well that we went straight in and dropped all our bombs in one salvo.

Flying Officer John 'Ginger' Garwell DFM did likewise, but his Lancaster was hit and caught fire. He crash-landed two miles west of Augsburg.[40]

The second formation of six led by Squadron Leader Sherwood encountered no fighters. All they saw was a single German Army Co-operation aircraft, which approached them and then made off quickly. Just inside Germany Flight Lieutenant Ernie Deverill DFM noticed a man in the uniform of the SS who took in the situation at a glance and ran to a nearby post office where there was a telephone.[41] A little further on the Lancasters passed over a squad of German soldiers doing PT. Their physical exercises were enlivened by a burst of fire from one of the rear gunners and 'the speed with which they took cover did great credit to their instructor.' Crossing a lake near the objective, the bombers passed over a small steamer and a German on deck discharged his Mauser at them without noticeable effect.

They reached the target at a few minutes past eight and at once saw the two aircraft, which were all that remained of the first flight, dropping their bombs. They flew straight in through heavy fire. Contributing to it was a solitary German on the top of the main building of the factory, blazing away with a machine gun. He was shot off the roof by one of the rear gunners. When still three miles away the Lancaster piloted by Warrant Officer Tommy Mycock was hit and set on fire in the port wing. Mycock was still far enough away to have turned and made a forced landing; but he carried on, dropped his bombs accurately on the target and then, the flames having spread so as to envelop the whole aircraft, crashed to earth.[42] The leading Lancaster, piloted by Sherwood, dropped its bombs before it too was set on fire. It was last seen a pillar of flame on the ground 10 miles from Augsburg. Another flew so low that it passed between two chimneys of the factory.[43]

The Lancaster piloted by Ernie Deverill, which had been hit in the starboard wing when approaching the target was hit again over it and a fire started in the pipes leading to the aft and mid turrets. It was extinguished by the wireless operator as the bombs were dropped in a short stick. On turning away, the port outer engine stopped but was successfully started again on the way home. Squadron Leader 'Darky' Hallows' aircraft was hit near the port petrol tank when above the Assembly Shop but his bombs reached the target. Altogether seven out of the twelve Lancasters did not return. But they accomplished their mission. Photographs show that the main Diesel Engine shops were severely damaged by a number of direct hits and by the subsequent fire and that at least three other buildings next door to them were demolished and four more damaged. Production appears to have been seriously affected for some time.

Winston Churchill sent a message to Harris, saying that,

We must plainly regard the attack of the Lancasters on the *U-boat* engine factory at Augsburg as an outstanding achievement of the Royal Air Force. Undeterred by heavy losses at the outset, the bombers pierced in broad daylight into the heart of Germany and struck a vital point with deadly precision. Pray convey my thanks of His Majesty's Government to the officers and men who accomplished this memorable feat of arms in which no life was lost in vain.[44]

In March and April the Ruhr suffered eight heavy raids in which 1,555 aircraft took part, besides three small attacks. In the same period Cologne was visited four times by a total of 559 aircraft. By the end of April about 75,000 square yards occupied by workshops in the Nippes industrial district had been damaged. Heavy bombs had completely destroyed buildings nearby covering an area of 6,000 square yards. The Franz Clouth rubber works, covering 168,000 square yards, had been rendered useless, much of it being levelled to the ground. To the east of the Rhine a chemical factory and buildings beside it occupying 37,500 square yards was almost entirely destroyed. Severe damage had also been caused to the centre of the city. All this was confirmed by the evidence of photo reconnaissance. Twice Dortmund was heavily bombed: on 14/15 April and again on the next night, a group of factories in the Weissenburger Strasse being extensively damaged. Hamburg endured five raids, those on 8/9 April and the 17/18th being especially severe. The raid on Cologne on the 22nd/23rd by 64 Wellingtons and five Stirlings, all equipped with *Gee* for blind-bombing, was largely experimental. Over 40 HE bombs and more than 1,200 incendiary bombs were dropped on the city – perhaps 12–15 aircraft loads – but others fell up to 10 miles away.[45] Two of the eight Wellingtons dispatched by 9 Squadron at Honington went missing in action. The Squadron lost a third aircraft when Sergeant Warren Thompson Ramey's Wimpy, which was badly damaged, crashed at Sapiston on the return. Sergeant P G Russell who was found injured and still in his rear turret in the back of a hedge the following day was the only survivor. 'Ray' Ramey, who proudly wore the 'RCAF' flash on the upper arms of his uniform and was from Whitefish Bay, Milwaukee, had successfully abandoned his Wimpy over Herne Bay, Kent while returning from the operation to Düsseldorf on 27/28 November 1941.

A Wellington of 75 New Zealand Squadron at Feltwell that was badly shot about by a Ju 88 night fighter on the raid on Cologne crash-landed on return to base. At Lakenheath nearby, *S-Sugar*, a Stirling on 149 Squadron that returned from Cologne, landed and swung onto uneven ground whereupon the undercarriage gave way and the bomber was wrecked. At least the crew was safe.

In Wisconsin, 'Ray' Ramey's wife Dolores received the telegram on behalf of the RCAF Chief of Staff bearing the terrible news that her husband was dead. It arrived only an hour after the mailman had brought her a new photograph of her husband with a cheerful note hoping that she and Steven, the son he never saw, were well.[46] Ramey and the four other members of his crew – two Canadian, a New Zealander and an Englishman from Birmingham, were laid to rest in All Saints churchyard near RAF Honington.

Ever since the successful raid on Lübeck in March, Harris had been keen to mount another series of fire raids against a vulnerable historic town where incendiaries could once again achieve the most damage. Rostock on the River Warnow south of the Baltic, which like Lübeck had become a powerful member of the Hanseatic League in the 14th Century and whose narrow streets characterized the *Altstadt* like those of Lübeck, offered up the same possibilities for success. For four consecutive nights beginning on the night of 23/24 April, Rostock was smothered with a carpet of incendiary bombs as had happened at Lübeck a month earlier, the only difference being that on the first three nights a small force of 18 bombers of 5 Group attempted a precision attack on the Heinkel aircraft factory on the southern outskirts of Rostock.

I H Davies, a Whitley pilot on 51 Squadron at Dishforth recalls:

On the 23rd April 1942 we were briefed for a 'fire blitz' on Rostock; we were told that the town was to be burned to the ground and that we should keep on going back until the job was finished. (In fact it took four nights and we were on the first and third). Rostock was a city built like a pair of spectacles: the old town to the East and the new town to the West. Because the lighter coloured buildings were in the new town and more easily seen, they were pasted on the first and second nights with relatively little damage to the old town. In our bomb dump we had a number of 250lb incendiaries which we were not then permitted to use because they were said to give-off noxious phosphorous fumes and the powers that be were afraid that we would be accused of using poisonous gas and face retaliation. But by then the German Air Force was, more or less, beyond giving trouble and my CO, Wing Commander Percy Pickard (one of the few outstanding bomber leaders of the war)[47] asked for permission to arm a couple of aircraft with 250 pounders to mark the target. Up until then we had used flares, but these were often shot down by the enemy light flak. Permission was received and my aircraft and Pilot Officer Lambert's were sent off first with two incendiaries to mark the old town. It is now history that the third and fourth nights finished the job (there was no need to mark on the fourth night).

In the first area-bombing raid on Rostock the concentration was very heavy, all the bombs dropped from about 140 aircraft falling within the space of an hour. From about 2 a.m. onwards, fires raged in the harbour and the Heinkel works and smoke presently rose to a height of 8,000 feet. Geoff Rothwell[48] recalls: 'We acted as the marker with an all-incendiary bomb load. It was an all-Stirling raid and we obtained a photograph of the aiming point.'

Flying Officer John Wooldridge on 207 Squadron, heading for the Heinkel factory on his first trip in a Lancaster, could see the fire of the town glowing from almost 100 miles away:

> It was an amazing sight. There hardly seemed to be any part of the town that was not burning. We dropped down to 5,000 feet and skimmed across the factory. Lurid coloured shells seemed to be whizzing past in every direction. A building went past underneath, blazing violently. Then the nose of the Lancaster reared upwards as the heavy bomb load was released. Even from 5,000 feet there was a clearly audible 'whoomph' as our heaviest bomb burst. As we turned to look, we saw debris flying high into the air. 'Look out, pilot,' shouted the navigator, as another stream of tracer shells shot up past the wing tips and we turned away to have a look at the target. All over the place, blocks of buildings were burning furiously, throwing up columns of smoke 3,000 feet into the sky. We lost height to about 1,000 feet and then flew across the southern part of the town, giving several good bursts of machine-gun fire. Sticks of bombs and incendiaries were crashing down everywhere and we certainly took our hats off to those anti-aircraft gunners. They continued firing even when their guns seemed to be completely surrounded by burning buildings. The last we saw of Rostock was from many miles away. We turned round and took a last look at the bright red glow on the horizon, then turned back towards England, very well satisfied with our first raid in our Lancaster.[49]

The navigator of a Lancaster arriving towards the end of the raid told his captain that the fire he saw seemed 'too good to be true' and that it was probably a very large dummy. Closer investigation showed that it was in the midst of the Heinkel works and the Lancaster's heavy load of high explosives was dropped upon it from 3,500 feet. Damage to the factory was considerable. The walls of the largest Assembly Shed fell in and destroyed all the partially finished aircraft within. Two engineering sheds were burnt out and in the dock area five warehouses were destroyed by fire and seven cranes fell into the dock.

Four bombers failed to return and three more crashed in England. The crew on a 218 Squadron Stirling at Marham that crashed at Clenchwarton in Norfolk were all killed. One of the crew of a Whitley on 51 Squadron at

Dishforth, which crash-landed at Hellifield, Yorkshire was charged two-pence by a farmer for a telephone call to base after he safely descended by parachute.

Photographs taken in daylight after the second attack by just over 90 aircraft on Rostock the following night, when 125 aircraft were dispatched, showed swarms of black dots near the main entrance to the station and thick upon two of its platforms. These were people seeking trains to take them away from the devastated city. Another 34 aircraft attempted the bombing of the Heinkel factory but it was not hit. A Wellington on 150 Squadron at Snaith crashed on take-off and three of the four man crew on a 420 Squadron Hampden at Waddington died when the aircraft crashed near Sonderby Klint.

The third attack on Rostock the following night by 110 aircraft was met by strengthened flak defences yet no bombers were lost on the raid nor on the one by 18 aircraft that attacked the Heinkel factory once more. Manchesters on 106 Squadron commanded by Wing Commander Guy Gibson DFC scored hits; the first time in the series of raids that the factory had been damaged. Rostock was bombed again on 26/27 April when just over 100 aircraft of seven different types split into two to attack the city and the Heinkel factory once more. The Official History described the raid as 'a masterpiece', with successful bombing by both parts of the force. And all for just three aircraft lost; one of which set course for Sweden after being disabled by flak and the 301 Polish Squadron Wellington crew was interned. The four crew of the Whitley V that was ditched in the Baltic also survived and they were taken into captivity. All eight crew on a Stirling which crashed in the sea were killed.

Any loss of aircraft and crews was felt deeply by friends and families and there was concern too for the inhabitants of Rostock, where by the end of the fourth attack two large areas of devastation had been caused in the old town. All the station buildings of the Friederich Franz Station had been gutted and the Navigational School and the town's gasworks destroyed. Only 40 per cent of the city was left standing. The Turkish Ambassador in Berlin told his Government that 'Neptune Shipbuilding Yard and the Heinkel factory have been completely destroyed from end to end.' Goebbels said almost hysterically: 'Community life in Rostock is almost at an end.' The Ministry of Economic Warfare declared: 'It seems little exaggeration to say that Rostock has for the time being ceased to exist as a going concern.' Rostock was one occasion in his fairly brief aircrew career when pity almost overwhelmed Australian Sergeant Cal Younger RAAF. The Wellington navigator/bomb aimer on Flying Officer R A P Jones' crew on 460 Squadron RAAF at Breighton, 15 miles south-south-east of York recalls:

Because so many of its buildings were old and built of timber, we carried incendiary bombs. We could see the blazing city from

140 miles away as we flew home in relative safety. True, night fighters claimed some victims but we did not see one and the flak over the target had worried us little. There had been no challenge, no battle to carry out on our mission and so there was awe and pity and guilt. In the years since the war many aircrew who survived must have looked at their consciences many times and looked away again. Certainly, I wondered how much blood I had on my hands, or whether I had any at all. After all, in early 1942 RAF chiefs were worried about the lack of accuracy of the bomb aimers of whom I was one. The bomb aimer was also the navigator at that time. Later the two tasks were separated. On several occasions I brought back photographs, which proved that we had been on the target, so it is likely that I caused some deaths at least. Mostly one felt dispassionate about bombing. Our job was to bomb a target and to do so we had to contend with fighters and flak and searchlights (which could be very unnerving). One did not really give much thought to people below. I suppose their chances of survival were better than ours.

In the air on operations we were in danger from the moment we took off until the moment we landed. Statistically we had small hope of surviving even one tour of operations. We became impersonal. We had been given a target and we faced in most instances, an awesome challenge from night fighters and from flak. Frequently we were pinned in the sky by a cone of searchlights, often consisting of one hundred or more beams. We felt naked and as vulnerable as a butterfly. The target, even if it was a city like Essen, became for us almost an abstract, engendering no more emotion than a clay pigeon. That ordinary people were below us seeking what shelter they could from our dreadful cargoes did not impinge on our minds. Over the target the battle was usually intense. We saw our friends shot down in flames and our relief when finally we left the target was immense. There was no room for regret. There was little if any discussion of feelings on the squadron at the time, just an occasional, 'I felt sorry for the sods' or some such remark. There were some sensitive types who must have suffered conscience but they kept their feelings to themselves. It is difficult to convey the atmosphere in the Mess. We all knew we were very likely to die. We had only to watch our friends disappearing. We lived on a permanent 'high' and did not talk about death except in joke. When we were not on 'ops' we headed for York. Most went to pubs and bars. I always went to the cinema, more often than not by myself. Some became regulars at the local village pub.

The ferocious raids on Lübeck and Rostock prompted the *Luftwaffe* into reprisal. Exeter was bombed on 23 April and on 24 April, Baron Gustav Braun von Sturm said, 'We shall go out and bomb every building in

Britain marked with three stars in the *Baedeker Guide*,' thus giving the series of raids their name.[50] After the RAF attacks on Rostock were those on Stuttgart on 4 and 5 May and Mannheim on the night of 19/20 May. Mannheim was the second largest inland port in Europe. Its docks were continually full of raw materials, tank parts, armour plating and other war supplies, which came to them down the Rhine from the Ruhr. There were also many industrial plants situated in or near the city. In the attack by 197 aircraft, 155 bombers reported hitting Mannheim but most of their bombing photographs showed forests or open country. One exception was the force of 31 Stirlings that dropped more than 4,000 incendiary bombs, which left many fires alight. Eleven aircraft failed to return.

460 Squadron – motto 'Strike and Return' – had been the third RAAF Squadron to fly in Bomber Command.[51] It had begun to form at Molesworth on 15 November 1941 with four officers and 117 other ranks transferred in from 458 Squadron. Their first commanding officer was Wing Commander A L G Hubbard, an Australian by birth but who had served with RAF squadrons prior to assuming his new posting. Initially, 460 became part of 8 Group but this had been changed later to 1 Group when they moved to Breighton. Soon 460 was the only one carrying the Australian name in the Command, for early in 1942, 458 Squadron moved to the Middle East and 455 Squadron transferred to Coastal Command. In 28 months of endless attacks on the enemy 467 Squadron lost 590 killed in action (including five commanding officers), 117 taken prisoner and 84 who were not captured thanks mainly to the evasion lines in the conquered countries. 467 Squadron lost the equivalent of 100 per cent of its complement of operational aircrew in its first seven months. In its 17 months attacking the enemy 463 Squadron, with similar strength, lost 350 killed in action, 92 taken prisoner and 77 evading capture. Three commanding officers were shot down: two were killed and one escaped capture. 463 Squadron lost more than 50 per cent in the first four months. Australians in Bomber Command fought with distinction yet in their home country they were often referred to as 'Jap Dodgers' and some received white feathers from Australia. Only a more or less constant supply of new aircraft factories and reinforcements from the training pipeline enabled them to continue.[52] The Dominion air men came from the 'Empire Air Training Scheme'; Australia sending few gunners and even fewer flight engineers to England. Sergeant 'Jat' Jones, who flew as the rear gunner on Pilot Officer Frank Lillecrap's crew, recalls:

I was very politically minded in those days. I was born of Protestant parents in the south of Ireland. My father was an Infantry Officer during the First War. For all that he was not by any means convinced of the righteousness of 'England's war'. We were farmers and had our own trade with England right through the 1930s. We bought coal from Germany because England refused to buy our meat. I went to sea and maybe two years of the North Atlantic on an aviation spirit tanker converted me or perhaps it was the sight of the long-range Sunderland flying boats meeting us inbound from Biscay. I saw something of the frightful war before I joined the Air Force and realised that one could not be neutral. I was the cadet officer of a ship (my last) called the *Van de Vilde*, which was hit by another in convoy off Newfoundland at night. We carried, amongst other things, 1,200 tons of TNT. Both holds were pushed in by the bows of the other ship and we strewed 59lb TNT (empty) boxes minus their contents half way across the Atlantic: The sea water came in and washed the boxes out! My first ship was torpedoed after I had signed off with the loss of twenty men including the boy who relieved me. I went through two separate Focke Wulf Condor attacks off West Africa on a homeward bound convoy from Freetown and every Atlantic crossing had *U-boat* attacks of one kind or another .[53]

In Australia the politicians were not pleased at the distribution of Australians 'across the length and breadth' of England. They still clamoured for a wholly Australian squadron or squadrons.[54] In early January 1942, 460 Squadron had moved north from Molesworth and had carried out its first operation on 12/13 March from Breighton. The village of Bubwith was so close against the airfield perimeter that some of the Aussie Squadron's Wimpys in the dispersal bays were almost parked in the village. It was just a mile's bike ride through the gates to the 'Black Swan', soon known as the 'Dirty Duck', and the 'Seven Sisters', which was known as the 'Fourteen Tits', or more decorously, the 'Fourteen Titties'.[55] Aircraft on 460 carried Australian names like *Anzac, Billabong Battler, Jumbuk, Kanga, Advance Australia* and *Jackass. K-Kitty* had a lion's head similar to the one that roars to introduce MGM movies.

On 29/30 May, Sergeant Cal Younger on Flying Officer Jones' crew on 460 Squadron RAAF prepared for their 13th Wellington operation:

Ironically, the target which caused me to jump for my life was believed to be more or less undefended. Nor, it was hoped, were French civilians in danger. It was the *Gnome et Rhône Ateliers Industriels de l'Air* factory at Gennevilliers, near Paris. At briefing we were told that our squadron was to provide four of twelve Wellingtons, which were to attack from 2,000 feet and illuminate the target for the heavies who would bomb from 8,000–10,000 feet.[56] (That the air chiefs believed there would be no casualties was proved the following night when the first raid of 1,000 bombers took place. Aircraft and crews from operational training units had to be scraped up to reach the magical 1,000 so casualties among experienced crews was neither wanted nor imagined). The four navigators worked out their flight plans together. Some time before midnight the four Wellingtons followed each other into a moonlit sky. I had a strange feeling, a presentiment of disaster. As we flew over Northampton, its roofs shining in the moonlight, I suggested to Sergeant Ken Mellowes the wireless operator that he should go to the astrodome to look at his home city. We flew over Reading, crossed the coast at Beachy Head then set course for Paris. As we neared our target we were stunned to see a network of tracer; a fireworks display on a scale I had never imagined. Perhaps we were unwise to stick to the height we had been given. It looked suicidal in the scintillating moonlight. We did not hesitate. As I prepared to go to the bombsight I heard a crunching sound behind me. We had been hit and the intercom had failed. I told the Skipper we would bomb on light signals. A blue, master beam of a searchlight had fastened on us and Sergeant George Loder our rear gunner fired down the beam. Eventually he put it out but not before a red line of tracer traversed the length of our starboard wing, almost as if the gunners were operating a garden hose.

Standing beside the pilot I could see that we were doomed. I took his parachute from its container and put it on his knee and then released Sergeant George Houghton the front gunner from his turret, gave him his parachute, opened the hatch and told him to jump. I clipped on my own parachute as I returned to the Skipper. He had managed to clip on one side of his parachute. I did the other for him.

He asked, 'Was there any chance?'

I told him 'No'. He smiled a gentle, almost serene smile and told me to jump. At that moment the aircraft went into a steep dive, screaming as if in agony or from some terrible frustration. I could see that the Skipper did not intend to bail out. He really had no time but also he did not know what had happened to the wireless operator and the rear gunner and would never have abandoned them. Loder had bailed out when he saw flames streaming past his rear turret. The wireless operator who had had been standing, watching from the astrodome was killed by the burst of fire amidships.

I felt a strange calm and I am sure I would have gone down with the Skipper had I not seen the front gunner standing by the open hatch. As he stepped down I yelled to him to jump. He didn't and thinking I had nothing to lose, I jumped. The parachute just broke my fall. I was unconscious for a time but suffered no injury. Eventually I got up and walked away. Eight days later, after many hard hours of walking at night, I was arrested by French police and handed over to the Germans. Several years later I repeated my trek and discovered from a hotelier who had been chief of resistance in the area that the police should have handed me over to him; I should have been hidden until flown to England in a surreptitious Lysander, perhaps to join in the battle once more and to add to my guilt.[57]

Notes

1. Sgt Telling was killed six months later, on 19 January 1942, when his Wellington broke up during a training flight near Thetford, Norfolk. Saich, Sgt Eric Trott and four others on *T-Tommy's* crew were KIA on the Berlin raid of 7/8 September 1941 when their Wellington was shot down by a German night fighter, believed flown by *Oberleutnant* Helmut Lent of 4./NJG1 near Terwispel in Holland. Four Wellingtons were lost on the Bremen raid. *Oberleutnant* Lent (4./NJG1), *Leutnant* von Bonin (6./NJG1) and *Unteroffizier* Benning of 1./NJG3 each destroyed a Wellington. Lent's victim has been identified as W5513 on 104 Squadron and von Bonin's as R1613 of 214 Squadron. *Unteroffizier* Benning's *Abschuss* was either T2737 on 149 Squadron or W5726 on 305 Squadron.
2. Needham and his crew were KIA on the operation to Essen on 7/8 August 1941.
3. Gilchrist, who returned to England by corvette, was recommended for DSO but received a MiD.
4. Two Whitleys on 10 Squadron were lost to crews of 1./NJG1 and 4./NJG1. *Leutnant* Linke of 4./NJG1 destroyed Hampden AD835 on 83 Squadron over Schiermonnikoog.
5. Sir Hugh Trenchard was Chief of Air Staff from 1918 to 1930 and the chief protagonist in the development of what became known as 'The Strategic Air Offensive' in which bombers would play the decisive role in any future war.
6. A detailed investigation into Bomber Command's operations in June and July that was carried out by D M Butt, a member of the War Cabinet Secretariat, concluded that of those aircraft recorded as attacking their target, only 1 in 3 got within five miles. Over the French ports, the proportion was 2 in 3; over Germany as a whole, the proportion was 1 in 4; over the Ruhr, it was only 1 in 10.
7. Three Wellingtons, 1 Halifax, 1 Hampden and 1 Stirling were lost. The 2nd and 3rd searchlight suppression Hampdens (AD97EA-O and AE126 on 49 Squadron), which FTR on 28/29 August, were shot down and crashed into the Waddenzee south of Ameland. *Oberleutnant* Helmut Lent, 4./NJG1 shot down AD971 at 03.40 hours for his 21st victory. P/O Bernard Fournier and his 3 crew KIA. They were buried in Nes General Cemetery. Ten minutes earlier AE126 piloted by P/O Thomas Pratt had gone down in the same area, probably shot down by flak at 00.43 hours in the Waddenzee. Three of the

crew were buried on Vlieland and Texel Islands and Sgt Arthur Charles Willis, under gunner, at Harlingen. In addition to the searchlight suppression losses, 3 Wellingtons, 1 Halifax, a Hampden and a Stirling of the Main Force on Duisburg were lost; probably all to flak.

8. *Chased By The Sun; The Australians in Bomber Command in WWII* by Hank Nelson (ABC Books 2002).
9. Adapted from article in the Bomber Command Assoc Newsletter No. 28, February 1995.
10. R1772 piloted by Sgt Rowland Bertram Dunstan Hill was shot down over Kiel Bay by a Bf 110. Hill crashed to his death. Five crew bailed out safely and were PoW. R1798 was shot down on its return from Berlin by *Oberleutnant* Helmut Lent of 4./NJG1 as his 23rd *Abschuss* at 04.58 hours, near Drachtstercompagnie in Friesland province, with the loss of all Sgt Ian Patrick McHaffie Gordon's crew.
11. This was the squadron that featured in the well-known wartime propaganda film, *Target For Tonight*. F/L Percy Pickard and Wellington *F- Freddie* took the 'leading roles' and for a short time Mildenhall was like a film set.
12. 56 Wellingtons, 13 Stirlings and seven Halifaxes were despatched.
13. Four Wellingtons and a Halifax were lost.
14. *The Great Escape* by Paul Brickhill.
15. *The Great Escapers* by Tim Carroll (Mainstream 2004).
16. *SS-Obergruppenführer* Dr. Ernst Kaltenbrunner, Himmler's deputy, issued the text of what became known as the 'Sagan Order'. He ordered that the *Kriminalpolitzei* hand over for interrogation to the *Gestapo* more than half of the recaptured officers and after interrogation they were to be taken in the direction of their original camp and shot *en route*. After the war many of the murderers were tried and convicted in War Crimes Trials in Nürnburg and Hamburg and sentenced to life imprisonment or death. Kaltenbrunner, along with other top *Nazis,* was hanged in October 1946.
17. Lord, like so many others, carried out a dozen or more operations before his 20th birthday and he was not 22 when, with 30 or so ops and a 'rest' in an instructional job as his reward, he was killed off Holland flying a Wellington of 23 OTU on the third and final 'Thousand Bomber Raid', on Bremen, on the night of 25/26 June 1942.
18. Just over 90 more bomber crews were given targets as far afield as the Essen and other areas, Ostend, Boulogne and Oslo, where 13 Halifaxes sowed mines.
19. *Handley Page Halifax; From Hell to Victory and Beyond* by K A Merrick (Chevron Publishing 2009).
20. See *Out of the Blue: The Role of Luck in Air Warfare 1917–1966* edited by Laddie Lucas (Hutchinson 1985). Siska was charged with high treason and espionage against the Third Reich but the attempt on

Hitler's life diverted attention and delayed his court martial in Torgeau. Sent to Colditz before being taken to another camp, Siska was saved from certain death in front of a firing squad when the camp was liberated by US troops. He was flown back to Manston on 15 March 1945, his 33rd birthday, and spent two years in hospital before returning to Czechoslovakia.

21. Hampden P1165 crashed 2km west of Winterswijk (Gelderland).

22. Aircrew who bailed out earned the right to join the exclusive Caterpillar Club. Established in the 1920s, its founder was Leslie Irvin who had made the world's first free-fall parachute descent in 1919 before establishing a factory for the mass production of parachutes in 1926. Parachutes from the factories of Irvin and GQ, another British parachute manufacturer, saved the lives of thousands of Bomber Command aircrew who bailed out over northern Europe. The Caterpillar Club continues to this day for all those whose lives have been saved by parachute, members receiving a certificate and a distinctive golden caterpillar badge. By the time of VE Day, 20,538 badges had been awarded.

23. Of 54 aircraft sent to bomb Bremen this night, only 28 claimed to have bombed the primary target. Two Hampdens and 1 Wellington were lost. Of the 38 aircraft dispatched to Emden, three Hampdens and a Whitley were lost.

24. 92 Wellingtons, 64 Hampdens, 37 Blenheims, 15 Manchesters, 13 Halifaxes, 11 Stirlings and 10 Boston bombers in 2 Group, which were not yet operational.

25. F/O Norman Worsley Richardson and his crew were killed on the operation to Stuttgart on 5/6 May 1942.

26. Peirse died in 1970 aged 78. *The Right of the Line* by John Terraine (Hodder & Stoughton 1985).

27. A town in northern Spain almost completely destroyed in 1937 by German bombers aiding General Franco's forces in the war of 1936–39.

28. During his long tenure Harris would often be referred to as 'Bomber' Harris or 'Butch' although there has long been some debate about it being an abbreviation of the word 'Butcher'. 'Bert', a name often used by his American contemporaries, is even more obscure. He had acquired it in Baghdad before the war in the Officers' Mess, which was full of ex-Royal Naval Air Service men. In the Navy, just as all Wilsons are 'Tug' and all Millers are 'Dusty', so all Harrises are 'Bert'. *The Thousand Plan* by Ralph Barker (Pan Books Ltd 1967).

29. It was reported that 300 bombs fell on the factory destroying 40% of the buildings. Production was halted for 4 weeks and final repairs were not completed for several months. A post-war American estimate said that the production loss was almost 2,300 vehicles. Just 1 aircraft (a Wellington) was lost.

30. It was not the first time Cartwright and his air gunner, Sgt David
    Nicholas, had encountered trouble with a Wellington. Both were
    veterans on the squadron, and on their sixth operation on the night of
    9 November 1941 they were involved in a dice with death while
    returning from a raid on Hamburg. Cartwright was flying as second
    pilot to Sgt Pendleton when their Wellington developed engine
    failure in the vicinity of the target. They returned to East Anglia
    on one engine but stalled and crashed in a wood near RAF East
    Wretham. The aircraft was totally burnt out but none of the crew
    suffered any lasting injuries. Cartwright was later given his own
    crew and Nicholas went with him.
31. *Pathfinders* by W/C Bill Anderson OBE DFC AFC (Jarrolds London
    1946).
32. *Pathfinders* by W/C Bill Anderson OBE DFC AFC (Jarrolds London
    1946).
33. *Bomber Harris* by Dudley Saward (Sphere Books 1984).
34. *Pathfinders* by W/C Bill Anderson OBE DFC AFC (Jarrolds London
    1946).
35. Two of them Hampdens, a Manchester on 61 Squadron, a Stirling
    and a Wellington.
36. F/O Sproule and his crew of Lancaster *R-Robert* were shot down
    in the target area on 11/12 June 1942 during a *Gardening* operation.
    Sproule and two of his crew were taken prisoner. The rest perished.
37. *Gunners' Moon* by John Bushby (Futura 1974).
38. F/L Charles Surtis Cranmer McClure DFC KIA on 8/9 May 1942 on
    the operation to Warnemünde.
39. All seven in Sgt George Thomas 'Dusty' Rhodes' crew were killed.
40. Garwell and two crew were taken prisoner. The four other crew
    members were killed.
41. S/L E A Deverill DFC AFC DFM was killed on 16/17 December
    1943 when his 97 Squadron Lancaster crashed near Graveley,
    Huntingdonshire, returning from Berlin. Only W/O Benbow DFM,
    who was injured, survived.
42. All seven crew were killed.
43. John Sherwood miraculously, survived and though recommended
    for a Victoria Cross, was awarded the DSO. His six crew were killed.
44. 37 aircrew, of which 12 became PoWs; 36 returned. S/L Nettleton,
    who landed his badly damaged Lancaster at Squires Gate, Blackpool
    ten hours after leaving Waddington, was awarded the VC. See
    Legend of the Lancasters by Martin W Bowman (Pen & Sword 2009).
45. Middlebrook.
46. Thorburn.
47. G/C Pickard DSO* DFC lost his life on the legendary attack by
    Mosquitoes on Amiens prison on 18 February 1944 when his Mosquito

was shot down by *Feldwebel* Wilhelm Mayer of II./JG26 (KIA 4.1.45) flying a Focke-Wulf 190.

48. After completing his first tour on 99 Squadron he had served as an Operational Liaison Officer with the USAAC in Alabama and Georgia in 1942 and on returning to England was posted to a 4-engine CU, which was equipped with Short Stirlings.

49. After service on 44, 76, 61 and 207 Squadrons, in 1942 Wooldridge became a flight commander on 106 Squadron under Guy Gibson. On 17 March 1943 Acting W/C John 'Jack' de Lacey Wooldridge DFC* DFM RAFVR took command of 105 Squadron. He spent 3 months in command of 105 and on 25 June he was posted to 3 Group at RAF Stradishall. After the war Wooldridge wrote *Low Attack* and having studied with Sibelius, he composed music, worked as a conductor, with the Philharmonia Orchestra especially and wrote many plays, orchestral suites and incidental film music and film scores. His most famous was *Appointment in London* (1952) for which he wrote the music and also the squadron song. Wooldridge died in a car accident on 27 October 1958. He was 39 years old.

50. These raids killed 1,637 people, injured 1,760 and destroyed 50,000 buildings.

51. The first was 464, which was formed at Feltwell, Norfolk on 1 September 1942 in 2 Group. 466 Squadron was formed in 4 Group at Driffield in Yorkshire on 10 October 1942.

52. Rollo Kingsford-Smith DSO AM DFC writing in *Reveille*.

53. From the article, *Aussies In England* by Kim Fawkes.

54. When 467 Squadron was formed at Scampton on 7 November 1942 over 90 per cent of its aircrew and most of its groundcrew were in the RAF at the outset. As Australians became available they replaced the British. 463 Squadron was formed on 25 November 1943 from 'C' Flight, 467 Squadron. 462 Squadron was formed at Driffield on 12 August 1944. There were 4,050 Australian casualties in Bomber Command in WWII (and 9,919 Canadians and 1,697 New Zealanders).

55. Nelson. 467 Squadron RAAF formed in 5 Group on 7 November 1942.

56. 65 Wellingtons, Lancasters, Halifaxes, Hampdens and Stirlings.

57. George Loder had arrived in Scotland from Australia by ship and had noted that the 'colours of the landscape [were] beautifully soft and moist, the green of the fields and the trees the gentlest I ever remember.' George finished his tour of 45 ops on 156 PFF Squadron at Warboys in late 1943 but he wanted to fly a few more trips so that his crew could all complete their tour together. F/L Loder DFC KIA on the operation to Frankfurt on 20/21 December 1943 when Lancaster JA674 *Q-Queenie* and F/L Michael Acton Sullivan DFC RNZAF's crew FTR. See *Chased By The Sun*. Two years later Loder's DFC was handed to the daughter he never saw.

CHAPTER 5

The Whirlwind

The Germans entered this war under the rather childish delusion that they were going to bomb everybody else and nobody was going to bomb them. At Rotterdam, London, Warsaw and half a hundred other places, they put that rather naive theory into operation. They sowed the wind and now they are going to reap the whirlwind.[1] We cannot send a thousand bombers a time over Germany every time as yet but the time will come when we can do so. Let the Nazis take good note of the western horizon, where they will see a cloud as yet no bigger than a man's hand but behind that cloud lies the whole massive power of the United States of America. When this storm bursts over Germany they will look back to the days of Lübeck and Rostock and Cologne as a man caught in the blasts of a hurricane will look back to the gentle zephyrs of last summer. It may take a year, it may take two but to the Nazis the writing is on the wall. Let them look out for themselves. The cure is in their own hands.

There are a lot of people who say that bombing can never win a war. Well, my answer to that it has never been tried yet and we shall see. Germany, clinging more and more desperately to her widespread conquests, whilst even seeking foolishly for more, will make a most interesting initial experiment. Japan will provide the confirmation.

ACM Sir Arthur Harris

Every evening since her Pilot Officer husband had left Sutton Bridge on Tuesday 26 May 1942, Denise 'Dinny' Johnson had telephoned through to RAF Feltwell and talked to him for a few minutes. Her husband David, who stood six foot three inches tall, had been captain of his school at Rugby and was a competitor at the junior tennis championships at Wimbledon. He was apprenticed to Daimlers in Coventry and at weekends he was a trainee pilot in the Volunteer Reserve. On the eve of war he joined the RAF. 'Dinnie' had been a photographer's, artist's and fashion model and had given it all up to follow David to Cambridge where he did initial training. They had got engaged in the summer

199

of 1939 and they married when both were 19. Early in 1942 David was posted as a staff pilot to the Central Gunnery School at Sutton Bridge near King's Lynn in Norfolk where he flew the Wellington Ia. He had found digs for 'Dinny' and six-month-old son Clive about a mile from the airfield. Johnson and two other pilots were told to take scratch crews to RAF Feltwell on the edge of the Fens and he took Flight Sergeants Josiah Connor, John McLean and G J Waddington-Allwright. At Feltwell he picked up a second pilot, Warrant Officer Oldrich Jambor, a Czech, and Flight Lieutenant Hector Batten, navigator.

Some pilots' wives were not accustomed to their men folk being taken from them in this manner. Pilot Officer Douglas Mourton's wife Maisie was. Her husband's 'final' letter had remained unopened; he had completed his tour of ops on 102 Squadron before being posted to 22 OTU just before Christmas 1941. They lived near the aerodrome at Wellesbourne Mountford where on 25 May they were in their garden looking down on the airfield when a Wellington crashed on landing into another Wimpy that was waiting to take off. Both aircraft went up in flames. Nine men were killed and three, including one of the instructors, were injured. Four of the dead on one of the crews were New Zealanders. The next day everyone was confined to camp and the rumour had it that something 'really big' was going to happen. On 27 May they heard that all of 22 OTU's aircraft were going to go on an operation, which was unusual. Almost everyone was 'crewed up' and Mourton considered that he was very fortunate not to appear on the crew list. The old Wellington Ia's were obsolete and Mourton was not alone in thinking that they would be sitting targets for the German defences. On 29 May orders were received to disperse 13 of the Wellingtons to Stratford (Atherstone) and 11 more to Elsham Wolds, 11 miles east-north-east of Scunthorpe, a grimy steel town, lying in the shadow of vast slag heaps. Sid Chinnery, an engine fitter on *A-Apple* piloted by Flight Sergeant David Chell was one of several ground crew who assembled in a hangar before being dispatched by road, unaware of their destination. Late in the day they arrived at Elsham. There was time for a meal and they were then shown to their billets. Despite the time of day and their weariness from the journey, they noticed that their individual aircraft had arrived and were at dispersal points. Chinnery still could not find out what the target was.

Top level consultations between Harris and his subordinate commanders had revealed that the raids on Rostock had achieved total disruption. Whole areas of the city had been wiped out and 100,000 people had been forced to evacuate the city. The capacity of its workers to produce war materials had therefore been severely diminished. Harris, who had written that 'on the night of 28/29 March the first German city went up in flames' had for some time nurtured the desire to send 1,000 bombers to a German city and reproduce the same results with incendiaries. His first choice was Hamburg but if any such raid were to go ahead he not only needed the support of his fellow Commanders, he would also need political support from Churchill. And so on the evening of Sunday the 17th Harris drove to Chequers to discuss his 1,000-plan with the prime minister. The C-in-C outlined the plan, emphasizing that the losses should not to be greater than 5 per cent because the raid would be concentrated into 90 minutes and would therefore, saturate the defences. Churchill listened intently and was enthusiastic. When Harris finally left at 3 o'clock that morning he had Churchill's blessing and his statement that he was prepared for a loss of 100 aircraft, or 10 per cent. Driving back to his headquarters in his Bentley Harris found himself humming *Malbrouck s'en-va-t'en-guerre*, which always came into his head whenever he had just left the prime minister. The spirit of Marlborough going to war seemed appropriate.

On 20 May, Harris wrote letters to his each of his five operational bomber groups and the two bomber training groups and to Coastal, Fighter and Army Co-operation Commands, explaining the details for the 'Thousand Plan'. Sir Philip Joubert C-in-C, Coastal Command offered Harris 250 aircraft, which on paper gave Harris 1,081 aircraft but before the transfer to east coast bases could go ahead the Admiralty, which controlled Coastal Command operationally, refused to allow them to take part in the raid. To help make up the disparity 91 OTU Group was combed for training crews with at least an instructor pilot, but 49 out of the 208 aircraft would have to take off with pupil pilots. On 25 May warning orders were issued for moving about 100 aircraft to southern and eastern England from their more distant training stations such as the Isle of Man and 20 OTU at Lossiemouth in Scotland where 14 Wellington Ic's were to fly more than 400 miles south to Stanton Harcourt, a satellite of Abingdon. At Harwell there were 20 worn-out Wellingtons and 10 more at the 15 OTU satellite airfield at Hampstead Norris. All the crews were called to the briefing room and told that 'there was something big on requiring a maximum effort'. The Flight Commander devised a scheme with playing cards to allocate aircraft and to create crews. When the final orders were ready on 26 May with the full moon approaching, Harris had only 940 aircraft. Even this figure was an optimistic one.

Next day Harris went down to the underground operations room at High Wycombe soon after 9 o'clock for his daily planning conference he liked to call 'Morning Prayers', with his Deputy Commander-in-Chief Sir Robert Saundby and his air staff officers. Hamburg, the C-in-C's first choice of target received a stay of execution, as the weather over north-west Germany especially was unfavourable for three days running. On Saturday 30 May, Harris decided to send the force to his second target choice, Cologne, where the cloud was expected to clear by midnight. The aircraft total rose to 980 and then to a thousand. He gave the order 'Operation Plan Cologne' to his Group Commanders just after mid-day so that 1,000 bombers would be unleashed on the 770,000 inhabitants. At his HQ at Exning House Air Vice-Marshal 'Jackie' Baldwin received the news with interest. He told his daughter Pamela, a WAAF officer, that Cologne was a target he had bombed in the last war and he added, 'I am going to bomb it in this.' It was a day of surprises for Pamela Baldwin. Normally, her father rode his horse on Newmarket Heath every morning before breakfast but this particular Saturday he had allowed her to ride in his place.

Baldwin, now 49 years old, was a former cavalry officer in the 8th Royal Hussars who had learned to fly at his own expense and had joined the RFC in 1914. By October 1916 he was in command of 55 Squadron equipped with the DH4 bomber. When his flying days were over, the veteran flier decided to leave the RAF as soon as he could retire on a full pension and devote his life to farming and the breeding of polo ponies. An opportunity came in August 1939. He left the service but 12 days later he was attending York races when he got a telegram recalling him to duty as AOC 3 Group whose Headquarters was at Exning House, an ornate Victorian mansion and the home of Lord Glanelly, a leading racehorse owner near Newmarket! Baldwin's love of horses characterized much of his thinking. After five Wellingtons were lost on the daylight raid on 14 December 1939 he was compelled to compare the disaster to the Charge of the Light Brigade.

On the Saturday afternoon Baldwin rang the Marham Station Commander, Group Captain Andrew 'Square' McKee and told him that he wanted to fly with 218 Squadron to Cologne that night. McKee asked the CO, 30-year-old Wing Commander Paul Holder, a tall, quiet South African, 'Who shall we put him with?' Holder replied, 'He'd better come with me.'

After dinner, cooked and served by Lord Glanelly's staff, Baldwin told Pamela not to wait up for him. Her mother lived at the family home at Stamford. Baldwin did not believe in married men having their wives with them on operational stations and he practiced what he preached. 'See you at breakfast' he said.[2]

All bomber stations throughout England were at a high state of readiness to get all available aircraft airborne for the raid. On paper the actual number of serviceable aircraft totalled 1,047 bombers – mostly Wellingtons (602) – almost 300 of which were clapped-out OTU aircraft. Forty-five Hampdens of 92 (OTU) Group were also detailed and even Whitleys had to be used. No Whitley squadrons were left in Main Force, partly because the last three had been transferred to Coastal Command. But 21 of these obsolete aircraft in total were found from 10 OTU at Abingdon and seven more at Driffield from the target-towing and gunnery flight and 1405 Blind Approach Training Flight. Rank has its privileges and Squadron Leader Russell DFC decided that he would take *H-Harry*, the best Whitley available on the Flight: it could climb more quickly. John Russell, 21-years-old, was a Scot born in Oban, Argyllshire. One of the most colourful personalities on the Station, he was artistic and high-spirited and though 'screened' from ops he relished every opportunity to fly a trip over enemy territory.[3] The raid would also include the first Lancaster operations of 106 Squadron at Coningsby, which was commanded by 24-year-old Wing Commander Guy Gibson DFC*, a leader who had already shown exceptional capabilities. All told, 5 Group detailed 73 Lancasters and 46 Manchesters and 34 Hampdens for the operation.

At Skellingthorpe, a satellite of Swinderby, three miles west of Lincoln, preparations were in progress to get 15 Manchesters on 50 Squadron ready for the operation. Sergeant Jim Wilkie and his crew had been recalled from leave on 22 May but they were not among the names on the squadron board. Neither was Leslie Thomas Manser's crew. The NCO pilot – not quite 19 – and the 20-year-old quietly spoken and recently promoted Flying Officer were from different backgrounds. Wilkie, a grammar school pupil from Altrincham in Cheshire, was working as an office boy when in June 1940 he tried to volunteer for the RAF when he was all of 16. His first attempt failed but he tried again. When he was asked for his birth certificate he told the recruiting sergeant that he had been born in India and it had been lost. It worked. Wilkie was accepted and he gained his wings on his 18th birthday, on 18 July 1941. Manser, the son of a civil engineer in Post and Telegraphs, had been born in New Delhi on 11 May 1922. On the family's return to England he attended St. Faith's school, Cambridge and Cox's House at Aldenham, Hertfordshire where the family took up residence in the village of Radlett. Sergeant Leslie 'Beve' Baveystock the second pilot had not flown with Manser before and was older. At first he thought that his 'too handsome features' and 'slender figure' made him appear a 'bit effeminate' but, he added, when his wife Bette asked about him, he was friendly and likeable and he was a good pilot who 'gets across'. Pilot Officer Bob Horsley the wireless operator from Yorkshire, who had finished his tour but agreed to fly one more operation, had found this out this first time he flew with him. Quick to sum up people he had thought that this 'fair-skinned young pilot who had what seemed a weak almost girlish mouth' was a bit of a 'cis'. He soon noticed how Manser brought his crew's attention to mistakes and omissions without mincing his words but quietly and without fuss. Pilot Officer Richard Barnes, better known as 'Bang On' Barnes because of his accurate navigation, having flown with Manser as a second pilot on Hampdens, had asked especially to stay with his Skipper and do a full tour as a navigator. Horsley thought that it was tempting fate to do this extra trip and he went back to his room after lunch, had a sleep and then tidied up his kit, just in case he did not make it back. It was not something he had ever done before. He was not the only one with doubt in his mind. Wilkie's navigator, Sergeant Alan Bee, usually so talkative and animated was strangely quiet. He and Wilkie had been through training and the Hampden operations together but when his pilot came back to the squadron after his conversion course he had an entirely new crew and Bee had only joined later. Sergeant Alastair Benn the mid-upper gunner was an Australian. Eddie Finch, a hardened cockney was the front-gunner. He was twice Wilkie's age and the only married man. His best pal was Sergeant Doug Baird the rear-gunner. Flight Sergeant 'Toby' Tobias, a Canadian, was the second pilot. Sergeant 'Jock' Campbell the wireless operator had completed his 32nd operation before the crew went on leave and he was asked to do one more trip. Their leave came after they had been hit by flak on the operation to Warnemünde but they had landed safely back at Skellingthorpe.

Early on Saturday morning both crews were called to the flight office. They were to collect *T-Tommy* and *D-Dog* – two spare Manchesters belonging to 106 Squadron at Coningsby – and to stand by to fly them that night.

The raid was to be led by the *Gee*-equipped Wellingtons and Stirlings of 1 and 3 Groups who were to operate in a fire-raising capacity.[4] They were allotted a time span of 15 minutes to set the centre of Cologne alight with loads of 4lb incendiary canisters. At Mildenhall 419 Squadron RCAF had 18 first line Wellingtons ready. The Canadian squadron was commanded by Wing Commander John 'Moose' Fulton DSO DFC AFC who in 1934 had travelled to Mildenhall to watch the start of the Great Air Race. At his RAF selection board in 1935 he claimed that he used to hunt moose and caribou in Canada, a claim made to impress his interviewers. Born on 4 November 1912 at Kamloops, Fulton had served as a policeman in Saskatchewan and he began his military career as a trooper in the British Columbia Hussars. Before arriving in Britain he had flown with Boeing before taking a cattle boat across the Atlantic to England. Appointed acting pilot officer he spent his early wartime career with the Instrument Armament Defence Flight before flying operationally on 99 and 311 (Czechoslovak) Squadrons, finally assuming command of 419 on 21 December 1941. 'Moose' recalls Flight Lieutenant, The Honourable Terence Mansfield, 419 Squadron Bombing Leader, 'was not one to take over someone else's aircraft and 419 were wholly equipped with Wellington IIIs and there were crews for every aircraft so he borrowed an elderly Ic from the Blind Approach Training Flight. This normally spent its time flying along our Lorenz-beam, training pilots to use it.'

At 12 OTU at Chipping Warden too an old drogue-towing Wellington Ic with a winch in the rear of the fuselage was among the Wimpys detailed for the raid. The unlucky pilot assigned to fly it was Pilot Officer 'Bob' Ferrer who was married and came from Stetchford, Birmingham. Four others on his crew were Canadian. That afternoon his wireless operator was taken ill and Flight Sergeant Ronald Grundy was detailed to fill the vacancy. Grundy had completed an operational tour as a WOp/AG before becoming an instructor at Chipping Warden where he and his pregnant wife had digs nearby in the same row of council houses in Wardington outside Banbury where Ferrer and his wife lived off base. Grundy had been offered a commission but he had turned it down as it would probably have merited a posting away from his wife. Besides, he had applied for training as a pilot, which had always been his sole ambition even though he had been turned down at the age of 19 in 1935. Grundy knew Ferrer vaguely but the two wives had got to know each other well. His immediate concern was the aircraft but it behaved well on air test. He took the trouble to check on the crew's training record. They too passed muster.

Squadron Leader Hughie Stiles, who after completing his first tour in 4 Group Bomber Command on 58 and 104 Squadrons had on 14 July 1941 become an instructor at 22 OTU at Wellesbourne Mountford, was also unhappy with the choice of aircraft:

The Wellingtons which had been put out to pasture at an OTU after perhaps 60 sorties on a squadron were certainly not as nimble as they once were. I was therefore, not too surprised to find the aircraft assigned to me would not safely become airborne with more than 1,000lb of bombs compared with 4,500lb currently carried by front line squadrons. In addition to an instructor wireless operator, the navigator, bomb aimer and rear gunner were assigned from pupils on the senior course. Some crews consisted entirely of senior pupils.

Douglas Mourton was dismayed to discover that he was a substitute for his very good friend Juggins who had been crewed up with four Canadians who had not yet passed out. Juggins had refused to fly, as he thought that after surviving so long he did not want to get killed with a crew who were not very proficient. Mourton recalls:

I went along to briefing and met my crew for the first time. They were obviously very inexperienced. The captain was Pilot Officer Lowe. The briefing took place in the afternoon and we waited expectantly for the arrival of the CO. As usual we jumped to attention when he entered, then the usual 'All right men; be seated.' The large map of Europe was on the wall and in due course the ribbon was stretched to mark Cologne as a target. When the number of air-craft taking part was announced there was a gasp of astonishment, especially as the raid was to be condensed into a relatively short space of time. The risk of collision was discussed and the Intelligence Officer said that it was projected that only two would be lost in this way. One wag shouted out 'Yes but which two?'

22 OTU would put up 35 aircraft including 24 Wimpys from Atherstone and Elsham Wolds, where the ground crews were up early that morning. After a quick breakfast they were taken by lorry to their aircraft. 'Everybody was busy readying the aircraft for its air test' recalls Sid Chinnery 'following which, bombs were loaded. The weather was very good in the afternoon and we lay about waiting for take-off at around 22.30 hours.'

Among the throng of RAF and Commonwealth airmen who went to briefings at their stations there were at least five Americans. At Stradishall 31-year-old Flight Sergeant Charles L Honeychurch, a Stirling gunner, sat with the rest of Sergeant Tonkin RAAF's crew. Honeychurch was from Brooklyn; he was a graduate of Erasmus High School and had spent two years at Brooklyn College. Flight Sergeant Campbell, a 23-year-old WOp/AG on a 405 'Vancouver' Squadron RCAF Halifax at Pocklington was from Pawling, New York. He had joined up in mid-1940. On every one of his 20-plus raids he wore the medallion of St. Christopher around his neck. At Bottesford, ten miles north-west of Grantham in Leicestershire, Flying Officer Frank Roper was a Lancaster pilot on 207 Squadron. On 214 Squadron at Stradishall 21-year-old Sergeant Barrie Phillip 'Bud' Cardinal from Fort Worth was a Stirling gunner. Sergeant Howard 'Tex' Tate Junior from Dallas, Texas, was on Sergeant Wilf Davis' Stirling crew on 218 Squadron at Marham.

At Honington Sergeant Harry Langton, a London policeman in peacetime, listened intently to the 9 Squadron briefing officer. Langton's wife Liz was a nurse. During his pilot training at Marshalls in Cambridge they had been on the receiving end when German bombs hit the Globe Hotel where they were living and they had lost everything they had. Langton was deeply impressed by the briefing; he could not remember hearing anything so precise and emphatic before but Bill Anderson wrote that the elephant of rumour had given birth to a miserable mouse:

'The town is an important centre, the second largest city in the Reich with a population of ____' We had heard this line of 'Bull' so often before. 'Our job is to carry incendiaries to start up fires for the other crews to bomb' – same old job in the same old Happy Valley. Why couldn't they think up something new for a change? After all the fuss and gefluffle of the last few days, we were looking for something really big.... 'The weather is expected to clear over the target'.... Base conditions on return should be good....'

'One more thing. There will be more than a thousand aircraft on the target.'

The climax was terrific and in a moment everyone was cheering and laughing. So this was IT. This was what we had been waiting for so long. The Hun had asked for it. Rotterdam, Coventry, London and now, by God, he was going to get it.[5]

At Balderton near Newark 408 'Goose' Squadron RCAF would drop parachute flares to light up the target for the main force. Flight Lieutenant Brian Frow, one of the Hampden pilots, recalled:

> At briefing we were told that aiming point for 5 Group was the square in front of Cologne Cathedral. It was well known that in area attacks against cities at night, the bomb pattern followed the design of a triangle, with the apex at the aiming point, widening and falling back along the inbound track of the raid.

In 1932 Frow went to the Hendon Air Show with a friend from his south-London prep school. A 'hostile fort was bombed with live missiles; balloons forming life-sized animal were chased by big game hunters in fighter aircraft and eventually shot down. It left him spellbound. In the school holidays he cycled to Croydon aerodrome to watch and record every aircraft he saw. His eldest brother Herbert had been killed in action on the Western Front but Brian had made the RAF his career. On arrival at the OTU at Cottesmore one of his first tasks had been to act as one of the escort officers at the funeral for five students who had crashed on the airfield the week before. More experienced now, as the briefing continued he noticed that there were no orders given for straight and level flight over Cologne. He believed that there should have been. Weaving to get out of the flak only increased the risk of collision.

Tom Dailey, a Wellington WOp/AG on 158 Squadron at Driffield, recalled:

> A collective sigh of relief eddied through the flight briefing room as the squadron leader announced 'Your target for tonight is Cologne.' The port city on the Rhine was in relatively easy reach, just two or three flying hours away and therefore less time for being shot down. A gasp followed his next utterance. 'It will be a big one. We intend to send over 1,000 bombers.' No air raid on this scale had ever been conceived before. AM Sir Arthur Harris was out to make an impression. Before we took off there was the usual banter, 'Can I have your bacon and eggs if you don't come back!'

Flight Lieutenant John Price was now an instructor at 10 OTU at Abingdon, doing the usual so-called 'rest' period of six months between ops, the idea being to give seasoned aircrew a brief respite from real operations and also to teach others.

> I found it ironic that so many of us got killed on the OTUs. Pilot error (the pupil was flying), navigational errors, bad weather over England in wintertime – the losses were horrendous. We had Whitley aircraft, which were unbelievably slow and climbed at about 125 mph

with a full bomb load. They had the same turrets as the Wellington. There was no protection for the poor old air-gunners front and rear, just perspex. I felt very sad. The target area was the centre of Cologne and the map clearly showed the red crosses of every hospital in the city. I would have nightmares after the war thinking about all the women and babies we had killed that night. It is now obvious to me that we in England were determined to save our land at whatever the cost and killing the enemy, of whatever gender, the only answer.

At the end of the briefings at each Station a message from Harris, a last rallying cry to his crews, was read out.

The force of which you form a part tonight is at least twice the size and has more than four times the carrying capacity of the largest air force ever before concentrated on one objective. You have an opportunity, therefore, to strike a blow at the enemy which will resound, not only throughout Germany but throughout the world. In your hands lie the means of destroying a major part of the resources by which the enemy's war effort is maintained. It depends, however, upon each individual crew whether full concentration is achieved. Press home your attack to your precise objective with the utmost determination and resolution in the foreknowledge that, if you individually succeed, the most shattering and devastating blow will have been delivered against the very vitals of the enemy. Let him have it – right on the chin.

Earlier that afternoon, at Glebe House Farm within the airfield boundary at Cottesmore seven miles from Oakham, Muriel Ramsay took tea with her pilot husband Tom, or 'Mac' as he was known. He was 30 when war broke out and as an architectural draughtsman, which was a reserved occupation, he had had some difficulty in joining the RAF. The Ramsays were Londoners though their home had been in Leeds. When 'Mac' had been posted to 14 OTU for operational training they had looked around for living-out accommodation. Glebe House Farm was ideal. Hampdens often taxied right past their bedroom window to the end of the run-way before taking-off. They shared the large house with a lady whose husband had been on 14 OTU but had been posted away, and their five children. Before walking across to the briefing room Ramsay told his wife that he would be night flying and might not be back home until daylight. She was not unduly concerned as night flying at an OTU was no more than routine. Ramsay left the briefing room at Cottesmore and walked across the airfield to his Hampden at its dispersal barely 250 yards from Glebe House Farm, where his wife Muriel got ready for bed. Ramsay and his upper gunner, Sergeant Falk, worked for the rest of the evening on swinging the compass, which had given trouble on air-test and both men missed their pre-flight supper. They did not even have time to call in at the farmhouse for coffee and biscuits before take-off when they would be joined by Pilot Officers' 'Bill' Gorton the tall, serious-minded observer and 'Vic' Woolnough the under-gunner who deservedly wore the ribbon of the DFM.[6]

As the time drew near at Elsham Wolds, coaches and lorries picked up the aircrew. Sid Chinnery's crew arrived and after a conversation with David Chell he watched, as one by one, each aircraft went through its ground test. 'After successfully undertaking the test our pilot signed the Form 700. The signal was given for *A-Apple* to taxi to the runway. When it came the turn of our crew to take off we gave them the thumbs up sign. As silence descended in the airfield we went into our Nissen hut to await the return of our aircraft.'

Take-off was a little before dusk to ensure complete darkness before arriving at the enemy coast, although it was a clear, moonlit night. The first aircraft off, at 22.30 hours, were the incendiary force: the Stirlings of 15 Squadron at Wyton in Huntingdonshire. At Marham where 18 Wellingtons of 115 Squadron and 17 Stirlings of 218 Squadron waited to taxi out, the weather forecast made it uncertain almost up to the last moment whether they should start. When the green light came none was more relieved than the 3 Group commander Air Vice-Marshal 'Jackie' Baldwin, who had borrowed 'Square' McKee's Mae West, para-chute harness and flying kit before climbing aboard Wing Commander Holder's Stirling. Only a direct order by the C-in-C would have pre-vented him going on the operation and Harris had not been informed. One by one the Stirlings and Wellingtons rolled down the runway. At ten minutes to midnight, Holder and Baldwin watched as HA-L, one of the Stirlings, bounced badly on take-off, ripping off its port wheel, which bowled into the corner of the field. No matter, Sergeant Falconer would worry about the landing when he returned. At Feltwell less than 10 miles further south, 47 Wellingtons on 57 Squadron and Flying Training Command were also getting airborne. Last to leave were David Johnson and the two other Wimpys of the Gunnery Flight. 'Dinny' Johnson had been taken to a dance at Sutton Bridge. She had tried to telephone Feltwell and was told that they were not accepting any calls. It was the first inkling she had that her husband was on op. At half past eleven she asked to be taken home. Her husband's aircraft was still on the ground waiting to take off. At Cottesmore Muriel Ramsay was asleep when her husband taxied his Hampden past their bedroom to the end of the runway for take-off.

At Binbrook 12 Squadron put up 28 Wellingtons and crews, more than any other single squadron. To accomplish this task however, all aircraft had to fly without second pilots and this placed added strain on the crews. They began taking off at around 22.42. As well as putting up the most aircraft the squadron suffered the heaviest casualties and no less than six of their Wimpys were forced to turn back with various problems. Twenty-five minutes later Sergeant George Everatt, one of the second pilots promoted to first pilot and captain especially for the raid, crashed near Lexham in Norfolk, apparently through engine failure. *B-Baker* caught fire and all the crew perished. Another aircraft that was among the first to take off from Binbrook was *C-Charlie* flown by 22-year-old Tony Payne, a flight lieutenant on his second tour. *C-Charlie* crashed on the outskirts of Amsterdam with the loss of the entire crew, probably a victim of fighters. Two more Wellingtons, one flown by Pilot Officer Alan Albert Waddell RAAF and the other by fellow Australian, Pilot Officer Bruce Shearer, went down over the Reichswald Forest. Shearer's crew numbered three New Zealanders and an Australian. All were on their first operation. Shearer, a 19-year-old Queenslander from Brisbane, had done five trips as second pilot. There were no survivors on Waddell's crew. Shearer too died valiantly, keeping the Wimpy airborne while his crew – all sergeants – bailed out. Bruce Brown the bomb aimer and front gunner from Sydney, who had been a taxi driver, kicked out the emergency hatch in the belly and jumped from there. Eddie Ansford the observer and 'Mac' McKenna the wireless operator bailed out through the main hatch just aft of the cockpit. All three men were soon captured. Meanwhile Geoff 'Kid' Gane, the 21-year-old tail gunner had turned his turret into position so that he could drop out backwards. But before he could get out the Wellington went into a violent spiral to port. Finally the aircraft rolled out of its spin and Gane was able to get out. When daylight came he was easily caught. A truck that took him into captivity contained three coffins in the back. They stopped by a cemetery and for a moment he thought he was about to be shot but he was asked to look in one of the coffins. The lid of the coffin was lifted and there, pale but otherwise unmarked, was the face of his pilot, Bruce Shearer.[7]

Every aircraft that 9 Squadron could muster at Honington was there at take-off, recalled Bill Anderson:

> They followed each other lurching round the airfield, a long line of giant, roaring beasts. Then one by one they swung on to the end of the runway and then went roaring and pounding off into the night. The sky was clear above, the ground was clear below and the coast of England stood out black against the sea. On the port beam trembled the Northern Lights, a glorious panorama of shifting colours. All the stars were out to greet us and as we turned southwards towards Cologne we could see flying along below to port, above and to starboard, other aircraft all pressing steadily onwards to the target. Here and there over the Dutch coast, a searchlight wavered and a few guns fired. From the farmhouses in Holland,

the V for Victory sign was flickered out to us. Soon we were into Germany and as we came up to the Ruhr, the defences sprang into life, A couple of dummies, areas of lights that twinkled like incendiaries on a target, complete with canopies of searchlights, were hopefully lit up to attract attention but we thumbed our noses at them and passed on. We were out to get Cologne.

Squadron Leader John Russell had taken *H-Harry* off from Driffield at 23.10 and he set course for the target. Four other Whitleys in his flight, which took off soon after, were forced to return with severe icing. Tom Dailey sat at his position in his Wellington at Driffield as his crew waited for the 'off':

A flash from an Aldis lamp on the darkened runway was the only signal for our five-man bomber to lumber into the air. The sound of a thousand engines would have been deafening as we passed over the east coast of England heading across the North Sea. But at 10,000 feet it was bitterly cold. There was no formation flying at night. Each aircraft was alone. I used Morse to obtain coded fixes, triangulated from ground control for the pilot to set our course. The atmosphere aboard was edgy. But no one was biting their nails. There was always fear of the unknown but you didn't show it. Training bolstered your spirits and we had already been bloodied on previous sorties.

'Moose' Fulton and Flight Lieutenant Terence Mansfield took off in their elderly Wellington Ic at 23.25 hours:

Although 419 were in the first wave, we were not. At approximately 50 mph slower than the IIIs our Ic was also handicapped by trying to get to the briefed height of 18,000 feet, 4,000 feet higher than I had ever been before in a Wellington. We made visual identification on arrival at Cologne and made one circuit of the city before our attack. We then flew round the target again as Moose had a pair of night binoculars, which were remarkably effective, but I made no notes of what I could see. I think I must have been more interested in looking down from what seemed such a great height; this being the occasion on which I had dropped bombs from over 10,000 feet. Our attack was made as ordered. Height; 17,500 feet. Night photograph taken and later plotted within 800 yards of the aiming point. The weather over the target was remarkably clear and not as we had come to expect from the Ruhr area.

Crews got their pinpoint south of the city and then turned north, with the Rhine to their right. Ahead of them were two central bridges, first the Hindenbergbrücke and then the Hohenzollernbrücke, which carried all passenger traffic from the main station to the east. Their aiming point was a mile due west of the first bridge, in the centre of the *Alstadt*. In Cologne the sirens had sounded an hour earlier. This was the 105th air raid of the war on the city and the population were accustomed to aerial bombardment. Cologne had public shelters for 75,000 people with 25 special deep bunkers for a further 7,500. Twenty-nine additional such bunkers were in the process of being built. A total of 42,000 small air-raid shelters had been provided under or next to houses and apartment buildings for residents. Fourteen auxiliary hospitals had been built, giving an extra 1,760 emergency beds.

Bill Anderson again:

> Ahead were the defences of the city, below and to the left, the River Rhine was shining like a strip of silver ribbon. Great cones of searchlights were building up and as we came in, the flak opened up and at the same time the first incendiaries began to fall. Half-way through our bombing run, the searchlights caught us and blinded us and a burst of flak holed us amidships. We turned off and came in again, so that by the time that we finally bombed, the 'party' was in full swing. The defences were hopelessly swamped. The search-lights were waving helplessly and many of them had gone out. All the guns seemed to have stopped firing except for one battery in the south of the town, which, ringed with glowing red fires, still blazed hopelessly away into the skies. Amongst the blinding white incendiaries and billows of smoke, lights were leaping as bombs fell amongst the burning buildings. And every now and then, an especially bright flash would be followed by a huge, slow mushroom of smoke as a 'cookie,' two tons of concentrated destruction, burst in the doomed city. And as we left the target, we could see behind us a great pall of smoke building up over the heart of Cologne.

As the procession passed over the city, stick after stick of incendiaries rained down from their bomb bays, adding to the conflagration. The defences, because of the attacking forces size, were relatively ineffective and flak was described variously as 'sporadic' and 'spasmodic'. Flight Lieutenant Pattison, who piloted a 419 Squadron RCAF Wellington, wrote:

> When I bombed there was a huge fire on the east bank of the Rhine and another just starting on the west bank. When I left the target area both sides were getting it thick and fast and eventually, large concentrations of fires were spread practically across the length and breadth of the entire built-up area.

A Wing Commander of a squadron of Wellingtons said:

> When we got there we saw many fires which had not yet taken real
> hold but I thought it had all the makings of a successful raid. It was
> easy enough to see the city, for we could pick out the Rhine and
> the bridges quite clearly. There was little or no opposition over the
> target, I think because there were so many aircraft that the ground
> defences could not cope with them. We did meet with opposition on
> the outskirts but it was very indiscriminate. Before I left I saw the
> fires growing larger and larger.

The Wimpy flown by Pilot Officer Lowe on 22 OTU had taken off at
20 minutes to midnight and then flown across the North Sea to the
target. Sergeant Douglas Mourton plugged into the intercom. Although
he could hear shrapnel hitting the side of the aircraft, there was no
conversation going on between the crew. The rear gunner was not giving
the pilot any instructions as to where the anti-aircraft was coming from
and so forth, so he decided to go up into the astrodome and see what was
happening for himself.

> We were flying along straight and level with anti-aircraft bursting
> on the port side. I immediately shouted to the pilot to corkscrew
> to starboard, which he did and almost immediately there was a
> near miss on the port side where we had been a couple of seconds
> previously. I shouted to him and to the bomb-aimer to drop the
> bomb and let's get out of it as quickly as we could. We were over
> the town and there was no point in hanging about, especially flying
> straight and level, which was a sure recipe for disaster. Also, we
> were flying much slower and lower than the four-engined aircraft
> above us and were attracting most of the ack-ack. Also, suddenly
> you would hear a big rumble overhead, be rocked about by an air-
> stream and see four engines just missing you; it was very stressful.
> There was also the danger of being hit by bombs being released by
> the aircraft above.

The Wellingtons were followed closely by the Stirlings. Air Vice-Marshal
'Jackie' Baldwin sitting in the second seat beside Wing Commander Paul
Holder, recalled:

> We had not been flying very long before we met much low cloud
> and this depressed me. The front gunner got a pinpoint on an island
> off the Dutch coast but the weather was still somewhat thick and
> there was an alpine range of cloud to starboard. Suddenly, 30 or

40 miles from Cologne, I saw the ground and then the flak. It grew clearer and clearer until, near the city, visibility was perfect. First I saw a lake gleaming in the moonlight and then I could see fires beginning to glow and then searchlights, which wavered and flak coming up in a haphazard manner. The sky was full of aircraft all heading for Cologne. I made out Wellingtons, Hampdens, a Whitley and other Stirlings. We sheered off the city for a moment, while the captain decided what would be the best way into the target. It was then that I caught sight of the twin towers of Cologne cathedral, silhouetted against the light of three huge fires that looked as though they were streaming from open blast furnaces. We went in to bomb, having for company a Wellington to starboard and another Stirling to port. Coming out we circled the flak barrage and it was eight minutes after bombing that we set course for home.

Still miles from the target, Tom Dailey's Skipper called him up to the cockpit:

'Tom, come and have a look at this.' It was astounding. The night sky was a swirling fire of red, orange and yellow. Cologne was alight. We were in the second or third wave and the bombers which had gone in ahead of us had dropped incendiaries. In our plane was a feeling of exultation. This was payback. We had suffered the *Blitz* for all those years and were full of venom and hate for all things German. I was 20-years-old and twice, before I joined up, I was nearly killed by bombs falling on London.

Victor Martin, a Halifax pilot on 1652 CU at Marston Moor, recalled:

Silence reigned until the navigator's voice came over the intercom with the words 'enemy coast ahead'. Shortly after crossing the coast we encountered the defensive line of searchlights and anti-aircraft guns set up to protect entry into Germany. The searchlights swept the night sky and should an aircraft be caught, the master searchlight immediately focused onto it, then all others would follow suit. The guns began what was called a box; they fired above, below ahead and astern and gradually reduced the box until the aircraft was hit or could take violent evasive moves to extricate itself. Silence once again as we entered enemy territory with its defences now on alert following earlier waves, broken only by the gunners as they quietly checked with each other regarding the sighting of a night fighter; we did not attack to give away our position but observed in case of a sudden turn for hostile action. The first wave had now attacked and in the distance a red glow was already visible in the sky. Above the fleecy lining of the clouds hiding the enemy below all seemed so peaceful; another aircraft appeared ahead and travelling at the same speed we were motionless. Suddenly the heavy anti-aircraft guns opened fire and the exploding shells shattered our world of peace. The aircraft ahead received a direct hit and with a blue flash was gone. Taking the immediate evasive action of undulating and banks to port and starboard, we continued our course.

Flying Officer Arthur 'Bull' Friend, a tall, 17-stone Rhodesian second pilot-navigator on a 97 Squadron Lancaster, recalled:

The dykes, the towns and sometimes even the farmhouses of Holland: we could see them all clearly as we flew towards Cologne soon after midnight. The moon was to our starboard bow and straight ahead there was a rose-coloured glow in the sky. We thought it was something to do with a searchlight belt, which runs for about 200 miles along the Dutch–German frontier. As we went through this belt we saw by the light of blue searchlights some friendly aircraft going the same way as ourselves and a few coming back. But the glow was still ahead. It crossed my mind then that it might be Cologne but we decided between us that it was too bright a light to be so far away. The navigator checked his course. It could only be Cologne.

Squadron Leader Hughie Stiles adds:

The two-and-a-half hours to the target were relatively uneventful; except that coaxing the aircraft all that time put me barely at 15,000 feet as I approached the target. It just refused to go a foot higher and I surmised that the other 999 were mostly above me and I wondered if the bombs coming down would exceed the flak coming up! Shortly before approaching any target one always wondered what the intensity of the flak and searchlights would be and who would be the 'Joe'. While I was making my run it seemed that at any moment there was always one aircraft, which the batteries of radar-controlled searchlights, maybe 30 or so to a group, would lock onto and form such a large area of intersection that it was almost impossible to fly out of it. And into which the heavy flak would be poured. I didn't have long to wait. My track was between two distinct groups of searchlights aimed more or less vertically into the sky. I kept my fingers crossed and hoped that I would sneak through while they were perhaps monitoring someone else. I was watching the increasing flak bursts ahead and above when in a single instant all the searchlights in both groups swung towards each other and coned me in a blinding zone of light. I was the 'Joe'. Seeking the comfort of the instruments for a second or two to rest my eyes from the shock, I put the aircraft into a steep diving turn to port in a frantic effort to escape.

Superimposed upon the myriad lights which followed wherever I went, I was uncomfortably conscious of the more mellowed colour of the shell bursts, which were so close I could hear the hissing thuds as they exploded. Instinctively I wrenched it over to a starboard turn, to no avail and I felt sure a direct hit was inevitable. Continuing down in the maelstrom of blinding noise, weaving from left to right, I noticed we were now down to 10,000 feet and moving at nearly 350 mph; over twice normal speed. Flattening out required some effort at that speed. As I banked again to the left in a fairly steep turn I felt and heard a terrific impact, which jarred the whole aircraft. The wireless operator reported that about three feet of the top of the fuselage behind the astrodome had just disappeared. As we were now well within the target area I instructed the bomb aimer to jettison, as it looked as though I was going to need all the performance I could get, any second. Then, as if to confirm my action I saw a jagged tulip-like shape appear on the top of the port-engine cover. I scanned the engine oil pressure and temperature gauges for a reduction in one and an increase in the other. It seemed impossible for a piece of flak to come out of the top of the engine cover without having first caused critical damage in its passage through the engine components.

Now at 9,500 feet the defences regretfully turned their attention to the next one on the 'Joe' list, while I set a course for home alternately praying and watching those port engine instruments. The thought of having to keep this thing in the air, on one engine, for over two hours filled me with a great deal of apprehension after my last experience on the Wellesbourne circuit but minutes ticked by with no unpleasant manifestations and I finally relaxed. The crew had suffered no injuries and everything was still working so what more could one ask?

Tom Dailey adds:

As we went in on our bombing run we had to observe W/T silence. Flak was bursting around us. Our bomb aimer, lying prone above the open hatch, was guiding the pilot. Left was always repeated twice, to avoid confusion. So it was 'left, left, right a bit'. Then the words we all waited for: 'bombs gone!' Two tons of high explosives and incendiaries in canisters had been delivered to their destination. We felt the aircraft lift and then tilt as the pilot put on full throttle and banked to the left, heading for the North Sea and home.

'Bull' Friend continues:

It looked as though we would be on top of it in a minute or two and we opened our bomb doors. We flew on; the glow was as far away as ever, so we closed our bomb doors. The glare was still there like a huge cigarette-end in the German blackout. Then we flew into smoke; through it the Rhine appeared a dim silver ribbon below us. The smoke was drifting in the wind. We came in over the fires. Down in my bomb aimer's hatch I looked at the burning town below me. I remembered what had been said at the briefing, 'Don't drop your bombs on the buildings that are burning best. Go in and find another target for yourself.' Well at last I found one right in the most industrial part of the town. I let the bombs go. We had a heavy load, hundreds of incendiaries and big high explosive. The incendiaries going off were like sudden platinum-coloured flashes, which slowly turned to red. We saw many flashes going from white to red and then our great bomb burst in the centre of them.

As we crossed the town there were burning blocks to the right of us and to the left the fires were immense. They were really continuous. The flames were higher than I had ever seen before. Buildings were skeletons in the midst of fires. Sometimes you could see what appeared to be frameworks of white-hot joists. The blast of the bombs was hurling walls themselves across the flames. As we came away, we saw more and more of our aircraft below us silhouetted against the flames. I identified Wellingtons, Halifaxes, Manchesters and other Lancasters. Above us there were still more bombers lit by the light of the moon. They were doing exactly as we did: going according to plan and coming out according to plan and making their way home.

'Bull' Friend would return from Cologne but would die piloting a Lancaster on the operation on Bremen on 27/28 June. Two of his crew were killed also; four men were taken into captivity.

Closing in on the target at Cologne, the intensity of the fire became more apparent to Victor Martin:

It was not the usual cluster of separate burnings; it appeared that the complete area below was ablaze in one large fire. A feeling of sorrow came but with a ferocious burst of anti-aircraft fire bouncing the aircraft about with explosions, concentration on the purpose of the mission became uppermost. With the most dangerous part now commencing, a level and steady course had to be maintained for accurate aiming, the navigator lying down over the bomb sight giving instructions for lining up the target – 'left, left, steady, right, steady, bombs away.' As all bombs were released at once, the aircraft, relieved of its heavy load, rose like a lift and with so many bombers above this could cause a serious problem unless quickly controlled. Later, back at base it was discovered the navigator had cuts on each side of his neck, probably caused by shrapnel during the steady bombing run in. If so, a slight waver could have proved fatal.

Course was set for home and the running of the gauntlet of ack-ack, searchlights and night fighters once again. Dropping down to an altitude below the range of the heavy guns and above light fire, we were suddenly in a ring of searchlights giving a most eerie feeling, a ghostly light filling the darkness of the cockpit. The tracer shells from the guns seemed to be still as you looked at them, coming up and then flashing past the windscreen. A bank to starboard gave the gunners a better view to return fire; the aircraft filled with the sinister sound of machine guns firing at a rate of several thousand rounds a minute. Searchlights were hit and the tracer shells coming up, like water from a hose pipe moving around to cover an area, also ceased.

When the Halifaxes arrived the raid had lasted for an hour. By this time Cologne was visible to late comers 60 miles away, first as a dull red glow over a large area of ground.

One Halifax pilot stated:

It was almost too gigantic to be real. But it was real enough when we got there. Below us in every part of the city buildings were ablaze. Here and there you could see their outlines but mostly it was just one big stretch of fire. It was strange to see the flames reflected on our aircraft. It looked at times as though we were on fire ourselves, with a red glow dancing up and down the wings.

A bomb-aimer who was lying prone in a Halifax made an interesting comparison: 'There were aircraft everywhere. The sky over Cologne was as busy as Piccadilly Circus. I could identify every type of bomber in our force by the light of the moon and the fires.'

The captain of one Halifax and his navigator thought that the fire towards which they were flying was too large to be anything but an especially elaborate dummy. The pilot of another Halifax thought that a heath or a whole forest must have been blazing. Ten miles off however, they knew that the glow came from a town on fire. As they drew near they could see more and more loads of incendiaries burning in long, narrow rectangles made up of pinpoints of bright, white patch, which swiftly blossomed each into a rose of fire. Like the others, the Halifaxes identified the target easily by means of the bridges over the Rhine.

One captain reported:

So vast was the burning that ordinary fires on the outskirts of the city or outside it, which I should usually have described as very big, looked quite unimportant. It was strange to see the flames reflected on our aircraft. It looked at times as though we were on fire ourselves, with the red glow dancing up and down the wings.

There were many awards truly earned over the holocaust of Cologne. Flying Officer Cyril Anekstein, a Londoner who had enlisted in the RAF as an Aircraftman Second Class in September 1939, was later awarded the DFC for continuing a run up to the target after his aircraft had been badly damaged by flying splinters. He got his aircraft over the target, saw the bombs away and then turned back and nursed his crippled bomber along hundreds of miles, most of it over hostile territory. He was back over Germany with another cargo of bombs a few nights later. Flight Sergeant Thomas Oswold 'Mac' McIlquhan, the Canadian rear-gunner on Squadron Leader Evan Griffiths' Halifax on 102 Squadron got one Focke-Wulf 190 at 9,000 feet by waiting until the night fighter had drawn in close. A second Focke-Wulf 190 fell to his guns later. For his feat McIlquhan deservedly wore the ribbon of the DFM a few weeks later. Sergeant Cyril Terry, a Londoner like Anekstein and a chauffeur in civil life, was front gunner in another heavy bomber. His sharp eyes, cool nerves and shooting skill accounted for two of the black-painted night fighters that swarmed in a vain attempt to break up the phalanx of bombers. Near the target he saw one of the bombers being attacked by a night fighter who had cleverly positioned himself for the attack. His tracers were pumping into the aircraft. Terry passed back instructions to his captain, who promptly manoeuvred into a position from which Terry could stalk the stalker. The distances between the three planes closed and when he was satisfied about the range, Terry pressed the gun-button. He was dead accurate in his sighting. The very first burst tore open the night fighter's engine and set it alight. The fighter went down in a dive and continued diving. Not long afterwards Terry stalked another night fighter who was moving in to attack a bomber. Again he beat the German airman in that ghostly game of follow my leader. For his work that night Terry got the DFM. He was back over enemy territory a few nights afterwards, when he destroyed a Focke-Wulf 190. He sent it down in the sea, blazing like a torch, just off the Dutch coast.[8]

The 'press on types' like Anekstein did so regardless. Leslie Manser was another in the same mould. *D-Dog* had performed well enough on air test but fully loaded, the Manchester refused to climb above 7,000 feet. Manser held the aircraft straight and level and carried on to the target. Sergeant Stan King dropped their cargo of 1,260 4lb incendiary bombs. Almost at once they were hit by light 20mm flak and a searchlight cone was shining through the cockpit roof. They were down to 800 feet before they finally escaped into the darkness. Sergeant Ben Naylor, the rear gunner, who was peppered by splinters in the shoulder, nose and toes during the attack shouted that he had been hit. Manser was completely in control and his voice was firm. On intercom he told him to 'hang on'. As fire and smoke billowed through the fuselage 'Beve' Baveystock went aft to see if any of the incendiary bombs had hung up but everything was dark and he could not see. Bob Horsley looked into the rear end and found that he could see straight through to the ground. The rear part of the bomb doors had been blown off by the flak burst but at least the bombs had gone.

Manser nursed the ailing Manchester up to 2,000 feet and 'Bang On' Barnes gave him a course for England. And then the port Vulture engine suddenly burst into flames. *Oberleutnant* Walter Barte of 4./NJG1 had intercepted the Manchester at low level in *Nachtjagd* Box 6A and he delivered the *coup-de-grace* with a burst in the engine before flying off to submit his claim for his fifth victory. But Manser was not finished yet. He feathered the propeller and ordered Baveystock to try to put out the fire with the extinguisher. Baveystock did but it was no use. Although he and his crew could have safely bailed out Manser was still determined to try to get them home. 'Let's wait and see if the fire goes out' he said in such a calm manner that it astonished his crew. In the next few minutes the metal panels round the engine burned slowly away and then the flames flickered and went out. Manser was steering for Manston on the Kent coast. 'Go aft and jettison everything you can' he ordered Baveystock. The Manchester was steadily losing height and Manser doubted if he would get to Manston but he might be able to make the Channel where he would ditch the aircraft and 'perhaps avoid capture'. Baveystock found Naylor lying on the rest bed and Horsley was bandaging his wounds. Baveystock stuffed everything moveable that he could find down the flare chute but it was clear that there was no hope of reaching England. Manser ordered the crew to put on their parachutes and prepare to abandon the aircraft. Horsley helped Naylor to the fuselage door while the rest of the crew went to the front hatch which Sergeant A McF Mills the front gunner had already opened. Baveystock shot a glance at the flying instruments and realized that with the speed down to 110 knots they were almost on the point of a stall. He tried to hand Manser a parachute but his Skipper waved it away. 'For God's sake get out – we're going down' he shouted. He could only hold the aircraft steady for a few seconds more. Baveystock crawled down to the front hatch, doubled himself up and dropped though the hole. The aircraft was now at 200 feet; no time for his parachute to open fully. In England Bette Baveystock and their 18-month-old daughter Jill, who had recently been ill with pneumonia, waited for news.

Twenty-three-year-old Pilot Officer Philip Ford on 49 Squadron had faced the same dilemma as Manser when he too was disabled by flak. Losing height rapidly Floyd held the Manchester steady while his crew proceeded to evacuate the aircraft. Sergeant John Valentine the 27-year-old navigator got down to the front compartment where he found Sergeant John Smith the front gunner hesitating about the jump. There was no time to lose and Sergeant D E Randall the Australian second pilot was behind him waiting to jump so Valentine decided not to wait for the gunner. But in his excitement he pulled the ripcord on his parachute while he was still inside the aircraft. Valentine gathered it up and dropped through the open hatch. Randall followed but in the next second the Manchester rolled over on its back and plunged forwards with Floyd and the front gunner still inside. The aircraft exploded on the ground at Mulheim-Oberhausen. Floyd and Smith were killed instantly. Randall, Valentine and the three other members of the crew who had bailed out were taken into captivity.

Jim Wilkie had trouble with his borrowed Manchester and could get no higher than 9,000 feet. He had considered turning back at the Dutch coast but with so many aircraft above him he, like Manser, thought that their lowly position might actually be an advantage. But when he was caught in the cone of searchlights and his port engine was hit they had lost height rapidly. Wilkie knew there was no chance at all of getting home. He applied opposite rudder and kept *T-Tommy* on a straight course so that the crew could bail out. Jock Campbell and Alastair Benn were the first to jump and both got down safely. 'Toby' Tobias as second pilot had chosen to go last and was about to jump when the Manchester hit the ground. Wilkie had belly landed on the airfield at Düsseldorf-Lobhausen and he survived. There was no sign of the other three men. Eddie Finch had wasted precious seconds checking the rear turret to make sure that his friend Doug Baird was clear and when they and Alan Bee jumped they were too low and their parachutes failed to open properly. Wilkie and his two crew members were marched off into captivity. All the crew on the fourth Manchester that was lost were killed.

Tom Dailey's Wellington returned safely:

> Apart from a few small holes in the fuselage we were unscathed. But dirty, dog-tired and sweaty. Beneath our sheepskin flying jackets we all wore three or four woollen vests to keep out the cold. At breakfast we had our bacon and eggs. But there were gaps around the Mess tables. Nobody mentioned them.

158 had lost two Wimpys and nine men, including Squadron Leader Donald Harkness DFC, a 26-year-old New Zealander, had been killed. Another of the gaps was Squadron Leader John Russell's scratch crew,

the only one of the 28 Whitleys dispatched that failed to return. Of the 21 Whitleys which went on the raid from Abingdon, all attacked the target and all returned safely, although one crash landed at Manston. Russell had managed to coax a little more than 120 mph out of *H-Harry* and had climbed to 12,000 feet for the flight to Cologne. They bombed the target and were on the way home when over Belgium the Whitley was attacked by a German fighter. After two attacks fires raged out of control in the port nacelle and inner wing and spread to the fuselage. Russell gave the order to bail out at 1,100 feet. The second pilot, Pilot Officer Dennis Grant Box, a New Zealander from Auckland handed him his parachute and immediately the port wing disappeared with a loud explosion. The aircraft turned onto its back and started to spin. Centrifugal force pinned the Scottish pilot to his seat:

> Flames now were everywhere. The cockpit was full of smoke and tangled up crew. I was feeling very dazed and stupid and still pulling at the controls to try and correct the spin. Suddenly, there was another explosion and I was alone in space with the moon, fields and canals etc chasing one another round and round. I was now very wide awake and cool and I had my parachute firmly gripped in my right hand. I clipped it on very gingerly and pulled the rip-cord. Two swings and I hit heavily breaking my right leg in two places. The aircraft (most of it) hit a few seconds later about 200 yards away.[9]

The Whitley had crashed near Hoboken in the south-west suburbs of Antwerp. Box and Sergeant Jim Godbehere, the Canadian navigator from Montreal, were thrown out in the explosion but had not been holding their parachutes. Dennis Foster DFM, the wireless operator, who was on a rest from operations, was the only other man to survive. He too was thrown out when *H-Harry* exploded. Russell concluded:

> The second pilot undoubtedly saved my life and lost his own through fetching my pack before trying to put on his. He and the navigator fell some distance away. Sergeant 'Bill' Orman the rear gunner was either killed or incapacitated by gunfire. His body was still in the turret with cannon shells through the thorax.

Tom Ramsay had arrived over the target soon after 1 o'clock. Bill Gorton got the bombs away. Ahead of them the defences seemed more active so Ramsay continued his turn off the target until he was heading north-west but the compass was playing up and after a while he discovered that instead of heading back for the Dutch coast south of Rotterdam, they were flying almost due north. The solitary Hampden was inviting disaster and it soon came. *Leutnant* Manfred Meurer of III./NJG1 in a

Bf 110 attacked and raked the fuselage with cannon fire. The port engine burst into flames and Ramsay called the crew several times on intercom telling them to bail out. There was no answer. Gorton and the two gunners, Vic Woolnough and Fred Falk, must have been killed in the fighter attack. Ramsay managed to extricate himself from the tiny cockpit and he bailed out. He was taken into captivity but it was five weeks before Muriel Ramsay learned that her husband was safe. Like Ramsay, Pilot Officer David Johnson and his scratch crew had bombed the target successfully but they too turned almost due north away from the target area, probably because of a faulty compass reading. They were attacked by a night fighter believed to be a Bf 110 flown by *Oberleutnant* Helmut Woltersdorf of III./NJG1. The Wimpy eventually crashed in flames in the Hessen Alle in Klarenbeck, 15 miles north-east of Arnhem at 02.30 that Sunday morning. In the burnt out wreckage were found the bodies of five of the crew. Among them was David Johnson. Only Flight Sergeant Waddington-Allwright the rear gunner survived. He was taken into captivity.[10]

By the time they reached Antwerp Harry Langton knew that they would never make it to Honington or even Manston. They had lost the port engine after the target and Langton ordered the crew to prepare for ditching. They opened all the escape hatches but when it was clear that they would not even reach the coast of Belgium, Langton, who insisted on flying as slowly as he could, just above stalling speed, belly-landed the Wimpy in a marshy field at Retie heading straight for a farmhouse. Langton was not wearing his seat belt and as they hit the farmyard he was thrown 30 yards from the aircraft, badly injured but alive. The rear gunner, 21-year-old Sergeant Ken Pexman was found dead in his turret. He had been a gunner on Defiant night fighters and had only arrived at Honington earlier that day where he had replaced the original tail gunner who was sick. He had confided in his wife Mabel of four months that he never expected to live to see his 22nd birthday. Flight Sergeant Graham 'Tiny' Welsh, the six foot-four observer who was on the last operation of his tour and who had been standing beside Langton when they crashed took a blow on the ankle but was relatively unscathed. Sergeant J Haworth who had a badly lacerated hand and Sergeant J Johnson who was uninjured, survived. All three men spent almost a week evading capture but they were taken when they were looking for a doctor for Haworth. Harry Langton was repatriated in an exchange of wounded prisoners two years later and subsequently made a full recovery.

On the return a Hampden collided with a Lancaster but both returned safely. Flight Lieutenant Brian Frow was more frightened of collision than of fighters. Half a mile ahead of him soon after passing over Mönchengladbach he saw a burst of tracer dart across the sky. Seconds later there was a bright glow in the sky and then a ball of incandescent light fell slowly and gently out of the stream. It was a signal for a furious increase in the weaving and corkscrewing of the bombers ahead. They were determined not to be caught in the same way. Frow warned his crew on intercom but kept the Hampden in straight and level flight. Then he noticed two aircraft not more than 400 yards ahead of him, one above the other. The top aircraft was a Stirling on 214 Squadron at Stradishall. The one underneath was a Wellington on 101 Squadron at Bourn near Cambridge, flown by Pilot Officer Anthony De Fay Gardner. As it weaved the Wimpy rose slightly while the Stirling sagged and then levelled out. Then the Wellington came up again under the Stirling, soaring this time just a few feet too far. As the two aircraft touched, the propeller blades of the Wellington cut the tail of the Stirling clean off. Both bombers lifted together and then hurtled down. The Wimpy blew up. There were no survivors. Frow watched the Stirling falling for several thousand feet and then it was lost from view. A few seconds later there was a vivid explosion on the ground where it went in.

In another collision, a 78 Squadron Halifax at Croft piloted by Pilot Officer Geoffrey Foers and a 14 OTU Hampden at Cottesmore flown by Squadron Leader Donald 'Uncle' Falconer DFC collided over the Cambridgeshire fens and crashed near March. Two of Foers' crew were killed and the rest were injured. Sergeant Harold Curtis the flight engineer managed to throw himself from the doomed aircraft, his parachute only just opening at 200 feet. Landing heavily he badly wrenched his left leg but still managed to hobble over to the wreckage and assist the local Home Guard to remove the dead and injured. An over-zealous Home Guard who, spotting a parachute flare among the debris, promptly evacuated the entire area, leaving Curtis stranded in the middle of the field. He had to limp back towards the main road almost a mile-and-a-half before being picked up by a local doctor driving an ancient Austin car. Falconer was the only man on the Hampden to escape death.

Foers, who had been a clerk in a Surbiton bank before the war and was a fine athlete, returned to operations that August. He was shot down by a fighter near Duisburg on the operation on Krefeld on 2/3 October and was killed with all but two of his crew. Donald Falconer returned later to operations, becoming a wing commander with an AFC to add to his DFC and completing a second tour with the Path Finders. On New Year's Eve 1943 Wing Commander Falconer volunteered to do an extra sortie from which he failed to return. The operation was to Cologne.[11]

Clive Saxelby, a New Zealander on 103 Squadron known as 'Bix Sax', had been the first man over the target from Elsham Wolds. Tall, pale, lean and casual, dark-haired and grey-eyed, he had trained as a pilot directly after leaving school and he had come to Britain in 1940 when still only 18. He had completed his first tour on 75 New Zealand Squadron at Feltwell flying as second pilot to Don Harkness and had then put in a year as an instructor. Not yet 21, Saxelby was now half way through his second tour. As they crossed the Dutch–German border and were approaching Eindhoven the Wellington was attacked twice by a night fighter, which raked the fuselage with cannon shells and set the aircraft on fire. There was a strangled scream on intercom and St Pierre, the French-Canadian in the rear turret was hit in the leg. His left flying boot was caked with blood, his intercom was dead and he crawled forward to see what was happening. Under the astrodome, leaning against the side of the fuselage was Sergeant George Roberts, recently arrived on the Station and, unknown to Saxelby and his crew, who had gone with them as second pilot for the experience, apparently taking it easy. St Pierre gave him a prod to attract his attention and Roberts slid in slow motion to the floor. He was dead. The navigator, Flight Lieutenant L C Pipkin, was nearest to the flames. He had no gloves on but he attacked them immediately with his bare hands. Flight Sergeant W J McLean, the wireless operator, helped Pipkin and between them they managed to extinguish the fire. Saxelby was having great difficulty keeping the aircraft airborne. As the aircraft became locked in a spiral, the ground was coming up fast. Pipkin disappeared and then came back with a rope, which he tied round the control column. Saxelby noticed that the skin on Pipkin's hands were shrivelled and burnt. Pipkin lashed the stick back and the Wellington levelled out. They made it back and force landed at Honington.[12]

One of the flight commanders on 103 was unwell and Group Captain Hugh Constantine, the 34-year-old Station Commander at Elsham, had flown as first pilot in his place. The navigator, 21-year-old Flight Sergeant H J 'Dizzy' Spiller 'the untidiest man on the Station' who rarely wore his aircrew brevet or his chevrons of rank, groaned: 'Old Connie's bound to write us off'. Spiller was short, round-faced and rosy-cheeked and he had lost one of his upper front teeth during an argument after a party. It had been a lucky punch because somehow the gap complemented his personality. He and the rest of the crew had proceeded to give a continual running commentary of advice over the intercom but Constantine had not silenced them. He knew that the change of Skipper had made them nervous and they were simply working it off. They made it back to Elsham safely.

As the planned time for *A-Apple* and David Chell's crew's return approached, Sid Chinnery and his fellow ground crew left their Nissen hut and went outside to listen:

Suddenly we heard the sound of aircraft approaching and joining the circuit. One by one they came in to land and taxied to their dispersals. We were still waiting for *A-Apple*. We watched the last aircraft with apprehension as it completed its landing run. Imagine our feelings as it turned and taxied to our side of the airfield. The crew climbed out of the aircraft, very pleased to be home. We were told to assemble in the hangar because the CO wished to speak to all ground crews. He told us that the previous night we had bombed Cologne and that a thousand bombers had taken part. He thanked us all for the hard work which we had put in that had made the raid successful. After two more days at the Station we saw our aircraft return home and then made our way back to Wellesbourne Mountford. It was a thrill for me and my friend 'Jock' to know that we had played a part in helping in the first thousand-bomber raid.[13]

When they had left the target area Douglas Mourton had returned to his wireless, plugged in and found that it was completely dead. He did not know for what reason but he realized that he would not be able to give the crew any assistance with courses to fly and he hoped that the navigator was sufficiently proficient to get them back home again. Unbeknown to him a piece of shrapnel measuring about three inches by two inches had gone through the aircraft where he usually sat and into the radio but obviously it had occurred when he was supervising at the astrodome. If he had been sitting there the wireless set would have been working perfectly but he would not have been. He recalls:

Actually things went well. We landed back at Wellesbourne just after 5 o'clock in the morning. We were debriefed and then went along to the mess to have the usual egg and bacon breakfast with two or three cups of sweet tea and always a couple of cigarettes afterwards, while we chatted away and I revelled in the fact that I had completed another trip; I had survived and everything had gone well. Juggins, whom I had replaced, was never seen again. He had been found guilty of LMF and stripped of his Flight Sergeant's stripes and crown and sent to another Station.

Squadron Leader Stiles landed back at Wellesbourne five hours and ten minutes after take-off:

Holes in the fuselage and flaps were fairly superficial but a major repair was necessary to replace the geodetic structure missing from the top of the Wellington's fuselage. There was much discussion as to how this damage occurred but as we were in a steep turn it must have been caused either by a falling bomb or an up-coming shell fused for a greater altitude. We concluded that the flak hole in the port engine cover could only have been caused by a piece of shrapnel passing through the propeller blades, missing the cylinders and coming out the top. There was obviously a lot of luck involved. Two of my friends who officiated at my wedding the previous month were captains of two Wellesbourne aircraft, which failed to return and I believe also one pupil crew.[14] A high price to pay for dropping about 3,000lb of HE on Cologne.

Out of 368 OTU aircraft, only 17 were lost so the grim forecast that many inexperienced crews would get killed was proved wrong. Even so 49 pupils and 40 instructors did not return. At Graveley 26 OTU lost four Wellingtons. Flying Officer William Robert Humphrey Whiting was shot down by *Hauptman* Walter Streib to take his score for the night to two, although both claims were for Whitleys. Whiting's Wimpy crashed west of Eindhoven with no survivors. The Wellington flown by 31-year-old Flight Sergeant Edwin Ford DFM, a former motor salesman, was shot down by *Leutnant* Helmut Niklas of 6./NJG1 and crashed at Leeveroi near Venlo. All but one of his crew were killed. The exception was the wireless operator Flight Sergeant Denis Caswell who was taken prisoner. Before the operation Ford had advised and befriended Warrant Officer Freddie Hillyer who took *O-Orange* off from Cheddington. They made it to the target and the bomb-aimer, 22-year-old Pilot Officer Cyril White, the son of a parson and the youngest man on the crew, got their bombs on target. Sergeant Hector Smith the rear gunner, the only married man on the crew, was the oldest. Short and tubby he would sit in his turret smoking his pipe in spite of repeated warnings from Hillyer. *O-Orange* was hit in the port engine over Cologne and was flying at barely 90 mph when Sergeant Dave Vincent the navigator gave Hillyard a course to steer. The diminutive pilot from Alresford in Hampshire had joined the RAF as a trainee flight mechanic before becoming a fitter and when war came, had re-mustered as a pilot. *O-Orange* was now a lame duck and *Oberleutnant* Horst Patuschka of 4./NJG2 in a Bf 110 delivered the *coup de grace*. He set the Wimpy's rear fuselage on fire and Hillyard gave the order to bail out. Just before he left the cockpit he glanced down and saw that the front turret guns were pointing sideways. The power for the hydraulics came from the dead port engine. This meant that Cyril White was trapped in the turret. Hillyer fought his way through to the turret and banged on the door as he grabbed the dead man's handle and tried to wrench the doors open. But it was jammed. There was no answer from turret. White must be dead. Hillyer got out before the Wellington crashed at Alem. He was the only survivor. Next day he was taken prisoner and driven to nearby Utrecht. Before being taken into captivity his captors drove him to the scene of the crash. He could see that all his crew had been killed in the fighter attack.

The fourth and final loss was the Wellington piloted by Sergeant John James Dixon who made it home only to crash near Soham flour mill at 04.35. Dixon and Sergeant Brian Camlin the rear gunner were killed. Three others were injured. *Z-Zebra*, an 11 OTU Wimpy at Bassingbourn that Flight Sergeant John Bulford, the 20-year-old instructor pilot had taken off from Steeple Morden, also failed to return. Bulford's crew was made up of a trainee navigator, a screened rear gunner and wireless operator and two New Zealand pupils who had recently arrived from initial training in their native country. *Z-Zebra* lost its starboard engine after the target and finally the dead propeller had fallen off. Bulford, who had only recently come off operations, got the ailing Wimpy to within sight of the Dutch coast where everyone bailed out. They were all taken prisoner.

P-Peter, a 25 OTU Wellington flown by Pilot Officer C G Hughes that took off from Finningley, crashed at Aslool, all six crew being taken prisoner. *O-Orange*, a Wellington Ic on 23 OTU at Pershore flown by Flight Sergeant William Ross Campbell Johnson RCAF, was shot down by a night fighter and crashed near Gravendeel in Holland. Johnson's body was found clear of the wreckage with his parachute open around him. About 200 yards from the main wreckage lay the tail section with Sergeant Ronald Arthur Broodbank, the Australian rear gunner, dead in his turret. Two other Australians and the English front gunner were cremated by the full load of incendiaries inside the aircraft. Only their identity discs were found.

Two Wellingtons on 15 OTU failed to return to Harwell and Hampstead Norris. One of these was piloted by Sergeant Jack Paul DFM, a tall solid Midlander from Coventry; a veteran of over 30 operations, who had returned from one week's leave and his honeymoon with his wife Joyce just the day before. He had completed a bombing tour on Wellingtons in the Middle East before becoming an instructor. Two other instructors and a student gunner made up the rest of the crew, which was to operate with a single pilot instead of the normal complement of two. Flight Sergeant Bernard 'Bunny' Evans DFM, the 35-year-old, Manchester-born, gunnery instructor took the rear gun turret for what was his 50th sortie. He too had completed a tour in the Middle East. The Harwell crews were driven to their aircraft at 20.00 ready for a take-off one hour later. Paul's crew had been allocated one of the better Wellingtons, but a serious magneto drop on one engine sent them rushing to R1791, the spare aircraft, one of the oldest and worst aircraft on 15 OTU, with many items missing. The crew had finally got airborne at 23.14. Jack Paul described the aircraft as 'a bit of a heap and we were so slow that we must have been one of the last to arrive over the target, which was a mass of flames that I could see for miles.'

On the way home R1791 was attacked near Charleroi in Belgium by *Leutnant* Helmut Niklas and his *Bordfunker*, *Unteroffizier* Wenning of II./NJG1 in a Bf 110. On the approach of the bombers they had taken off from St-Trond and flew to the radio beacon just to the north-west of their allocated fighter control station. Wenning later recalled:

In our area we did not have long to wait. At 3,000 metres we encountered the first, which we recognised as a Wellington, 500 metres away. At almost exactly the same time the Tommy spotted us. He made a sudden turn to the right and then turned away from us. We went after him, but his fire was so strong that we could not get into a firing position and we overshot the Wellington. Again we moved into a position behind the target and, from short range, we pumped shells into the bomber's left wing. It caught fire and we could see the flames. By this time our victim was down to 2,000 metres. Again we closed in. We fired another burst into the fuselage and wings and the flames burnt brighter. Then we moved out for a while, waiting to see whether it would be necessary to go in again.

The Wimpy's intercom was rendered useless and 'Bunny' Evans' rear turret was badly damaged. The turret could not be turned fully and one of the guns was useless. Paul pulled the bomber into a hard turn and the fighter overshot allowing the student front-gunner, a pupil named Sergeant James McCormack, to open fire. When the Bf 110 returned for a second attack Evans opened fire with his one serviceable gun, but he was wounded in the hand. The Wellington suffered further damage, with fire breaking out near the port engine and this quickly spread. Without the intercom, further instructions could not be passed so Paul shouted to Flight Sergeant Tommy Lyons the wireless operator to tell the crew to bail out. After the second attack 'Bunny' Evans realised that the aircraft was severely damaged. He opened his turret door and crawled into the fuselage. He could see flames but no sign of life up front. Without communication he assumed that they had bailed out. (His pilot was slumped over the control column, unconscious). Evans grabbed his para- chute, clipped it on and as the Wimpy passed through 2,000 feet he dropped through the diamond-shaped escape hatch in the rear of the aircraft, kicking it out as he went.

Niklas and Wenning watched for a short time as the Wellington flew on, the blaze growing the whole time. Then it flipped over and went down, trailing sparks like a comet. Close to the ground it exploded, lighting up the surrounding countryside. Niklas climbed back up to his operational altitude and reported to their ground station that they were ready for the next target. Almost immediately they were guided into position behind a second Wellington and sighted it 700 yards in front:

He was weaving but he did not open fire. Had they seen us? We went straight into the attack. The target grew larger until, suddenly, it seemed enormous. My breath almost stopped: we were going to ram him. From short range we opened fire, hitting him on the wings and on the fuselage. We could see the glow of the flashes on the rear fuselage. I was about to call out 'He's on fire!', when suddenly *Leutnant* Niklas shouted 'I've been hit, breaking off immediately!'

I had mistaken the muzzle flash from the rear turret for the glow of hits. We could not bother with the Tommy any more – we had our own problems.

Niklas's left arm had been smashed and was unusable and also it was bleeding profusely. Unable to reach the controls from his position in the rear of the 110, Wenning improvised a tourniquet and tied it round Niklas's arm; then he set about the difficult task of directing his pilot back to St-Trond while the latter drifted in and out of consciousness. Wenning continues:

> That was how we flew back to our airfield. *Leutnant* Niklas was almost over the lights before he caught sight of them. It was too late to land on the runway. So, with a sideslip, he tried to get down on the emergency strip. Trees passed just below us. 'We're too low!' Niklas murmured, 'I can't go on any longer' and slumped forward. There was a scraping sound and soil was flung against the cabin. We skidded over the ground for what seemed an eternity. I sat there tensely. So this was what a crash landing was like; I had always imagined that it would be different. The crashing and splintering grew louder; there was a jerk-and everything was still. Then Niklas shouted: 'Let's get out of here!' He had hit his head but had regained consciousness. He leapt from his seat, trying to run and at the same time to release his parachute harness. But it was no good and he fainted. I laid him out gently on the grass and opened his blood-soaked flying suit. Soon a doctor and others appeared and they carried him away. I was surrounded by a lot of people, who began to ask questions; I realised just how lucky I had been.[15]

'Bunny' Evans had landed in a plum tree in the back garden of a miner's cottage in the village of Mont-sur-Marchienne near Charleroi. After landing, he heard windows opening and voices, so he decided to get clear of the area. He eventually came to a house with a light on and knocked at the door and after explaining that he was a British aviator, he was welcomed inside. He was given a drink and his wounded hand was dressed before he was moved to another house where he was fed and hidden in an attic. During the day, the Germans searched all the houses with the exception of his hiding place. Later that evening he was collected and transferred to Charleroi. Members of the Belgian Resistance movement had seen his parachute descent in the bright moonlight and he was soon in the hands of the *Comète* escape line.

Jack Paul remained unconscious as the Wimpy crashed into a house in the village of Montigny-le-Telleul, knocking down one side of the building completely, depositing his body in the ruins and then carrying on into an orchard on the far side of the road where it steadily burnt itself out. Remarkably, Jack Paul and the occupants, who were asleep, lived and they soon rescued the badly injured Paul. Warrant Officer Stan Green the navigator, McCormack and Tommy Lyons had been killed before the aircraft crashed. The Germans arrived and after a visit from a doctor they took Paul in an ambulance to a German hospital in Charleroi where he had an operation on his broken legs and where an English woman, Ruby Dondeyne, who had married a Belgian, nursed him. She told him that three of his crew were dead and one was missing and asked if he wanted to send a message home. The pilot scribbled a few words to Joyce on a prescription slip and signed it with a drawing of the Leslie Charteris 'Saint', which he had always used when writing to her. He never thought that Joyce would receive the message but she did. At first she thought that a telegram which had arrived telling her that he was missing was a mistake. It was only when she heard the news on the wireless at lunch time on Sunday that she realised he must have been on the Cologne raid.

Paul meanwhile, received word from 'Bunny' Evans on a scrap of cigarette paper that he was 'in good hands'. The rear gunner was taken later to Louvain with two other airmen and with help of the *Comète* line, finally made it to the Spanish border. He arrived in Gibraltar on 18 August and within 24 hours was flown to Whitchurch airfield in a BOAC Dakota. He was debriefed by officers of MI9 and was able to give valuable information about the German gun defences on the road between St-Jean-de-Luz and Hendye. The Deputy Director of the MI9 Prisoner of War Section recommended that Evans be awarded a Mention in Despatches for his successful and resourceful evasion. He commented on the file, 'His good luck was the result of a good effort to get going.'[16]

After a few days Jack Paul was moved to a hospital in Brussels. In the next ward he was astonished to recognise his close friend and pilot, 26-year-old Warrant Officer Jack Hatton, who had been too badly wounded to escape although the Belgian Resistance had offered to hide him. Hatton, an ex-Cranwell apprentice, was believed shot down by *Oberleutnant* Reinhold Knacke of 3./NJG1 at Waasmont Brabant in Belgium. Hatton's wireless operator, Sergeant Bob Collins, an Australian from Brisbane, also reached Gibraltar and he was flown home on 21 July. The rest of Hatton's crew had been taken prisoner.

Pilot Officer 'Bob' Ferrer and his 12 OTU crew had bombed Cologne about half-way through the raid but soon after the target they were attacked by a Bf 110, which fired cannon shells into the fuselage and badly wounded Flight Sergeant John Draper McKenzie the Canadian rear gunner. Ferrer put the old drogue towing Wimpy into a dive to shake off the fighter, finally levelling out after losing 10,000 feet and their pursuer. Somehow they managed to cross Holland and the North Sea but the aircraft's faltering port engine finally gave up the ghost and Ferrer ditched off Harwich. Ron Grundy suffered multiple injuries in the crash.

The bodies of Bob Ferrer and Pilot Officer Alvin Luckie the navigator, who was of Polish extraction, were never recovered. Grundy, McKenzie and Sergeant Kenneth Buck, the 19-year-old front gunner and bomb aimer, were picked up by a motor vessel and taken to the Royal Naval Hospital at Shotley (HMS *Ganges*). Ironically, Grundy, who never flew again, received confirmation of his place on a pilot's course while recovering at the RAF Hospital, Ely. Kenneth Buck later joined 102 Squadron at Pocklington. He was killed on 4/5 May 1943 on the raid on Dortmund. All the crew of the Halifax died.

Thirty of the 53 bombers that were lost were believed to have been shot down by night fighters in the *Himmelbett* boxes between the coast and Cologne. It was estimated by Bomber Command that 16 of the 22 aircraft that were lost over or near Cologne were shot down by flak. One of these was Stirling *N-Nan* flown by Pilot Officer Arthur 'Wilf' Davis on 218 Squadron at Marham which approached Cologne from the north-west at 18,000 feet and was coned by 30 to 40 searchlights. Flak riddled the aircraft, a piece of shrapnel hitting Sergeant Albert Smith, the 29-year-old WOp/AG in the mid-upper turret in the chest just above the heart. It exited at the left shoulder blade without killing him. Incredibly, Smith bailed out and he survived the parachute descent and was taken prisoner. The only other man to survive was 'Tex' Tate, who had gallantly shared his parachute with Flight Sergeant 'Joe' Borrowdale, the 23-year-old navigator from Cumberland whose chute had been torn to shreds by flak. There had been no time to interlock their harnesses and as soon as the shared 'chute opened Borrowdale slipped to his death. A second Stirling was written off at Marham when Sergeant Falconer was forced to belly land HA-L, which had been damaged on take-off. There were no injuries to the crew and within a few weeks Falconer had been awarded a DFM.[17] *R-Robert*, a Wellington on 115 Squadron flown by Sergeant Emrys Edwards was the only other aircraft that failed to return to the Norfolk bomber Station. All the crew was lost without trace. It was however, a happy return for 'Jackie' Baldwin and Paul Holder. Ninety miles from the target and within nine minutes of the coast, Holder turned and did a complete circuit so that Baldwin could take a final look at the glow that was Cologne. At times drifting clouds obscured the moon and later a black pall of smoke rising to 15,000 feet spread like a thick blanket over the city. Two war correspondents reported:

We had the impression that Cologne had been visited by an earthquake. We could see clearly that the walls of buildings were collapsing, not from direct bomb hits but from air pressure and even more from the ground vibrations. The chaos in Cologne was indescribable. The ground defences gradually lost all sense of the direction of the attacks. Most of the RAF losses occurred during approach and while flying away after releasing the bombs. Machine guns and aerial guns strafed numerous searchlight batteries and flak positions. From the 55th minute of the attack onward, we all had the impression that we were flying over an active volcano.

Baldwin echoed these thoughts:

> The fires seemed like rising suns and this effect became more pronounced as we drew further away. Then, with the searchlights rising from the fires, it seemed that we were leaving behind us a huge representation of the Japanese banner. The fires then resembled distant volcanoes.

Harris soon found out that his 3 Group Commander had flown on the operation and for the next 1,000 bomber raid, on Emden, he would add a postscript to his executive signal: 'No AOCs to fly without my permission and none tonight.' Baldwin was knighted in January 1943 and this was followed by promotion to the rank of air marshal.[18]

Pilot Officer Arthur William Doubleday on 460 Squadron RAAF was one of the Wellington pilots on the Cologne raid. The 30-year-old second son in a family of five girls and three boys enjoyed country life and had farmed at Wagga, New South Wales. He had no intention or thought at all of doing other than living a life on the land. In February 1933 all that had changed. Young Arthur loved cricket and when he went to Sydney to see the fifth test in the 'bodyline' series, which England controversially won, he went out to Mascot aerodrome, paid his ten shillings and took a flight over the city. His second flight, seven years later, was with the Royal Australian Air Force.[19] In a *Daily Mirror* press cable Doubleday, who had flown on his Aussie squadron's first raid on 12/13 March, said of the raid on Cologne:

> It was five times larger than the biggest brushfires I have ever seen. Earlier arrivals had set the place well alight. We had a perfect target and it was impossible to miss. We dropped ton after ton of bombs right in the middle of the blazing factories. My cobbers said they were able to see the fires and smoke from the Dutch coastline approximately 200 miles distant. The flak was murderous as usual till towards the end of the raid. The Hun gunners practically gave up the ghost. They must have got sick of shooting at us. The Hun night fighters were pretty active. My gunners squirted at a couple, which quickly sheered off and did not molest us again.

A Wellington on 150 Squadron at Snaith crashed at Faldingworth in Lincolnshire; all the crew were killed. Two crews on 101 Squadron at Bourn failed to return. One of them was *Z-Zebra* flown by Flight Lieutenant Reece Read, the 28-year-old pilot who was on his first trip as captain of an aircraft. He had been a mining engineer for eight years and was in West Africa when war broke out. One of the engines had developed a fault just after take-off and as they approached the Dutch coast both engines overheated. Read ordered his crew to bail out. All the crew were taken prisoner. A few weeks later Read heard of the death of his brother Ambrose, killed in a flying accident at 12 OTU at Chipping Warden. He had encouraged his brother to join the RAF. Behind the wire Read went to pieces for a time but then he began to study medicine. Before the war he had wanted to be a doctor but he had never had the money to finance his way through university.

American Flight Sergeant Campbell's St. Christopher had worked its magic and he and his crew on 405 'Vancouver' Squadron came through safely. So too did Frank Roper. 'Bud' Cardinal made it too but he would be killed later, on 7 June on the operation on Emden, with all his crew. Sergeant Tonkin's crew on 214 Squadron returned safely to Stradishall but their tour was short lived. They were shot down on a *Gardening* operation on 11/12 June and taken into captivity. Sergeant 'Hal' de Mone RCAF on 16 OTU at Upper Heyford had a very short but interesting career as an air gunner. He had completed a month's air gunnery course but had never seen an operational aircraft nor even sat in a modern gun turret. Neither had he flown at night. Sent to England immediately after his short course had finished, he had barely arrived at Upper Heyford before he found himself on the operation to Cologne manning the rear turret of a Wellington. Attacked on the way back de Mone shot down their attacker. Two nights later he was shot down on the second thousand bomber raid on Essen. Two of his crew were killed and two were taken prisoner. 'Hal' de Mone bailed out and successfully evaded. He made it to Paris with the help of the *Comète* line where on 7 June he met up with two of the five evaders from Leslie Manser's crew. One of them was Bob Horsley and the other was Leslie Baveystock, who incredibly, had survived the 200 foot jump when he had hit a dyke. The four or five feet of water had broken his fall.

Baveystock had peeled off his Mae West and harness and ran across to the burning wreckage of the Manchester which crashed three miles east of a small Belgian village called Bree near the Dutch border. But it was impossible to get near it, so fierce were the flames. A clump of trees around the crash site had caught alight and ammunition was exploding with frightening rapidity. It was clear that Manser, holding on for those few extra seconds to give his crew a chance to escape, had been killed instantly as the Manchester ploughed in. Barnes was injured in the fall from the aircraft and was unable to avoid capture. Horsley, having landed in a marshy area of Belgium, a few kilometres north-east of Bree, was able to dry his wet clothes in a farmhouse. The farmer took him by bicycle to the house of a doctor in Tongerloo where he met Naylor and Mills. As the resistance was unable to move all three men together

Naylor and Mills were taken to a windmill at Dilsen, 15 kilometres south of the crash site. Horsley was later reunited with Baveystock and Stan King, who had turned an ankle on landing. On the night of 12/13 June, Baveystock, Horsley and Hal de Mone were taken across the Pyrenees to San Sebastián from where they were driven to Madrid. A few days later Mills and Naylor, now fully recovered, were moved from Brussels and they too passed along the *Comète* escape line to Paris and St-Jean-de-Luz and then over the Pyrenees to San Sebastián. Finally, on 6 July all six men sailed home from Gibraltar on the *Narkunda*.[20] The award of a posthumous Victoria Cross was made to Leslie Manser on 20 October 1942 after testimonies from all five of the crew.

His CO, Wing Commander R J Oxley DSO DFC said.

> When I told the squadron how Manser showed his determination by attacking the target with one engine out of action and then gave up his life to save the lives of the rest of the crew, we all felt humbled by what he had done. We realized that he had set an example, for the rest of us to live up to and that he had established a tradition for the squadron. He was one of the most competent captains we have ever had on 50 Squadron. Whatever task was set him, he did it willingly and without question. All who met him became his friends and everyone in the squadron felt his loss as a personal blow.

In all, 898 crews claimed to have hit Cologne and almost all of them bombed their aiming point as briefed. Fifteen aircraft bombed other targets. The total tonnage of bombs was 1,455, two-thirds of this tonnage being incendiaries. Post-bombing reconnaissance certainly showed that more than 600 acres of Cologne had been razed to the ground. The Air Ministry reported after reconnaissance had been made that:

> In an area of seventeen acres between the Cathedral and the Hange Brücke forty or fifty buildings are gutted or severely damaged. Buildings immediately adjacent to the south-eastern wall of the Cathedral are gutted. There is no photographic evidence of damage to the Cathedral, although the damage to the adjoining buildings suggests that some minor damage may have occurred. The Police Headquarters and between 200 and 300 houses have been destroyed in another area of 35 acres extending from the Law Courts and the Neumarkt westwards almost to the Hohenzollernring. An area of three and a half acres between St. Gereon's Church and the Hohenzollernring has been completely burned out.

The fires burned for days. In his report to Chief of Police Himmler, Gauleiter Grohé recorded that 486 people were killed, 5,027 injured and

59,100 rendered homeless, 18,432 houses, flats, workshops, public buildings and the like were completely destroyed, 9,516 heavily damaged and 31,070 damaged less severely. 'The immense number of incendiary bombs dropped' had caused 12,000 fires of which 2,500 had been major outbreaks. Albert Speer, Minister for Armaments and War Production, was with Goering at the Veldenstein castle in Franconia when the Reichmarschall was told of the reported weight of the attack. Speer said that Goering shouted: 'Impossible! That many bombs cannot be dropped in a single night!'

It was estimated that from 135,000 to 150,000 of Cologne's population of nearly 700,000 people fled the city after the raid. In the early hours of 31 May the roads to Cologne started to fill with lorries bringing relief supplies – 34,000 items of clothing for adults, 50,000 items of clothing for children, 61,000 sheets, 90,000 boxes soap powder, 700,000 cakes of soap, ten million cigarettes and 100,000 metres of curtain material. A small army of 3,500 soldiers, 2,000 prisoners of war and 10,000 labourers arrived to assist the 5,200 workmen in Cologne detailed to clean up the city. As a result almost all routes, except in the city centre, were able to function under temporary repair within ten days of the raid. To help in this process of recovery the schoolchildren were immediately sent on holiday because all school buildings that had survived the bombing were needed as emergency centres. Some 370,000 claims were submitted for war damage. Dr. Josef Goebbels, Hitler's Propaganda Minister, shrugged off the implications of the raid and wrote in his diary, 'Naturally the effects of bomb warfare are horrible when one looks at individual cases but they must be put up with.'

Squadron Leader Stiles concludes:

It seemed to us the whole thing was a propaganda ploy aptly summed up by a cryptic announcement in the *Daily Telegraph* the following day: 'At a Bomber Command Station, Sunday. On the 1001st day of the war more than 1,000 RAF bombers flew over Cologne and in 95 minutes delivered the heaviest attack ever launched in the history of aerial warfare.'[21]

The following descriptive account was published by the American *Associated Press* in May 1942:

The moon was on our right and in the sky ahead of us was a rosy glow. 'How long until we get there, navigator?'

'About ten minutes,' he replied.

Good, that's all we need to know. The red glow is Cologne. Those chaps have lit themselves quite a fire.

The sky was full of antiaircraft projectiles, tracer fire, bursting shells and searchlight beams, so that it looked like a fireworks display at a country fair. The Germans were firing on all barrels. Viewed through the bombsight, Cologne glowed in the dark like the tip of a huge cigarette. Then our plane stood directly over the fires and the pilot ordered: 'Bomb bays operational.'

'Bomb bays operational' came the reply. The pilot spoke again: 'Damn it, hold on a minute. There's no point in wasting the stuff on buildings that are already burning. Let's look for a dark spot.' Block after block of city buildings blazed up under our aircraft; smoke drifted past the wings, which stood out distinctly against the flames. In the firelight we could make out structural skeletons of white-hot steel. A tiny dark speck appeared on the west bank of the Rhine. 'That must be the Elektra steel-wire plant,' said the pilot. 'Let's have a go at it.' We had an anxious moment as we approached the target. Then the bomb-gunner pressed the button and our aircraft zoomed upward, freed of its heavy payload. Jubilant shouts came over the intercom. We had completed our mission. It was a breeze from there back to our home base. Our Short Stirling heavy bomber sent out a call and the control centre informed the pilot that he was fourth in line to land; he was told the altitude at which he should circle before landing. The bus carried the cheerful crew to debriefing head-quarters, along with other men who had just come back from Cologne. A slender pilot with a sunburnt face and white eyebrows said laughing: 'Well that was the only time I've been glad to be over Cologne – and it was my fifth flight; God, what a nice little fire.' 'A damned fine sight,' others agreed. The debriefing was over; the crews took off to eat a special food allowance of ham and eggs.

When the *Kölnische Zeitung* resumed publication three days after the raid 'those who survived' it said 'were fully aware that they had bade farewell to their Cologne, because the damage is enormous and because the integral part of the character and even the traditions of the city is gone forever.' In a wireless broadcast after the raid George Orwell said that:

In 1940 when the Germans were bombing Britain, they did not expect retaliation on a very heavy scale. They were not afraid to boast in their propaganda about the slaughter of civilians which they were bringing about and the terror which their raids aroused. Now, when the tables are turned, they are beginning to cry out against the whole business of aerial bombing, which they declare to be both cruel and useless. The people of this country are not revengeful but they remember what happened to themselves two years ago and they remember how the Germans talked when they thought themselves safe from retaliation.

Bomber Harris received messages of congratulation from Sir Archibald Sinclair the Secretary of State for Air and as far afield as Lieutenant-General Golovanov, his Soviet opposite number. Harris responded in kind. 'We will not cease our efforts until Hitler's Germany cries, "Enough!"'

In England squadrons repaired and patched their damaged bombers – no less than 116 aircraft suffered damage, 12 so badly that they were written off – and within 48 hours they were preparing for another 1,000-raid, this time against Essen. (The weather had proved unsuitable immediately after the raid on Cologne). Flight Lieutenant John Price at 10 OTU recalls. 'Real bombs were not used on an OTU Station so I was a bit shaken to see them rolling onto our airfield. At briefing we were told our part in the operation was to kill as many of the workers as possible. Other bombers would go for the Krupps factory itself.' At nightfall on 1 June, 956 aircraft including 347 aircraft from the Operational Training Units, took off and headed for Essen. Despite a reasonable weather forecast, crews experienced great difficulty in finding the target. The plan was similar to the recent raid on Cologne except that many more flares were dropped by the 'raid leaders' flying in Wellingtons of 3 Group. Seven of the 22 Halifaxes on 76 Squadron were briefed to attack the precise aiming point, a large shed in the centre of the Krupps Works. Twenty Wellingtons were to pinpoint their position and then release flares to illuminate the entire target area for the fire raisers of the marker force. The remaining 120 Halifaxes were to join the Main Force attack. But the target-marking force had great difficulty finding the aiming point because the ground was covered either by the industrial haze or a layer of low cloud, and results were poor, with bombing scattered over Essen and at least eleven other towns, particularly Oberhausen and Mülheim, in or near the Ruhr.[22]

Essen itself escaped lightly and Krupps was once again almost untouched. Although seemingly lacking the concentration of the earlier raid on Cologne the bombing nevertheless was effective enough to saturate the defences. One Skipper went as far as to say that the fires were more impressive than those of Cologne. A belt of fires extended across the city's entire length from the western edge to the eastern suburbs. Many fires were also spread over other parts of the Ruhr. Of the 37 bombers lost on the second 1,000-bomber raid on Essen, 20 were claimed by night fighters. On return a 218 Squadron Stirling crash landed at Marham and a Wellington on 305 Polish Squadron at Lindholme crashed at Billingford near RAF Swanton Morley in Norfolk. Forty-three-year-old Wing Commander Robert Juliusz Hirszbant OBE DFC and his crew all died in the crash. Hirszbant, who had flown the Cologne raid, had been born in Warsaw in 1899 and was a university-trained engineer. At the time of the

German invasion he was a major in the Polish Air Force. Essen was his 23rd trip.

After Cologne and Essen, Harris could not immediately mount another 1,000-bomber raid and he had to be content with smaller formations. On 2/3 June just 195 aircraft, 97 of them Wellingtons, carried out a follow-up raid on Essen. The story is told of how one morning at planning, after spending his usual quarter of an hour looking at the photographs of the previous night's raid and the Met charts, Harris glanced up and said, 'Essen'. Saundby coughed a little deprecatingly and murmured, 'Excuse me, sir but I think the boys are getting a little browned off going to Essen every night.' Harris summed up the situation in two words, 'So's Essen!'[23]

On the night of 3/4 June, 170 bombers were dispatched on the first large raid to Bremen since October 1941. Crews reported only indifferent bombing results and 11 aircraft failed to return – eight of them shot down by *Nachtjäger*. One of these was a Manchester on 50 Squadron at Skellingthorpe flown by Flying Officer John Heaton, which took off at 21.10 hours on 3 June. The Manchester lost power crossing the Dutch coast and refused to climb higher than 9,000 feet but Heaton still managed to bomb the target and even completed two circuits to obtain the mandatory photographs. On the way home over the Veluwe in central Holland the Manchester was attacked and set on fire by a Bf 110 night fighter and crashed near Apeldoorn. Sergeant Ken Gaulton the wireless operator recalls:

I switched to the aircraft inter-communication system to advise the pilot that we were cleared to return to our base, this information having been received on the 02.30 broadcast from Group HQ. A Messerschmitt 110 attacked us. The starboard wing of our aircraft was burning and the pilot advised that he was going to dive in an attempt to 'blow out' the fire. This did not succeed. The German aircraft did a victory roll near the tail of our aircraft and Sergeant Peter Buttigieg our tail gunner shot him down. I was amazed to hear the yelling from the tail gunner who was engaging the Me 110 with his guns. After diving for thousands of feet I requested the pilot's permission to have the tail gunner and mid-upper gunner join me to prepare the rear escape hatch for evacuation. This was done and we jumped in turn; firstly the tail gunner (the only married man on the crew) then the mid-upper gunner and then came my turn. The aircraft kept on diving and crashed, killing Heaton, Pilot Officer John Steen, second pilot, Pilot Officer Harold Sheen, navigator and Sergeant Stan Thomas, front gunner, all of whom were in the front of the aircraft. I left the aircraft when it was slightly below 1,000 feet, quickly pulled the ripcord and was promptly knocked out by the chest parachute striking me under the jaw. I landed in the Zuider Zee on an ebbing tide and speared up to my chest in mud. An Alsatian dog woke me by licking my face and its owner took me to a medical doctor at about 05.30. I was unable to walk. The doctor quickly established that the man was a collaborator and was therefore unable to hide me. I was transported by car to Arnhem where I was interrogated by the *Gestapo* and then by train to Amsterdam, where I was gaoled in the Amsterdam watchtower for four days. While I was there a German captain from the fighter squadron visited me about 6 June and advised me that our aircraft had crashed on a hunting lodge owned by the Dutch Royal family near Apeldoorn. He told me that we had shot down one of his aircraft, killing two airmen. He claimed the Germans were two up as four of our crew had been killed.[24]

On 5/6 June in the raid on Essen by 180 bombers, 12 aircraft – eight of them Wellingtons – failed to return and the bombing was scattered over a wide area.[25] On the night of 6/7 June a force of over 230 aircraft was dispatched to Emden. A Wellington on 9 Squadron crashed and caught fire shortly after taking off from Honington and burnt out, but the crew were safe.[26] One of the three Wellingtons that were shot down on the operation was a 150 Squadron Wimpy flown by Flying Officer Malcolm James Larke Blunt RAAF, which was downed by *Oberleutnant* Ludwig Becker of 6./NJG2 and crashed into the North Sea off Ameland. All the crew perished. Becker was also credited with shooting down a 7 Squadron Stirling, one of two that failed to return. All of Flying Officer N L Taylor's crew survived and were taken prisoner. The other Stirling, a 214 Squadron aircraft flown by 26-year-old Flight Lieutenant Reginald Turtle DFC who was a veteran of 46 ops, was shot down by *Oberleutnant* Prinz Egmont zur Lippe-Weissenfeld of II./NJG2 and crashed off Terschelling with no survivors. Turtle was posthumously awarded a DFC. Two missing Manchester Is were from 49 Squadron at Scampton, three miles north of Lincoln, and a third, flown by Pilot Officer 'Don' Beatty RAAF and his all-Australian crew on 50 Squadron at Skellingthorpe, ditched off the coast of the Dutch Friesians after developing engine problems. Beatty recalls:

We could only climb to 9,000 feet with a bomb load, when bombs dropped on target we always put the nose down and headed for the deck to avoid night fighters and flak and to also fire at searchlights when necessary. We flew north of the Friesian Islands at low altitude when one engine packed up. The propeller would not feather, causing excessive drag and as I was in the front turret and the ocean getting too close I climbed back up behind the pilot while the two pilots struggled to control the aircraft. We were perhaps only 200 feet above the water and could not gain height, when the port engine stopped and the aircraft crashed nose first into the drink. I saw the second pilot [*Sergeant Ronald Burton*] hit the dashboard and then we were under water. Both he and I were not strapped in. I picked myself up off the floor and got kicked in the face by the navigator [*Pilot Officer Fred Allen*] as he pushed open the escape hatch. I followed him and was about to jump into the water when I saw the navigator's curtain bobbing up and down in the escape hatch. I tore it off and helped the pilot who was badly injured out and helped him swim around to the dinghy on the starboard side of the aircraft, which was half submerged. The tail section had broken behind the mid-upper gunner's turret. The dinghy had inflated upside down and the mid-upper gunner cut it free, which was probably just as well as the aircraft sank in a couple of minutes. I heard the wireless operator [*Sergeant Arthur Tebbutt*] calling in the dark that he could not see so I swam to where he was calling from and brought him back to the dinghy. We all got in the dinghy, which was upside down, as we did not want to lose anybody in the dark. We spent a wet and most uncomfortable night, as there were six of us who had survived. The 2nd pilot had a horrific head wound [*Burton died from his injuries on 10 September*]. The navigator, we found later, had a broken thigh. The wireless operator had a split lip and eyebrow and I had a head wound and badly bruised left side, arm and leg.

When daylight finally arrived we had to all get back into the water and the two uninjured gunners turned the dinghy over and helped us all back in stiff and sore. About an hour after daylight two Me 109s on patrol spotted our florescent trail in the water, flew low over us, waggled their wings and disappeared. A very old biplane seaplane arrived, landed and picked us up. The injured were put on stretchers. The dinghy was slashed to sink it and we were flown to Nordeney where we were put into the *Luftwaffe* hospital for a week and were very well treated. We were covered in oil and florescence. The two uninjured were put in the cooler until we were fit to travel. One of the blond 109 pilots came to see me, gave me cigarettes and shook hands. As neither of us understood each other, I tried to thank him for his courtesy and in saving us. We joined the two gunners[27] and were then taken under escort by train to Frankfurt to *Dulag Luft* for interrogation. There we joined up with a number of Commonwealth and RAF aircrews and placed on a guarded train to *Stalag Luft III* at Sagan in Silesia, where we arrived 16 June 1942.

On 20/21 June, Emden received another visit, this time from 185 aircraft. But only part of the bomber force identified the target and only about 100 houses were damaged. Eight aircraft, three of them Wellingtons, failed to return. One of the Wimpys was *J-Jane* flown by the CO of 9 Squadron, Wing Commander Leslie Vidal 'Jimmy' James DFC who was on his second tour of operations. Twenty-five-years-old, married and sporting a typical RAF 'handlebar' moustache, James had completed a tour on 149 Squadron and many ops had been in his Wellington *The Ozard of Whiz*, with said character depicted on the nose as a prominently uddered dancing cow. James had arrived on 9 Squadron, bringing with him Pilot Officer John Baxter DFM, his second-tour observer. Bill Anderson, who would make a name for himself as a wing commander in the Path Finder Force, recalled that at briefings they would all sit down and the CO would stand up with a long slip of paper in his hand, which he began to read 'in a dull, rather monotonous tone, as if he were just a little bored with the whole business'. To Anderson 'it sounded odd coming from such an impressive figure, six feet of toughness with a shock of black hair and a pugnacious chin that earned him the nickname of "Hammer of the Hun" .' When he flew ops James never seemed to choose the 'nice, easy trips'. Wearing a helmet and a flying-suit, he:

> Seemed no longer a 'Wing-Co' in charge of a squadron but just a man, completely in command of himself and the situation. Nobody who operated with him could help being affected by the utter simplicity of mind and singleness of purpose with which he attacked a target. To say that he took risks is beside the point; he apparently never considered them. He had a load of bombs aboard, which he was going to deliver to a German address and no power on earth, least of all the German defences, was going to stop him.[28]

James and Baxter and the rest of the crew of *J-Jane* were killed in a one-sided battle with *Oberleutnant* Egmont Prinz zur Lippe-Weissenfeld, who shot down another Wellington and a Halifax over Holland on the same sortie.

North of Bergen, Pilot Officer James Cowan, who was flying another 9 Squadron Wimpy, was attacked by a Bf 110 night fighter from 600 yards dead astern. After one burst Sergeant Brown's rear guns jammed and the enemy fighter proceeded to make about 10 more attacks, mostly from the port quarter. On instructions from Brown, Cowan, a New Zealander from Hastings on the shores of Hawke's Bay, made sharp diving turns into the attack, losing height rapidly, pulling out into climbing turns in the opposite direction in an attempt to break off the engagement. The Wimpy suffered damage to the port engine and starboard wing and a petrol tank received 15 holes but Cowan made it home, where he was reunited with his younger brother Pilot Officer William Bruce Cowan who was also a pilot. Flight Lieutenant James Cowan DFC completed his tour having survived a crash in a Wellington full of incendiaries and being blown clear, and in another incident he flew through the blast of an exploding mine. He was posted to 1663 Conversion Unit, leaving William to fly his ops and return to New Zealand a squadron leader with the DFC. A third brother, Neville, would also become a squadron leader DFC after a tour on Wellingtons on 148 Squadron. On 12 March 1943, 30-year-old James Cowan was flying a Lancaster which crashed, killing all eight men and two ground crew.[29]

On 22/23 June, 144 Wellingtons, 38 Stirlings, 26 Halifaxes, 11 Lancasters and eight Hampdens attacked Emden again for the third night in a row. 'Good' bombing results were claimed by 196 of the crews but decoy fires are believed to have diverted many bombs from the intended target. Six aircraft – four Wellingtons, one Lancaster and a Stirling – were lost.[30] Emden reported that 50 houses were destroyed, 100 damaged and some damage caused to the harbour. Six civilians were killed and 40 were injured.

As he looked around the crowded bar at Scampton on the evening of 24 June, Sergeant (later Flying Officer) John Bushby, the 22-year-old tail gunner in Sergeant (later Pilot Officer) 'Dick' Williams' Lancaster crew on 83 Squadron, realized that there were many new faces on the squadron and many familiar ones that were absent. Operations had been taking their toll and even in his absence of just under a month at Gunnery Leader's School, the change was evident.[31] Bushby was an aviation-mad teenager who in the 1920s had seen *Hell's Angels* and *Dawn Patrol* at the local cinema. Once the famous Alan Cobham Circus had come to town and Bushby had watched in awe as the formation of odd biplanes thundered over to advertise its arrival. In the thirties, living in London while working in a Fleet Street advertising agency, he was able to visit the annual Hendon displays by the Royal Air Force. Bushby became a 'Saturday afternoon airman' in the Auxiliary Air Force on a fighter squadron near London and in 1940 he had been accepted for training as an aerial gunner. In September 1941 Bushby 'crewed up' at 25 OTU Finningley. Crewing up, the RAF's tried and trusted method, where men were put in a room and told to '*Sort yourselves out and get yourselves crewed up!*' was known as 'The Marriage Bureau'. Men would stand in huddles to see what was on offer while others milled around like wallflowers at a village dance. Bushby's pilot was a stocky, powerful looking man remarkable for a huge moustache and a rich Cockney accent. This was the young air gunner's first contact with the man with whom he would fly on Wellingtons and then Manchesters and now Lancasters and get to know better than his own brother, on the ground and in the air, at war and peace for a long time ahead. Williams was married, who in the time-honoured tradition said, 'But don't tell the wife I'm a bomber pilot. She thinks I play the piano in a brothel!'

A briefing called on 25 June had everybody buzzing with surprise. It was another 'Thousand Bomber Raid', the third and final 'thousand' effort in the series of five major saturation attacks on German cities. At Scampton Dick Williams' crew were given L-*London*[32] for their first Lancaster operation. Their OTU instructor, Flight Sergeant Harold Hopper 'Whitey' Whitehead DFM who after a first tour of operations had done his 'six months hard' at Finningley, would pilot another 83 Squadron Lancaster. 'Whitey' by then coming up to almost his 50th operation, was a regular, who before becoming a pilot he had been, of all things, a cook and butcher. If ever a man's character was belied by his appearance it was Whitey's. Slightly built and with a sharp, pinched face and pale complexion, he looked more like a seedy clerk than a bomber pilot. He had 'nerves of steel and a sort of cold, dedicated courage.'[33] Williams' and Whitehead's Lancs were among the 1,067 aircraft that would attack Bremen that night, 25/26 June. Although only 960 aircraft, including 272 from the OTUs, became available for Bomber Command use, every type of aircraft in Bomber Command was included, even the Bostons and Mosquitoes of 2 Group which, so far, had only been used for day operations.[34] Bomber Command never before, or after, dispatched such a mixed force. After Churchill had intervened and insisted that the Admiralty allow Coastal Command to participate in this raid, a further 102 Hudsons and Wellingtons of Coastal Command were sent to Bremen but official records class this effort as a separate raid, not under Bomber Command control.

Flying Officer Harry Andrews was one of the many instructors involved in the 1,000 plan. After completing an anti-shipping tour of ops flying Hudsons on 224 Squadron, Coastal Command, he was posted to 1 (C) OTU at Silloth as an instructor on Hudsons in early 1942:

The monotony of training was temporarily broken for us when 30 or so Hudsons took part in the 1,000 bomber raid on Bremen. The instructors flew the aircraft but most of the crews were trainees, many of them from establishments in Canada. The Bremen raid was their first taste of operations. I think that many of us welcomed the news of the operation as a break from months of instructing. The ceaseless 'circuits and bumps', the constant reminders to student pilots to lead with the port throttle to prevent swing (and, to the over-confident type, a graphic description of the burn-up that often followed an uncontrolled swing). The warnings to 'watch your air-speed' on the approach, the fighting down of ones reaction to take over the controls when the student was holding off too high at nearly stalling speed and, not least, an encouraging word to the student whose white knuckles gripping the controls too tightly and whose knee tremors indicated both stress and determination. And later on when the student pilots had soloed on Hudsons teaching them low flying over the sea and holding one's breath at their first attempt to fly at 50 feet or so. Certainly we had no conception of the seriousness and moment of the 1,000-bomber raids operation. Looking back I find it almost unbelievable how ignorant we all were on what was happening: in short, what it was all about and what part we were playing in the overall plan.

After the abortive stand-by for the Cologne raid in May no one really took the orders for special operations on 23 June seriously until we flew to Squires Gate late on that day for bombing-up: ten 100lb GP bombs – the maximum load a Hudson could take with the fuel required. We then flew on to Thornaby arriving late at night. The next day (24 June) was spent in the seemingly inevitable hanging about and it was not until the late afternoon that we were released from standby: another anti-climax. On the morning of 25 June we were briefed that Bremen was the target: 1,000 aircraft would be taking part, the risk of collisions over the target was virtually nil if everyone kept to their timings and flight paths. Briefing included weather, night fighter tactics, anti-aircraft flak concentrations and other standard Bomber Command data. All of us had a Coastal Command background involving anti *U-boat*, reconnaissance and anti-shipping operations. The Bomber Command type of briefing was entirely new to us. Many of the student navigators had been trained overseas and had little or no experience of night flying or European weather. The specific briefing for the Hudson crews was to climb to 10,000 feet after take-off, cruise at 140 knots to the target, bomb and then immediately descend to 1,500 feet and return to base at that level. If I remember correctly, the designated targets were the Focke-Wulf aircraft works and the *U-boat* construction yards at Deschimag in the waterfront area of Bremen.

The tactics were basically similar to the earlier 'thousand' raids except that the bombing period was now cut from 98 minutes, which was a feature of the Cologne raid, to 65 minutes. Bremen, on the wide River Weser, should have been an easy target to find and the inland penetration of the German night fighter belt was only a shallow one. There were doubts about a band of cloud which lay across the Bremen area during the day but this was being pushed steadily eastwards by a strong wind. Unfortunately the wind dropped in the evening and the bomber crews found the target completely covered for the whole period of the raid. The limited success which was gained was entirely due to the use of *Gee*, which enabled the leading crews to start fires, on to the glow of which many aircraft of later waves bombed. 696 Bomber Command aircraft were able to claim attacks on Bremen. Generally the results were not as dramatic as at Cologne but much better than the second 'thousand' raid to Essen. Once again, as at Essen, a layer of cloud intervened between the force and its objective. Most aircraft in the first wave bombed blind on *Gee* and the glow of the fires thus caused reflected in the cloud and aided identification for the succeeding waves. Bremen reported a strengthening wind at the time of the raid which fanned the many fires throughout the town, increased the extent of the damage and left whole areas of houses in ruins. Twenty-seven acres of the business and residential area were completely destroyed. The RAF plan to destroy the Focke-Wulf factory and the shipyards was not successful, although an assembly shop at the Focke-Wulf factory was destroyed by a 4,000lb bomb dropped by a 5 Group Lancaster. A further six buildings at this factory were seriously damaged and 11 buildings lightly so. Damage was also experienced by the Atlas Werke and the Vulkan shipyard, the *Norddeutsche Hütte* and the Korff refinery and by two large dockside warehouses.[35]

Flight Lieutenant Terence Mansfield, the 419 Squadron RCAF Bombing Leader and 'Moose' Fulton's navigator/bomb aimer was on the 30th and final operation of his tour. Mansfield recalls:

> We took off at 23.25 hours. Although briefed for a greater height, we found the target area completely covered by cloud and came down to 12,000 feet in the hope of getting some visual identification from which we could start a timed run. We ended up doing what others did, namely bombing what we thought was the most likely place. Not very satisfactory and nor were the results.[36]

The heavy bomber crews were given the opportunity of bombing the red glow of the fires, using *Gee* as a check, or proceeding to a secondary target in the vicinity of Bremen. The cloud conditions prevailed at many of the targets of opportunity and many crews, unable to bomb, brought their lethal cargoes home. Flying Officer Harry Andrews continues:

> The old Hudson I had, like many others, suffered from the faults brought by the hard usage from OTU training. Rate of climb at full throttle was something less than 1,000 feet a minute and 3 or 4° of lateral trim was required to fly level. Weather was good for the first 200 miles or so. The sky was clear and the surface of the North Sea was dark against the lightness of the sky. With some envy I could see the silhouettes of Halifaxes and the odd Stirling flying high above us and overtaking on a roughly parallel course. The weather then turned treacherous (as was not uncommon over the North Sea). Low stratus covered the entire sea long before we reached the enemy coast and medium and heavy cloud developed in layers. We were navigating solely on dead reckoning and had only a general idea of our position, flying in and out of cloud (no radar, *Gee*, LORAN or H_2S[37] in those days, at least for our Hudsons). We saw groups of light and medium flak to port and starboard with a heavier

concentration ahead, which we assumed to be Bremen (a pious but hopeful assumption since we had not been able to fix our position on crossing the coast). In a somewhat detached frame of mind I noticed the coloured AA tracer start slowly then corkscrew past one's line of sight almost unbelievably quickly. Cloud cover was such that no positive identification of the target could be made.

A few minutes after our dead reckoning time over target the turret gunner shouted that a night fighter with an orange light was astern of us (we had been warned at briefing that some German night fighters carried a red/orange light – purpose unknown). It disappeared as quickly as it came and it may well have been the exhaust flame of one of our own aircraft. However, at that time violent evasive action seemed to be the prudent order of the day. Some minutes later we saw through a gap in the clouds a port complex which, from its geographical features, we took to be Wilhelmshaven. Since we were now well behind our scheduled time over target and Wilhelmshaven was a designated alternative target and, not least, mindful of the other 999 (theoretical) aircraft milling around in the general area we released the bombs. With some relief we dived to just above the lowest layer of stratus and set course for home. Fifteen or so minutes later a gap in the cloud layer showed us for a fleeting moment to be over a coastal airfield with one runway lit by flares. A few minutes on we had a glancing sight of one of the islands off the coast but we were too low to identify it and an uneventful flight home was made at low level. Not a heroic flight or one that made even a minuscule contribution to the defeat of Germany. The contribution made by Coastal Command OTU Hudsons in the main must have been to public morale – the 'magic' figure of 1,000 bombers had simultaneously attacked a German city.

The risk of collision and enemy fighter activity proved a constant threat and crews had to be ever watchful. Squadron Leader Denzil Lloyd Wolfe's Wellington on 419 'Moose' Squadron RCAF was involved in an engagement with a Bf 110 night fighter north of Borkum at 4,200 feet over the North Sea. Wolfe was a Canadian who had joined the RAF prior to the outbreak of war. Sergeant Roy Gordon Morrison opened fire and the enemy fighter's port engine was seen to burst into flames, which almost at once engulfed the entire wing. It dived into the sea, leaving a large circle of fire around the point of impact.[38]

The total of 48 aircraft lost (including five Coastal Command aircraft)[39] was the highest casualty rate (5 per cent) so far.[40]

At Scampton two 83 Squadron Lancasters failed to return. One was S-Sugar flown by that 'dour seasoned veteran' 'Whitey' Whitehead who had recently been commissioned. Whitehead and his crew were lost without trace, as John Bushby recalled:

Of all the people to get the chop on a trip like this! What could it have been which got him? Surely not flak, for Whitey seemed to have a sixth sense as to where the flak was going to burst next. A fighter? Maybe.... Whatever it was, we felt his loss keenly and none more so than Dick to whom he had, so to speak taught the art of self-survival in a dangerous trade. For a day or so afterwards Dick lost some of his Cockney good humour and became irritable and impatient.[41]

Sergeant Harris B Goldberg, born in Boston, Massachusetts, had trained as an air gunner in the RCAF and in October 1941 had arrived in Scotland before joining a Wellington crew. He flew the 1/2 June *Millennium* raid on Essen and the 25/26 June raid on Bremen:

We went in at 12,000 feet, got hit and damn near fell to pieces. We went down to 2,000 feet and sort of stumbled home at about 90mph. I don't really know how we got home. All my crew were English. We used to have some pretty wild arguments about the States staying out of the war. After that night over Bremen we argued but we never really got mad any more. Going through something like that brings you pretty close.[42]

Although the raid was not as successful as the first 1,000-bomber raid on Cologne, large parts of Bremen, especially in the south and east districts, were destroyed.[43] The German high command was shaken but 52 bombers were claimed destroyed by the flak and night fighter defences for the loss of just two Bf 110s and four NCO crewmembers killed or missing. A total of 1,123 sorties (including 102 Hudsons and Wellingtons from Coastal Command) had been dispatched and 50 Bomber Command aircraft and four from Coastal Command were lost. This time the heaviest casualties were suffered by the OTUs of 91 Group, which lost 23 of the 198 Whitleys and Wellingtons provided by that group. All but one was manned by pupil crews. As an instructor John Price at 10 OTU had been ordered to go but as there were not enough instructors to fill the aircraft pupil pilots were called upon – ditto navigators and air gunners.

My pupils – 18-year-old boys – pleading with me to let them go besieged me. I knew that half of them would not come back but I chose my dozen or so then prayed for their safety.
None came back.[44]

Notes

1. Hosea 8:7.
2. See *The Thousand Plan* by Ralph Barker (Pan Books Ltd 1967).
3. See *The Thousand Plan* by Ralph Barker (Pan Books Ltd 1967).

4. 1 Group provided 156 Wellingtons and 3 Group, 88 Stirlings and 134 Wellingtons. A total of 131 Halifaxes were provided by 4 Group.

5. *Pathfinders* by W/C Bill Anderson OBE DFC AFC (Jarrolds London 1946).

6. *The Thousand Plan* by Ralph Barker (Pan 1967).

7. See Barker.

8. *Bombers Fly East*. Squadron Leader Anekstein's luck would finally run out on the operation to Mönchengladbach on the night of 30/31 August 1943. *J-Johnny*, his 7 Squadron Lancaster, was shot down in the target area and he was killed.

9. See *Nachtjagd: The Night Fighter versus Bomber War over the Third Reich 1939–45* by Theo Boiten (Crowood 1997).

10. Woltersdorf was KIA on 2 June 1942 when he crashed into parked aircraft at Twente after being attacked by an e/a while landing with his *Bordfunker* Heino Pape (WIA). Woltersdorf had scored 24 victories.

11. 14 OTU lost a third Hampden when returning over Norfolk. F/L Wilfred Lawrie Cameron and his crew were killed trying to land at Horsham St. Faith, near Norwich.

12. See *The Thousand Plan* by Ralph Barker (Pan Books Ltd 1967).

13. Adapted from *Operation Millennium* by Ian Frimston (*Wingspan* Magazine April 1988)

14. Two crews – those of F/L Al Hamman DFC*, a South African from Cape Town who had already completed two tours, one in the Middle East and one in the UK, and F/O Harold Roger Blake DFC RNZAF – were missing from the ten who took off from Elsham. Hamman and three of his crew died. There were no survivors from Blake's crew. A 22 OTU crew captained by F/Sgt Cyril James Mathews, which took off from Waddington were the other crew lost. All were killed. On 103 Squadron F/Sgt William Onions and crew were lost over Germany and Sgt Leslie William Flowers crashed on take-off from Kirmington next morning after being diverted. Both pilots were on their first trip as first pilot and captain. There were no survivors from Onions' crew. Flowers and three others were killed; two men were injured.

15. Niklas recovered from his wounds, but he was killed in January 1944 after an engagement with USAAF bombers on a daylight raid.

16. Bernard Evans award was gazetted on 1 January 1943. He returned to Harwell to continue his tour as an air gunnery instructor and was commissioned in January 1943. He visited Buckingham Palace on 23 December to receive his DFM, continuing as an instructor at various OTUs, eventually becoming the gunnery leader at 20 OTU based at Lossiemouth. *Men Behind The Medals* by Air Cdre Graham Pitchfork (Sutton 2003).

17. Falconer died while on active service on 8 May 1944.

18. Ralph Barker.

19. *Chased By The Sun; The Australians in Bomber Command in WWII* by Hank Nelson (ABC Books 2002).

20. On 6 October Baveystock, Horsley, Mills and Naylor were awarded the DFM. The award of the DFC to Baveystock followed on 25 January 1944 and he received a bar to his DFC on 25 August. De Mone was awarded the DFM on 1 September 1942. *RAF Evaders: The Comprehensive Story of Thousands of Escapers and their Escape Lines, Western Europe, 1940–1945* by Oliver Clutton-Brock (Grub Street 2009). F/L Baveystock DSO DFC DFM later served on 201 Squadron in Coastal Command as a Sunderland pilot. On 7 June 1944 he sank *U-955* in the Bay of Biscay north of Spain and on 18 August he sank *U-107* in the Bay of Biscay, SW of St-Nazaire. Baveystock was awarded the DSO on 13 October 1944. Flight Lieutenant Robert Horsley DFC later became a pilot on 617 Squadron and survived the war. His brother, Squadron Leader Hugh Horsley, was killed on 1 February 1945 when his Lancaster crashed on take-off at RAF Skellingthorpe.

21. Stiles' navigator, S/L T Hillier-Rose recalled that Stiles was 'ticked off' for having flown on the raid. At the time he was recovering from a severe wound to an arm, sustained in a crash whilst flying a Mosquito.

22. *The Bomber Command War Diaries: An Operational reference book 1939–1945.* Martin Middlebrook and Chris Everitt. (Midland 1985).

23. See *Pathfinders* by W/C Bill Anderson OBE DFC AFC (Jarrolds London 1946). This attack was also widely scattered with just three HE bombs and 300 incendiary bombs falling in the city, and 14 aircraft failed to return.

24. Peter Buttigieg, a Maltese national, Gaulton and F/Sgt John Farquhar the WOp/AG bailed out and Manchester VN-Z L7432 crashed in flames at Beekbergen near Apeldoorn at 02.33 hours. German radio traffic on the morning of 4 June referred to a Bf 110 crashing at Deelen. Buttigieg tried to get back to England but was betrayed and fell into the clutches of the *Gestapo*. He survived the war.

25. 12 aircraft – 8 Wellingtons, 2 Stirlings, 1 Halifax, 1 Lancaster FTR. *Nachtjagd* was credited with 8 victories.

26. A Halifax on 405 Squadron was abandoned on the return to Pocklington due to both outer engines losing power, and crashed near Binbrook. All the crew bailed out successfully. *RAF Bomber Command Losses of the Second World War, Vol. 3 1942* by W R Chorley (Midland 1994).

27. Sgt Alan F Scanlan and Sgt Ronald Buchanan – and the 6th member of the crew, navigator, Sgt R F Davies.

28. *Pathfinders* by W/C Bill Anderson OBE DFC AFC (Jarrolds London 1946)

29. See *Bombers First And Last* by Gordon Thorburn (Robson Books, 2006).
30. Two of which were destroyed by *Oberleutnant* Rudolf Schoenert, *St Kpt* 4./NJG2.
31. *Gunner's Moon* by John Bushby (Futura 1974).
32. R5773.
33. *Gunner's Moon* by John Bushby (Futura 1974).
34. 472 Wellingtons, 124 Halifaxes, 96 Lancasters, 69 Stirlings, 51 Blenheims, 50 Hampdens, 50 Whitleys, 24 Bostons, 20 Manchesters and 4 Mosquitoes. Five further aircraft provided by Army Co-operation Command were also added to the force. The final numbers dispatched, 1,067 aircraft, made this a larger raid than that on Cologne at the end of May. The entire 5 Group effort – 142 aircraft – were to bomb the Focke-Wulf factory. Twenty Blenheims were allocated the A G Weser shipyard; the Coastal Command aircraft were to bomb the Deschimag shipyard; all other aircraft except for 5 Group were to carry out an area attack on the town and docks. This raid was the last flown operationally by Manchesters, after which the type was withdrawn.
35. *The Bomber Command War Diaries: An Operational reference book 1939–1945.* Martin Middlebrook and Chris Everitt. (Midland 1985).
36. W/C 'Moose' Fulton and Terence Mansfield landed back at Mildenhall at 04.45 hours. Mansfield had completed his tour and later became Bombing Leader on a squadron of Lancasters. After his death in action on the operation to Hamburg 28/29 July 1942, 'Moose' Fulton's nickname was incorporated in the official title of the unit.
37. H_2S was a 10cm experimental airborne radar navigational and target location aid developed by Dr. Lovell at the TRE (Telecommunications Research Establishment) at Malvern, Worcestershire, which produced a 'map' on a CRT display of a 360° arc of the ground below the equipped aircraft. It was first used in January 1943.
38. S/L Wolfe DFC and five of his crew on 405 'Vancouver' Squadron RCAF at Gransden Lodge were killed on the night of 13/14 July 1943 when their Halifax was attacked by a night fighter and disintegrated near Asten, Holland on the operation to Aachen.
39. Altogether, 29 Wellingtons, four Manchester Is, three Halifaxes, two Stirlings, one Hampden and one Whitley were lost.
40. Of the 31 No. 1 (C) OTU Hudsons on the Bremen raid, two returned early owing to cowling and engine trouble; 29 crews reached the target area. AM794 was shot down by *Oberleutnant* Egmont Prinz zur Lippe-Weissenfeld, *St Kpt* 5./NJG2, E of De Kooy airfield. AM762 VX-M on 206 Squadron crashed at Frel near Heide; shot down by *Oberleutnant* Werner Hoffmann, *St Kpt* 5./NJG3 for his first night victory of the war. F/Sgt Kenneth Douglas Wright (22) pilot, WOp/AG and an air gunner KIA (2 PoW). AM606 VX-S flown by S/L Cyril

Norman Crook DFC (29) crashed into the sea S of Fehmarn Island, shot down by *Leutnant* Hans-Heinrich 'King' Koenig of 8./NJG3. No survivors. Hudson flown by F/L Derek Hodgkinson (later ACM Sir Derek Hodgkinson, KCB CBE DFC AFC) of 220 Squadron, CO of the temporary Operational Hudson Squadron, shot down by two unidentified Bf 110s attacking simultaneously on the return leg over the Dutch coast. Hodgkinson skillfully ditched his burning aircraft off Ameland, where he and his badly wounded navigator were taken prisoner next day. In all, 24 OTU sent 16 aircraft. Three FTR. Wellington T2723 on 20 OTU from Lossiemouth flown by Sgt N W Levasseur RCAF was shot down into the sea off Terschelling in an encounter with *Oberleutnant* zur Lippe-Weissenfeld. Levasseur and one other member of the crew survived and were taken captive; the three other crew members perished.

41. *Gunner's Moon* by John Bushby (Futura 1974).
42. After flying 273 operational hours in the RAF and surviving a crash in a 'Wimpy' in the Sinai desert in November 1942, Goldberg transferred to the 8th Air Force.
43. 5 Group destroyed an assembly shop at the Focke-Wulf factory when a 4,000lb 'Cookie' scored a direct hit. Six other buildings were seriously damaged.
44. Four Whitleys on 10 OTU were lost. One of the five-man crews which ditched in the North Sea were rescued.

Index